Readings on Elementary Social Studies

E*Readings on* lementary S**ocial** S**tudies**
Prologue to Change

Edited by

JOHN R. LEE

Director, Social Studies
Curriculum Center,
Northwestern University

JONATHON C. MCLENDON

Professor of Social
Science Education,
Florida Atlantic University

ALLYN AND BACON, INC.   BOSTON, 1965

Library of Congress Catalog Card Number: 65–24797

PRINTED IN THE UNITED STATES OF AMERICA

RARELY, IF EVER before, have those responsible for elementary school social studies faced such opportunities and challenges as they do now. Social forces are merging with trends in education to set the stage for major changes in the schools' programs for leading children to examine and understand human relationships. Several schools and many individual teachers, some textbook publishers and various leaders in the field have developed significant modifications of elementary social studies content and activities. Proposals and experiments that should lead to further change and improvement are being reported monthly in the professional journals.

There would be less need for this book of readings if every school system had a complete and up-to-date library at the disposal of its teachers, or if there were enough copies of pertinent journals in college libraries so that every student had an opportunity to read as widely as his professors would like. But not every school has an adequate library, nor does every college have multiple copies of journals and books for its prospective teachers. This type of book is designed to fill such gaps.

Books of readings have two advantages that an inclusive textbook lacks. An up-to-date selection of well-chosen readings can draw together recent articles of importance and get them into print quickly in a time marked by urgency; the author of a text must take more time to digest the ideas of others, test them against his own ideas, and reform them in his own work. Readings can present a range of ideas that—no matter how they are organized—may be reorganized and interpreted as teachers and professors wish to use them. A textbook, on the other hand, usually assumes a particular point of view, for it is on particular points of view that professional reputations are made.

We feel that our rationale, our selection of articles, their arrangement, their direct applicability to immediate problems, and their range of differing viewpoints will make this reader a most useful book. We have surveyed textbooks, other professional publications, and courses of study, and have made our selections from a variety of outstanding professional journals and books. Many of the nation's leading authorities in the social sciences and the social studies have been included. Their writings present a variety of styles, approaches, and points of view.

The arrangement of selections facilitates their use as a basic text-book or as a supplemental reference for college courses; the breadth and pertinence of the arrangement makes the book equally useful to the elementary school teacher and the curriculum worker. The selections stress current and emerging trends in social studies; they consider in depth the social, psychological, and professional elements that undergird social studies programs and instruction; they extract from the social sciences a number of ideas that may be distilled for use with children; and provide insight into a number of curriculum proposals. Further, the readings offer help in planning for instruction, guiding activities, and evaluating learning; and they deal with the uses of textbooks and other materials. In short, these selections deal with the challenges and responsibilities we all share for improving the social studies. They will be of use, then, to both the pre-service and the in-service teacher seeking resources to aid their efforts with the social studies.

No effort has been made to favor a particular approach to elementary social studies; a balance of divergent and sometimes conflicting views is intentionally included. The criteria for including selections were confined to an author having something significant to say, saying it with force and logic, and revealing a commitment to improvement of elementary school social studies. The editors were less concerned with promoting their own preferences in instruction and programs than they were with providing others with a range of proposals and methods from which choices might be made. Ideas ought to generate creative thinking in a general intellectual market; our book of readings brings current ideas into that marketplace for readers who might otherwise not find them easily available.

Grateful acknowledgement is due many individuals and groups, particularly to the original authors and publishers who are credited as their contributions appear in the readings. Stimulus for the kind of professional interest that has resulted in this publication derives from the former graduate advisors of the editors: Paul R. Hanna of Stanford University and Edgar B. Wesley, Professor Emeritus of the University of Minnesota, and from E. T. McSwain and B. J. Chandler, Deans of Education while both editors were faculty members at Northwestern University. Mr. Gene Rooze, a teacher in the Evanston elementary district, aided in gathering selections; Mrs.

Betty Rand and Mrs. Patty Yates of Northwestern took great pains with the typing of introductions and articles; Miss Susan Dwight, of Allyn and Bacon, edited our copy as if it had been her own. Several librarians at Northwestern University furnished essential aid. The editors' wives (as is so often true) made this work possible because of their skill in running homes occupied by preoccupied professors.

A book of readings really ought not to be dedicated to anyone, for editors have little right to speak for the original authors. But we know many of these authors, and we know of their work with teachers in courses, workshops, institutes, and professional organizations. We know who is on their minds as they teach their courses and write their articles. They think of children, and of that reappearing figure, the elementary teacher who faces his or her almost impossibly diverse tasks with devotion and courage, and with a desire to improve the lives of others. For the authors whose works we edited, we rededicate this reader to the teacher, the eternal strength of American education.

JOHN R. LEE
Evanston, Illinois

JONATHON C. McLENDON
Boca Raton, Florida

❧ CONTENTS

Part A – Purposes, Programs, and Trends

Part B – Foundations of the Social Studies

Part C – The Social Sciences and the Social Studies

Part D – The Multidisciplinary Nature of the Social Studies

Part G – Professional Improvement of the Social Studies Curriculum

Readings on Elementary Social Studies

⤙ PART A ⤚

Purposes, Programs, and Trends

T HE FIRST FOUR selections—two from major councils and two from outstanding writers—focus on the purposes for and results of instruction in the social studies. Ralph W. Tyler forcefully identifies our task: improve an inadequate curriculum! The National Council for the Social Studies and the American Council of Learned Societies pinpoint a major issue and amply demonstrate that men disagree most over those ideas they most value. And Ralph C. Preston sounds the hopeful note that signs of change are evident. The talent that produced these selections provides eloquent testimony to the intellectual potential which promises change in the social studies.

The articles by Dorothy M. Fraser and Donald L. Barnes specify the topics most commonly taught in elementary school social studies programs. Harold D. Drummond then takes up the question of whether the social studies should be taught as separate or merged subjects. He states his preference, but he also insists that our primary concern should be for the quality of the learner's experiences. Edgar B. Wesley raises the often unconsidered question of whether organization of content by teachers really facilitates pupils' learning at all.

The last three selections in this section provide us with examples of designed programs. Paul R. Hanna recommends a change from loosely organized programs to a systematic approach to scope and sequence. Theodore Kaltsounis offers a modification of Hanna's plan. Joseph C. Grannis then reports two new approaches to organizing social studies programs. There will be more programs proposed in the next decade, but the ideas presented in these articles seem dominant now—and their influence is bound to continue.

✍ An Assessment: The Edge of the Future
Ralph W. Tyler

> *Ralph Tyler, whose interest in the social sciences has been as persistent as his contributions have been brilliant, sets the stage for a consideration of trends in the revitalization of the social studies. His examination of current inadequacies in the social studies and his identification of the role that scholars must play emphasize two themes that will reappear several times in the articles that follow. His entire article, and indeed all of the brief book it has been taken from, is well worth the most careful reading.*

ALTHOUGH THERE ARE some notable exceptions, on the whole, the social studies are the least effective educationally of any of the basic areas taught in the American public schools. This sweeping generalization is supported by a variety of evidence, the most recent of which is the report by Martin Mayer (1) of his visits to the classrooms of teachers in various parts of the country. The instruction given in these classrooms had been identified by teachers and administrators as superior illustrations of social studies teaching. The data from standardized-interest inventories place the social studies in the lowest quarter of school subjects in terms of the interest pupils express in courses they are taking in this field. High-school alumni questionnaires indicate a similar low rating by high-school graduates of the courses they took in the social studies. My own observations over the years in many schools found some excellent courses and excellent teaching in this field, but these cases were in the distinct minority. Commonly the classes were dull, spiritless, and lacking in clearly defined content or method.

INADEQUACY IN THE SOCIAL STUDIES

There are several reasons for the current inadequacy of the social studies. In the first place, the American public and school people are

Used by permission of Scott, Foresman and Company; from *The Social Studies: Curriculum Proposals for the Future*. Chicago: Scott, Foresman and Company, 1963, pp. 121–132. Ralph W. Tyler is the director of the Center for Advanced Study in the Behavioral Sciences.

both confused about the educational purposes for teaching the social studies. For example, history is often confused with the communication of myths or the indoctrination of students in the prejudices of their communities. Thus, the state histories in many Southern schools teach children things which are directly in conflict with what children in Northern states are taught. History is sometimes regarded and taught as a body of proved facts, rather than an account of developments, an account which is a subject of continuing inquiry and reinterpretation in the light of new information and knowledge.

As another example, geography is sometimes considered to be a listing of places on a map, sometimes a subject for explaining the location of peoples and industries in terms of climate and other physical features. Sometimes it, too, is treated as a description of foreign people and places which emphasizes the esoteric features. Wonder and surprise are likely to be overplayed at the expense of accuracy and understanding. Economics is often treated as a set of doctrines explaining the superiority of American life, sometimes as a set of exercises in calculating rent, interest, insurance costs, and the like, and rarely as a science for studying the allocation of resources. Civics, too, presents confusion, sometimes treated as a detailed description of the American political structure, sometimes as a subject for debating current political issues, without benefit of necessary knowledge and tools of analysis, and sometimes as a means of understanding aspects of the political process. The confusion seen in psychology arises from courses which try to be a sophisticated Dorothy Dix in providing advice on personal problems, while other courses impress one as a kind of distorted or "fractured Freud." Still other courses appear to be a pseudo-psychometrics, with students taking a variety of cognitive and personality tests, and thus getting a "scientific" description of themselves. The subjects of sociology and anthropology rarely appear in the social studies curriculum.

The state of confusion regarding the educational objectives of the social studies is widespread throughout the country. Popular magazines and newspaper editorials reflect deep misunderstanding of the educational potential of these subjects. Discussions with parents reveal a similar misapprehension. This confusion is not limited to laymen. Teachers and administrators also share the uncertainty about the functions of this field.

A second reason for the current inadequacy of the social studies is the fact that the schools have had inadequate intellectual resources upon which to draw in developing the educational program in this field. This lack of resources is understandable. Several of the social sciences have come of age only recently and, until now, they had very little to offer of solid content or effective methods of inquiry. Heretofore, there have been few efforts made to involve highly competent social scientists in curriculum work with teachers in the schools. During the depression of the 1930's particularly in connection with the Eight-Year Study, the Commission on the Secondary School Curriculum of the Progressive Education Association had been able to interest a few recognized scholars in the social sciences who worked effectively with high-school teachers in beginning the development of a social studies curriculum. . . . However, the Second World War brought this endeavor to a halt. Since that time, the schools have not had these intellectual resources to draw upon.

The social studies curricula have been poorly planned. This is a third reason for their current inadequacy. Because the educational purposes have not been clear, there has been no well-defined aim to guide us in deciding on the emphasis to be given, the kind of materials to be used, the sequence to follow, and the way in which social studies should relate to other school subjects. As a result, most courses lack unity and emphasis. The materials used are often ineffective in stimulating and maintaining active student learning. Students complain both of repetition in content from grade to grade, and of the lack of depth possible through sequential treatment. They see few connections between their work in this field and the other subjects which they study.

A fourth reason for the inadequacy of social studies is the fact that the social studies are very frequently assigned to teachers whose major field of interest lies elsewhere. In the social studies, more than in any other basic subject, teachers are likely to be assigned in terms of their having an extra period or two during the day when they are not working in their major field of interest and preparation. This curious method of assigning teachers arises, at least partly, from the fact that not many social studies teachers have been well educated in fields other than history. At the high-school level, history is the only subject in the social studies which is commonly offered for more than one year. Most colleges do not provide a major sequence to prepare teachers for courses involving anthropology, economics, political science, psychology, and sociology.

Another factor in the assignment of teachers may be the common attitude on the part of school people as well as the public, that the social studies have no important content which is not part of the common-sense experience and knowledge of every college graduate. With such a view, special preparation in the social sciences is not deemed essential.

THE ROLE OF SCHOLARS

This pictures the present sorry condition of the social studies, but it should not cause us to conclude that the social studies field is hopeless. . . . The time has come when the state of the social studies can be greatly improved.

Now that we are conscious of our confusion in aims, we can select consistent, central purposes. In doing so, however, we must keep in mind that the role of the subject fields in education is not as ends in themselves, but as resources which can be used to equip the student with ways of thinking, feeling, and acting which can help him to live more effectively and with greater dignity and satisfaction. For us to use each subject in this way, we need to understand what the subject really is, at its best, so that we can avoid prostituting it in a caricature for school children. This kind of understanding can be obtained only from serious scholars and scientists who are actively involved in the subject.

Competent historians, for example, do not find history primarily a list of items for memorization, but, to them, history is a study of developments taking place over time. History offers us a way of looking at questions in terms of the time dimension; it offers us methods of inquiry for studying development; it enables us to work out explanations which are always subject to reinterpretation in the light of new knowledge; and it also offers us a way of gaining appreciation for contributions of man's past experiences. Similarly, serious anthropologists, economists, geographers, political scientists, psychologists, and social scientists can help us see potential intellectual and emotional contributions which the study of their subjects can give. None of these subjects give immediate or final answers to important questions, but rather they can contribute to understanding through inquiry, and to appreciation through understanding and the emotional concomitants of active efforts to learn.

In emphasizing the importance of involving scholars and scientists with school people in the task of selecting consistent, central educational purposes for the social studies, I do not mean to imply that the potential contributions of each subject are to be considered in a vacuum. Since we have so little time for school learning, not everything of value can be taught there. A careful selection of those things most important to learn must be made. In judging importance, we need to consider the demands and opportunities of contemporary life. What students learn should assist them in meeting the demands of life, or enable them to take advantage of the opportunities available to them for self-realization. We need also to assess the extent to which what is proposed can be effectively learned in the school by the students in question. Finally, our selection of what is to be taught in the social studies, as well as in other fields, must take into account the extent to which it makes a contribution to the human values cherished by the school, such as helping to develop in each student a concern for others, respect for the dignity and worth of every human being, independence, and the ability to use intelligence in solving human problems. But the point I am stressing here is that the social studies cannot really aim at what the disciplines are not honestly able to contribute.

References

(1) Martin Mayer, *Where, When, and Why* (New York: Harper & Row, 1963).

THE ROLE OF THE SOCIAL STUDIES

This statement of role serves as a benchmark in the history of the National Council for the Social Studies. The position of the Council's committee on the ultimate goal of education in the social studies comes through clearly. Although some may disagree with this article's definition of social studies, or with its description of the relationship between citizenship and scholarship, the committee makes clear its concern for both intellectual development and the transmission of the values of our heritage.

THE SOCIAL STUDIES are concerned with human relationships. Their content is derived principally from the scholarly disciplines of economics, geography, history, political science, and sociology, and includes elements from other social sciences, among them anthropology, archaeology, and social psychology. The term *social studies* implies no particular form of curricular organization. It is applicable to curricula in which each course is derived for the most part from a

Used by the permission of the author and the National Council for the Social Studies, from *Social Education*, 26:315–318, October, 1962. This statement was prepared by a committee composed of Jack Allen, George Peabody College for Teachers; Howard R. Anderson, University of Rochester; William H. Cartwright, Duke University; Dorothy McClure Fraser, College of the City of New York; John M. Haefner, State University of Iowa; and Samuel P. McCutchen, New York University.

single discipline as well as to curricula in which courses combine materials from several disciplines.

The ultimate goal of education in the social studies is the development of desirable socio-civic and personal behavior. No society will prosper unless its members behave in ways which further its development. Man's behavior tends to reflect the values, ideals, beliefs, and attitudes which he accepts. . . . In a free society, behavior must rest upon reasoned convictions as well as emotional acceptance. Knowledge and the ability to think should provide the basis on which American children and youth build the beliefs and behavior of free citizens. . . .

A number of considerations grow out of the brief description of the social studies and what they are good for. Instruction in the social studies is part of the education which should be provided to everyone. The kinds of behavior, beliefs, knowledge, and abilities mentioned in this statement are needed by all members of a free society. To attain the goals suggested, a comprehensive program of instruction in the social studies is required throughout the elementary and secondary school. . . .

The complex task of teaching the social studies involves a heavy responsibility. The effective teacher must have some understanding of all of the social sciences. A comprehensive program for the education of young citizens clearly cannot be limited to instruction in one social science. It is also clear that in a world of rapid and continual change it is impossible to prescribe a fixed and immutable content for the social studies. Even though most of the information currently taught will remain valid and useful, the total body of content will require frequent updating and sharpening as new problems arise and new ways of dealing with persistent problems are discovered.

In summary, this statement includes four major considerations: 1) The ultimate goal of education in the social studies is desirable socio-civic and personal behavior. 2) This behavior grows out of the values, ideals, beliefs, and attitudes which people hold. 3) In turn, these characteristics must be rooted in knowledge. 4) For the development and use of knowledge, people require appropriate abilities and skills. The perpetuation and improvement of our democratic way of life is dependent upon the development of individuals who achieve these goals.

THE BEHAVIORAL NEEDS IN A FREE SOCIETY

. . . In approaching the problem of behavior the school recognizes that in a democratic society responsibility for appropriate behavior must be assumed by individual members. A democratic society depends upon self-discipline and upon societal discipline approved by a majority. In any free society individuals must be willing and able to participate effectively in the solution of common problems. They must also be willing at times to arrive at decisions reflecting compromises among different points of view. Such compromises are acceptable when they help society to advance toward desirable goals, but the compromises must not result in the sacrifice of those inalienable rights, principles, and values without which democracy cannot survive. . . .

Among the behavioral patterns which may be identified as essential for the maintenance, strengthening, and improvement of a democratic society are the following:

1. Keeping well informed on issues which affect society, and of relating principles and knowledge derived from the social sciences to the study of contemporary problems.
2. Using democratic means in seeking agreement, reaching solutions, and taking group action on social problems.
3. Assuming individual responsibility for carrying out group decisions and accepting the consequences of group action.
4. Defending constitutional rights and freedoms for oneself and others.
5. Respecting and complying with the law, regardless of personal feelings, and using legal means to change laws deemed inimical or invalid.
6. Supporting persons and organizations working to improve society by desirable action.
7. Scrutinizing the actions of public officials.
8. Participating in elections at local, state, and national levels and preparing oneself for intelligent voting in these elections.
9. Opposing special privilege whenever it is incompatible with general welfare.
10. Being prepared and willing to render public service and to give full-time service in emergencies.
11. Engaging in continual re-examination of one's personal values as well as the value system of the nation.

The responsibility for the development of patterns of democratic behavior in pupils falls in large measure upon the social studies program. Behavior grows from the intellectual acceptance of new ideas, changes in attitudes, and the formation of a personal commitment to values which are basic to our society.

THE BELIEFS OF A FREE PEOPLE

Values may be defined as the beliefs and ideas which a society esteems and seeks to achieve. They inspire its members to think and act in ways which are approved. To the extent that actual behavior is consistent with the values claimed, a society is meeting the standards it has set for itself.

A fundamental premise of American democracy is that men and women can be taught to think for themselves and to determine wise courses of action. In choosing a course of action they need to take into account the values which are basic to our society. These values are rooted in the democratic heritage and provide a stabilizing force of utmost importance.

In meeting new situations Americans not only must consider whether possible courses of action are consistent with democratic values but they may need to re-examine the values themselves. Although the basic values of American democracy are permanent, secondary values are subject to change. Furthermore, there is always need for adjustment whenever one value is in conflict with another, as, for example, liberty and authority.

Other agencies than the schools obviously have responsibility for the inculcation of basic values. Nevertheless, a primary objective of instruction must be the development of a better understanding of our value system. At all grade levels, instruction in the social studies should concern itself with the attainment of this objective. To the extent that Americans have a thorough understanding of the values underlying their way of life, and accept this code as their own, they will be able to do their part in achieving the great goals which they have set for themselves.

Among the values which instruction in the social studies should seek to engender in youth are:

1. Belief in the inherent worth of every individual—that each person should be judged on his merit.
2. Belief that all persons should possess equal rights and liberties which are, however, accompanied by responsibilities.
3. Belief that all persons should have maximum freedom and equality of opportunity to develop as they desire, consistent with their capacities and with the general welfare.
4. Belief that individual and group rights must be exercised in such a way that they do not interfere with the rights of others, endanger the general welfare, or threaten the national security.
5. Belief that citizens should place the common good before self-interest or group or class loyalty, when these are in conflict.
6. Belief that freedom of inquiry, expression, and discussion provide the best way for resolving issues; that the will of the majority should govern; that the rights and opinions of the minority should be respected and protected.
7. Belief that citizens should be willing to act on the basis of reasoned conclusions and judgments, even though personal sacrifice is involved.

8. Belief that government must be based on properly enacted law, not on the caprice of men holding office; that government has a responsibility for promoting the common welfare.
9. Belief that people are capable of governing themselves better than any self-appointed individual or group can govern them, that political power belongs to and comes from the people; and that the people have the right, by lawful means, to change their government.
10. Belief that the freest possible economic competition consistent with the general welfare is desirable; that government has the obligation to stabilize economic growth and reduce gross economic inequalities.
11. Belief that both competition and cooperation are essential to the democratic process and to our national well-being.
12. Belief that the separation of church and state is essential.
13. Belief that maximum individual freedom, under law, throughout the world is the best guarantee of world peace.
14. Belief that change in relations between nation states should be accomplished by peaceful means, and that collective security can best be achieved within an organization of nation states.
15. Belief that Americans should work to achieve a world in which justice and peace are assured to all mankind.
16. Belief that Americans should have reasoned devotion to the heritage of the past, and a commitment to perpetuate the ideals of American life. . . .

THE ROLE OF KNOWLEDGE

The attainment of goals in the social studies depends upon the acquisition and utilization of information, facts, data. Each of the social sciences, in effect, is a reservoir of knowledge to be used. But the kind and amount of knowledge which can be used from one or more disciplines is necessarily determined by curriculum requirements associated with a particular stage in the educational process. In any event, one cannot be concerned with the goals of social studies instruction without being drawn immediately into considerations of content. The National Council for the Social Studies, consequently, has made frequent examinations of content areas, notably in its Yearbooks to which distinguished social scientists have contributed.

In the last few years the National Council for the Social Studies has recognized the necessity for making a more comprehensive study of the social studies curriculum. One report, issued in 1957, carries the title: *A Guide to Content in the Social Studies.* This report listed 14 themes which were proposed as guidelines for the selection of content. A second report, published in 1958, is called *Curriculum Planning in American Schools: The Social Studies.* The group which prepared this report showed special interest in the advances made by social science research in recent decades and was concerned that these findings be reflected in school programs in the social studies. Beyond noting some limited illustrations of these advances, the report underscored the need for cooperative effort among social scientists, educators, and teachers in the planning of the social studies curriculum. In such planning a fundamental problem would be the development of agreement on principles to be used in the selection and grade placement of content. . . .

THE ROLE OF ABILITIES AND SKILLS

. . . The purpose of teaching skills in social studies is to enable the individual to gain knowledge concerning his society, to think reflectively about problems and issues, and to apply this thinking in constructive action.

The need for the systematic teaching of social studies has become increasingly urgent for a number of reasons. With the development of modern media of mass communications and the expansion in the amount of scholarly material, there has been an enormous increase in the quantity and variety of social data that the citizens must deal with in locating and selecting information that is pertinent to a given issue. With the refinement and increasingly pervasive use of persuasion techniques in many areas of daily living, there is a correspondingly greater need for skill in appraising information and evidence and the sources from which they come. With the complicated forms of social organization which develop in an urbanized society, new skills of group participation are essential for effective action.

The development of some of these skills is the special responsibility of the social studies, such as those involved in understanding time and chronology. Others are shared with other parts of the school program, but have special application in social studies. The list of proposed objectives centering on abilities and skills includes both types, for students need both to deal with social studies materials. . . .

The objectives listed in this statement involve abilities and skills needed for effective behavior; the abilities peculiar to the social science disciplines must be developed further as the college student pursues his specialized studies.

I. Skills centering on *ways and means of handling social studies materials*

    A. Skills of locating and gathering information from a variety of sources, such as:

using books and libraries effectively, taking notes, using the
    mechanics of footnoting and compiling bibliographies
listening reflectively to oral presentations
interviewing appropriate resource persons and observing and
    describing contemporary occurrences in school and com-
    munity

B. Skills of interpreting graphic materials, such as:
using and interpreting maps, globes, atlases
using and interpreting charts, graphs, cartoons, numerical data,
    and converting "raw data" into these graphic forms

C. Skills needed to develop a sense of time and chronology, such as:
developing a time vocabulary and understanding time systems
tracing sequences of events
perceiving time relationships, between periods or eras and be-
    tween contemporaneous developments in various countries
    or parts of the world

D. Skills of presenting social studies materials, such as:
organizing material around an outline
writing a defensible paper and presenting an effective speech
participating in a discussion involving social problems

II. Skills of *reflective thinking as applied to social studies problems*

A. Skills of *comprehension,* such as:
identifying the central issues in a problem or argument
arriving at warranted conclusions and drawing valid inferences
providing specific illustrations of social studies generalizations
dealing with increasingly difficult and advanced materials

B. Skills of *analysis and evaluation* of social studies materials, such as:
applying given criteria, such as distinguishing between primary
    and secondary sources, in judging social studies materials
recognizing underlying and unstated assumptions or premises,
    attitudes, outlooks, motives, points of view, or bias
distinguishing facts from hypotheses, judgments, or opinions,
    and checking the consistency of hypotheses with given in-
    formation and assumptions
distinguishing a conclusion from the evidence which supports
    it
separating relevant from irrelevant, essential from incidental
    information used to form a conclusion, judgment, or thesis
recognizing the techniques used in persuasive materials such
    as advertising, propaganda
assessing the adequacy of data used to support a given con-
    clusion
weighing values and judgments involved in alternative courses
    of action, and in choosing alternative courses of action

C. Skills of *synthesis and application* of social studies materials,
    such as:

formulating valid hypotheses and generalizations, and mar-
shalling main points, arguments, central issues

comparing and contrasting points of view, theories, generalizations, and facts

distinguishing cause-and-effect relationships from other types
of relationships, such as means and ends

combining elements, drawing inferences and conclusions, and
comparing with previous conclusions and inferences

identifying possible courses of action

making tentative judgments as a basis for action, subject to
revision as new information or evidence becomes available

supplying and relating knowledge from the social studies as
background for understanding contemporary affairs

III. Skills of *effective group participation*

A. Assuming different roles in the group, such as gadfly or sum-
marizer, as these roles are needed for the group to progress

B. Using parliamentary procedures effectively

C. Helping resolve differences within the group

D. Suggesting and using means of evaluating group progress

Certainly a major purpose of social studies instruction is to place
emphasis on the development of those abilities which encourage the
accurate and intelligent utilization of social science data and which
make habitual the orderly processes of mind necessary to carrying on
reflective thought and to taking action based on such thinking.

LOOKING AHEAD

This preliminary statement of goals for the social studies is but a first
step in a process that looks forward to making recommendations for
the social studies curriculum in our schools. There remains for the
future the major task of working out a logical sequence of grade
placement that will present a systematic overview for the social
studies curriculum. Here, there must be concern for a sequential
development of the essential knowledge, skills, and attitudes that
should be acquired by pupils going through the school program. Also
consideration must be given to programs for pupils of widely varying
abilities. Some experimentation with programs seeking to achieve all
the objectives set forth will in all probability be called for in order to
evaluate their effectiveness. Finally, it should be recognized that there
is no single way in which the materials can be best organized in
arriving at the goals, but that several alternative patterns might well
be suggested.

◆§ Issues: Social Studies and the Social Sciences   *Bernard Berelson*

The American Council of Learned Societies has expressed considerable interest in the substance and pattern of social studies instruction. Berelson, in this selection taken from a volume of articles by A.C.L.S. members, considers a number of issues that disturb both academicians and educationists. His plain talk and good sense do much to remove irrelevant prejudices and to leave us with solid tasks whose solutions call for the best that the social scientist, the educationist, and the teacher have to offer.

Should the social studies curriculum aim to produce good citizens, or knowledgeable students of the major fields of learning? At first glance, it would appear that there is a genuine difference of opinion on this matter among our [social science] authors, or certainly between some of them and the position of most social studies teachers. . . .

My own impression is that this is largely a spurious issue that will go away if it is put in a different semantic frame. As a starter, suppose we were to say that we—all of us involved—want to give high school students the best introduction we can, within limits of practicality, to the best available knowledge from the social science disciplines *as a means to the end* of producing responsible citizens. That single sentence, which I think would be agreed to by many participants on all sides of the debate, may go a long way toward resolving the issue. . . . There are a few more points that need to be made in this connection.

In the first place, the scholars are quite clear that "preparation for responsible citizenship" ought not be used as the facade for "how to do it" courses in the social studies—not on commercial education or business problems in economics . . . , not on personal adjustment in psychology . . . , not on family living in sociology . . . , and in area

Abridged from Bernard Berelson's "Introduction" to *The Social Studies and the Social Sciences*, pp. 6–15 sponsored by the National Council for the Social Studies and the American Council of Learned Societies, © 1962, by Harcourt, Brace & World, Inc., and reprinted with their permission. Bernard Berelson is a leading author of scholarly works in the social sciences.

studies not on the "trouble-spot approach. . . ." In every case, the scholar would naturally prefer his subject to be presented for its own intellectual sake, in the spirit of the liberal arts; and he goes on to argue that that is indeed the best "preparation for responsible citizenship" so far as his field is concerned. Understanding, they feel, should precede and underlie application; and at this stage in education, the time available should be devoted to basic understandings, illustrated by their applications to past and present societies.

There are two additional reasons why this seems indicated. . . . The first is that for a large proportion of high school students, this will be the last exposure to these fields in a formal educational program. Many will not go on to college at all, some will start in college but soon drop out, some will go on in fields that leave little opportunity for further work in the social sciences. So the social studies curriculum in the schools will have to serve not only as the introduction for those continuing in formal education but as all there is for the others—or, put another way, as the platform for adult education. Hence, the more representative of our best knowledge it can be, the better. If there is time for only a beginning, that beginning ought to be fundamental in nature, not peripheral.

The second reason takes us back to the objective of the social studies curriculum if stated as "responsible citizenship." In order to specify that condition for students in secondary schools, it is desirable if not necessary to look ahead, as well as we can. If there is one thing we know about the decades ahead in which today's high school students will be "responsible citizens"—perhaps the only thing we may know with some certainty—it is that they will be a time of change. . . . Who will now venture to say just what that time will bring in the way of specific, concrete demands upon "responsible citizenship"? The only safe prediction is that they will be sharply different from today's issues and conditions. Most of the students being trained in the high schools now will be participants in that world, and some of them will be the leaders of it. So we are training now for the twenty-first century. How can we do better for our students than to give them a fundamental, intellectual preparation that will last, rather than a vocational or utilitarian preparation geared to today's situations that will become outmoded so soon?

What would such preparation mean? In the first place, students would come to know, or at least be exposed to know, a number of things not now presented to them generally or systematically. If we were to follow only the suggestions set down in these papers—not that the authors thought that they were setting down prescriptions—here is just a sampling from the disciplines:

The regional concept, the geography of population, and the use of the culture concept, in geography

The biological bases of human behavior, perception, learning, and personality, from psychology

The nature of economizing and the market system, from economics

Socialization and social control, from sociology

Social function and structure, from anthropology

Political history and the development of governing institutions, from political science

Historical diversity and the great revolutions, from history

—not to mention a range of themes from the area programs. This is a tall order, and it remains so even when we recall that there is a certain amount of overlap among the illustrative recommendations made by our nine authors: between political science and history, for example, or between anthropology and history, or anthropology and the area programs, or psychology and sociology, or geography and history, or economics and political science. Such overlaps, incidentally, are encouraging instances of convergence that speak well for the prospects of putting together a coherent curriculum.

Before asking whether and how such a program could be put into effect, however, I wish to call attention to three special aspects of "what the social studies student should know" as they appear in these pages. Each of them, it seems to me, warrants a moment's extra look.

The first has to do with cultural diversity: explicit attention to differences among human ways of life. This theme appears in the papers on geography, on sociology, on anthropology, on history, and of course strongly in the case of the area programs. In each case, the author argues, it is of particular importance for the student to see himself and, in the literal sense, to appreciate himself in an objective relation to the rest of the world. . . .

The second point is closely related to the first; indeed, it may be the general point of which the first is a special case. That is the desirability of leading the student to an appreciation of what he thinks he knows that is not so. . . . Certainly a sober appreciation of this point is the beginning of wisdom, and if this is soundly done, it could be among the most important consequences of the social studies curriculum.

And third, partly as a way of realizing that end, there is . . . the desirability of giving the student some familiarity and even experience with the research methods by which knowledge is gathered. . . . This approach may be the channel for introducing the high school student to the kind of statistical reasoning and quantitative analysis that characterizes these fields, and that constitutes a great innovation in the study of man within the past several decades.

There remain a few issues that seem to be peculiar to the social studies. At any rate, they do not occur with similar force in such fields as physics, mathematics, biology, or even English.

The first has to do with the high school student's readiness for such a course of study. . . . Will he unduly personalize psychology and sociology or make direct applications to himself and his environment that may not be justified? Ought such matters to be saved until he is more mature, until he has more background against which to evaluate this material? Now such questions do not typically arise in the impersonal case of mathematics or even in the case of biology, but they do in connection with the social studies. Are the students ready?

There is some difference of opinion among our authors on this score, but in general they believe that the students are readier than the teachers. . . . Our authors are willing to go cautiously ahead, to take it for granted that the students are indeed ready, and to focus on the central question of what they should be offered. Their assumption is that high school students can benefit from such material, that they can learn it in a scholarly way if it is properly taught, that they already do in the social-problems course as well as in experimental courses in anthropology and social psychology (plus, of course, the traditional historical, governmental, and geographical courses).

The second issue of peculiar importance to the social studies as compared, say, with mathematics or physics, is not unrelated to the first. It is that this field involves sensitive issues of social, political, economic, even personal policy. Behavioral norms are directly involved here in a sense that they are not in other fields, and that fact can lead to both practical and intellectual difficulties. Note, for example, only some of the problems that would come up and would require dispassionate attention and analysis: the Civil War in history, race differences in anthropology and certain area studies, child rearing and sex matters in psychology, the welfare state in economics, class differences in sociology, Communism in political science and the Soviet area, national aspirations in the Asian area. Beyond such matters, there are questions about the role of values in social studies—questions, incidentally, that the scholarly disciplines themselves are still debating. . . .

Certainly such matters are necessarily involved in any proper course of social studies. What else, indeed, are they about if not the richness, the complexity, the controversy of human life? But where else can the student get a better introduction to such delicate yet important issues than in a classroom properly led by a teacher knowledgeable in the subject and dedicated to its objective analysis? . . .

But perhaps the concern over the matter of values has less to do with indoctrination of the students than with pressures from various minorities in the community. Here the high school teacher may feel somewhat vulnerable and exposed to attack, from whatever quarter does not sympathize with the particular point of view or even the particular fact presented: evolution decades ago, parts of the social studies today. . . . In a sense, it is the very controversiality of many parts of the social studies that requires some systematic attention in the schools for the health of the society.

The third issue centers on the organization of the social studies curriculum. In a sense, it is a political issue, what a friendly observer has characterized as "the League of Nations problem," in that the disciplinary claims for inclusion are as many and profound as the countering pressures of time. . . . In the social studies . . . psychologists must somehow come to terms with political scientists, sociologists with historians, area specialists with geographers, economists with anthropologists. It is not an easy prospect, though in view of the agreed-upon urgency of the goal, it is by no means an impossible one either. . . .

There are two more important points on which our authors appear to agree. The first is that if the social studies must choose between coverage and thoroughness—and given the practicalities of the situation, that choice is probably built in—it should choose thoroughness. As Strayer says, "there is always a temptation to try to do too much, and thus to do nothing very well . . . ," and he advocates within history what is required even more in the wider program, namely, "judicious sampling. . . ." This is a hard choice to make, but a necessary one if an ambitious curriculum is not to thin itself out to the vanishing point.

The other agreement is that the secondary school curriculum should and must stand on its own feet. It is not to be considered as a watered-down version of the college curriculum nor as necessarily having the same objectives—any more than the colleges would consider that their purposes were subordinate to those of the graduate and professional schools. This is not to say that a revised social studies curriculum would not have implications, and even repercussions, upon the work of the college and the graduate school; but the social studies program should be determined by its own demands, its own ends.

ᴥ§ THE SOCIAL STUDIES: NATURE, PURPOSE, AND SIGNS OF CHANGE   *Ralph C. Preston*

*What, after all, is the basic nature of the social studies? What
are our purposes for teaching the social studies? What are the
agents of change operating in our lives today? What shifts are
taking place in the substance and pattern of social studies instruction? Preston helps us answer these questions—and gives
us a warning. He cautions us that careful thought and rigorous
experimentation must enter into coming changes if we are to
escape the mere swinging again of the old familiar pendulum.*

WHAT THE SOCIAL STUDIES ARE

The social studies are those portions of the social sciences that are
selected for use in teaching. The question then arises: What are the
social sciences? The social sciences are the fields of knowledge which
deal with man's social behavior and his social institutions. The three
social sciences which are most frequently and most appropriately
drawn upon by elementary school social studies are the following:

Geography: Geography is the study of the regions of the earth with
special emphasis upon man's relations to his habitat (its land,
climate, and other physical features), and of how these relations are
influenced by, and to some extent may influence, man's energy,
imagination, technical skill, aesthetic instincts, traditions, and beliefs.
The trend among geographers is to define and classify regions in
terms of areas which are relatively homogeneous with respect to
cultural features.

History: History is "the totality of what has transpired," only a
small portion of which, of course, has been recorded. Even the
recorded portion is too vast to be mastered by a single historian,
and the portion to be incorporated in the social studies of the elementary school is necessarily quite restricted. It must be confined to those
events, personalities, and traditions which will enable the child to

From *The National Elementary Principal*, 42:8–13, April, 1963. Copyright 1963,
Department of Elementary School Principals, National Education Association.
All rights reserved. Dr. Preston is professor of education at the University of
Pennsylvania and the author of books and numerous articles on elementary
social studies.

understand better his present world by recognizing in it familiar elements from the past (1). So far as American history goes, authoritative opinion among historians holds that the period of exploration and the Colonial period should receive the heaviest emphasis (2), so far as world history goes, the background of a sampling of other cultures should be studied (3).

Economics: Economics is the study of the production, distribution, and consumption of commodities. It deals with "the ways in which, as a people, we manage our productive human and natural resources and the goods and services which result from the employment and use of these resources" (4). In the elementary school, economics takes up the conflict between unlimited wants and limited resources; the factors which influence each individual in a free society in deciding on what and how much to buy; the impact of consumer choice on production patterns; and the interaction of supply and demand (5).

The elementary social studies program draws also upon other social sciences but in a more limited way. Thus, the field of government makes contributions (largely through history) to the study of political institutions ranging from the role of town or city governments in supplying local public services (schools, police and fire protection, sanitation, etc.) to the national government in supplying postal, military, park, and a vast number of other services. Another fruitful source of elementary school social studies is anthropology. It makes obvious contributions to studies of the early American Indian and other primitive groups, and of how institutions such as the home differ in contrasting cultures.

It is thus evident that the social studies are derived directly from recognized academic disciplines. The term "social studies" does not necessarily imply a unified treatment of the social sciences, as is sometimes mistakenly believed. It is a label which describes programs in which the social sciences are taught whether unified (fused) or distinct and separate (e.g., as geography or history). . . .

OBJECTIVES OF THE SOCIAL STUDIES

George Bernard Shaw is credited with defining a fanatic as one who, having lost sight of his objectives, redoubles his efforts. Teachers who lose sight of their objectives often react similarly. In teaching, as in other fields of human endeavor, the slighting of objectives is a calamity. Exertion of "effort," however conscientious, fails to compensate for lack of purpose and sense of direction.

Those who are in the most authoritative position to indicate social studies objectives are the social scientists themselves. The objectives discussed below are drawn from the writings of a group of them (6).

Knowledge and Understanding:

Of the broad factual structure of each subject and topic pursued. (The suitability of a social studies textbook or curriculum guide can be determined by the care and authenticity with which it presents such structures.)

Of the cultural history, traditions, and values of the child's own society

Of the cultural history, traditions, and values of selected societies representing varying beliefs and practices

Of man's culture in varying environments and its influence upon his relations to his habitat

Of society's management and use of its economic resources, both natural and human

Of some of the methods employed by social scientists in their pursuit of knowledge in their respective fields.

Attitudes:

Toward the subjects and topics under study—curiosity about, and interest in, their subject matter

Toward evidence—respect for it and acceptance of the rules which govern it

Toward man—appreciation of human dignity and sensitivity to the feelings of others

Toward the child's community and country—devotion to their welfare and development of a sense of responsibility with regard to them

Toward generalizations about human behavior—critical reaction and discrimination.

Skills:

In examining data on human beings and their societies with objectivity

In judging the validity and relevancy of data

In compiling and classifying data

In interpreting maps, globes, and graphic material which present social data

In practicing some of the social scientists' methods in collecting firsthand data. . . .

AGENTS OF CHANGE

The emergence of an aggressive public mood toward education. The feverish race over outer space, popularly heralded by the launching of the Soviet Union's first Sputnik in 1957, jolted the public's complacent, easy-going attitude toward education. . . .

The uneasiness promoted by Sputnik also provided a wider hearing of the criticisms and proposals of such groups as the Council for Basic Education which for years had been airing their highly critical views with only limited effectiveness. Many citizens became persuaded that our schools were in need of fundamental curriculum changes. Editors, commentators, and other publicists reflected the new mood by repeating the charges and keeping them to the fore. Although some of the criticisms were groundless and unfair, few school officials escaped the resultant pressure to raise educational standards.

Expanded research and experimentation. Research funds became available. The United States Congress allocated funds for "Project Social Studies" designed to underwrite basic and applied research projects and "curriculum study centers" to redefine the nature and aims of the social studies curriculum and improve teaching methods and materials (7). Private groups, such as Educational Services, Incorporated (producers of the revolutionary physics program of the Physical Science Committee), are tackling the social studies.

Participation of social scientists in curriculum programs. The traditional aloofness of scholars to curriculum problems of the elementary and secondary schools is giving way to expressions of active interest. Their participation in California's social studies program, although limited, is an encouraging indication of the possibilities (8). Reference has already been made to the production of a notable volume by a group of social scientists who joined six professors of education in its preparation (9). It is reasonable to predict that it will wield influence in clarifying the objectives and content of the social studies.

The effect of television and increased travel upon children's concepts. The pace at which children now advance beyond the narrow confines of their communities is much more rapid than before the advent of television and before the rapid expansion of family travel over weekends and during vacations. Although in many respects television is an intellectual "wasteland," as critics of the industry have maintained, it cannot be denied that television-viewing, as well as travel, equips children with large amounts of information. Teachers are now reporting that they can assume a larger background of experience on the part of children than in former years, that their vocabularies are larger, and that more advanced concepts can hence be taught.

The advent of programmed instruction. Only a fraction of the programmed materials now available deal with social studies, and the degree of eventual application of programming to the social studies can only be conjectured. Nevertheless, programming has been sufficiently impressive in certain other fields to have influenced, if only indirectly, the preparation of social studies textbooks and the teaching of social studies. . . . The interest which programming has aroused has caused publishers and teachers to become acutely conscious of the desirability for systematic, careful introduction of facts and skills with frequent interspersion of readily self-corrected exercises to provide children with many opportunities for reinforcement of their learning.

Widening interest in team teaching. Team teaching is an organizational scheme wherein several teachers divide responsibilities for teaching a group of children. Each teacher is afforded the opportunity to specialize to some extent in one or two subject areas. Team teaching and other forms of departmentalization in the elementary school are finding favor in a number of influential school systems. Their chief advantage is that "the deeper the teacher's understanding of his subject, the greater the likelihood of excellent instruction." (10) Departmentalization or semi-departmentalization with young children has certain questionable features, and there are those who think the team teaching concept may prove to be a fad (11). In any case, the present experimentation with the concept is giving fresh emphasis to the importance of the quality of teacher scholarship and preparation.

NATURE OF THE CHANGES

The preceding section, with its emphasis on the forces which are yielding change, hints only sketchily what the changes themselves are. Three already discernible shifts can be described.

1) Increased emphasis on subject matter. There is greater recognition of the value of content, per se, and correspondingly greater stress upon it. There are more valid frameworks of content and better schemes of sequence of subtopics. The content of the primary grades, while properly including community institutions, workers, and processes, is beginning to extend beyond the community; it is slowly divorcing itself from platitudes and sentimentality. In the intermediate grades, the subjects of geography and history are given greater identity—in unified programs as well as in programs which treat geography and history as entirely separate subjects.

2) Increased availability and use of authentic, up-to-date in-

formation. There is a narrowing of the gap between the curriculum in the elementary school and available scholarly knowledge. The "notorious lag between new advances in scholarship and their appearance in our elementary and secondary schools" is gradually being reduced (12). What scholars believe to be of primary significance in their fields is beginning to find its way into the classrooms. By way of example, better materials on other cultures are available and are finding their way into the classroom. Consequently, the archaic and otherwise unreliable stereotypes often associated with them are giving ground to more realistic portrayals.

3) Increased insight into how children may become aware of the challenging nature of the social studies. There is a growing recognition that a purely descriptive approach to social studies is not an approach which "preserves the connection between knowledge and the zest of life." (13) The recent emphasis in the newer elementary school arithmetic programs upon the importance of self-discovery by children has relevance to the social studies, too (14).

4) Increased understanding of how to teach citizenship. A more realistic view is emerging concerning the relationship between teaching social studies and teaching citizenship. Much of the teaching of citizenship via social studies in the past has been sentimental, contrived, self-conscious, and ineffective. . . .

Teachers are becoming increasingly aware that the social studies have built-in elements which develop traits of good citizenship quite naturally—and more successfully than . . . contrived devices. . . . Social scientists have pointed out that the knowledge and methods of the social studies in and of themselves are the best preparation for responsible citizenship (15). They can be organized and taught so as to impart a disciplined way of analyzing, classifying, and judging data. The importance of the types of thinking underlying such activities when applied to public decisions is obvious. Furthermore, the social studies, when rigorously taught, develop a belief in the desirability of free inquiry, of comparing and evaluating sources of data, and of weighing conflicting data. Such a belief perhaps is the best defense against propaganda and subversion.

It is also better understood today than a few years ago that knowledge of the social studies contributes to citizenship in other ways. (a) The knowledge provides a basis for viewing current affairs with perspective, i.e., for appraising situations realistically, avoiding undue optimism or undue pessimism and avoiding the provincial outlook. (b) By providing understanding of preceding generations, the knowledge promotes in the child a sense of continuity. He will be better able to live and work tolerantly with the generations which overlap his. (c) Through the knowledge, the child is brought to feel more at home in his world and to sense how his homeland is related to other lands. The surface of things may appear to him as chaotic, but study of the content will reveal the presence of some order. For example, there may be classifiable motives or patterns; and many of man's activities are governed (and explicable) in terms of season, climate, and topography. An understanding of such matters is part of the basis of true adjustment.

The foregoing elements of citizenship, then, can be taught indirectly rather than through a frontal attack on citizenship itself. Lessons in citizenship are byproducts of straight social studies well taught.

In closing, the writer wishes to issue a warning. Periods of change are not only periods of challenge. They are also periods of danger. They are exploited by sloganeers and faddists. If the social studies are to emerge sound and strong from the current ferment, it will be necessary for each new proposition to be scrutinized carefully and experimented with critically—particularly those propositions which are largely organizational in nature. Otherwise we may find in fifteen years that, instead of having made progress, we have simply experienced another ride on a pendulum.

References

(1) Strayer, Joseph R. "History." *The Social Studies and the Social Sciences.* (Edited by Bernard Berelson *et al.*) New York: Harcourt, Brace & World, 1962. pp. 20–41.

(2) *Ibid.* That historians have been consistent in this position may be seen by referring to the Report of the Committee on American History in Schools and Colleges of The American Historical Association, *et al. American History in Schools and Colleges.* New York: The Macmillan Co., 1944.

(3) Strayer, *op. cit.*

(4) Lewis, Ben W. "Economics." *The Social Studies and the Social Sciences, op. cit.*, p. 108.

(5) Edwards, Edgar O., and Senesh, Lawrence. *How to Maintain Economic Freedom*, Part II. Hartford: Connecticut Council for the Advancement of Economic Education, 1957.

(6) This list of objectives is based to a considerable extent upon ideas furnished by the social scientists who contributed to *The Social Studies and the Social Sciences, op. cit.* They wrote with the secondary school in mind, but most of their discussion of goals applies in large part to the elementary school as well.

(7) "Announcement for Project Social Studies." *Social Education* 26:300; October 1962. "More About Project Social Studies." *Social Education* 26:411; November 1962.

(8) *Report of the State Central Committee on Social Studies to the*

California State Curriculum Commission. Sacramento: California State Department of Education, 1961.

(9) *The Social Studies and the Social Sciences, op. cit.*

(10) Anderson, Richard C. "The Case for Teacher Specialization in the Elementary School." *Elementary School Journal* 62:253–60; February 1962.

(11) Wynn, D. Richard, and De Remer, Richard W. "Staff Utilization, Development and Evaluation." *Review of Educational Research* 31:393–405; October 1961.

(12) Petrovich, Michael B. "Teaching about Russia and Eastern Europe." *The Social Studies and the Social Sciences, op. cit.,* p. 241.

(13) Whitehead, Alfred North. *The Aims of Education and Other Essays.* New York: The Macmillan Co., 1929, p. 139.

(14) See Wirtz, Robert W., and Botel, Morton. *Math Workshop for Children: General Guide.* Chicago: Encyclopaedia Britannica, 1962.

(15) *The Social Studies and the Social Sciences, op. cit.,* pp. 6–7, 107.

◄§ Scope and Sequence of Content in Social Studies Programs   *Dorothy McClure Fraser*

The major elements of the scope and sequence of social studies for the elementary grades are reported in this selection. Note particularly the mention of an earlier shift in the upper grades from such topics as "transportation" and "communication" to more content drawn from history and geography. Then note that the primary grades are still organized around "food," "transportation," and similar topics.

Since the expanding-environment or expanding-geographic-areas plan for establishing sequence in content selection is predominant, it is not surprising that centers of interest assigned to given grades in elementary social-studies programs show considerable similarity from one school to another and from one part of the country to another. Table 2 summarizes recent research concerning the themes and topics commonly utilized at each grade level in social-studies programs today.

Used by permission of the National Society for the Study of Education; from "The Organization of the Elementary School Social Studies Curriculum," *Social Studies in the Elementary School,* Fifty-Sixth Yearbook, Part II, Chicago: University of Chicago Press, 1957, pp. 142–147. Dr. Fraser is a professor of education at Hunter College and the author of numerous works for pupils and teachers of the social studies.

Table 2. Commonest Subject Matter in Elementary Social-Studies Programs *

COMMONEST OFFERINGS	AS FOUND BY BOTH PRESTON AND HODGSON	AS FOUND BY PRESTON ONLY	AS FOUND BY HODGSON ONLY
GRADE I	Home, school, pets	Farm life	
GRADE II	Community helpers	Transportation	Farm life, pets
GRADE III	Food, clothing, and shelter	Community; other communities; transportation; communication; Indians	
GRADE IV	Type regions of world; U.S. history; community	State	Indians, Eskimos
GRADE V	U.S. geography; U.S. history	Latin America; Canada	
GRADE VI	Latin America; Canada; Asia; Europe	World geography; old world backgrounds; transportation; communication	

* From Ralph C. Preston, *Teaching Social Studies in the Elementary School*, chap. iii. New York: Rinehart & Co. (revision in preparation).

These findings are not materially different from those reported by Burress (1), who studied twenty-one courses of study issued between 1946 and 1950, or Wesley and Adams, whose most recent listing was published in 1952 (2). Nevertheless, examination of courses of study issued since 1953 and statements from the fourteen specialists cited above indicate that some gradual changes are taking place in the content areas assigned to each grade level as well as in the topics suggested for implementation of the grade-level themes.

For the kindergarten and Grades I and II, the theme of "home, school, and community" is almost universally utilized. In the kindergarten the emphasis continues to be placed on group living, holidays, getting acquainted with the school, and exploring the immediate neighborhood. In Los Angeles County it is suggested that a beginning be made in studying "Workers who help us at home, at school, and in the neighborhood." (3) The guide developed by curriculum committees in Aberdeen (South Dakota) moved somewhat away from the customary pattern for the kindergarten to include some study of community helpers and transportation as well as more customary materials on home, school, and holidays (4).

There seems to be an increasing tendency to treat aspects of the "community-helpers" theme throughout the Kindergarten–Grade II sequence, rather than concentrating this material in one year, and to focus on services people need and use rather than on the "helpers" themselves. Playground attendants, ministers, doctors, nurses, dentists, and shoe repairmen may be studied along with the milkman, the postal worker, and the policeman. Units on the farm and aspects of transportation and communication continue to be used in the sequence from kindergarten through Grade II.

Specific attention is given to safety in the Kindergarten–Grade II sequence, often through "units" or "interests" on "How people meet their health and safety needs," "Learning to grow healthfully and to practice safety," "Safety in the home," or "Safety on the farm." Often some science elements are woven into these health and safety units. Other science experiences commonly suggested in connection with social studies are study of the weather, seasonal changes and their effects on ways of living, and plants and animals of the immediate area. Aspects of conservation are sometimes brought into such experiences. Science information related to transportation and communication is frequently included, also.

Holidays and other special days, once the major social-studies content in the first school years, continue to be celebrated. Other long-used approaches to the development of understanding and acceptance of national traditions continue to be employed. They include studying about the flag and its symbolism, learning and reciting the pledge of allegiance, and hearing stories of great Americans of the past and present.

In Grade III a continuation of the community study which is begun as early as the kindergarten seems likely to become the predominant theme in place of the "food-clothing-shelter" theme carried out through culture units. However, any change from the content previously followed at this level may be less drastic than the change in statement of the theme would suggest. In some cases the community is studied through investigation of the ways in which basic human needs are met within the home community and then in other communities. The "basic needs" are likely to be limited to those for food, clothing, and shelter, although in some cases it is suggested that others such as recreational, educational, and religious needs be considered. Sometimes attention is given to conservation of natural resources in connection with the food, clothing, and shelter units.

The "other communities" studied in Grade III may be contemporary and within the United States, or they may be remote in time and/or space. Study of Indians continues to appear at this level with some frequency. Sometimes the topic is recommended as an example of a primitive, "simple" culture in which the basic needs must be met; in this case, other "culture units" dealing with far-away lands may also be included. In some cases the community study in Grade III involves a historical approach. Then, Indians are likely to be studied as part of the investigation of the community's past, with a block of work on colonial or pioneer life following.

Perhaps the most definite change that is occurring in content placement in elementary social-studies programs is in Grade IV. More recent curriculum guides and the reports of specialists indicate that study of the state, or of "the community within the state," is winning considerable popularity. However, study of type regions, which has long served to introduce formal geography at this level, persists in many schools. In a number of cases there seems to be a compromise, with attention to both the home state and various regions of the world. Thus, the suggested program for Grade IV in Newark (New Jersey) begins with study of "other communities" in New Jersey and of the history of the state and concludes with geographic units on the Netherlands, the Belgian Congo, the Arabian Desert, and the Far North (5).

In Grade V, while content drawn from the history and geography of the United States is usually treated, there is no general agreement as to whether the emphasis shall be historical or geographic, and whether other parts of the Americas shall be studied along with the United States. One arrangement includes study of the earlier periods of the national history (discovery, exploration, settlement, and westward movement) along with attention to the economic geography of the various regions. Another utilizes study of the regions as the framework, starting with ways of earning a living in each region today and drawing in historical background. The United States and Canada, the United States and its neighbors to the north and south, and the United States and the other American lands today are other arrangements of content that are found in Grade V.

The almost universal use of United States history content in Grade V undoubtedly reflects legislative or other legal requirements for the teaching of the national history in the elementary school as well as a traditional curriculum arrangement inherited from the nineteenth century. Hodgson found that, of 40 cities having local legal requirements for the study of United States history in the elementary school, 57.5 per cent required it in Grade V (6). A survey conducted by the Research Division of the National Education Association in 1953 indicated that 18 states had statutory or regulatory provisions for the teaching of American history and government that would almost certainly affect the intermediate grades. An additional 21 states have adopted provisions such as those requiring instruction in American history to begin not later than Grade VIII, making it mandatory for all elementary schools to teach United States and state history and civics (7).

More variation exists in the content placed in the sixth grade. There is fairly even division between study of the western hemisphere continued from Grade V and study of the eastern hemisphere with emphasis on Europe. Where the focus is on Europe, considerable historical content is included along with some geography. One specialist, for example, reported that the most frequently studied topics in the sixth-grade classes in her geographic area were: prehistoric times; Europe and the Middle East, yesterday and today. It seems significant that specialists reported this historical emphasis as current practice much more frequently than it was recommended in recent curriculum bulletins. The "old-world-backgrounds" material, once so generally taught in the intermediate grades, apparently persists in many schools, probably modified by fusion with geographic content. A third arrangement found in Grade VI uses "world geography" as the basic content. In some cases this seems to be the traditional country-by-country examination of physical features, products, and so on. In others it involves the study of selected regions and comparisons with appropriate regions of the United States. If the United Nations is studied in the elementary-school program, it is found most frequently in the fifth or sixth grade, usually in connection with the interest of the United States in world affairs.

Writing in 1941, Turner noted some trend toward placing "general" topics, such as transportation, communication, inventions, arts of man, and money and trade, in Grades V and VI as substitutes for the history and geography previously studied there (8). Today such topics are found in a few programs, but the overwhelming emphasis continues to be on historical and geographic materials.

References

(1) Robert N. Burress, "A Desirable Social-Studies Curriculum for the Middle Grades," pp. 66–67. Unpublished Ph.D. dissertation, George Peabody College for Teachers, 1951.

(2) Edgar B. Wesley and Mary A. Adams, *Teaching Social Studies in Elementary Schools*, pp. 44–46. Boston: D. C. Heath & Co., 1952 (revised edition).

(3) *Educating the Children of Los Angeles County, op. cit.*, pp. 86–87.

(4) "Learning through Action: A Guide Book for Social Studies," Part I, "Kindergarten-Primary Area." Aberdeen, South Dakota: Public Schools, 1954 (mimeographed).

(5) *Social Studies in Our Schools, op. cit.*

(6) Hodgson, *op. cit.*, p. 220.

(7) "Statutory and Regulatory Provisions for the Teaching of American History and Government." Information Bulletin of Research Division of the National Education Association, August, 1953 (mimeographed).

(8) Turner, *op. cit.*, p. 603.

ᎧᎦ What Are We Teaching in Social Studies?
Donald L. Barnes

One of the more difficult questions in considering the social studies is: What is being taught? The casual observer finds himself quickly bewildered at the tremendous variety of topics "covered" in the elementary grades. Barnes' findings bring a degree of order to the question, but they also indicate the tremendous variety within and among grades. Some topics appear to be duplications. For example, what is the difference between a study of the "home" and of the "family"? And what is the meaning of "other" in the many places where that term appears? Barnes' findings confirm what many have long thought to be true—that social studies programs often look like patchwork quilts. And although patchwork quilts may have kept some of us warm on cold winter nights, their patterns were not logically sound. Quilt patterns do not demand logic, social studies patterns do.

In the heat of argument surrounding present controversies over curricular offerings in American schools, zealots on all sides frequently resort to sweeping statements based upon limited observations.

The . . . national survey reported in this article . . . [was] con-

Reprinted from the October, 1960, issue of *Education*, pp. 121–123. Copyright, 1960, by The Bobbs-Merrill Co., Indianapolis, Indiana. Dr. Barnes is an associate professor of education at Ball State Teachers College.

ducted in an effort to piece together a more accurate picture of current offerings in social studies . . . in cities and towns throughout the United States. Sixty-two cities in forty-two states from Maine to California co-operated in the study.

SOCIAL STUDIES

Completed tabulations in social studies reveal that there is much similarity among the programs on various grade levels. Programs begin with studies of people and things close at hand and expand as children's interests expand. The percentage of school systems offering each topic at each grade level is as follows:

> *Grade One:* Family, 30 per cent; Home, 84 per cent; School, 82 per cent; and Other, 16 per cent.
>
> *Grade Two:* Community, 42 per cent; Neighborhood, 44 per cent; Community Helpers, 44 per cent; and Other, 20 per cent.
>
> *Grade Three:* Indians, 22 per cent; Pioneers, 10 per cent; Food, 24 per cent; Shelter, 24 per cent; Clothing, 26 per cent; Transportation and Communication, 22 per cent; Our City, 68 per cent; and Other, 18 per cent.
>
> *Grade Four:* Our State, 40 per cent; and Beginning Readiness for History and Geography, 78 per cent.
>
> *Grade Five:* United States, Past and Present, 90 per cent; Western Hemisphere, 12 per cent; and Other, 4 per cent.
>
> *Grade Six:* Old World, 42 per cent; Other Nations, 42 per cent; Eastern Hemisphere, 12 per cent; and Other, 14 per cent.
>
> *Grade Seven:* U. S. Geography, 24 per cent; World Geography, 48 per cent; State Geography, 24 per cent; State History, 26 per cent; and Other, 24 per cent.
>
> *Grade Eight:* U. S. History, 82 per cent; Citizenship, 14 per cent; and Other, 16 per cent.
>
> *Grade Nine:* World Geography, 18 per cent; World History, 26 per cent; Civics, 58 per cent; and Other, 8 per cent.
>
> *Grade Ten:* World History, 88 per cent; World Geography, 28 per cent; and Other, 4 per cent.
>
> *Grade Eleven:* U. S. History, 82 per cent; Sociology, 10 per cent; Government, 16 per cent; and Other, 27 per cent.
>
> *Grade Twelve:* Economics and/or Sociology, 54 per cent; Government, 60 per cent; and U. S. History, 26 per cent.

In the absence of a centralized governmental control agency similar to those found in European countries, it is surprising to find such great similarity among the offerings in the various school systems. A partial explanation of the phenomenon may lie in the fact that most large publishers in the United States enjoy nation-wide distribution of their school-texts—a reflection of common values held by citizens throughout the country.

Approximately 90 per cent of the cities in the study indicated that they used the unit method in teaching social studies. The units incorporated panels, group and committee work, films, pupil-teacher planning, audio-visual materials, and trips through the city or area in which the school was located. Most units consisted of an introduction, a study or mastery period, and an evaluation period. The length of units varied from two to six weeks.

ஐ SEPARATE OR MERGED—SOUND EXPERIENCES ARE VITAL *Harold D. Drummond*

Professor Drummond takes a close look at a persistent problem: Should history and geography be organized and taught as separate subjects, or should they and other social sciences be merged and coordinated into the social studies? He then discusses three factors that must be taken into account as a faculty or school district makes a decision on this problem. The plea that Drummond makes in his final paragraph is worth some research on the reader's part. The teacher has both the right and the obligation to prepare original materials to substitute for weak spots in textbooks or to fill in areas that text authors have ignored.

FOR THIRTY YEARS or more, discussions about social studies teaching in educational literature and in faculty meetings have frequently focused on organizational problems. Much attention has been devoted by teachers, principals, and curriculum workers, to say nothing of publishers of materials, to the question: "Shall history and geography be taught separately, or shall they be merged or fused into social studies?" As so often is the case, much of the discussion probably has been seeking answers to the wrong question.

Any program for young learners which limits instruction in social education to only the time-honored fields of history and

From *The National Elementary Principal*, 42:27–30, April, 1963. Copyright 1963, Department of Elementary School Principals, National Education Association. All rights reserved. Harold D. Drummond is the chairman of the Department of Elementary Education, University of New Mexico.

geography—as necessary as those fields are—is cheating the young-sters. Either these separate fields *must* be much more broadly defined than they are traditionally—to include learnings from eco-nomics, sociology, anthropology, and political science—or another organizational structure or framework to carry the learning load must be adopted. Moreover, much of the program must be viewed as affective in nature. How a youngster feels about himself and others as a result of his experiences in social studies influences greatly his subsequent behavior in the social realm.

In the main, two different approaches to social studies instruc-tion have been utilized. Those school systems holding to separate instructional periods in history and geography (the number of these may be gaining slightly at present) have included some learnings from economics and anthropology in "geography." Some concepts from political science and sociology have likewise pervaded the "history" programs. The great majority of school systems, however, have adopted another structure—the social studies—drawing upon the social sciences for content but providing instruction through units of work of several types.

For many years, teachers of young children generally seemed to agree that units of work (focusing on the community, social processes, a period of history, or a region-culture) were useful ways to organize learning experiences in the social studies. . . .

FACTORS TO CONSIDER

What factors need to be considered in planning a program of social education? . . .

1. *The culture surrounding the school must be considered.* If the youngsters are new arrivals from Cuba or Puerto Rico, or if they live in an Indian Pueblo, what can and should be done at school is something different from what can and should be tried in an upper middle class suburban community. The school's problems in some ways may be greater in the latter case—especially if parent expecta-tions are very high, if opportunities for the child to explore, to experiment, and to make decisions have been rigorously curtailed at home by apartment house living, new carpets which must not be soiled, or the sterile cleanliness of suburbia.

Principals and teachers must continuously remind themselves that each child brings to school, in part at least, *his* learned way of responding to adults, to other children, and to new experiences. School staffs which, because of their own values, create in-school expectancies far removed from out-of-school realities should expect that many youngsters will fail to learn—whether history and geography are taught separately or merged. Acceptance of this point of view does not mean that "standards" should be sacrificed or that basic values and concepts should not be sought and taught. It does mean, however, that the school staff's *action* may vary considerably from school-community to school-community.

2. *Individual differences among learners must be considered.* This statement has been written so many times in the past quarter-century that it almost has become a cliché. The facts remain, however, cliché or not! . . .

Whether there are separate periods for history and geography, or whether the program is organized as the social studies, provisions for *individuals* must be made. As is true of many organizational questions, what happens *after* the decision is made is of greater importance than the choice. It is possible to provide needed learnings in citizenship education geared to unique individuals under either organizational structure. The converse is also true—the structure does not guarantee that instruction will be carefully planned in terms of the needs of each child. . . .

3. *The materials selected for use, and the activities provided, make a difference.* For a considerable period of time, proponents of the two organizational structures have, at least superficially, separated themselves into factions on the use of textbooks in teaching. The proponents of the separate history and geography periods have supported, generally, the idea that every child should have a copy of the same basic textbooks. By contrast, the social studies adherents have recommended frequently, although by no means universally, ten or so copies of several available textbooks, so that a wider selection of material is available for use. Both groups support, basically, the use of audiovisual materials, including films, filmstrips, maps, globes, and television programs when appropriate.

Let no one deny—the materials available for use *do* make a difference. Textbooks which are well organized, factually accurate, up-to-date, and well written are better than textbooks full of contrived stories, stereotypes similar to those on travel posters, and little or no emphasis on skills and content. Whichever structure is selected for use, good instructional materials make it more possible for teachers to help youngsters learn the important concepts and master the needed symbols. Moreover, there is nothing inherent in either structure which mitigates for or against materials which seem at first glance to have been organized primarily for use in one of the two structures. Good textbooks are useful in either structure, if used properly as tools rather than as bibles. . . .

Learning activities—the experiences learners have—also make a difference in what is learned. Regardless of the organizational structure, learning activities can be well selected, vital, intellectually challenging, and educationally sound. By contrast, activities in either organizational plan can be wooden, lifeless, emotionally sterile, and dull. As the scope of knowledge increases astronomically each year, it becomes increasingly apparent that not all that is known can be taught to children and youth. *Selection* of key ideas which provide an understandable structure to the disciplines seems essential now and for the foreseeable future.

Structural approaches to a field, while they will undoubtedly help the learner, do not guarantee the development of ways of thinking utilized by scholars in a field. We know so little, in fact, about how such ways of thinking develop that jumping on the structural bandwagon at this period in history seems fundamentally an action which should be considered carefully. Moreover, the lasting results of changes in approach are not likely to be apparent in the thinking patterns of youngsters for several years. Marked improvement in achievement as measured by standardized tests should probably not be expected. Achievement scores may even drop initially as less attention is devoted to knowledge, per se, and more to processes of seeking and learning. The shift in emphasis toward structure will require a search for new kinds of evidence concerning the extent of learning. We will become less interested in memorization of facts and regurgitation of them at appropriate times and more concerned about the ways youngsters approach problems, seek information concerning the problems, and utilize rational processes in coming to solutions.

WHICH STRUCTURE, THEN?

On the basis of the foregoing analysis, it must be obvious that I believe that instruction in the whole broad area of social education, regardless of the terms used to describe it, can be improved. Furthermore, I believe it can be improved markedly, regardless of the organizational structure utilized.

My own conviction, after a quarter-century of working with teachers and children, is that the social studies approach is fundamentally better with children than the attempt to separate the disciplines. Too frequently, when the separate discipline approach is utilized, the instruction becomes wedded to a single source of information. Too frequently, when the separate discipline approach is utilized, teachers move away from sound involvement of learners in planning and carrying out learning activities which teach ways of seeking knowledge, and move toward the dullest sort of verbal repetition of answers which have been conveniently packaged in the textbooks. Too frequently, when the separate discipline approach is used, unnatural and unwise attempts are made to separate related factors. History and geography *are* related—and these disciplines are related also to resources, social organization, political structures, and culture, broadly defined.

As yet, however, I have not seen a truly excellent textbook for use with children which provides satisfactorily both geographical and historical perspective. When one *is* developed, it may lack perspective from economics, anthropology, or political science. In other words, the basic books probably will continue to be written from a particular perspective of human society. In the foreseeable future, therefore, teachers and children will need to use a number of textbooks in their search for knowledge in the social studies. And that is sound, it seems to me, for that is what scholars do. Scholars do not rely on a single source of information—even if the source contains their names as the authors! They use *many* sources. Moreover, scholars share their concerns with other scholars and learn ways of working from other scholars. Should not youngsters learn this way, too?

Although I must frankly admit that some of the poorest teaching I've seen has been done by teachers who had not mastered a unit approach to teaching the social studies, I must simultaneously observe that in every case the *best* teachers *were* utilizing that approach. These truly excellent teachers were, in the finest sense of the term, learners themselves. They were continually seeking increased understanding of their world and interpretations of it from several vantage points. It seems likely, then, that teacher education, at both pre-service and in-service levels, should devote more concern to extending teachers' basic grasp of the total field encompassed by the social studies—but at the adult level. Few colleges, universities, or school systems are structured and staffed to perform this vital task.

A slight improvement in teaching practices may result when a public school system moves from whatever structure is now used to another—at least for a time. But the basic questions which must be answered are not fundamentally related to structure or organization. The basic questions are: How vital are the learning experiences provided? How useful are they in helping young learners take sound steps toward independent inquiry in the field? In other words, whichever organizational pattern is utilized, sound learning experiences—those which challenge, free, and lead the learner toward inquiry—are vital.

More of our energies should be spent creating better materials which may be used fruitfully in either approach, developing better ways of differentiating instruction based upon individual needs, and planning more effectively for the particular group of youngsters in terms of the experiences which they have daily out-of-school. Separate or merged—sound learning experiences are vital.

DOES ORGANIZATION OF CONTENT FACILITATE LEARNING?   *Edgar B. Wesley*

Do the social studies need to be highly structured programs of specified scope and articulated sequence? Do topics within programs need to be highly organized and carefully coordinated? Wesley asks these questions in a manner that raises even more basic questions about the difference between the teacher's organization of his lessons and the pupil's own organization of his experiences. If Wesley is both serious and correct, what changes should be made in existing programs? If his tongue is partially in his cheek, when should we be planning for and when with pupils?

FROM TIME IMMEMORIAL teachers, speakers, and writers have assumed that the logical and systematic organization of their product facilitates understanding. They have struggled valiantly to provide an artistic structure that rises from a firm foundation and towers into the blue of color and appeal. At times they seem to reflect Flaubert or Walter Pater and imply that organization is more important than content. They have assumed that they were taking all this trouble for the sake of the learner.

Assuming that units, chapters, and topics call for the same elements as a story or a drama, their creators have spent enormous energy to achieve a symmetrical organization, one that would presumably facilitate understanding and retention. Consequently a unit

Used by permission of the author and the publishers; from the *Indiana Social Studies Quarterly,* 12:14–16, Autumn, 1959. Edgar B. Wesley is emeritus professor of education, University of Minnesota.

or a chapter is expected to have chronological, or some other kind of sequence, an orderly development, an inductive logic, a dramatic high point, a recurring reminder, and a closing clincher.

Dramas and stories may require a rather strict adherence to some predetermined structure, but it is doubtful that narratives, descriptions, and expositions—the typical content of the social studies—require the faithful following of any rules of organization. There is considerable doubt as to whether the organization that appeals to the author and on which he expends great care has much value for the learner. In fact, the organization may in some instances not only not facilitate learning; it may distract, confuse, and mislead the potential learner. He may be impressed by the form and assume that it is the essence of what should be learned. Even more likely, he admires and tries to appropriate the organization as well as the content, thus failing to perform an imperative of learning, namely, reorganization in terms of the learner. In such instance the neat, appealing organization has not only not facilitated learning; it has distracted and misled the potential learner by causing him to assume that he should and could appropriate the categories as well as the contents provided by another.

Organization is an indispensable step in the learning of an extended, complicated, or involved matter. The memorizing of the state capital may involve merely a mechanical recall, but the memorizing of fifty state capitals requires some order, plan, system, or structure. Without some kind of sequence one would not know when he has reached the fiftieth state. Thus organization of some kind is a necessary step in learning that involves any significant content.

Both the nature and importance of organization in learning are strikingly revealed in Morrison's unit method. His fourth step is devoted to organization, and it is the organization of the scattered, unassembled, and unsynthesized materials of the unit *by the student*—the learner—and not by the teacher. In Morrison's second step—presentation—the teacher hints at the contents of the unit and foreshadows the organization, but he very carefully refrains from presenting an organization. That is the glorious privilege, the inescapable obligation, and the fostering opportunity of the learner, not the prerogative or obligation of the teacher. The teacher who presents the organization which the student should achieve is robbing him of his chance to learn. Thus the presentation of an organization not only does not facilitate learning; according to Morrison it actually forestalls learning.

Ask a person as he emerges from a lecture hall to report upon the speech to which he has just listened. In most instances he will be unable to give a systematic review or even a synthesized idea of the speech. After a period of stammering confusion he may chuckle over a joke, repeat a phrase, or refer to a story. His inability to present an intelligible summary is due to the fact that he has not organized or reorganized the speech. Naturally, he can seldom remember both the major ideas and the organization and in many cases he remembers neither. The speaker probably labored carefully over the outline of his speech but it did not greatly aid the hearer in recalling its contents.

Organization does make one very tangible, though not a basically important, contribution to learning. It serves as a model. The intelligent learner becomes somewhat mindful of the form in which the material is presented. While he seldom appreciates the full relevance of all parts of the structure, he often perceives its general nature, appropriates some portions of it, and synthesizes them into the pattern or organization that he himself evolves. Thus the table of contents does serve as a sort of model; it is an example of what is in some form as necessary for the learner as it was for the author. But it is quite clear that the true learner as differentiated from the memorizer supplies eventually his own structure, no matter how aptly, cleverly, or charmingly the teacher or author may organize the content.

Thus it appears that authors, teachers, and lecturers have overemphasized organization. Textbooks, units, and courses of study have been prepared on the assumption that their structure as well as their content is to be understood, accepted, and retained. It is almost an article of educational faith that a beguiling organization is a prerequisite to learning. It does not seem to be widely recognized that organization belongs primarily to the author or teacher rather than to the learner.

If the foregoing analysis is sound, educators may relax a little and not worry quite so much about the logic, sequence, form, or structure of their materials. In fact, teachers, speakers, and authors may pour their ideas into a heap and trust students to select, sort, classify, rearrange, and reorganize. The learner will do much of the work that the teacher assumed he had to perform. The teacher and author need organization, not primarily for the sake of the learner, but for their own guidance. The nature of the product rather than the needs of the learner determines the importance and nature of the organization.

Even though organization may not materially facilitate learning, it is still highly desirable that speeches, chapters, and units have intelligible organizations. A framework, a structure, a sequence guides the author or speaker in arranging his content, serves as a touch-stone of relevance, and satisfies the dramatic urge. Thus organization will continue to attract supporters, upholders, and devotees. Its shrine will not be deserted.

✔ REVISING THE SOCIAL STUDIES: WHAT IS NEEDED? *Paul R. Hanna*

What are the basic human activities and the expanding communities of men? How are these two ideas used to provide a framework for social studies instruction? These two ideas have been both misinterpreted and misapplied in some school districts, but they persist as valid ideas for organizing social studies programs. Both Fraser and Barnes reported on the patchwork nature of many programs; their reports clearly indicate that parts of the activities and communities show up here and there in the curriculum. In this article, Hanna provides insight into a manner of combining these two ideas to structure a program for use in the elementary grades.

THE LACK OF DESIGN

Very few current projects begin with an over-all design. A few even reject any coordinated approach. One looks in vain for proposals on scope and sequence that have institutional or organizational support. Not since the National Council for the Social Studies brought out in 1939 its volume entitled *The Future of the Social Studies* have we had available in one source a variety of proposals for structuring the school social studies offering (1).

What we have today are many efforts at revision of the social studies, each proceeding without benefit of "systems approach," "set theory," or old-fashioned concern for curriculum balance, coordination, and articulation. Lacking any such planning, it seems to me the possibility is small of ever bringing order out of these scattered and unrelated starts (2).

Let it be understood at the outset that few if any social studies

Used by permission of the author and the National Council for the Social Studies, from *Social Education*, 27:190–196, April, 1963. Dr. Hanna is the Lee Jacks professor of child education at Stanford University; he is the author of many books for children and has written widely for teachers.

theorists would advocate one and only one grand design for all schools. We have prospered nationally by diversity. We do not here advocate "all or none." . . .

We advocate launching our nation-wide efforts to improve the social studies program with major attention to alternate systems approaches. These alternate designs should be as comprehensive, as wholistic, as balanced as we can make them. Granted, we must create in each design the continuous mechanisms: 1) to evaluate the program in action in classrooms; 2) to scan the social sciences and history for new or refined content and process, and 3) to feed back our findings to improve each design. . . .

A PROPOSAL FOR STRUCTURE

With these intentions and principles in mind, and again insisting that there must be alternative structures proposed, we now sketch one possible structure for a social studies program from the primary school through the secondary school grades.

In the elementary schools, by following the wholistic and co-ordinated approach to the study of men living in societies, we de-sign our program as follows: The sequence of themes or emphases is drawn from the fact that each of us lives within a system or set of expanding communities that starts with the oldest, smallest, and most crucial community—the family placed in the center of the concentric circles—and progresses outward in ever widening bands through the child's neighborhood community; the child's local com-munities of city, county, and/or metropolis; the state community; the regions-of-states community; and the national community. This set of communities—family to nation—is a highly interdependent system: e.g. the problems and possible solutions of the family group are always colored by the larger communities of which the family is the smallest but core group. Even the national community reaches inward through all of the intervening bands of lesser communities to influence the life of the family group.

The rationale for each of the expanded bands of the system is found in the necessity and the desire of the lesser communities to join other similar lesser communities in forming a larger commu-nity to provide through united effort means of carrying on basic human activities not possible within the resources of each of the lesser communities working in isolation. One can understand each of these interlocking communities better by studying the system: ultimately the American family can only be understood within the cultural complex that we know as the national personality; or the state community can be seen much better if one knows the composite characteristics of the family communities and of the local communities that have come together to form the particular state community under study. . . .

Suggested grade assignment of emphases. The logic of the expanding-communities-of-men design suggests that each larger component community be studied *in sequence* by the child. In the first grade, the child might start his study of the system with emphases on his own family and his own school. As he studies each of these communities, he learns what phases of life are properly the concern of himself as a member of these small intimate groups. He also learns that families need to join families to provide, through neighborhood apparatuses, fire protection, food and clothing, schools, etc. Consequently, the child moves naturally to the third emphasis in the sequential structure—the neighborhood community which exists to provide services not available to families or to the school in isolation.

This particular social studies design may assign the study of the neighborhood to the second grade. However, the grade assignment of the community to be emphasized is relatively unimportant; following *the sequence* from the lesser community to the next larger is the governing principle here.

The sequence typically followed in schools adopting this structure is as follows.

GRADE	EMPHASIS
One	1. The child's family community
	2. The child's school
Two	3. The child's neighborhood community
Three	4. The child's local communities: country, city, county, metropolis
Four	5. The child's state community
	6. The child's region-of-states community
Five	7. The U. S. national community

The grid of basic human activities (social science disciplines). Over this set of expanding communities of men, we now lay a grid of clusters of human activities. Universally, men in groups have in the past, do now, and no doubt will continue to carry on basic human activities, here catalogued under nine headings: protecting and conserving life and resources; producing, exchanging, and consuming goods and services; transporting goods and people; communicating facts, ideas, and feelings; providing education; providing recreation; organizing and governing; expressing aesthetic and spiritual impulses; and creating new tools, technics, and institutions. Note the similarity of the names given these clusters and the names used to designate social science disciplines: "producing, exchanging, and consuming" might as well be labeled *economics;* "organizing and governing" could be replaced by the term *political science.*

The point to stress here is that the grid of basic human activities (essentially the regrouping of the content of the social science disciplines) is laid over each of the expanding communities of men: the child studies the ways men in groups carry out the several basic human activities in each community. While it is to be expected that the class, in studying its state, may focus first on one cluster of activities and then another, this structure encourages the wholistic approach to the community being studied. All the interlocking social science disciplines are seen as part of the seamless web that we experience in living in family or state or nation.

The place of geography and history. Another dimension of this proposed structure for the social studies program is of great significance. Each of these expanding communities has both 1) a spatial dimension that we know as geography, and 2) a time dimension that we know as history. The child who studies his national community in grade five, for instance, must know the geographic arena within which the national life is rooted. The physical location of the United States national community must definitely be known; the arrangement of physical and cultural features cannot be neglected or the study of our nation will not take into account place-to-place differences or similarities. Likewise our nation cannot be known and appreciated unless the history of its origins, its values, its periods of struggle, and its successes are background against which we assess the present and chart the future. But in this proposed framework of the social studies program for the first five grades, geography and history are not offered in separate courses, but contribute their content and processes to the expanding communities of men as each community in turn is studied to discover how it carries on the basic human activities to supplement the work of the lesser communities.

Possible emphases beyond the United States national community. But our suggested design for the elementary school social studies is, to this point in our statement, incomplete. We have yet to complete our particular logic of expanding communities of men beyond the national community. Modern science and technology made obsolete the once defensible notion that the nation is the ultimate boundary of the system of expanding communities of men. We know today that nations cannot exist as islands: some multinational values, institutions, laws, and customs are even now appearing, while others wait for the birth time when men shall find it desirable and possible to welcome larger-than-national communities.

What we face today is a new set of *emerging* communities of nations that are increasingly important to the survival of the lesser national communities. These larger-than-national communities can be identified and assigned sequentially to school grades in some such pattern as this: . . .

EMPHASIS
8. U.S. and Inter-American Community
9. U.S. and Atlantic Community (3)
10. U.S. and Pacific Community
11. U.S. and World Community

Let it be re-stressed that the sequential order of the emphases is more important than the assigning of the study of a given community to a particular grade. One school district or state might telescope and assign both the national and the Inter-American communities to grade five; the Atlantic, the Pacific, and the world communities to grade six. Or another district might stretch the design through grade seven, or grade eight, or even grade nine, depending upon the decisions to be made in the remaining grades of the secondary school.

Several strategies of this design should be noted here. When the child moves beyond his national community, he is now focusing on the need for multinational solutions. The social studies program need not take each and every one of the more than 20 nations in the emerging Inter-American community for detailed study. The child should begin to observe the nearly half-billion people living on the American continents, working together through multinational action to create private and public solutions to their common problems. The U.S.-Canadian joint efforts could be studied realistically. The Alliance for Progress could be examined as one possible approach to the concern all of us have for economic, social, and political development of our neighbors to the south. Attention would be given to the nature of power and international policy as well as to cultural comparisons. The history we have in common in the Americas of ten thousand years of Indian culture, 300 years of European colonization, and 100 years of struggle for freedom and independence is probably of greater use to our youth than a detailed study of the history of any single neighbor nation. The design calls for the larger and more universal pictures of emerging multinational communities.

Another strategy of this social studies design should be explained here. The pupil is not encouraged to jump about aimlessly from community to community or from culture to culture. He does not, in this structure, make the difficult and often meaningless leap from an emphasis in grade two on the study of his neighborhood and other U.S. neighborhoods to a comparative study of Japanese neighborhoods that are part of a totally different cultural pattern. Such cultural contrast and comparison has its place in the total design. But is it not more appropriately assigned to Emphasis 10, the U.S. and Pacific community? A neighborhood community in Japan clearly reflects its national community which in turn reflects the cultures of the Orient. Is it not a preferable sequence to move systematically through the expanding communities from family through nation; then, having gained considerable knowledge of the several closely interrelated communities of which an American child is a citizen, is he not ready to compare and contrast meaningfully those far-away lesser communities that are a part of a very different national and world-regional culture?

We do not intend by this design-control to preclude that exciting content which emerges from the living current scene and invites side excursions into places and times not strictly related to the community assigned to a particular grade. Such enriching experiences make life varied and challenging. But the teacher has the obligation to prevent these side interests from displacing the main theme as set out in whatever design on which the district or state has agreed.

References

(1) We have several excellent discussions of structures in the separate social disciplines; the best of these is the recent publication entitled *The Social Studies and the Social Sciences*, sponsored by the American Council of Learned Societies and the National Council for the Social Studies. New York: Harcourt, Brace and World, 1962.

(2) I acknowledge that the opposite view is advocated by competent persons. These contend that a design in the beginning tends to be rigid and thus confining and limiting of the final results. They advocate much preliminary work on the parts; then they would proceed inductively to group, to systematize, to evolve a design. While I find myself in disagreement with these colleagues for reasons which I have tried to state, I strongly support their efforts to attack a problem which can profit from diverse logic.

(3) There is logic to support a reversal of Emphases 8 and 9 on the grounds that the Atlantic Community is of greater significance to us.

A Modification of the "Expanding Environment" Approach *Theodore Kaltsounis*

This selection reports several studies of children's knowledge about their world and suggests some guidelines for modifying the expanding environment concept as the key to sequence in the social studies. Are there really any basic differences between Kaltsounis' ideas and those of Hanna? What are the implications of those differences for the classroom teacher? What other modifications of the expanding environment idea might be made to answer the questions raised about the length of time it takes a child to get to some study of his nation and other parts of the world?

Almost every authority in the teaching of Social Studies or in the elementary school program in general is dissatisfied with the status quo of the Social Studies program. There are criteria on the basis of which broad themes are being selected, but beyond this very little (if anything) is settled.

If this is the situation with Social Studies content in general, the content in the first three grades of the elementary school is more vague and less valid. As reported by Preston and Hodgson (1) the most common subject matter in Social Studies for the first, second and third grades is home, school, pets, community helpers, food, clothing, and shelter. Several educators (save the outsiders) do not appear to be happy with this content. Celia Stendler (2) wrote that "studying 'community helpers' occupies a large part of the primary curriculum in most systems; yet . . . young children already know a good deal about the work of firemen and policemen—perhaps as much as they need to know at that level."

Dorothy Fraser (3) states the same complaint in the following words: "A major problem in the handling of the commonly used themes is that in an effort to provide a program grounded in the child's experience, the content presented might be unduly restricted. It may become repetitious and lacking in challenge." Herrick and others (4) pointed out that "it is remarkable that so little has

From *The Social Studies*, March, 1964, 55:3, 99–102. Used by permission of *The Social Studies*. Dr. Kaltsounis is a professor of education at the State University of New York, College of Education, Oswego, New York.

been done to identify the organizing elements which underlie the development of sequence in social studies."

There seems to be no doubt that the content presented in the first three grades is important, but it appears that in this age of television, radio, inexpensive and everywhere available printed materials, of at least one car in each home, and of more time for vacations, the children learn most of the conventional Social Studies content before formal instruction takes place. Why, for example, should pupils in a third grade of a particular section of the country study about building materials, when they often watch these materials being advertised through television? Why should children in the primary grades study about the grocery store, in the way in which they usually do, if for years, since they were babies, they were informally studying this store while their mothers were shopping? Many questions of this nature can be asked.

The claim that a large amount of Social Studies content is known to primary grades children prior to instruction is also supported by the very few existing related research studies. Charlotte Huck (5) in an effort to find out what information was possessed by first grade children with respect to certain areas of Social Studies, how this information was acquired, and how accurate it was, found that they knew a large amount of it. She concluded that "Teachers should refuse to teach the over-simplified, the child's 'false world'." John McAulay (6) found that second-graders knew most of the material, which they were going to study during the year, prior to instruction. This writer (7) conducted a study in which he found that third-graders knew about thirty-seven per cent of the third grade Social Studies cognitive content, as it appears in five major Social Studies text books, prior to formal instruction.

In a time in which the amount of knowledge is enormous, curriculum workers must exercise selectivity. The phenomenon of teaching things just because they used to be taught in the past can no longer be tolerated. For many years now, since the time the logical organization of the content progressively gave way to the psychological organization, the "expanding environment" or the "expanding horizons" or the "widening horizons" approach was used for the selection as well as the placement of the Social Studies content. It is advocated through this approach that instruction should deal first with the immediate environment of the child. Then it should move outward as the child advances from grade to grade. It should start with the home and school and then move to the neighborhood, the community, the state, the nation, the western hemisphere, the world.

Theoretically this approach is sound, but it allows too much emphasis on the "here and now" of the child. The result of this over-emphasis is repetition and lack of challenge in the beginning grades. This in turn results in loss of interest in learning. Children come to school with high expectations. They come to school to face new and challenging things. They become disappointed when they run into an over-simplified curriculum.

To eliminate unnecessary repetition this writer proposes a modification of the "expanding horizons" approach. The elements of this modified approach are not entirely new. However, they suggest a systematic strategy to be used in the selection of the content. Two parts in the child's environment should be recognized. One is that part which the child explores before he comes to school plus that part which he is capable of exploring by himself while he is in school. The other is that part in which the child needs the help of the school. The schools should carefully draw the lines between these two parts of the child's environment and avoid being concerned with the first one except for purposes of motivation. The principle of the "expanding horizons" modified as suggested here would look in a diagrammatical form as follows:

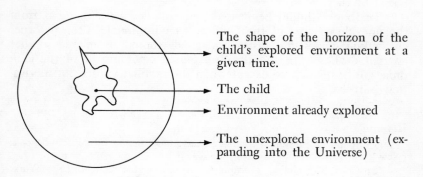

The shape of the horizon of the child's explored environment at a given time.

The child

Environment already explored

The unexplored environment (expanding into the Universe)

The child is in the center. Around him is his immediate environment which he explored to some extent before entering the elementary school. The irregular line enclosing the child marks the boundaries of the child's already explored environment. The irregularity of the line shows that the child has advanced more in his explorations in some areas while he is behind in others. This is due mostly to the special interests which the children have developed. It should be emphasized that the distance of the boundaries between the explored and unexplored environments is different from child to child. Also, the irregularities of the boundaries are different from child to child. These kinds of differences, determined on an average basis, would also be present from group to group or from grade to grade.

If the school is to do an effective job, it has first to find the distance of the boundaries and determine their irregularities, and then proceed from there. In other words, what is demanded here is an intensive diagnostic procedure which will provide a Social Studies curriculum not of what is close to the child in terms of the familiar, but of what of the unknown is close to the child in terms of its association with the familiar. A program designed in this way will be challenging and at the same time will take into consideration the past experiences of the youngsters.

As a conclusion the following suggestions are offered: All those concerned with the development or teaching of the primary Social Studies curriculum should realize that children in the primary grades know more of the Social Studies content than is usually assumed.

All teachers should carefully diagnose the children's knowledge in connection with a topic before undertaking the teaching of this topic.

The outside sources contributing to Social Studies learnings should be identified and recruited systematically in the teaching of Social Studies.

Textbooks should be revised and enriched with material from the unexplored area of the children's environment. Also, all other curriculum guides and instructional aids should be revised so that content dealing with the already-explored environment of the children will be eliminated except when the familiar is used for motivation purposes.

References

(1) Ralph C. Preston, *Teaching Social Studies in the Elementary Schools.* (New York: Rinehart and Company, 1958), p. 33.

(2) Celia B. Stendler, *Teaching in the Elementary School.* (New York: Harcourt, Brace and Company, 1958), p. 277.

(3) Dorothy M. Fraser, Chapter VI. "The Organization of Elementary School Social Studies Curriculum," *Social Studies in the Elementary School.* The fifty-sixth Yearbook of the National Society for the Study of Education, Part II (Chicago: The University of Chicago Press, 1957), p. 148.

(4) Virgil E. Herrick, *et al. The Elementary School.* (Englewood Cliffs, N.J.: Prentice-Hall, Inc., 1956), p. 210.

(5) Charlotte Huck, "Children Learn from their Culture," *Educational Leadership*, XIII (December, 1955), pp. 171–175.

(6) John D. McAulay, "Social Studies in the Primary Grades," *Social Education*, XVIII (December, 1954), pp. 357–358.

(7) Theodore Kaltsounis, "A Study Concerning Third Graders' Knowledge of Social Studies Content Prior to Instruction." (Unpublished Ph.D. dissertation, University of Illinois, 1961).

❧ THE FRAMEWORK OF THE SOCIAL
STUDIES CURRICULUM   *Joseph C. Grannis*

*This article discusses two major proposals for curricular change
in the social studies. These proposals are being viewed with
interest by a large number of school districts across the nation.
The themes proposed in these projects suggest an interesting
question: What can a teacher, or a prospective teacher, do to
prepare himself to teach such varied and exciting subject matter?*

HOW OFTEN HAVE YOU heard it said, or said yourself, that from history
we can learn from whence we have come and (with less certainty)
where we are going? This has always been a profound argument for
the study of history, though some historians themselves have been
more skeptical about the "meaningfulness" of history than any dis-
enchanted school boy. Today, no less than a half century ago, there
are many scholars and perhaps an even greater proportion of laymen
who feel that chronology should provide the basic framework for
social studies in the nation's schools. . . .

Another familiar approach to social studies, the "expanding
communities" scheme, is equally concerned with making connections
in experience. The frame of reference here, however, is more spatial
than temporal. It attempts to establish relationships within and among
the various socio-geographic regions of our lives. The expanding
communities curriculum, especially in the elementary grades, tends
to ask where things *come* from before asking from whence they
came. . . .

No one who has read John Dewey's *The School and Society*
(1899) can fail to see that the expanding communities approach to
social studies stems in part from a long developing realization that
modern life is fragmented in certain ways. Our learning and working,
the satisfaction of our needs, and so on, are not integrated through
household and neighborhood activities as effectively as they are in
less complex societies. Thus it is argued that the school should try
to bridge these discontinuities in our lives. . . . This approach is

From *The National Elementary Principal*, 42:21–26, April, 1963. Copyright
1963, Department of Elementary School Principals, National Education Association. All rights reserved. Dr. Grannis is on the faculty of the Graduate School of
Education, Harvard University.

strongly supported by many social studies educators today, perhaps partly because of a growing awareness that the disintegration of personal experience which Dewey sensed at the turn of the century has become even more pronounced in our own time.

If the framework of the social studies curriculum were to be determined simply on the basis of how best we can "cover" everything, it would be a toss-up. No scheme can begin to cover (or at least *un*cover) everything, though some persons might profess to see more possibilities one way or the other. It is far more important to recognize that the chronological and the expanding communities approaches each attempt to open up a basic dimension of human experience. *Both* the temporal and the spatial must be active in the social studies curriculum. Ironically, neither dimension truly emerges when either one is treated inflexibly. . . .

STRUCTURE AND DISCIPLINES

If one wonders why the academic disciplines are becoming increasingly involved today in education, the simplest explanation relates to that elusive word that is heard more and more frequently, "structure." The word has to do with how things are related to one another, be they numbers, the parts of an atom, or the heroes and villains of a novel. Why should structure command our attention? Very plainly, the crux of education *is* relating things. We have been talking about structure from the first word of this article. But it is also the stuff of the academic disciplines.

In now turning to the disciplines, we are asking what basic ideas they can suggest that might help us, both child and adult, to discover relationships. This is not to say that the historian or economist or anthropologist who works primarily in one discipline, who must produce for scholarly journals and so forth, has interests identical with ours. Nor can we suppose that we would receive, store, or recover information under the same conditions that the scholar does. Nevertheless, as recent developments in mathematics education would suggest, some of the most fundamental principles and concepts of the social sciences may be equally important to social studies. Let us look again at the structure of the curriculum from this point of view.

THE ACLS-ESI PROJECT

. . . Since June 1962, a group of some fifty scholars, most of them from the social sciences and humanities, have been developing plans for a new K–12 social studies curriculum in a primarily chronological framework. Under the joint auspices of the American Council of Learned Societies (ACLS) and Educational Services Incorporated

(ESI), an interdisciplinary scheme has been proposed for a colossal curriculum development project. . . .

The ACLS-ESI scholars are centrally concerned that the child be involved as much as possible in a thoroughgoing inductive approach to "raw data." Their plans call for extensive use of specially prepared films, reproductions of artifacts, maps, etc., as well as a variety of written materials produced by scholars and eye witnesses of the events to be studied.

For grades 1–3, the project proposes to develop units dealing with evolution, primate behavior, and hunters and gatherers. Present plans call for devoting all of grade 1 to a study of the Netselik Eskimo. From materials about his environment, his skills, art, myth, and social organization, the children would attempt to figure out how and why the Eskimo's culture ticks. Grade 2 would compare the lives of a Bushman group (a primitive people of the Kalahari Desert in Bechuanaland) and a group of Australian aborigines. Materials about free-ranging primates (especially baboons and chimpanzees) and about prehistoric cave men would be introduced in grade 3 and involved with the material of the two previous years in a study of the problem of evolution.

The next three years in the ACLS-ESI sequence involve respectively (grade 4) the origins of husbandry in the Near East and Middle America (grade 5) the origins and development of urban life in the Near East and elsewhere, and (grade 6) the beginning of the Western tradition in the Aegean world of Minoan Crete, Mycenean Greece, and Troy.

The overarching theme proposed for grades 7, 8, and 9 is "Man-in-Community," ranging from medieval manor castles to contemporary efforts at supranational community. Grade 8, entitled "From Subject to Citizen," is to be a series of case studies of 17th and 18th century England and America. Grades 7 and 9 are less clearly defined but seem to be an effort to "post-hole" Western developments between ca. 500 B.C. and ca. 1600 A.D., and then from ca. 1800 to the present.

There can be no doubt that this project intends to produce materials that will set high standards of authenticity, boldness, and imagination. As we have already recognized the essential rationale for such a curriculum, let us notice here a couple of questions about it.

First, we might ask how effectively the ACLS-ESI scheme ties in with children's own experience. We need not cling to the indefensible proposition that, *ipso facto*, things farther away from a child in time and space will be more difficult for him to understand. It still seems that a social studies curriculum should relate more directly

than does this one to the child's everyday firsthand-plus-television
sources of information, feelings, *mis*information, and questions. This
is not to deny what we have said earlier about the necessity to go
beyond superficial relationships between subject and learner. It does
assert, however, that *the choice of content itself* should reflect our
convictions about the applicability of basic social science principles
and concepts to the learner's experience.

A parallel question might be raised with respect to societal
problems, in the larger sense. At least in the plans so far, the ACLS-
ESI scheme seems highly susceptible to the sort of historical rational-
ization that we mentioned earlier. This would be a most ironic
outcome since anthropology, perhaps the least conservative of all
the social sciences, has strongly influenced the ACLS-ESI elementary
sequence. However, the curriculum relies heavily on the children's
being able and inclined themselves to apply what they learn to the
world in which they live. This is rather hazardous on two counts.
1) The little that we know about transfer of training suggests that
one must actually teach for transfer to get it. 2) One of the most
fundamental ideas of all in the social sciences, especially history, is
that generalizability is limited, or that basic social science concepts
and principles take on special meanings in each separate context.
Thus it would seem prudent for a social studies curriculum to sample
not only the basic ideas of the disciplines (there are many more of
these, too, than one could cover!) but also the contexts to which
they will be applied. A chronological frame of reference need not be
construed so rigidly that it does not "get to" the modern world
before grade 9. . . .

THE HARVARD-LEXINGTON PROJECT

. . . For several years, this writer has been engaged with the teachers
of two elementary schools in Lexington, Massachusetts, and with his
colleagues and students at Harvard in exploring ways of combining
the advantages of the chronological, expanding communities, and
problems approaches to social studies. *We began with a sequence of
generalizations,* proposed by a member of the Harvard-Lexington
research and development staff, Mrs. Beverly Simpson Stone. These
generalizations, selected from a number of sources, . . . were recommended *not as summary statements of content* but as points of convergence and departure for social studies inquiry. A number of
generalizations were suggested for each grade level, together with
several units and a general theme for each grade. Through the generalizations, we have intended to relate questions and problems

arising out of present experience to both the spatial and temporal dimensions of man's career.

The Harvard-Lexington social studies proposal has developed considerably since 1960 and now extends to more grades (K–9) than the range of the Lexington pilot schools (1–6). A majority of the units in the outline that follows have not yet been tried in the class-room. For each unit that is suggested here, many alternatives would be possible and, further, the number of units that might actually be studied in a given year could vary more than has been indicated. In examining the outline below, the reader must realize that it attempts to represent two planes simultaneously: the general themes to be investigated and, again, units that *might* be developed through these themes. For instance, the theme for grade 6 could equally well be employed to examine Far Eastern civilization. That we have chosen to emphasize ancient and medieval Western history indicates that the chronological approach has also been brought into play. However, grade 6 remains governed primarily by its general theme, through which the past is to be related to our own experience.

THE HARVARD-LEXINGTON GENERALIZATIONS

K. The ways of man are more flexible and inventive than the ways of other animals. Shelter; Tools; Domestication of animals; Communication. (The children would examine and compare human and animal life in detail throughout the year.)

1. Men have many different ways of meeting similar needs. Work; Training and schooling; Celebrations; Art and play. (Home and neighborhood life in one or two foreign places, e.g., Mexico or Japan, would be compared with life in the children's own community. These studies would attempt to trace some of man's activities to basic human needs they fulfill.)

2. Human groups and institutions involve various patterns of norms, interactions and feelings. Healing and medicine; Markets; Work-shops and factories; Courts. (Again, the children would compare life in their own community with life in one or two foreign places. The units would focus on the interrelationships among people in various kinds of shared experience.)

3. Primitive societies have adapted to a variety of natural habitats. A horticultural people, the Hopi Indians; A herding people, the Masai; A hunting and fishing people, the Copper Eskimos; A rice growing people, the Tanala of Madagascar. (The units would focus on the relationships between the traditional cultures and the climate, terrain, biotic resources, etc., of the regions in which they are established. The incursions of modern culture should not be ignored.)

4. *Man finds new ways to control his relationship to his environment.* Water; Agriculture; Metals; Fishing and whaling; Textiles. (The units would contrast relatively primitive and modern beliefs and practices, emphasizing the latter. The material could range quite widely through time and around the globe.)

5. *The industrial revolution has changed the production and distribution of goods and services and has created new opportunities and problems for human society.* Power and technology; Natural resources; Trade; Food and population; Cities. (These units would be concerned primarily with the ongoing industrial revolution and its effects, and secondarily with its historical origins. The materials might concentrate on just a few countries, e.g., the United States, Great Britain, India, and China.)

6. *Man's acts of inquiry, creativity, and expression evolve from and influence his total way of life.* Writing and measurement, the Fertile Crescent; Drama, Greece; Architecture, Rome; Universities, Europe; Exploration, the Renaissance. (Each unit would examine in detail a context from the history of Western civilization and would attempt to relate the past to the present. The children might ask, e.g., What can we learn about ancient Rome from its architecture and, then, what is reflected in the architecture of our own society?)

7. *The need for law and order in community life, man's ambitions for power, and his desires for freedom and opportunity have all shaped his political institutions.* Monarchy and parliament; Colonies and territories; The frontier; Towns and plantations; Revolution. (The main context of these units would be England and her American colonies in the 17th and 18th centuries. Materials about the history of Africa could be correlated with these studies, e.g., the children could compare the experiences of Africans and the American colonials with local self-government.)

8. *The government and economic development of a nation are interrelated.* The establishment of a national constitution; Migration and settlement; Civil War; Industrialization; The modern development of a region. (These units would explore topics from United States history, from ca. 1785 to the present. The units would also include related materials about Latin America, e.g., about the economic development of north-east Brazil.)

9. *There are a variety of patterns of rivalry and cooperation among the nations of the world.* Warfare and military alliance; World government; Cultural and technological exchange; Economic interdependence; Modern science. (The involvement of the people of the United States with other nations from ca. 1910 to the present is the main context of these units. Materials about Europe and Asia would be especially appropriate.)

This proposal must be analyzed from a number of angles before its general structure begins to come clear. It moves almost immediately to people and places beyond the child's firsthand experience, but it also establishes bases for relating to this experience. It tries to respect the general principle of involving successively more complex contexts from one year to the next, but there is also an effort to have the learning be more cumulative conceptually from year to year than in the expanding communities approach. Although it employs chronology, it moves more freely through time than a rigorous chronological sequence. And though the curriculum is interdisciplinary, each of the major social science disciplines can be brought into focus at various junctures.

Foundations of the Social Studies

PSYCHOLOGY REMAINS a long way from providing a precise theory of learning that might be applied to all children, all subjects, all classrooms. But psychological data do provide us with a foundation for teaching that is clearly superior to trial-and-error probing. Lavone Hanna and Neva Hagaman draw on child growth and development data in identifying some principles useful in instructing youngsters in the social studies. Ralph H. Ojemann discusses the nature of the child and the experiences available to him as major factors in concept development. W. Linwood Chase and Gilbert M. Wilson report a number of studies on that most elusive of topics—children's preferences in studying social studies. Shirley H. Engle expands on the articles that identify principles and preferences by focusing our attention on the process of individual decision making by youngsters.

The social foundations of the instruction are thought to include social, economic, and political trends as well as the historical and philosophical matrices in which these trends are set. Both John R. Seeley and Alice Miel discuss these forces and identify some of their implications for teaching the social studies. William E. Vickery takes up the difficult topic of intergroup relations and ties it to the subject matter of the social sciences. Peter Odegard closes this section with an examination of the status of the social sciences and an analysis of the pressures on social scientists to find answers to our social problems.

◂§ ACTION PRINCIPLES FROM STUDIES OF CHILD DEVELOPMENT

Lavone Hanna and *Neva Hagaman*

Hanna and Hagaman, sensitive to the role that growth and development principles play in planning and providing instruction, summarize the growth characteristics of children, dealing with their physical, social, and intellectual development. Then they draw from these data a number of principles that should be applied to the teaching of the social studies.

KNOWLEDGE ABOUT CHILD growth and development has increased greatly in recent years. Research carried on by Prescott and his colleagues at the Institute for Child Study at the University of Maryland, by Jean Macfarlane's group at the Institute of Child Welfare of the University of California, by the Committee on Human Development of the University of Chicago, by the staff of the Horace-Mann Lincoln Institute, and by staffs at other child study centers have added to and substantiated the findings of psychiatrists, cultural anthropologists, biologists, physicians, psychologists, and behavioral scientists about how children grow and develop, are socialized and acculturated, and acquire the social learnings needed to live in today's world. As Giles says,

> . . . The young sciences of the past twenty-five years have given us research material which has the most powerful meaning, if it were but generally known and used. Slowly it is beginning to be known, yet development of its understanding, and still more of its use, is painfully behind the need (1).

Teachers need to know how children grow and develop in order to provide optimum learning experiences in terms of their needs and interests; they need to understand the developmental tasks which occupy all children at certain stages of their development. They need to understand the major role which inter-personal relationships and environment play in helping children develop healthy personalities and resolve the personal-social conflicts which all children must resolve if they are to become all they are able in terms of their potentialities and environment. Teachers also need to recognize the relationship of self-perception and learning.

GROWTH CHARACTERISTICS OF CHILDREN

Teachers in most elementary schools are faced with groups of 25 to 35 children all of approximately the same chronological age. But this is usually the only characteristic the children have in common. Any group of children will vary in all other characteristics—they will be

Used by permission of the authors and the National Council for the Social Studies; from its Thirty-Second Yearbook, *Social Studies in the Elementary School*, 1962, pp. 32–46. Lavone Hanna is a professor of education at San Francisco State College. Neva Hagaman is a supervisor of elementary education in the Long Beach City Schools.

tall, short, fat, thin; with blond, red, black, or brown hair; with white, yellow, brown, and black skin; they will be gifted, bright, average, dull, active, quiet, restless, withdrawn, brave, fearful, shy, aggressive, loved, rejected, healthy and undernourished; and they come from rich, average, and impoverished backgrounds.

Each child's development is influenced by characteristics which he has inherited and by everything that has happened to him since conception. And while all individuals normally pass through the same developmental stages in an orderly manner, the rate of growth varies from individual to individual. Each child has his own time clock which was punched at the time of his conception and little can be done to change it. Growth also is asymmetrical and uneven: large muscles before small muscles, some organs before others.

Each child is unique and varies from all other individuals not only in physical characteristics, rate of growth and experiential background, but in temperament, intelligence, interests, and sensory acuity. Moreover, research suggests that part of an individual's uniqueness is due to the selections he makes of the things in his environment to which he reacts. No two children, consequently, learn exactly the same thing or in the same way.

> The human organism has a highly selective awareness and idiomatically patterned perception with emotional and affective response, which operate seriously to alter the seemingly objective stimulus situation or problem for each subject. . . . Each human being may learn in a different way from the same situation or lesson or experience. He selects what is to him highly relevant and individually significant and may ignore all else (2).

Because children in elementary school are grouped according to chronological age, teachers tend to generalize about first graders and fourth graders. But there is danger, Ambrose and Miel warn us, in generalizing too broadly about general growth patterns. Growth usually follows the same sequence but some children may depart from what is considered "normal development." What is typical behavior and growth for one individual may not conform to the normal growth pattern for the majority. By the time children reach school age these differences in maturity are obvious. Some six-year-olds may not be ready for reading physically; others may lack readiness because of deprived environments or unfavorable interpersonal relations. Experiences which facilitate development and learning for some children may retard or inhibit it for others.

> When generalizations about needs or developmental tasks are applied inflexibly, the teacher creates a situation similar to that in

which he mistakenly assumes that all can profit from doing the same exercise in an arithmetic book. Children do not approach their tasks or work upon their needs in the same way. Some may not have had opportunity to use their powers for effective interaction in the outer world. Some may not have had the kinds of interpersonal relations needed at certain points in their development. In Allport's terms they have "unfinished business" as they approach new tasks which markedly influence their perceptions of the tasks and the help they need from their teachers (3).

Early elementary childhood. When children enter kindergarten at five years of age, their growth rate is not as rapid as previously and for the next five to seven years, or until the pre-adolescent growth spurt, it will continue to be slow and steady. Girls at six years of age are usually as mature skeletally as the seven-year-old boy. . . .

SOCIAL DEVELOPMENT. A child during the primary grades moves from being egocentric, playing by himself, concerned with what touches him, and wanting his own possessions to cooperating and playing in small groups. Acceptance in the peer group is usually based upon skill in an approved game. Although boys and girls play together, sex differences, often imposed by the culture, appear in their interests and in their games. Primary school children are already aware of different sex roles: boys attempt to be "manly" and not show tenderness or weakness; girls already know what is considered "lady-like" behavior. The gang becomes important to seven- and eight-year-olds and the opinion and approval of their pals is often more important than that of adults. Children love the rules, secret language, secrets, and rituals of the gang; and play for them, too, is often ritualized. Young children seem unaware of racial or class differences. The primary child grows in being an independent human being able to go to school alone, to make his own way with others, to run errands, to have opinions, to select his own friends, to be trusted. As he finds more support from the group, he becomes less dependent on adults.

INTELLECTUAL DEVELOPMENT. All children are curious about objects and want to learn: What is it? What is it for? How is it made? What does it do? What makes it tick? They want to see, touch, smell, and taste things. They want to construct, to make things, to take them apart. Their curiosity is almost insatiable. Children want specific answers to their questions and the interests of eight-year-olds have expanded to include more than their immediate environment.

Young children begin to use abstract terms but they have difficulty with abstractions. They need many concrete experiences to give meaning to what they read and hear. They begin to understand simple cause and effect relationships, to differentiate between fantasy and reality, to understand simple space and time concepts, to take responsibility, to distinguish between right and wrong, and to be aware of the feelings of others. Their interests are transitory and self-centered and their attention span is short.

Children in the middle grades. Children in the middle grades are usually freer from disease than at any other age. Their growth continues to be slow and steady; eyes have matured enough for close work; eye-hand coordination is good and they like to work with their hands, to build, do, and perform. They have boundless energy and courage, are easily overstimulated, and need adequate rest and relaxation.

SOCIAL DEVELOPMENT. An important characteristic of children in the middle grades is their reliance upon the gang. Boys and girls no longer play together and girls may not be allowed in the gangs which often have secret names and "hide outs" from girls as well as adults. The gangs may be of short duration and with changing membership. Girls also form clubs but are usually satisfied with fewer close friends. Both boys and girls turn more and more to their peers for ideas, for support, and for companionship and are less dependent upon adults for ideas and sanction. Yet adult approval and support are necessary, and children need to know that they are loved, understood, and accepted.

Both boys and girls like to collect a variety of things from match folders to stamps. Membership in such groups as Cub Scouts and Camp Fire Girls under adult leadership satisfy their need to be with their pals and at the same time give them goals to work for and help them improve their skills and deepen their interests. Children in the middle grades are more selective in their friendships, exclude some children from their gangs, are aware of the socioeconomic stratification in their community, and may use common stereotypes in assigning status to their classmates. Exclusion by boys may be due to the ineptness of the excluded in physical skills needed to excel in games and physical activity. A boy who does poorly is considered a "sissy." Other reasons for exclusion are often hard for both boys and girls to explain, other than "we don't like him" or "she's not one of us." Children usually reflect the opinions and prejudices of the adults with whom they live and grow—their parents, their friends' parents, and their neighbors (4).

Children at this age have a fairly critical sense of justice, fair play, and right and wrong. There is an increase in their ability to assume responsibility and self-direction. They are perfectionists and want to do well, but become discouraged easily and dislike being nagged or pressured. They are usually cooperative, friendly, sympathetic, and responsive, and have a sense of humor.

MENTAL DEVELOPMENT. Children in the middle grades are still eager to learn and have insatiable curiosities. Their interests vary, yet are more stable than those of younger children. Children at this age collect facts about many things. They like to discuss problems and argue, and are eager to extend their horizons intellectually. Toward the close of this period, children show great interest in far-away countries and people of different times and places. Hero worship and a desire for adventure are characteristics of this age. They have a keen interest in science and want to know how things are made, how they work, and why. Rockets, missiles, and outer space fascinate them as do airplanes, automobiles, and machinery generally.

Girls generally forge ahead in mental development and make better grades than boys, but individual differences among members of both sexes become more pronounced than earlier. Some children need more concrete, firsthand experiences than others; some forge ahead in their ability to use vicarious experiences, to do abstract thinking, to generalize, to solve problems. For most of them, abstract thinking is still rudimentary and they need many firsthand, concrete experiences from which to generalize. Their understanding of time and space concepts has increased but is still immature. They have more understanding of cause and effect relationships, can make comparisons, and can anticipate the consequences of various courses of action. Their vocabularies have greatly increased, and many of the concepts needed for daily living are formed during this period. But Havighurst says,

> In middle childhood intellectual curiosity is channeled more in the areas of impersonal relations, things, processes, and exploration of the surrounding world than in the area of human relations. The latter are problems of immediate experience for the child, but not of intellectual curiosity. He is *feeling his way* in human relations while he is already *thinking his way* into the world of nature (5).

Pre-adolescents. The elementary school ends at the sixth grade for some children but for others the seventh and eighth grades are considered part of the elementary school. During these years a majority of the girls and about one-third of the boys enter the "pubescent growth spurt." Individual differences increase and girls tend to be taller and heavier than boys. Girls are ready for heterosexual activities, while the majority of the boys want nothing to do with girls. Rapid growers are often restless, lazy, and fatigue easily. Emotional responses are intensified. These children are sensitive to criticism, often moody, and irritable, worry about the normalcy of their development, feel insecure, and use cover-up techniques to conceal their insecurity. Health habits are apt to be at their worst. Awkwardness, bad posture, and poor muscle coordination often accompany uneven and rapid growth. Many have trouble with acne, oily hair, and excessive perspiration; they eat incessantly; and have low resistance to minor diseases. Often they are self-conscious about body changes and have trouble adjusting and even accepting them.

SOCIAL DEVELOPMENT. About half of the children at this age are still little boys and girls with the interests and characteristics of middle grade children. The other half, the early adolescents, have reached sexual maturity and are experiencing many of the psychological and physical changes which accompany it. Gangs continue with group loyalty stronger than ever. Conformity to peer standards and culture is a dominant characteristic of the adolescent. They want desperately to "belong" and need the security that comes from being one of the gang.

Adolescents are ambivalent toward adults: sometimes defiant, uncooperative, and overly critical; at other times, compliant, cooperative, and eager for help. They are both conformists and individualists; their behavior is sometimes unpredictable; they are secretive and want their privacy and possessions respected; desire money of their own—either an allowance or money earned by running errands, babysitting, or paper routes; and object to parent's rules about late hours, study, manners, punctuality, and the like. The early adolescent is egocentric, the world revolves around him and his interests. His problems are so serious to him that he thinks his parents should understand him, accept him, and know what he wants even when he does not know himself. His behavior is often erratic and vaccilating. He goes to extremes in clothes, sometimes wearing sloppy, even dirty, clothes to school but being fastidious with his appearance if he has a date. One day his behavior is childish, the next day mature. His bizarre behavior is often a cover-up for his insecurity; he continually experiments with social behavior and often uses attention-getting devices with various degrees of success.

MENTAL DEVELOPMENT. Early adolescents are concerned with a realistic picture of the world. School studies, movies, television, and other experiences have expanded their world and their interests. Their primary interest, however, is themselves, who they are, their place in the school, the community, and the world. They strive to establish themselves in the order of things and events, to understand themselves and their behavior, to reconcile events or happenings with idealistic teachings and their concept of right and wrong. Their interests are often unstable and boy's and girl's reading, recreational, and intellectual interests differ markedly. Early adolescents are restless and some have difficulty concentrating for long periods of time; their interest span is relatively short. They tend to procrastinate in starting tasks and have difficulty finishing them. There is marked discrepancy between their intentions and their deeds.

Early adolescents are increasingly able to work independently and in small groups. Their ability to solve problems, to generalize, to find information, to understand and use graphic materials, and to handle abstract concepts has greatly expanded. They are more facile in communicating their ideas and opinions. They love to argue, to question authority, to demand proof, but they do not like to listen. They have increased understanding of time and space concepts, but these take time to develop and are still not fully developed. They like to plan and can project plans for several weeks; they can take responsibility and can be self-directing but need to be held to commitments. Because of their own insecurity and confused feelings about themselves, early adolescents need an orderly, stable environment in which to grow and learn. . . .

References

(1) Giles, H. H. *Human Dynamics and Human Relations*. New York: New York University Press, 1954. p. 1.

(2) Frank, Laurence K. "Children's In-School and Out-of-School Teachers." *Educational Leadership* 12:294–96; February 1955.

(3) Ambrose, Edna and Alice Miel. *Children's Social Learning*. Washington, D.C.: Association for Supervision and Curriculum Development, a department of National Education Association, 1958. p. 61.

(4) Trager, Helen G., and Marion Radke Yarrow. *They Learn What They Live*. New York: Harper and Brothers, 1952. pp. 113–227.

(5) Havighurst, Robert J. *Human Development and Education*. New York: Longmans, Green and Co., 1953. p. 82.

⤚§ How Concepts Develop   *Ralph H. Ojemann*

There has been more than a little research on the development of concepts, and Dr. Ojemann has long been known as a specialist in children's learning processes. In this selection, he reviews a number of studies and uses their conclusions to illustrate the soundness of a number of generalizations about concept development. This selection has particular pertinence today when so many professors and teachers are talking about a "concept-centered curriculum." Ojemann's six generalizations should be held in mind as a reader considers the many concepts suggested for the elementary school social studies in later parts of this book.

IN THE DISCUSSION of the development of concepts we have two factors to consider: a) the nature of the child, and b) the experiences that are available to him. The importance of both factors has not always been recognized. Those who have been primarily concerned with experiences have often placed concepts at a given grade level without reference to ability of the child to incorporate them in his development. On the other hand, those who have been interested in studying the nature of the child and the development that one finds under present conditions have often neglected to consider what experiences the child has had and whether other experiences would have been equally or more satisfying and produced a different level of development. . . .

In a discussion of development, it is well to include a reminder about the complexity of concepts. A concept is essentially a group of meanings put together under one label. Thus, when we refer to a child's concept of time we may include many aspects. We may put the emphasis on sequence, such as prior to and following certain events, time of day by the clock, day of the week, the month, the year of a century, or centuries. In addition, we may consider duration such as an hour, a day, a week, a year, the sweep of centuries. This complexity of concepts is quite important in considering their development.

Studies of the development of concepts have suggested the following:

1) Not all aspects develop at the same rate. The four-year-old, under our usual cultural conditions, can indicate that something took place before or after a meal but cannot indicate the time of day or the day of the week (1). The ordinary six-year-old in our culture has

Used by permission of the National Society for the Study of Education; from "Social Studies in Light of Knowledge about Children," *Social Studies in the Elementary School*, Fifty-Sixth Yearbook, Part II, Chicago: University of Chicago Press, 1957, pp. 86–95. Dr. Ojemann is a professor at the State University of Iowa and director of the Child Welfare Research Station there; he is known for his research with youngsters and through his wide writings on growth and development.

some conception of length of the school day but cannot give a very meaningful description of the length of a year. Children tend to refer to the present before referring to the future, and to the future before the past.

Springer investigated the ability of children four to six years of age to perform such tasks as telling the time at which certain familiar activities come in their daily schedule, telling the time by the clock and setting the hands of the clock to indicate a given time. Forty-seven per cent of the five-year-olds and 80 per cent of the six-year-olds could tell the time their school starts, but only about 25 per cent of the five-year-olds and 33 per cent of the six-year-olds could set the hands of the clock to indicate a given hour (2). Studies by Friedman (3) and Bradley (4) provide further data.

An indication of the development of children's ideas of historical time is found in a study by Oakden and Sturt. They asked children to arrange names of outstanding historical personages in order of chronological sequence. They found that not until age eleven or so were concepts of historical time sufficiently developed to carry out an activity of this type (5). . . .

The development of some aspects of a concept may depend upon the growth of other concepts. In a study of the development of time concepts in 160 children from kindergarten through third grade, Harrison found that some of the concepts are dependent upon number meanings and relationships. For example, it is difficult for a child to develop a conception of "month" until he has some appreciation of what 30 or 31 means. Similarly, the concept of a year involves the idea of twelve months (6). It is, of course, possible to develop these concepts without direct reference to the number, such as "a year is as long as from one summer to the next," or "from one Christmas to the next," or "from one of your birthdays to the next," but even here the importance of basic number concepts tends to enter.

2) *Differences in development within a given age or grade level are usually greater than among successive age levels.* Lacey's study of 125 common social concepts in the first three grades found that, although there tends to be a continuous development in children's concepts from grade to grade, the differences within a grade group seem to be of more importance than the differences between grades (7).

Harrison, using a group of fifty common terms relating to time, found that the *high*-intelligence level in kindergarten achieved almost as many correct responses as the *low*-intelligence group in the third grade. The high-intelligence group in the first grade achieved a higher per cent of correct responses than the low-intelligence group in the third grade (8). . . .

3) *Since there is no intrinsic or inevitable connection between the meaning of a concept and its label, it is quite possible for a child to use the label with a minimum of meaning or the wrong meaning.* This phenomenon is well known under the name of "verbalism" and requires no extensive documentation. Scott and Myers, for example, found that children may give correct answers to direct questions, as in a class recitation, even though they had only a vague or incorrect conception of their meanings. Many children were able to give the names of two explorers but were then unable to describe what was meant by an "explorer." (9)

Aitchison found not only vague meanings but also many misconceptions among sixth, seventh, and eighth-graders as to the meanings of such words as "torrid," "temperature," and "frigid." (10)

Horn reports a number of studies by his students in which the meaning elementary-school children had developed of such concepts as "many people," "very irregular," and "a great deal" was investigated. The interpretations by fifth-grade pupils of "many people" as used in "many people in Alaska are engaged in the fishing industry" varied from 50 to "as many people as Chicago has." Fourth-graders interpreted "thick cap of ice" in the sentence, "Most of Greenland is covered with a thick cap of ice and snow which never melts away," with such meanings as "one inch," "three feet," "fifty feet," "thousands and thousands of feet." (11) Similar findings are reported by Preston (12).

4) *Some concepts are developed by experiences which the child gets out of school as well as in school, while other concepts depend more on school experiences.* Burton, in a study of children's specific information, found that such a concept as "legislator" was learned primarily through school experiences, whereas the term "divorce" seemed to be developed primarily through out-of-school experiences (13). Eaton, in a study of pupil achievement of sixth-grade pupils found that the amount of understanding children develop with respect to concepts ordinarily considered in the social studies in school is not directly related to the amount of time devoted to such topics in the school program (14).

In this connection, Harrison points out that, in developing concepts of time, teachers and parents have to be careful in the use of such phrases as "just a minute." (15) As one child expressed it to her mother, "In one of *your* minutes, Mother."

5) *Concepts that have a personal reference or those that deal with something immediate and personal tend to be more readily learned than concepts dealing with something more remote.* Farrell, in a study of time-relationships in five-, six-, and seven-year-old children of high intelligence quotients, found that time questions involving the personal and immediate were better answered at the lower chronological- and mental-age levels than questions that involved the remote and nonpersonal (16).

6) *The development of concepts depends upon both the experiences the child has and his level of development.* . . . An important problem that arises in the development of concepts in social-studies teaching is the question of when the child's concepts of time, geographical location, and distance are sufficiently developed so that he can profit from a study of history and geography. Since the development of a concept depends on both the nature of the child and the experiences he has had, this question cannot be answered in the same way for all children of a given age or grade level since the experiences they have had will differ greatly. Most of the studies of the development of concepts, such as those of the concepts of time, have examined children without reference to the experiences they have had. Furthermore, as Preston has indicated, there are many devices the teacher can use to help the child develop a concept of historical time that make use of something closely related to the child, such as "the time when your father was born" or "the time when your grandfather was a boy." (17) Baker found that, in the spontaneous discussion of children in the second grade, 83 per cent of the material contributed was obtained through "personal presence" (i.e., events they had directly experienced). At the sixth-grade level, this figure stood at 25 per cent (18). None of the studies of the development of the concept of time has asked the question, "What concepts *can* the child develop when he is placed in an environment in which there are many uses of such meaningful and enriching experiences?" Furthermore, as investigators become interested in such a question, our ability to devise ever more meaningful experiences will very probably grow, and children will be able to develop meanings that we now consider too difficult for them.

    Present studies of the concept of time have shown that at the kindergarten level the child is aware of such differences as before and after lunch (morning or afternoon), before and after certain activities, and a general "tomorrow" and a general "yesterday."

Practically all of the children in kindergarten in our present culture can learn to give the name of the day (i.e., Monday, Tuesday, etc.). By the time they have learned some of the number concepts, that is, when they are about seven years of age, they can learn the number of days in a month, can tell the approximate time by the clock, and give the seasons of the year. By eight or nine years of age, such concepts as "a year is as long as from one Christmas to the next" or "as long as from one of your birthdays to the next" appear to have considerable meaning. By the time the fifth and sixth grades are reached, such concepts as "a hundred years ago" can acquire some meaning, provided the meaning is developed from experiences which have meaning for the child, such as "when your grandfather was a boy" or "when the first railroad was built" or a series of sequences such as a series of meaningful events on a time line. From our discussion of concepts, it appears that providing meaningful experiences closely related to the activities of the child deserves more emphasis than a timetable to be applied to all children.

A somewhat similar statement can be made with respect to the development of such study skills as ability to read maps, ability to interpret graphs, and ability to find additional information in reference books. Studies such as those of Howe (19), Thomas (20), and Wrightstone (21) show that the elementary-school child has considerable difficulty in using geographical and historical tools and that the growth in ability to use such tools continues well into the high school. However, as such studies as those by Thorp (22) and by Whipple and Preston (23) indicate, systematic teaching hastens growth in ability to use social-studies tools. Here again, as Preston (24) and Bruce (25) point out, more ingenuity is needed in devising methods of teaching which take into account the backgrounds of the children with whom one is working and which break up the process of learning the use of complicated tools, such as maps, into a series of simpler learning tasks. The first maps may be maps of the immediate neighborhood with which the child is familiar. The first maps may also show only one or two major points. When these have been mastered more can be added.

References

(1) L. B. Ames, "The Development of the Sense of Time in the Young Child," *Journal of Genetic Psychology*, LXVIII (March, 1946), 97–125.

(2) Doris Springer, "Development in Young Children of an Understanding of Time and Clock," *Journal of Genetic Psychology*, LXXX (March, 1952), 83.

(3) K. C. Friedman, "Time Concepts of Elementary-School Children," *Elementary School Journal*, XLIV (February, 1944), 337–42.

(4) N. C. Bradley, "The Growth of the Knowledge of Time in Children of

School-Age," *British Journal of Psychology*, XXXVIII (December, 1947), 67–78.

(5) E. C. Oakden and M. Sturt, "Development of the Knowledge of Time in Children," *British Journal of Psychology*, XII (April, 1922), 309–36.

(6) M. Lucile Harrison, "The Nature and Development of Concepts of Time among Young Children," *Elementary School Journal*, XXXIV (March, 1934), 507–14.

(7) Joy Muchmore Lacey, *Social-Studies Concepts of Children in the First Three Grades*, New York: Bureau of Publications, Teachers College, Columbia University, 1932.

(8) Harrison, *op. cit.*

(9) Flora Scott and G. C. Myers, "Children's Empty and Erroneous Concepts of the Commonplace," *Journal of Educational Research*, VIII (November, 1923), 327–34.

(10) Allison E. Aitchison, "Torrid, Temperate, and Frigid Zones: Sources of Error in Children's Thinking," *The Teaching of Geography*, pp. 483–85. Thirty-second Yearbook of the National Society for the Study of Education. Chicago: Distributed by the University of Chicago Press, 1933.

(11) Ernest Horn, *Methods of Instruction in the Social Studies*. New York: Charles Scribner's Sons, 1937.

(12) Ralph C. Preston, *Teaching Social Studies in the Elementary School*. New York: Rinehart & Co., 1957 (revised).

(13) William H. Burton *et al.*, *Children's Civic Information, 1924–35*. Los Angeles: University of California Press, 1936.

(14) M. T. Eaton, "A Survey of the Achievement in Social Studies of 10,220 Sixth-Grade Pupils in 464 Schools in Indiana," *Bulletin of the School of Education, Indiana University*, XX (1944), 1–14.

(15) Harrison, *op. cit.*

(16) Muriel Farrell, "Understanding Time Relations of Five-, Six-, and Seven-Year-Old Children of High I.Q.," *Journal of Educational Research*, XLVI (April, 1953), 587.

(17) Preston, *op. cit.*

(18) H. V. Baker, *Children's Contributions in Elementary-School General Discussion*. New York: Bureau of Publications, Teachers College, Columbia University, 1942.

(19) George F. Howe, "A Study of the Ability of Elementary-School Pupils To Read Maps," *The Teaching of Geography*, *op. cit.*, pp. 486–92.

(20) Katheryne Colvin Thomas, "The Ability of Children To Interpret Graphs," *The Teaching of Geography*, *op. cit.*, pp. 492–94.

(21) J. W. Wrightstone, "Conventional versus Pictorial Graphs," *Progressive Education*, XIII (October, 1936), 460–62.

(22) Mary Tucker Thorp, "Studies of the Ability of Pupils in Grades Four to Eight To Use Geographic Tools," *The Teaching of Geography*, *op. cit.*, pp. 494–556.

(23) Gertrude Whipple and E. J. Preston, "Instructing Pupils in Map Reading," *Social Education*, X (May, 1947), 205–8.

(24) Ralph C. Preston, *op. cit.*

(25) Paul Bruce, "Vitalizing United States History," *Social Studies*, XLV (April, 1954), 137–39.

∾§ CHILDREN'S PREFERENCES
W. Linwood Chase and *Gilbert M. Wilson*

What means of learning do children like best? What kinds of writing projects do they favor? What are the most interesting topics in the social studies? What do children want to know about the world? What obstacles do they see to keep them from learning? Chase and Wilson report a number of studies dealing with these questions. This report should give the reader a number of ideas for planning for and with youngsters.

ONE OF OUR EARLIER studies on activities was initiated to determine how children regard certain methods in handling assignments (1). Using a situation test Stewart gathered her data from 546 children in grades four, five, and six. It was designed to reveal which assignments are most interesting: use of a single text or several texts; small group or single pattern participation; and pupil or teacher selection of material. It further explored children's preferences for reading, drawing, constructing, writing, or talking activities.

Stewart's general conclusions:

1. Multiple texts were favored more than the single text.
2. Group participation was selected by older children and upper intelligence levels. Partner participation was chosen by the slow learning and younger children.
3. Self-direction was more favored than teacher-direction.
4. Reading activity was not the most popular choice in any grade but was most popular in grade four and least popular in grade six.
5. Writing activity was in low favor in most of the preferences and had its greatest popularity in grade six. More girls than boys preferred writing.
6. In all groups drawing was either first or second choice. The top and lowest quartiles in intelligence preferred it to any other activity.
7. Constructing was generally the top choice among all activities.

Used by permission of the authors and the publishers; from the Journal of Education, a publication of the Boston University School of Education, "Preference Studies in Elementary School Social Studies" by W. Linwood Chase and Gilbert M. Wilson, 140:1–28, April, 1958. Dr. Chase is former dean of education at Boston University, where Professor Wilson is chairman of the Department of Elementary Education.

8. Talking was the lowest in choice of activities by grades. More grade six girls than boys preferred talking activities.

FIFTH AND SIXTH GRADE ACTIVITIES

Foley (2) used a check list to find out how sixth grade children felt about doing certain activities with social studies material. In order to have the check list reflect children's ideas and not wholly teachers' thinking, Foley asked her previous year's class to name the things which they like to do in social studies and those which they disliked. These were supplemented by suggestions from other sources.

There resulted a check list of thirty-eight items on which the children were to indicate their preferences by circling one of the following for each activity:

> X   I have not done this
> L   I like it very much
> N   I neither like nor dislike it
> D   I dislike it very much

After they had completed checking they were asked to go back over all the items, choose those which they best liked to do by putting 1 in front of the first choice, 2 in front of the second choice, and 3 in front of the third.

The check list was completed by all of the 398 sixth grade children in a Connecticut town, of whom 203 were boys and 195 were girls. It may be worth noting that less than twelve per cent of all activities judged (398 x 38) were categorized as disliked very much.

Table 7. Per Cent in Preference Categories of 203 Sixth Grade Boys and 195 Sixth Grade Girls for 38 Social Studies Activities

	X	L	N	D	F*
BOYS	11.06	51.20	24.53	12.61	00.60
GIRLS	13.39	50.35	25.56	10.12	00.58
TOTAL	12.20	50.79	25.03	11.39	00.59

* Failure to mark or mark correctly.

The thirty-eight activities have been arranged in the order of preference when the 398 children checked those they liked very much. The first twenty-five activities were liked by more than half of the children.

Table 8. Rank Order of Activities When Chosen by 203 Boys and 195 Girls in the Category of "I Like It Very Much"

RANK	ACTIVITY
1	Take a trip to the museum in connection with unit
2	See films, filmstrips, and slides about unit
3	Make up plays about interesting happenings
4	Find a play and act it out
5	Work with a group on a mural or picture
6	Have quiz contests on the most interesting facts
7	Make exhibits to go with the study
8	Draw pictures to illustrate the unit
9	Listen to reports
10	Work in committees on a project or assignment
11	Learn new words
12	Make a relief map, using materials such as salt, flour, etc.
13	Study maps of the country being talked about
14	Discuss films, filmstrips, and slides about unit
15	Collect pictures, poems, and stories to go with the unit
16	Construct models of interesting things studied
17	Dramatize important events studied in a unit
18	Fill in an outline map
19	Draw a map and show products, important cities, etc.
20	Use many different books in social studies
21	Study exhibits which go with the unit
22	Make up your own stories about the unit
23	Make individual booklets on the unit
24	Have discussions in charge of pupils
25	Work by myself on an assignment
26	Make a class booklet about the unit
27	Give reports to the class
28	Read social studies and answer questions made by the pupils
29	Prepare reports for the class
30	Use an outline made by the class for study
31	Use the same social studies book that each child in the class has
32	Make individual outlines for study
33	Use a question guide made by the class for discussion
34	Write out answers to questions placed on the blackboard
35	Read social studies and answer questions made by the teacher
36	Write summaries of important ideas
37	Have a test on the unit when it is finished
38	Have short tests on the day's discussion

There are six activities "liked very much" which show a statistically significant difference between boys and girls. Four of them are in favor of the girls:

17 Dramatize important events studied in a unit
4 Find a play and act it out
15 Collect pictures, poems, and stories to go with the unit
23 Make individual booklets on the unit

Two of the significant differences favor boys:

13   Study maps of the country being talked about
14   Discuss films, filmstrips, and slides about unit

In the total 38 activities, 23 were liked by a majority of the boys and 27 by a majority of the girls.

The relationships in popularity of the various activities change somewhat if the order of preference is taken from tabulations of choices when children have been asked to indicate their first three choices out of all the thirty-eight activities. In this choice pattern the boys and girls have been limited to only three choices as compared with being able to check as many as they wished in the category of "I like it very much." Because of scattering choices among so many activities this means that those activities chosen the greatest number of times may have only a small percentage of the actual total choices made. The exact percentages are indicated in parentheses after each activity.

1   Take a trip to the museum in connection with unit (11.22)
2   See films, filmstrips, and slides about unit (11.22)
4   Find a play and act it out (7.79)
12   Make a relief map, using materials such as salt, flour, etc. (4.94)
19   Draw a map and show products, important cities, etc. (4.52)
3   Make up plays about interesting happenings (4.44)
8   Draw pictures to illustrate the unit (4.27)
6   Have quiz contests on the most interesting facts (3.94)
5   Work with a group on a mural or picture (3.69)
10   Work in committees on a project or assignment (3.60)

None of the ten least popular activities had more than one-half of one per cent of combined first, second, and third choices, meaning that Activities 26 and 37 each had only six choices while Activity 36 had one first choice and no second or third choices among 398 children. Arranged in order from last choice upward they were:

36   Write summaries of important ideas
33   Use a question guide made by the class for discussion
30   Use an outline made by the class for study
34   Write out answers to questions placed on the blackboard
28   Read social studies and answer questions made by the pupils
38   Have short tests on the day's discussion
32   Make individual outlines for study
21   Study exhibits which go with the unit
26   Make a class booklet about the unit
37   Have a test on the unit when it is finished

Foley had all the children indicate subject preferences as was done in the 1947 Subject Preference Study. The results were nearly identical in first choices for social studies—9.40 per cent in the 1947 study and 9.82 per cent in her study.

One year later (1952) Duval (3) repeated the Foley study with all of the fifth grade children, 261 boys and 275 girls, in the same Connecticut town used by Foley. Duval duplicated the Foley study exactly. As one might expect the fifth grade preferences were in somewhat different rank order from the sixth grade. But when one examines the per cent of choices they vary little on most activities even though the rank order be different. On only five activities were the percentage differences great enough to say they were significant.

Activity 31 in favor of grade 5 giving it a higher preference
Activity 20 in favor of grade 6 giving it a higher preference
Activity 6 in favor of grade 5 giving it a lower preference
Activity 18 in favor of grade 5 giving it a higher preference
Activity 16 in favor of grade 5 giving it a higher preference

When Table 7 is compared with Table 9 it will be noted that the percentages of choice in the various categories is very similar.

Table 9. Per Cent in Preference Categories of 261 Fifth Grade Boys and 275 Fifth Grade Girls for 38 Social Studies Activities

	X	L	N	D	F
BOYS	13.52	49.90	23.12	12.88	00.57
GIRLS	14.64	50.06	24.78	10.31	00.21
TOTAL	14.09	49.99	23.97	11.56	00.39

When preference order for fifth grade is determined on the basis of choosing the three activities most preferred, it is not dissimilar to the sixth grade pattern. Seven of the first ten activities are the same although the order varies some. Activities 14, 16, and 18 were in the first ten in the fifth grade but not in the sixth grade; while Activities 6, 10, and 19 were in the upper ten of sixth grade choices but not fifth. There were only two differences in the bottom ten. Activity 28 was found in grade six and Activity 35 in grade six. . . .

PREFERENCES IN SOCIAL STUDIES SUBJECT-MATTER

Very little is known about what children would choose to study in the field of the social studies if given the opportunity to make choices. Out of all the topics which the field of social studies encompasses, what would children indicate as their preferences for study? What would they want most to learn about? A study by Bresnahan (4) sought an answer. It was necessary to construct an instrument which would reveal children's preferences. A master list of topics that could be a part of a social studies program was compiled. The topics were grouped into nine categories.

Category 1: *People*. Includes all people: famous people, every-day people, professional people, any person who has an individual occupation, and children.

Category 2: *Group occupations*. Includes any occupation in which a group of people contribute to an industry.

Category 3: *Progress through inventions*. Includes anything that has been invented which has helped us to progress in science, medicine, engineering, home life, and the like.

Category 4: *Periods of time*. Includes whole periods of time such as pioneer days, colonial days, or Middle Ages.

Category 5: *Cultural aspects*. Includes situations of freedom, human rights, cultural contributions by other peoples.

Category 6: *Aesthetic aspects*. Includes the development within a country of art, literature, and music.

Category 7: *Social aspects*. Includes reform by religion and political change and its effect on the human being.

Category 8: *Natural resources*. Includes the wealth or lack of wealth that nature has given that country.

Category 9: *Geographic aspects*. Includes size, climate, location, and topography and the effect they have had on particular peoples.

Statements were written at each grade level for each of the categories and then set up in pairs so the pupil could indicate his preference or interest. Thirty-six pairs compared each category with every other category, but, in order to eliminate the possibility of children checking the first statement too frequently, the thirty-six pairs were reversed in the second half of the check list, making seventy-two paired comparisons in all.

ILLUSTRATION FROM GRADE IV

If you had to choose, which would you rather study about?

( ) What the weather has to do with the way people live?
    or
( ) How machines have helped in traveling?
( ) The work of farmers in different countries of the world?
    or
( ) How we got the alphabet we use today?

Bresnahan secured preferences from 4,129 pupils in Grades II through VI. In Table 10 the number of children and per cent of

choices at each grade level are given for each of the nine categories.
Rank order at each grade level is also shown.

Table 10. Per Cent of Preferences in Social Studies Subjects Areas of 4,129 Pupils in Grades II through VI

CATEGORIES	II-703	RANK	III-767	RANK	IV-905	RANK	V-972	RANK	VI-777	RANK
PEOPLE	50.30	4	44.16	9	61.42	2	61.98	1	58.04	1
GROUP OCCUPATIONS	51.98	3	46.32	6	51.05	4	45.72	7	47.17	7
PROGRESS THROUGH INVENTIONS	48.94	6	51.13	4	41.42	8	42.92	8	40.98	9
PERIODS OF TIME	56.60	2	59.12	1	64.99	1	59.29	2	53.65	3
CULTURAL ASPECTS	60.50	1	56.73	2	48.56	6	51.76	3	52.01	4
AESTHETIC ASPECTS	38.76	9	48.79	5	44.67	7	51.65	4	56.91	2
SOCIAL ASPECTS	44.98	8	44.74	8	37.17	9	37.88	9	43.26	8
NATURAL RESOURCES	50.02	5	52.88	3	48.77	5	47.49	6	50.75	5
GEOGRAPHIC ASPECTS	47.92	7	44.94	7	51.82	3	48.74	5	47.21	6

At first glance it would appear that all the percentages are so high in Table 10 that there really is not too much difference in preferences for categories. One might conclude that choices between pairs in the original checking instrument were distributed so widely that it tended toward an average. On the other hand, if one follows the percentages paralleling the rank order in each grade they vary quite widely from first to ninth place—from 60.50 per cent to 38.76 per cent in the second grade, from 59.12 to 44.16 in the third grade, from 64.99 to 37.17 in the fourth grade, from 61.98 to 37.88 in the fifth grade, and from 58.04 to 40.98 in the sixth grade.

Some of the changes in rank order of a category from grade to grade seem difficult to account for. Other categories are fairly consistent like "Periods of time" and "Social aspects." The investigators made no attempt to determine the course of study being pursued by the children in the various towns from whom the preferences were collected. It is possible that what the children were "having" might influence what they thought they would like. It is also possible that choices were in directions away from what they were having in social studies because the grass looked greener in the other pasture. Perhaps the distribution of choices may simply illustrate the wide range of interests of children.

Such studies of children's interests emphasize wide individual differences, also. Every teacher is faced every day with a group of children who differ widely in their experiences, desires, drives and degrees of alertness in relation to the materials and content of the social studies. Unless the teacher is sensitive to these factors, our schools will go right on developing many children who are indifferent to or have a distaste for social studies.

WHAT CHILDREN WANT TO KNOW ABOUT THEIR WORLD

Many educators believe that children's interests expressed in their questions bear implications for those who are concerned with curriculum. A research project in 1952 collected questions from children in grades four, five, and six with respect to *What Children Want to Know About Their World* (5).

The directions read to children said: "If someone had the time and knew enough to answer all your questions, what questions would you ask? Perhaps you have seen something, heard something, read something, or just thought about something which made you wish someone could answer questions for you about those things. On your papers write down all those questions you would like to have answered. Spell all words the best you can."

The categories used in classifying the questions were the same thirty-three categories and their sub-divisions which Baker used (6).

A total of 54,389 questions were collected from 4,740 children. Eleven of the thirty-three categories can be classified as social studies. Table 13 shows those categories with the distribution of questions according to boys and girls.

Table 13. Number and Per Cent of 54,389 Questions Asked by 2,401 Boys and 2,339 Girls in Grades 4, 5, and 6, Which Can Be Classified in Each of Eleven Social Studies Categories

	BOYS		GIRLS		TOTAL	
CATEGORIES	NO. OF QUES.	PER CENT	NO. OF QUES.	PER CENT	NO. OF QUES.	PER CENT
1. MAN AS A SOCIAL BEING	2112	7.84	2128	7.75	4240	7.80
2. AMERICAN HISTORY AND GOVERNMENT	1285	4.77	1142	4.16	2427	4.46
3. COMMUNICATION	1636	6.08	2131	7.76	3767	6.93
4. TRAVEL AND TRANSPORTATION	1588	5.90	693	2.52	2281	4.19
5. INVENTIONS	699	2.60	402	1.46	1101	2.02
6. GEOGRAPHY OF THE U.S. AND ITS TERRITORIES	600	2.23	559	2.04	1159	2.13
7. DISTANT LANDS AND PEOPLES	974	3.61	1039	3.78	2013	3.70
8. INDUSTRIES AND COMMERCIAL PRODUCTS	1688	6.27	1902	6.93	3590	6.60
9. THE LOCAL COMMUNITY	422	1.57	408	1.49	830	1.53
10. RECREATION	1293	4.80	1428	5.20	2721	5.00
11. WAR	1593	5.92	1058	3.85	2651	4.87
TOTALS	13890	51.59	12890	46.94	26780	49.23

Table 13 shows that 49.23 per cent of the total number of questions asked fall in the categories classified as social studies. Science had 27.95 per cent of the total questions.

Table 14 shows the distribution of the 26,780 social studies questions by grades and the percentage of those questions classified under each of the eleven categories.

Table 14. Number and Per Cent of Social Studies Questions Asked by 1,485 Fourth Grade Pupils, 1,811 Fifth Grade Pupils, and 1,444 Sixth Grade Pupils in Each of the Eleven Social Studies Categories

	GRADE 4		GRADE 5		GRADE 6	
	NO. OF QUES.	PER CENT	NO. OF QUES.	PER CENT	NO. OF QUES.	PER CENT
1. MAN AS A SOCIAL BEING	1194	14.45	1647	16.09	1399	16.89
2. AMERICAN HISTORY AND GOVERNMENT	772	9.34	979	9.56	676	8.16
3. COMMUNICATION	1158	14.02	1352	13.21	1257	15.18
4. TRAVEL AND TRANSPORTATION	587	7.11	848	8.28	846	10.22
5. INVENTIONS	239	2.89	587	5.73	275	3.32
6. GEOGRAPHY OF THE U.S. AND ITS TERRITORIES	364	4.41	541	5.29	254	3.07
7. DISTANT LANDS AND PEOPLES	691	8.36	511	4.99	811	9.79
8. INDUSTRIES AND COMMERCIAL PRODUCTS	1360	16.46	1533	14.98	697	8.42
9. THE LOCAL COMMUNITY	346	4.19	268	2.62	216	2.61
10. RECREATION	1009	12.21	929	9.07	783	9.46
11. WAR	542	6.56	1042	10.18	1067	12.88
TOTALS	8262	100.00	10237	100.00	8281	100.00

In a comparison of the Clark study with that made by Baker it was found that the average number of questions asked per child was much greater, 11.47 to 6.06. In every category in the social studies area the percentage of children asking questions exceeded that of the Baker study. In that study, the category *Animal Life* in the field of *Science* ranked first, but in the present study the category *Man as a Social Being* in the *Social Studies* area ranked first.

References

(1) Dorothy H. Stewart, "Children's Preferences in Types of Assignment." Unpublished Master's thesis, Boston University, 1945.

(2) Harriet M. Foley, "Preferences of Sixth Grade Children for Certain Social Studies Activities." Unpublished Master's thesis, Boston University, 1951.

(3) David P. Duval, "Preferences of Fifth Grade Children for Certain Social Studies Activities." Unpublished Master's thesis, Boston University, 1952.

(4) Virginia W. Bresnahan et al., "Preferences of Children in Grades Two through Eight in Social Studies Areas." Unpublished Master's thesis, Boston University, 1952.

(5) Edythe T. Clark et al., "What Children Want to Know About Their World." Unpublished Master's thesis, Boston University, 1952.

(6) Emily V. Baker. *Children's Questions and Their Implications for Planning the Curriculum.* New York: Teachers College, Columbia University, 1945.

✌§ DECISION MAKING: THE HEART OF SOCIAL STUDIES INSTRUCTION   *Shirley H. Engle*

Unfortunately, too many teachers of the social studies are satisfied to assign readings and then hold recitations to see if pupils have memorized certain facts. Equally unfortunately, too many otherwise fine teachers fall back on this beginner's device whenever they deal with a topic that is controversial. Engle argues sharply against such primitive instruction and learning. He presses hard for a shift to decision making based on a synthesis of all available facts and knowledge of values. His ideas are not restricted to any particular organization of content, but can be applied to any topic in the social studies.

MY THEME IS a very simple one. It is that, in teaching the social studies, we should emphasize decision making as against mere remembering. We should emphasize decision making at two levels: at the level of deciding what a group of descriptive data means, how these data may be summarized or generalized, what principles they suggest; and also decision making at the level of policy determination, which requires a synthesis of facts, principles, and values usually not all found on one side of any question.

In order to make my case, it is useful to draw certain distinctions between the social sciences and the social studies. The social sciences include all of the scholarly, investigative work of historians, political scientists, economists, anthropologists, psychologists, and sociologists,

Used by permission of the author and the National Council for the Social Studies; from *Social Education*, 24:301–304 and 306, November, 1960. Dr. Engle is associate dean for graduate development at Indiana University.

together with such parts of the work of biologists and geographers as relate primarily to human behavior. Closely related fields include philosophy, literature, linguistics, logistics, and statistics. The social studies, including the content of the textbooks, courses of study, and whatever passes in the school for instruction in civic and social affairs, are based on the social sciences but they clearly involve always a selection of and distillation from the social sciences—they encompass only a minor portion of the social sciences.

SELECTIVITY AND PURPOSE

Selectivity, therefore, is one of the features which distinguishes the social sciences from the social studies. To social science, knowledge is useful for its own sake; all knowledge is of equal worth; there is no concern for immediate usefulness. To the social studies, a central consideration must always be that of determining what knowledge is of most worth. If all of the knowledge of a field of study is to be boiled down into one textbook, what is to be emphasized? If all of the knowledge of the area is to be boiled down into one course of study, what is most important?

There is a more basic distinction to be drawn between the social sciences and the social studies than merely that of selectivity. The impelling purpose of the two is quite different. The orientation of the social scientist is that of research. The more scientific the social scientist, the more specialized becomes his interest, the more consuming becomes his desire to know more and more about less and less, the less concern he shows for broad social problems. He is far more inclined to analyze, dissect, and proliferate than to unite, synthesize, and apply. His absorbing interest is to push back the frontier of dependable knowledge in some limited sector of the social scene.

In marked contrast to the meticulous research orientation of the social sciences, the social studies are centrally concerned with the education of citizens. The mark of the good citizen is the quality of decisions which he reaches on public and private matters of social concern. The social sciences contribute to the process of decision making by supplying reliable facts and principles upon which to base decisions—they do not supply the decisions ready made. The facts are there for all to see but they do not tell us what to do. Decision making requires more than mere knowledge of facts and principles; it requires a weighing in the balance, a synthesizing of all available information and values. The problems about which citizens must reach decisions are never confronted piecemeal, the facts are seldom clearly all on one side, and values, too, must be taken into consideration. A social problem requires that the citizen put together, from many sources, information and values which the social sciences treat in relative isolation. Thus in the social studies the prevailing motive is synthesis rather than analysis. The social studies begin where the social sciences end. Facts and principles which are the ends in view in the social sciences are merely a means to a further end in the social studies. The goal of the social studies lies not merely in information but in the character of people. The goal is the good citizen. . . .

DECISION MAKING AND LEARNING THEORY

If the purpose of the social studies is to be education for citizenship, if its primary concern is to be the quality of the beliefs and convictions which students come to hold on public questions, and if we are to be concerned with the development of skill at decision making, then there are some things which it becomes imperative that we do in teaching the social studies. I would like to develop briefly some of these imperatives.

We must abandon our use of what I shall call the ground-covering technique, and with it the wholly mistaken notion that to commit information to memory is the same as to gain knowledge. By ground covering I mean the all too familiar technique of learning and holding in memory, enforced by drill, large amounts of more or less isolated descriptive material without pausing in any way, at any time, to speculate as to the meaning or significance of the material, or to consider its relevance and bearing to any general idea, or to consider its applicability to any problem or issue past or present. Even when such material is interesting, and it sometimes is, merely to cover it in this uncritical, matter-of-fact fashion robs the material of its potential for accurate concept formation or generalization which will be useful to students in understanding events and conditions in other times and places in which like data appear. Simply reading and remembering the stories about Indians in our history, no matter how many times repeated, has never insured the development of accurate concepts about Indians or correct generalizations about the relationships between people of divergent cultures and histories. Or, if in our haste to cover ground, we refuse to deal contemplatively and critically with the material we are covering, the student may generalize haphazardly and may, without our help, arrive at totally erroneous conclusions. . . .

The ground-covering fetish is based on the false notion that remembering is all there is to knowing or the equally false notion that one must be well drilled in the facts before he can begin to think. M. I. Finley, noted British historian, says about ground covering that "a mere telling of individual events in sequence, no matter how accurately done, is just that and nothing else. Such knowledge is meaningless, its mere accumulation a waste of time. Instead, knowledge must lead to understanding. In the field of history this means trying to grasp general ideas about human events. The problem is to move from particular events to the universal; from the concrete events to the underlying patterns and generalities."

Equally fallacious is the background theory of learning, or the notion that we must hold the facts in memory before we are ready to draw conclusions from them or to think about their meaning. This theory is at considerable variance with recognized scientific method and the ways in which careful thinkers approach an intellectual problem. The thinker or scientist frequently engages in speculation or theorizing about possible relationships, from which he deduces tests or possible facts which, if observable, verify his theory. . . .

What happens in our classrooms from too strict an adherence to ground covering is that the number of facts committed to memory is reduced to a relatively small number. These are the so-called basic facts which we learn, and just as promptly forget, over and over again. Thus ground covering actually works to reduce and restrict the quantity of factual information treated in our classes. What is needed instead is a vast multiplication of the quantity of factual material with which students are asked to deal in the context of reaching a reasoned conclusion about some intellectual problem. Such an enrichment of factual background will come about when we turn from our preoccupation with remembering to a more fruitful concern for drawing conclusions from facts or for testing our speculations and ideas about human events with all of the relevant data we are able to collect.

For ground covering, or remembering, we should substitute decision making, which is reflective, speculative, thought provoking, and oriented to the process of reaching conclusions. My thesis is simply this, decision making should afford the structure around which social studies instruction should be organized. The central importance of decision making in the social studies has been cited earlier. The point here is that students are not likely to learn to reach better decisions, that is, grounded and reasoned decisions, except as they receive guided and critically oriented exercise in the decision-making process.

CLASSROOM ACTIVITY

Decision-making opportunities in the social studies classroom may run the entire gamut of difficulty, from very simple situations which take the form merely of posing questions for class consideration which require some thought and a synthesis of information supplied in a single descriptive paragraph to very complex social problems involving questions of public policy or individual behavior. . . .

Some decisions involve essentially matters of fact. For example, suppose we are reading about the building of the transcontinental railroads in the 1870's, 1880's, and 1890's and how the government gave large grants of land and money to the railroad companies to encourage them to build the railroads. We read further that subsequently the railroads, or most of them, went into bankruptcy but also that following their construction the country experienced a great expansion of agricultural and industrial wealth whereby our exports of wheat and corn multiplied tenfold in 20 years, and in the same period the value of our manufacturers' products increased 200 percent, 180 new factories were being built in Philadelphia alone. We have these and many other facts. But the decision rests in concluding what these facts mean. What do they all add up to? Which of the following generalizations accurately summarize these facts? Government subsidization of key industries brings a vast multiplication of other industries under private ownership; private investors will not take the extraordinary risk necessary to start a really new industrial development; one industrial development inevitably leads to other industrial developments; industry in which the government interferes is always inefficient and will fail in the end; private industry can never be expected to provide the transportation facilities needed for an expanding economy; government participation in industry tends to dry up the growth of private industry; industry resulting from government spending is uneconomical and is doomed to fail in the end; if the government had foregone the tax money used to aid the railroads, private individuals would have had money which they would have invested in the railroads. Clearly, the making of decisions among the alternatives listed above is essentially a matter of sorting out and applying facts until a conclusion is reached which honestly and accurately summarizes all facts that are relevant to the problem.

Other decisions, perhaps we should say most decisions, involve values as well as facts. Thus, in dealing with the issue of which of two proposed solutions to the problems of farm surpluses is best, one may conclude, factually, that government support of farm prices leads inevitably to inefficiency in agriculture and to unnecessarily high cost for food and fibre which the farm produces. This much is a factual conclusion. But this does not necessarily get us out of the woods, for one might still prefer government-supported agriculture to an unregulated agriculture because he feared the control of large agricultural corporations (which will almost inevitably follow the removal of governmental restrictions—another factual generalization) more than he fears governmental controls. The latter decision is a value judgment, though one fraught, as are all value decisions, with still further implications which could be grounded factually. For instance, in a hierarchy of values, the *greatest degree of individual freedom* may be the value sought or agreed upon by all involved in the decision. From this premise a factual investigation could be conducted of the relationship between government regulation and individual freedom on the one hand and between corporate control and individual freedom on the other. Thus, though the decision as to value is not in this way resolved, the exact issue over values is clarified by such a factual investigation of the alternatives.

CLASSROOM IMPLICATIONS

If decision making is to be the focus of social studies instruction, we will need to introduce vastly larger quantities of factual information into our classrooms. Drill to the point of memory on a few basic facts will never suffice. The superficial coverage of one textbook will never be enough. The very moment that a conclusion, such as any of those suggested above, is reached tentatively, the natural demand is for more facts with which to test the conclusion. This means almost surely the introduction of large quantities of supplementary materials, with far too much content to be committed to memory. . . . It may mean in the end the abandonment of textbooks and the substitution of numerous, more substantive, more informative, and more exciting books and other materials.

If the quality of decision making is to be the primary concern of social studies instruction, we must take steps to up-grade the quality of intellectual activity in the social studies classroom. . . . Among the common errors in logic easily observed in social studies instruction is the acceptance of an assertion as if it were a fact, the confusing of fact with opinion, the validation of the truth of something on authority, the acceptance of a merely plausible explanation for a sufficient explanation, the failure to agree on the meaning of key words (frequently value laden) before engaging in an argument in which the meaning of the word is essential as, for instance, to argue over whether the first Roosevelt was a good or a strong President without first agreeing on a common meaning for "good" and for "strong," and the confusing of questions which must be referred to facts for an answer and those which defer to values for an answer. The persistent practice in our classrooms of errors in logic of the kind mentioned can lead only to intellectual confusion and irresponsibility. If we are really concerned with effective citizenship, we must not only provide the opportunity for decision making but we must see to it that decisions are made in keeping with well known rules of science and logic and that students get practice in making such decisions.

Lastly, if responsible decision making is the end of social studies instruction, we must recognize values formation as a central concern of social studies instruction. Real life decisions are ultimately value decisions. To leave a student unaware of the value assumptions in his decision or to leave him untrained in dealing with value questions is literally to lead an innocent lamb to the slaughter. Such a student could, and he frequently does, return to our fold and say, "But you didn't tell me it was this way." Or he may quickly sink into cynicism or misbelief. The question of what values he should hold probably cannot be settled in the classroom, but values can be dealt with intelligently in the classroom. The nature of the values which people hold can be made explicit, the issues over values can be clarified, and the ends to which holding to a particular value will lead can be established factually to some extent. . . .

To duck the question of values is to cut the heart out of decision making. The basic social problem of America today is a problem of value. In simple terms the problem may be stated as to whether we value more the survival of a free America which will require sacrifice for education, for materials of defense, etc., or whether we value more our right as individuals to spend our resources on extra fins for our cars and for all the other gadgets of conspicuous consumptions. It is not impossible to predict the outcome of hewing to either choice. It is not at all certain that our students are being prepared to make the right decision and to make it in time.

My thesis has been a very simple one. It is that quality decision making should be the central concern of social studies instruction. I could cite many renowned people as having essentially supported the position I have here tried to state. Among the ancients these would include Socrates, Plato, and Thucydides, the father of objective history. These would include the great modern philosopher Alfred North Whitehead and such modern critics as the economist Peter Drucker and President Robert F. Goheen of Princeton. But to quote these would continue the discussion over-long, as I suspect I may have done already. So may I quote instead a simple statement from the noted modern scientist Hans Selye, who has said that "facts from which no conclusions can be drawn are hardly worth knowing."

&S FACTS OF LIFE   *John R. Seeley*

Is there a conspiracy of silence to keep the facts of our eco-nomic, social, and political life from youngsters? Professor Seeley's discussion of this question sparkles with wit and wis-dom. The article makes a further point: without the substance of truth, content becomes myth and dreams. If the social studies are to be improved, the teachers of the social studies must become better informed about the social, economic, and political foundations of our lives—and thus of how they are reflected in classrooms.

WHEN I AM asked what the schools should do that they are not now doing, I reply, "Level with the kids."

My views are received usually with kindness and enthusiasm. But nothing happens. I conclude that, despite repetition of my simple message, I have not been understood, perhaps because I have not spoken plainly enough. This lack of understanding de-mands a new attempt.

As I write this, through my window I can see the modern school my younger sons attend. Without a break of fence or boundary, its play-yard abuts a strip of greenbelt, which abuts my home lawn. This is no accident, but a powerful symbol of a significant reality. No longer is there the sharp, designed break between the soft, warm protections and illusions of home and the harsh, cold prac-ticalities and "realities" of school.

No longer does home represent the glad way the world ought to be, and the school, the sad way it is. Emotionally as well as physi-cally, each child moves across that undivided greensward, from "his"

Reprinted from *The Education Digest*, XXVIII (February, 1963), 1–4; con-densed from *The Toronto Education Quarterly*, II (Autumn, 1962), 1–7. Used by permission of the *Education Digest*. John R. Seeley is the chairman of the Department of Sociology, York University, Toronto.

lawn to "our" greenbelt, to "their" school. It is hardly a weaning; the break, if there is one, is minuscule.

And when he gets there, the child encounters as decent a society as he is ever likely again to encounter: as good and decent a society as his home, if he comes from a good one; far better, if he comes from a bad. The world he meets is largely scaled to his size, tailored to fit him, tolerant within reasonable limits of his odd angles and corners, impunitive, warm and bright, unconstrictive—a place fit for a child to live.

It is regrettably true that as we go up the school grades the infusion of humanity and decency steadily diminishes, so that in the higher reaches we are not much more than medieval; but I am consoled that further changes are largely a matter of time.

With all the qualifications and exceptions that might be made, with all the pointings to the margin between intent and performance, it is my judgment that teachers and administrators of education together have built an institution better and more enlightened and humane for its day than any other in the society.

How, then, can a body so praised be open also to devastating criticism, especially from the same source?

What I have to say is that what I regard as the best of institutions is the worst of *educational* institutions—if education is any way involved with what is formally communicated. What the school *does* is, to a large and creditable extent, based on the twentieth century; what the school *says* is lost somewhere in the mists of the sixteenth century—or the twelfth.

The school is a good society, or as nearly so as the surrounding society will permit. But its central function—which, I believe, is to tell the child the way the world is—has been sacrificed. All else it does with distinction; only this it fails to do.

I am not here joining in the cry for excellence, though I do not doubt, if we do not overdo it, that excellence is excellent. I am only saying in the simplest way that the school fails formally to teach the child which end is up, what are the facts he needs to know about the world in which he lives. If that is not a function—the central function—of the school, of course the charge fails.

The indictment is that, with respect to all major matters, the school stands today where it (and the family) stood with reference to the matter of sex a generation or two ago. In that matter, home and school, indeed the whole adult world, maintained a conspiracy of silence against the child. Where the silence could not be maintained, the adults lied or misled. If the child came at all to any sane appreciation of the leading facts his sources of information were informal and essentially bootleg.

The costs of this now largely abandoned procedure we surely know. Many of them we are paying yet. Knowledge that is bootleg in origin retains its bootleg character in utilization—that to which it refers retains forever considerable coloration of the darkness from which it came.

But that era is, for the most part, over. No one needs to be taken seriously who disputes that children should be informed about sex as fully and decently as their growing understandings will permit.

KEY FACTS OF LIFE

The facts suppressed today are, now even more than before, the key "facts of life": facts about the nature of human nature, about the nature of society generally and the state of ours particularly; facts about power, wealth, the state of ethics and philosophy in our age; the facts about themselves; even the facts about the school and the educational enterprise. Of course, it is *only* the key facts of life that are suppressed, and every society suppresses these. But who tells the children that?

How and where does the child learn the brute facts about power? How it is seized and maintained? How it is served by institutions ostensibly designed to stand against it? When do they read Machiavelli, Mosca, Laswell and Marx?

How does the child learn the brute facts about money? How it is made—not in the niggling amounts that represent pay or salary for work done, but in the really large chunks that come out of pipelines, large electrical combines, or cartels, trusts, or oligopolies? How and when does he learn how business, big business, is actually done as against some image based on a seventeenth-century Hanseatic merchant?

Where and when do children learn the actual nature of their own natures and what is now known about these? Who helps them understand and cope with the deeper, more inaccessible aspects of the human personality, the profounder motives, the more hidden drives? When do they encounter Freud, Piaget, George Herbert Mead, or even Gesell?

How and from whom do children learn about social class? About the function of myth in society generally and about leading myths of their own? If they can read travelogues in the lower grades that merely make strange folk look quaint, can they not have then, or soon after, the deliverances of modern anthropology translated into language within their grasp? Can they really grow up into the world as we know it as if Boas, Malinowski, Ruth Benedict, and Margaret Mead had never existed?

Let it not be said that we do not teach these things because children are incapable of comprehending them. Nor because the facts are "still in dispute" or too uncertainly founded. Nor because we do not know the facts ourselves.

As to the first, not only do the children easily understand such things, but they are the stuff of life they want to learn about and discuss. Here as elsewhere just *how* to introduce them to the truth is merely a pedagogical technicality; the commitment to do so is a moral decision.

If the school taught only facts certain or beyond dispute it would teach nothing at all; the very geometry we taught yesterday is seen today as having a false foundation logically. The same is true for calculus and, notoriously, yesterday's fundamental physics.

As to not knowing the facts ourselves, we should, of course, learn them if we were committed to communicating what they are about.

No, the reason they are not taught is because they *do* matter. They are not taught because there is a vested interest in ignorance about them; because, like most truths worth hearing, they are uncomfortable and they ruffle composures. They are not taught because in favoring freedom and a better life they threaten order and a safe and easy hegemony for those already having the most of whatever there is to get.

The point is that what we have learned about men and society since the seventeenth century is either withheld from the child, or mediated to him in an expurgated, misleading, and false fashion.

The answer to "He gets all this when he gets to college, doesn't he?" is: "Perhaps, but by then it is too late."

The reason why university is too late (apart from the fact that not everyone gets to a university) is that the kind of knowledge I am speaking of is fundamental, not superstructural. It is the kind of knowledge that transforms life as it is experienced—and should transform it early. Such knowledge is properly a foundation block—not a coping stone. It can no more be left as a finishing gesture than the notion of numbers could be left for introduction in grade 13.

I ask, why not tell our pupils and students the facts of life from the beginning? Every society, as I mentioned earlier, suppresses or attempts to suppress the key facts of life. How can I now ask that our society do other?

I believe that our society is, actually or potentially, a different society, in at least one respect. Perhaps this is not the first society with selfconscious, powerfully organized, professional educators, though it is different in degree in that respect also. But it is the first society with a busy, selfconscious, dedicated cadre of social scientists whose business it is, in part, to report social reality, *what is* rather than *what we should like it to be.*

Their presence makes it more difficult to bury heads in the sand—they keep drawing attention to what is not visible from that position. So educators who wish to know may know what it is they are joining with powerful interest to suppress. Educators may not be able to avoid knowing. And once they know these things, they are brought into conflict with their own powerful professional goals. They can no longer be unwitting conspirators for ignorance. They may not be willing long to be witting ones.

There seems but one answer compatible with duty—and it goes far beyond tinkering with the curriculum to get in more science or mathematics earlier or better. The answer is to redesign the school experience so that what is most important to all—an adequate orientation to the human world in which the children live—has not only a place, but, without question or qualification, the place of priority—the first place—that it deserves.

✍ SOCIETAL DEMANDS AND CHANGING SOCIAL PROBLEMS *Alice Miel*

This probing discussion is important in guaranteeing that the demands of our society play a part in decisions affecting the content and organization of the social studies. Miss Miel discusses the delicate problems of balancing individual freedom with order in society, and of maintaining a society while ensuring justice for every individual. She further adds some words of wisdom about the ways children learn to live democratically while building knowledge about democracy.

THE EXPRESSION, *demands of society*, often calls up a picture of a stern parent or teacher standing over a child demanding compliance

Used by permission of the author and the National Council for the Social Studies; from its Thirty-Second Yearbook, *Social Studies in the Elementary School*, 1962, pp. 17–25. Alice Miel is a professor of education, the head of the Department of Education, and the head of the Department of Curriculum and Teaching at Teachers College, Columbia University.

with a specific request. Although the term is rather misleading, it is well established and requires clarification lest curriculum planning in its name be misguided. It is true that in tradition-oriented societies the individual can be taught specific rules of conduct ready made for application to specific types of human relationship. The demands of democracy, that is what the society asks or expects of the individual, are of a quite different order. In fact, it is more accurate in a democracy to speak not of what the society needs but of what the *individual needs and wants to become* to live usefully and with satisfaction in his society. In a democracy it is not a case of the society against the individual or the individual against the society. The interests are mutual. The society is a good society if individuals can flower in it and they can flower only if the society provides the conditions of *order* made up of freedom and restraint and of *justice* made up of respect for the individual and the rule of law.

THE OVERARCHING DEMAND OF A DEMOCRACY

A democracy makes a unique demand on its members. Such a society is oriented only in part to maintaining honored traditions and preserving the basic social inventions which give it its special character. Those very inventions provide for the possibility of response to changing conditions. A democratic society invites its members to subscribe to basic values and to conform to the law of the land and to ways of living together found useful over generations. At the same time it lays upon its members the responsibility for protesting arrangements that have outlived their usefulness, of challenging instances in which the society is not living up to its ideals, and of inventing better ways of realizing the potential of democracy. To play his part in maintaining-advancing his society in this way, the individual is required to exercise judgment in one situation after the other. The individual freedom which democracy is designed to protect and enhance carries with it the pleasure and pain of making choices and the obligation to assume due responsibility for the consequences of the choices. In this activity the individual is guided, outside of the law, by only the most general set of ideals and a few flexible and approximate rules of conduct. A man enjoys (has the benefit of) freedom only if he enjoys (finds joy in) freedom, only if he sees choice making as a stimulating, fulfilling experience. Therefore, the mental health of the individual in a democracy depends upon his feeling of adequacy in making the decisions he is called upon to make and his feeling of satisfaction in the decision making process.

THE DEMANDS OF A DEMOCRACY IN MORE DETAIL

In a democracy the individual must decide or help to decide many difficult questions. Examples of those having special importance for his society are:

How much and what kinds of difference and likeness to encourage: the question of how to view respect for people.

How to reconcile private interests and public interests: the question of how to view the common welfare.

How to use fruitfully both majority and minority views: the question of how to view consensus.

How to maintain harmony between individual autonomy and external authority: the question of how to view authority.

Each of the questions is a special form of the basic problem of maintaining the delicate balance between the requirements of the individual and the requirements of the group, a balance which is the central and unique idea of democracy.

As he makes choices of behavior in a democracy other problems arise for the individual:

Maintaining such a balance between giving and receiving that sharing takes place.

Sending and receiving different forms of messages and sharing meaning in such ways that communication is achieved.

Maintaining individuality while cooperating to achieve purposes important to a wider group.

Participating as a group member, leading and following as appropriate.

Demonstrating loyalty through protesting against the society's actions deemed unjust or ill advised while conforming to the arrangements by which the society maintains order.

Exercising citizenship through claiming rights and taking responsibility.

This is an outline form of only one way of looking at the task of socialization in a democracy (1). There are others and it matters not which of several useful formulations is adopted provided that those responsible for the quality of elementary school social studies programs have a clear conception of the nature of their society. This is a necessary prerequisite to helping children arrive at an orderly view of democratic beliefs, which surely is one task of the school. No one can predict the precise moment when a child or group of children will be in a position to take the step of abstracting a systematic view from a series of more or less scattered generalizations. The points when attention to such a task will be fruitful can be determined only in the course of direct work with children. However, something is known about the order of events leading up to building with young people a theory of democracy. Liberal amounts of mutually reinforcing firsthand and vicarious experience promising a high yield of generalizations about democracy are necessary. Careful examination of the meanings of such experience is also necessary to cause the generalizations to emerge in the form of statements which can be communicated clearly to others. Only when several generalizations earned by children in such a manner are available can it be hoped that children will achieve an organized view of democracy which they deeply understand and care about.

CHANGING SOCIAL PROBLEMS AS SOURCES OF CURRICULUM CONTENT

Even the more detailed problems of decision making in a democracy outlined in the previous section are not met in such abstract form in real life. Always, as they appear to the individual, they wear a different guise, depending upon the persons involved and the time and place of the encounter. The elementary school has a choice, in planning its social studies curriculum, of trying to build generalizations about democracy that are destined to remain glib and empty phrases and that tend to close the door to further thought, or of seeking to build a quality of knowledge and commitment and active follow-through on beliefs and concerns that is adequate for functioning in today's complicated world.

If the latter course is chosen, an intelligent approach would be to study *what the society is becoming* to locate the promising specifics of experience out of which useful generalizations may grow.

As a people goes along living its history, the observers in the group begin to call attention to shortcomings and to note distressing trends. They imply the useful question: "Do we like what we are becoming?"

What the people are becoming: the darker side. When this section was first outlined, the nation was just getting over its shock at the extent of rigging of quiz shows on television. Fresh outbursts of anti-semitism were occurring. Juvenile crime was said to be on the increase. Mothers of young children in the South were abusing parents who sent their children to newly desegregated schools. Cars were sporting bigger and better tailfins, not only using up valuable metals but also, it was claimed, diverting money from such public services as health and education. School and community libraries were being combed by superpatriots for text and other books considered unsafe. Undue conformity and lack of excellence were being deplored. The rootlessness of an increasingly mobile population was a matter of concern. Fear was expressed over the dehumanizing effects which seem to accompany living in a crowded, pushbutton world. It was held that the public generally was altogether too apathetic about maintaining democracy at home and abroad. Representatives of youth groups at the 1960 White House Conference on Children and Youth accused their elders of having failed to .set an example of living guided by decent and humane values.

Some of the problems were quickly replaced by others differing only in the specific form they took. For example, ghostwriting of term papers and theses soon took the headlines away from quiz show exposés. Other problems were already on the way to correction by the time of writing. Smaller cars trimmed of excess adornment became the mode, though it could not be demonstrated that the savings thus achieved were applied to the support of community services.

If one has an eye only for the darker side of the picture, one can find quite a catalog of human failings that have persisted over the centuries. Is there any hope through social education? An affirmative answer is based on assumptions for which there is considerable foundation in fact: 1) there is a brighter side to what the people of the United States are becoming; 2) there are available in the society ways of tackling conditions needing correction.

What the people are becoming: the brighter side. The same newspapers which report the shortcomings of man also reflect individual and group achievements which are themselves gains for the human race and which also continue to demonstrate what man might be. Success stories in this category are agreement with other nations on a declaration of universal human rights followed by a declaration of the rights of children, civil rights legislation, reduction of economic inequality and growing social security, and virtual achievement of universal education.

In addition, a new mood is developing. The very expression of the concerns outlined in the previous section is one step in facing the underlying conditions and moving to correct them. When a new, young, and vigorous president called upon the people of the nation to be strong and to make sacrifices, a readiness had already developed. Awareness had been growing that there were other people in the world, that they would welcome help in developing their human and material resources, and that the United States of America had an important world role to fill. Once their elders began to show that they cared about human values and respected human intelligence, the youth of the nation showed themselves quite ready to bring their idealism out from under cover and to give way to their very real interest in learning. The response to the idea of the Peace Corps showed a shift from an earlier preoccupation of young people with enclosing themselves and their families in safe little nests supported by safe jobs with regular hours. The generosity and community-mindedness that had long been characteristic of the people of the United States was given new outlets. . . .

What the United States of America can count on. The nation has been fortunate in its location on the globe and in its natural resources. But it has been even more fortunate in the conception of a society to which it has been able to give living form. The values declared before the world in its basic documents may be imperfectly realized but they remain the stated commitment of the society, available as ideals to give direction to future development. The processes of democracy may not always work as intended but they are available to be used in correcting the evils growing out of man's shortcomings. As long as there is room for protest, for the minority peacefully to try to convert the majority, democracy will maintain its self-correcting nature.

The United States of America also has at its disposal a great fund of knowledge relating to human potentialities and how they may be developed. It is realized more with each day that highly developed intelligence, creative power, and skill in a population is the only hope in a world where this nation is outnumbered many times over by forces unsympathetic to individual freedom. . . .

EMPHASIS ON SOCIAL LEARNING

As men seek to learn the ways in which they are alike and seek to build on their common interests, in their efforts to create a peaceful world, there are two dangers. One is that the mediocre or worst rather than the best features of various cultures may be selected for survival. The other is that likeness may be valued more than difference and that constructive cultural variety may not be kept alive. Making judgments with regard to aspects of a culture is part of a larger requirement. Essentially, the world needs to learn how to judge a man. What is deeply offensive in terms of basic human values? What is a surface difference offensive only because of the habits or sights or odors to which one is accustomed? Within the differences in language, dress, foods, and forms of recreation which have grown up around the world, what is the constructive core of human likeness which tells one man that he has found in another a kindred soul?

Knowledge and judgment are incomplete without deep feeling for people. There is, as yet, only partial understanding of how an individual becomes a participating member of a society, in the sense of caring about what the society stands for, caring where the society is going, caring about what happens to individuals in it, and investing himself in efforts to make the society better. Those growing into membership in the society will be called upon to discover ways of relating to one another suitable for modern conditions (vast numbers of people trying to share limited resources and space). Can their teachers help them to learn to use their resources and the time released by advances in technology to be creative, in the many ways man can be creative, to savor the wonder of living by finding joy *within experience* as well as in anticipated outcomes?

If the social studies are to serve their function in the elementary school as one means of contributing to the socialization process, that is, of helping children to become more intelligent, useful, and committed members of their society, then those responsible for providing opportunities for experience within this area of the curriculum must be responsive to the peculiar nature of the demands made on the individual by the type of society doing the educating and to the current forms of the perennial problems which that society faces.

The social studies are about people. Can teachers and their advisers keep that one fact foremost in all their planning? Can they make the social studies a genuine search for meaning, not just of terms or even of relationships between sets of facts but of human existence and what it might become? That would truly be education for excellence.

References

(1) For a more detailed development of these ideas see Miel, Alice and Peggy Brogan, *More Than Social Studies*. Englewood Cliffs, New Jersey: Prentice-Hall, Inc., 1957. Chapters 1 and 2.

≼§ EDUCATING CITIZENS FOR DEMOCRATIC INTERGROUP RELATIONS, 1960–1980   *William E. Vickery*

Vickery lists a series of concepts based on a few sets of key ideas. These concepts—although drawn from social psychology, sociology, and anthropology—all focus on intergroup relations. Vickery's syntheses are particularly useful examples of how ideas are tied to each other, and how they can be used to structure social studies content and instruction.

PROGRAMS OF INTERGROUP education in the coming years will be built around basic concepts rather than around outlines of subject matter. The same concepts will be developed at different grade levels and in a variety of subject fields.

In current educational thought and practice, a sound program of intergroup education is best organized within the framework of existing courses, not superimposed on them in the form of special units of work. It utilizes the subject matter of established fields of knowledge. It is not a new subject, requiring a separate sequence of courses. Rather, at its best it is an emphasis in the curriculum, valuable in itself and giving richness and depth to the program of general education traditionally provided by elementary and secondary schools.

How can intergroup education be made an intrinsic part of existing fields of study, organized so that learning takes place in an orderly, logical sequence and is cumulative in its effects? How can knowledge be balanced with cultural sensitivity, social skills, and rational, objective ways of thinking so that the pupils' behavior in "we-they" situations is improved?

The experimental studies of the Project in Intergroup Education demonstrated that instruction in intergroup education can be organized effectively around certain key concepts or focusing ideas. These key ideas can be incorporated readily into three persistent themes that run through elementary and secondary education: home and

Used by permission of the author and the National Council for the Social Studies; from its Thirtieth Yearbook, *Citizenship and a Free Society: Education for the Future,* 1960, pp. 165–169. William E. Vickery is the director of the Commission on Educational Organizations of the National Conference of Christians and Jews.

family living, community studies, and the rise and development of a distinctive culture in the United States. A fourth set of key ideas was developed during the course of the Project for an important educational theme found in only a few school programs, a theme which may be called characteristics of human groups and studies in social relationships. The first three sets of basic concepts give fresh emphasis to familiar fields of study. The fourth set adds some badly needed and much neglected subject matter, readily adaptable to existing social studies and group-guidance programs.

In many schools, the study of home and family living initiates the reading program and the social studies in the primary grades. Often this theme is repeated in the seventh-grade or ninth-grade general education program and is again included in the 12th-grade elective "problems course." The key concepts needed for an effective program of intergroup education, therefore, can be developed really without changing the established sequence of course work.

Some concepts useful in developing an understanding of both family life and intergroup relations are:

1. *Family patterns in all national and cultural groups are both alike and different in many ways.* All families face the same general problems and serve the same basic needs. How the problems are met and the needs served depends on the circumstances, traditions, and cultural learnings of the group.
2. *All families have problems and conflicts.* All families also try to solve these conflicts, though in different ways.
3. *Individuals play different social roles in different families.* In the general pattern, the father earns the living and the mother keeps house. But there are many variations.
4. *Families live more happily if each family member is treated as a unique individual,* if his likes and dislikes are respected, if his talents are fostered and his ambitions recognized.
5. *We learn our behaviors, values, and ways of living.* We learn to do what brings approval and friendship from our families, friends, and adults (1).

To this list might be added a sixth helpful concept:

Anyone can change his behaviors, values, and ways of living as he learns better ways.

Plainly these key ideas seek to develop in children the understanding, respect, and acceptance of individual and group differences indispensable for good intergroup relations. At the same time, they underline the essential similarities of the human family and provide a basis for cross-cultural studies free of invidious, ethnocentric comparisons. These ideas may be developed in many different contexts, through a variety of subject matter, and at various levels of complexity suited to the intellectual and emotional maturity of the pupils.

Community studies, like studies of family living, recur at different grade levels of the elementary and secondary school. From the "community helpers" sequence in the primary grades through the studies of urban and rural life in the final year of high school, units of work are found that deal with the community. Among the concepts related to this important educational theme are:

1. *Differences exist in communities just as they do in people;* differences are caused by dominant work patterns, the use made of physical environment, and the tradition of the people.
2. *Interrelationships in communities are important.* Communities are as much a network of people as of houses and streets; one person's work depends upon what someone else does; difficulties in one area create problems in the next; failure in one activity or service jeopardizes others.
3. *Community culture largely determines people's activities, choices, and values;* poor housing helps to produce uncleanliness, unhappiness, conflict with a landlord; the father's work affects family life; people's roles and expectations in community life are determined largely by social position.
4. *Community history and tradition, plus current forces, dictate the quality of the life and relationships within it;* the historic sequence of immigration has affected the status of various ethnic groups; the role and reputation of neighborhoods have changed with shifts in industrial patterns; distortions in institutions are caused by changes in people they serve.
5. *All people work, and all kinds of work are necessary and important to the community; people's lives are greatly affected by their occupations; jobs are interdependent* (2).

These concepts are only a sample of the many that can be formulated to give point and vitality to a program of intergroup education. Yet this sample accurately reflects two persistent features of a program that seeks to improve group relations through community studies. One feature, and perhaps the more important, is a constant effort to reduce the segmentation that characterizes city life by showing the interdependence of people, neighborhoods, and work patterns. A second feature is the systematic study of the multiple causes for differences in community ways of living. These studies are designed to develop objective, nonstereotypic ways of thinking about people who live in different neighborhoods or who are newcomers to the community. To facilitate communication and relationships among people is always emphasized as a main goal of instruction. Descriptive, statistical, and historical studies are geared to that purpose and never conceived of as ends in themselves.

By far the most sustained educational theme in elementary and secondary schools is developing the pupils' understanding of the American culture. To develop such an understanding, teachers have relied mainly on courses in American history and literature. These courses, or units and topics related to them, are offered at almost every grade level. Full courses in American history generally recur in the fifth, eighth, and 11th grades. None of the educational themes offer more or richer opportunities for intergroup education than do the American history and American literature sequences.

Through the history and literature sequences, a number of important concepts in intergroup and human relations can be developed:

America is a land of many cultures, and the present culture pattern is a fusion of many. This blending has enriched American life.

Some people who came here found opportunity and freedom and a chance for advancement. Others found discrimination and prejudice. All found obstacles, such as confusing languages, different customs and dress, and a tendency on the part of the inhabitants to belittle newcomers, especially immigrants.

Inequality in one area of living produces inequality in another. Majority as well as minority groups are affected by these inequalities.

All newcomers to America had certain common problems. All people had to make adjustments. All were treated as different. All found they had to win acceptance. All had some difficulty in becoming part of the new community.

These adjustments may vary with circumstance. Moving from one school to another in the same city presents one set of problems. Moving from the country to the city presents another set of problems. And moving from one country to another presents still another set of problems.

The adjustments newcomers have to make may depend on the time in history, and the degree of difference between the culture of the old place and the culture of the new place (3).

Many similar focusing ideas can be formulated around which the subject matter of history and literature may be organized easily and naturally to develop an understanding of the American culture. The concepts listed above emphasize the movements of people, migrations within the country, and immigration. The idea that newcomers have to make adjustments when they move and settle down in a different place is a particularly vital one in a nation where one family in five changes its place of residence each year. History takes on fresh and deeper meaning for many children when their studies help them to compare and contrast their own families' migration with that of the people who emigrated to the United States or took part in the westward movement.

Other concepts, also connected with the pupils' personal experiences and interests, can be formulated in such subject areas as the economic patterns in American life, civil rights and civic responsibilities, and international affairs. Intergroup relations are central issues in all of these subject areas and provide an appropriate focus for study. Such a focus does not, as some allege, distort the subject matter of history and literature or water down the content of existing courses. Human groups and their relationships *are* the content of the social studies. Literature is mainly concerned with human thoughts, human feelings, human behavior, and human problems. Understanding human beings, the multiple and complex causes of events, and the possible consequences of different courses of action are the chief purposes of both subjects in programs of general education.

Schools in general have not yet found a place in the curriculum for a systematic study of social groups and social relationships. Some institutions of higher learning have experimented with general-education programs built around human-relations concepts (4), but the disciplines that contribute data and ideas to such programs—psychology, sociology, and cultural anthropology—all too often are taught as if they were only subjects for specialists.

Effective teaching sequences to develop an understanding of social relationships can be built around such concepts as these:

> *All people gain satisfaction from belonging to groups.* Being left out always causes psychological distress and often produces undesirable behaviors, such as aggressiveness or indifference.
>
> *There are conflicts of standards and values within all groups.* Variations in standards and values are normal, and harmonious group life can exist without suppression of them. The narrower and more rigid standards are, the less is learned by those who hold them and those who deviate from them.
>
> *People learn behavior from one another.* What they learn depends on the atmosphere of the group, and the behavior of all other individuals in the group. We cannot achieve adjustment if we expect adjustment only of the individual and not also of the group.

Organizing programs of intergroup education around key concepts or focusing ideas makes possible the development of an orderly, logical sequence in learning that results in changes in behavior, changes that cannot be effected by isolated units of work, short-term projects, and occasional assembly programs. The use of focusing ideas in developing curriculum also provides a way to introduce intergroup education easily and naturally into a variety of subject fields, each supporting and enriching the other's work. In programs so organized, the goal of making intergroup education an integral part of existing school work can be realized without introducing new courses or drastically altering present curricular patterns.

References

(1) Taba, Hilda; Brady, Elizabeth; and Robinson, John T. *Intergroup Education in Public Schools*. Washington, D.C.: American Council on Education, 1952, p. 80.

(2) *Ibid.*, p. 85–86.

(3) *Ibid.*, p. 93–94.

(4) See, for example, Cabot, Hugh, and Kahl, Joseph A. *Human Relations: Concepts and Cases in Concrete Social Science*. Two volumes. Volume 1, *Concepts*, 333 p.; Volume 2, *Cases*, 273 p. Cambridge: Harvard University Press, 1953.

THE SOCIAL SCIENCES IN THE TWENTIETH CENTURY   *Peter Odegard*

Recent emphasis upon the social sciences as the major source of subject matter for use in the social studies has tended to make many of us forget that not all social scientists are in agreement about the major concepts or the methods of inquiry of their disciplines. Odegard identifies this conflict and considers a number of propositions about the roles of value, specialization, and analysis in the social sciences. His words should be borne in mind in considering the often fervent proposals for fuller utilization of the social sciences in the social studies.

THE FACT-VALUE SYNDROME is but one cause of present discontent among scholars and scientists, especially among social scientists. Others arise from increasing specialization that has characterized the so-called Age of Analysis in which we live. The span of attention

Used by permission of Scott, Foresman and Company; from *The Social Studies: Curriculum Proposals for the Future*. Chicago: Scott, Foresman and Company, 1963, pp. 25–40. Peter Odegard is a professor of political science at the University of California, Berkeley.

or at least of sustained interest among scholars and scientists has progressively narrowed. Yet it is only because scientists have been content to learn more and more about less and less that the world in general has learned more and more about everything. Without specialization, it is unlikely that the so-called knowledge explosion of our own generation could have occurred.

THE ROLE OF ANALYSIS

The age of science is not only an age of specialization, but, as Morton White has said, it is an age of analysis (1). Analysis means to "unloose . . . , to dissolve . . . , to separate" anything, whether an object of the senses or of the intellect, into constituent parts or elements. In every branch of science, specialists have succeeded in pulling our world apart. The physical world has been reduced to smaller and smaller particles. So, indeed, has the world of man and society been reduced to an almost infinite number of cultures and subcultures, systems and subsystems, classes, groups, and interests forever clashing in a kind of Hobbesian state of nature. The individual is reduced to an impersonal psychoörganism, pushed this way and that, by forces beyond his ken or control—strictly according to Newton's Second Law—or he disappears altogether in the *role* or *roles* he is compelled to play in the great pageant of human life.

In this process of analysis, social scientists have laid such stress on measurable psychophysical forces at work both in the person and in his environment that the role of reason and of freedom to choose have had short shrift. The 18th-century model of the free, rational citizen has all but disappeared, and human behavior is increasingly conceived as nonrational and determined. When reason is admitted at all, it comes into our calculations only as a special kind of conditioned (i.e., determined) behavior or as an indeterminate variable not yet wholly understood.

Analysis, as I have said, means to dissolve, to disintegrate—not to integrate, and the progressive disintegration of the physical world and of man and society poses some difficult problems. One of these is the gap between appearance and reality. When John Doe is reduced to his basic elements and placed in neatly labeled bottles on a laboratory shelf, one is driven to ask where or what is the real John Doe? When the political community is reduced to a series (whether continuous or discontinuous) of systems and subsystems, each seeking to maintain its own inner equilibrium and to maximize its own interest, what happens to the community? When individual voters, doctors, lawyers, even professors become merely impersonal roles, moving like shadows in a cave or masks in a pageant, with differential arithmetic values, what happens to individual persons with their distinctive names and personalities? Are the rights and privileges, the goals and aspirations referred to in the literature of free societies attributes of real, living, individual men and women or of groups, or systems, or merely *roles* within systems?

SYNTHESIS AND CONCEPTS

Specialization and analysis thus pose still another problem, the establishment or reestablishment of order, unity, and even meaning among otherwise disparate and meaningless particles of information. Otherwise we are left in a kind of nihilistic wilderness in which, as it were, "Ye shall know the facts and the facts shall be sufficient unto themselves." Analysis may clarify but it does not, as such, create knowledge. Knowledge comes not from more and more information about less and less but from the facts of life seen in some meaningful context. To meet this problem, social scientists, as I have said, strive constantly to conceptualize, i.e., to find concepts which will restore some unity and meaning to the fragments of reality their analysis has revealed. The business cycle, imperfect, monopolistic or oligopolistic competition, national income and gross national product in economics; culture, status, stratification, role, social mobility, socialization in sociology; intelligence and aptitude, conditioned response, Gestalt, drive, anomie, id, superego and ego in psychology; bureaucracy, public opinion, decision-making, pressure politics, power elite, geopolitics, left, right, and center in political science are examples. . . .

New and useful concepts, however, are relatively few and far between. Most fruitful social science research has been concerned with the analysis of concepts long established and uncritically accepted. Concepts like capitalism, competition, laissez faire, the laws of supply and demand, value and price in economics; political power and influence, the state, sovereignty, pluralism, oligarchy, democracy, federalism, parliamentarism, balance of power, and national interest in political science are being subjected to more rigorous and systematic empirical study and analysis. In the process, social scientists have borrowed from one another and from the natural sciences such concepts as equilibrium or homeostasis, input, output, feedback, system, subsystem, even nuclear fission which have been put to new uses in the analysis of man and society. . . .

We are, in fact, confronted in all this with a central paradox of modern times. The very specialization and analysis that have been pulling man and his world apart have at the same time made men everywhere more interdependent. That each man is his brother's keeper is no longer a question but a condition. Disintegration through analysis has made integration not only inevitable but urgent if we are not to fly apart. Indeed the rediscovery of a sense of direction and purpose has become a matter of life and death for the human race. Central to this rediscovery is a continuous restudy of those basic concepts that lie at the core of human knowledge.

THE FACT-VALUE PROBLEM

Concepts, like other things, come in many shapes and sizes and with varying degrees of significance. They also play different roles. Some merely seek to describe and define what *is*, some to outline what *ought* to be, and others to *predict* what will be or *could* be under certain circumstances. In general, contemporary hard-nosed social scientists, in their zeal to be value free, eschew the use of concepts of what *ought* to be or even of what *might be*, if people were of a mind to have it so, in favor of concepts of *what is*. What this posture overlooks is that neutralism and indifference toward what *ought* to be not infrequently align the scientist with values and social forces least compatible with the freedom without which science itself cannot survive. Moreover, it tends to reduce the scientist to the role of technician and to sacrifice a philosopher's crown for a servant's cap.

It is obvious, of course, that a value-free science—a science without goal or purpose—becomes merely a form of random behavior which makes a mockery of the term. A scientist without values is like a fanatic who redoubles his effort after he has lost his aim. Nor is it enough to say that his values are merely methodological or procedural, concerned with means and not ends, except only the objective pursuit of truth. For truth wears many faces and, except as it is arbitrarily defined in terms of meter readings, can be as elusive as liberty, equality, and fraternity. Moreover, to discover what is true or false is not unrelated to the discovery of what is good or bad. A scientific concept can be true or false in the degree to which it corresponds to the norms or standards of science itself—i.e., to meter readings. So, too, it may be good or bad in the degree that it contributes to or corresponds with the basic needs and goals of human life. Unless science is merely random behavior or idle curiosity without purpose, it has a responsibility to discover and to serve these basic human needs.

This lays a special obligation on the social sciences because they are by definition concerned with man and society. So-called behavioral science, whether hard-nosed or soft-nosed, has no mandate to be indifferent to human goals or values. One of its major assumptions is that human behavior is goal-directed, and in striving for these goals, men choose among alternative modes of conduct. It assumes also that in choosing, they are conditioned not merely by the physical world and the pressures of appetite and instinct but by formal education in rational modes of thought and behavior. Rationally induced changes in human behavior thus become as reasonable, i.e., as scientific, as rationally induced changes in the physical environment. There is nothing unscientific in social scientists who seek to change those conditions of character and environment that impair man's ability to make rational choices among alternative modes of behavior.

There is nothing sentimental or sloppy in social scientists committed to the rational analysis and eradication of poverty, pestilence, and war, ignorance, fear, and hate. There is nothing unscientific in economists who are as much concerned with the components as with the size of our Gross National Product. Moreover, I suspect that integration of the social sciences and better lines of communication with the natural sciences will come as quickly through cooperation on problems of this kind as in conferences on scope and method.

Not less important is the task of social scientists, by precept and example, to encourage in every way possible and in every one they can reach a conscious and continuous reflection on the human condition and on alternative roads to the basic goals for which all men strive. This continuous and rational reflection on contemporary patterns of thought and behavior is but another definition of social ethics, without which men become but creatures of custom and habit, little better than beasts. Scientists are not immune from the responsibilities of other citizens. They need to be reminded that their attitudes of olympian indifference and skepticism toward moral and ethical problems in a society that has all but canonized the scientist can issue in apathy and cynicism among others; attitudes dangerous alike to science and a good society.

In a daring book called *Daedalus*, published forty years ago, J. B. S. Haldane said:

> I think that the tendency of applied science is to magnify injustices until they become too intolerable to be borne. . . . I think [also] that moral progress is so difficult that any developments are to be welcomed which present it [i.e., moral progress] as the naked alternative to destruction, no matter how horrible may be the stimulus which is necessary before man will take the moral step in question (2).

Have we now reached a point in history where the alternatives to moral and political progress are so horrible that we may at long last be willing to put forth the effort necessary to guide mankind into a more orderly and humane society? Unless we do so, we shall surely die.

References

(1) Morton White, *The Age of Analysis* (Boston: Houghton Mifflin, 1955).

(2) J. B. S. Haldane, *Daedalus* (New York: Dutton, 1924), p. 86.

ᵈ§ PART C §ᵇ

The Social Sciences and
The Social Studies

G. D. LILLIBRIDGE discusses the nature of history and the value of studying it; as an historian, he sets the stage for two articles on the teaching of the subject. In the first of two articles, Vincent R. Rogers looks at the structure of history in the elementary grades; in the second, he deals with the use of source materials with young children.

A British geographer, G. H. Gopsill, describes a number of positions that geographers have taken on the nature and scope of their subject. Henry J. Warman identifies a number of ideas that give structure to geography and to the geographic strand of the social studies. Zoe A. Thralls, both geographer and educator, then takes up the tough question of developing geographic concepts with elementary school children.

Sir Norman Angell stresses the power of ideas in the operation of governments and the necessity of political education in a nationalistic, nuclear age. Franklin Patterson deals with the causes of political alienation; his three suggestions provide sound approaches to creating an awareness of political reality in children. And Gloria Cammarota reports the findings of two political scientists interested in the political attitudes of elementary school pupils.

Social studies programs have long covered content purported to be economic in nature. Two authors—the economist, Lawrence Senesh, and the educator, Harold J. Bienvenu—have raised a number of questions about the fuzzy character of such economic units as those on "community helpers." In their articles, each illustrates what he feels to be sound economic content and teaching for the elementary grades. George D. Spindler, a professor of anthropology and education, points to the role that cultural anthropology can play in the social studies, and suggests some ways that the busy elementary teacher can prepare himself to deal with anthropological content. E. Merle Adams, Jr. explains the meaning of a number of key concepts from sociology and indicates ways that they might be used in teaching the social studies. Wilbur C. Miller and Joel E. Greene concentrate on the idea of interaction among men, and stress this

111

idea as a key concept for use in elementary school social studies programs.

✎ History in the Public Schools
G. D. Lillibridge

What is history? Why is history as a subject so lacking in appeal to so many pupils? What is the value of studying history? Lillibridge examines these questions from the viewpoint of a professional historian. His article sets the stage for Rogers' more specific suggestions for teaching history in the elementary grades.

The study of history, as practiced in the American educational scheme, has long been regarded as one of the most repulsive and fruitless of subjects—a judgment which (who knows?) may well be deserved. We are all familiar with the spectrum of contempt which ranges from bored indifference to wrath and indignation that such torture should be inflicted upon the young in what is supposed to be a humane society.

There are a number of possible explanations for these disagreeable attitudes toward the study of history. For one thing, historians are not generally noted for the liveliness of their writing—a fault observable not only in monographic studies but in textbooks as well. It would not, indeed, be too much to say that the number of historians who write with verve and wit can be counted on the fingers of a one-toed sloth. The profession of historical writing sees all too rarely these days the almost poetic tone which Turner gave to *The Significance of the Frontier in American History* or the fine precision and splendor of language which dominated the Beards' study of *The Rise of American Civilization*.

In part this fault stems from the immense extent of specialization which is naturally to be found in the oldest and broadest of the fields of human knowledge. For it is quite obvious that a detailed analysis of the role of hog production in the fourteenth district elec-

Used by permission of the author and the National Council for the Social Studies; from *Social Education*, 22:110–115, March, 1958. Dr. Lillibridge is an associate professor of American history at Chico State College in Chico, California.

tion of the State Assembly of North Dakota in the year 1903 is not going to be fraught with opportunity for bold and rich writing.

Furthermore, the dullness so traditionally associated with the study of history can be explained in part by the fact that the study of history simply does not easily lend itself to the same kind of exciting experiences for the student that many other studies offer. In the laboratory, for example, when one wishes to become acquainted with some physical material of the world, he can—as often as not—pick it up, handle it, examine it from all angles. Unhappily, one cannot do the same with historical material—say, for instance, with Cleopatra. . . .

Moreover, it is often possible to transmute the knowledge of the laboratory into products whose practical application and worth can be literally seen. An example might be penicillin which has, indeed, the added advantage that it can be felt as well. But one cannot take the Turner thesis of American history and convert it into some physical material which can be mass-produced and its utility statistically measured. This is in one way unfortunate, for the inability literally to see and touch the past oftentimes wipes out the excitement, the practicality, the value in learning which comes, as it were, from the very feel of things. At the same time, we must not forget that the lack of these advantages can be a decided stimulus to learning, for their very absence forces the imagination (one of man's most precious gifts) to go to work.

Nevertheless, it would seem clear that the handicaps under which the study of history operates have created, to use the most charitable word, a remarkable *indifference* to history. Unfortunately, indifference does not lead to knowledge but rather to ignorance. Little wonder, then, that ignorance about the past is as widespread as it is among the American people.

I had this brought home to me (and dropped heavily on the head) several years ago while riding through Illinois with Professor Merle Curti of the University of Wisconsin. To speed the time away, Professor Curti began idly to speculate which of the many small towns through which we were passing might have hosted one of the famous Lincoln-Douglas debates. Finally, about dusk, we pulled into a small town centered around a square distinguished by neatly-clipped grass, inappropriate statues, and numerous indecipherable plaques. We stopped in front of a restaurant, went in, and took a table by the window. At that point, Professor Curti took up again the day-long game, remarking "This must be one of the towns in which Lincoln and Douglas debated. My guess would be that they spoke right out there in the square." Just then the waitress, an attractive young lady, swept up to our table to take our orders. Turning to her for confirmation of his deduction and gesturing casually toward the square, Professor Curti asked, "Was that where the Lincoln-Douglas debate was held?" The girl hesitated momentarily, and then replied, "Well, I—I really wouldn't know, you see I only came on duty at six o'clock."

The study of history—like history itself—would seem to be in a sorry way. Yet I am not altogether sure that uninspired writing, specialization, or the lack of thrilling historical learning experiences can alone account for contempt or indifference to historical study. There are two other major factors of importance.

For one thing, it seems to me that history has been generally so unappealing to students largely because we have failed to suggest some meaning and purpose for the study of history which can make its value and practicality apparent to the student. Now this is no easy task. We all know, as one historian has noted, that history has been used and abused in many ways—that, in the passage of time, there have been a multitude of approaches to history, a multiple of meanings assigned to it.

History has been viewed, for example, as providing lessons of good or evil learned from the past. History has been regarded as ordered by a series of immutable laws governing the behavior of men which, if we can only discover them, will provide us with the blueprints for the future. History has indeed even been ignored completely. Henry Ford is reputed to have said that history began this morning at eight o'clock, and even so sensitive a poet as Carl Sandburg once wrote that "The past is a bucket of ashes."

Even though the study of history has been complicated by these attitudes, and many more, I think we should try to find some broad meaning and purpose to the study of history with which most of us might agree.

We might well begin by asking ourselves to imagine a social problem or situation which could be comprehended or understood at all, much less intelligently approached for solution or resolve, without knowing something of the historical environment in which it rests. Would it be possible, for example, to comprehend, simply to grasp what is meant by the problem of the Cold War unless we have some understanding of the conflicting historical forces, institutions, and ideas involved on both sides? Is it not indeed our historical understanding (whether imperfectly realized or not) of these things which has drawn us in the first place to the conclusion that a conflict in fact exists between these varied forces, institutions, and ideas of the United States and the Soviet Union? But this is only a part of the problem. How, for instance, can we expect to resolve this conflict unless we have some understanding of the forces and ideas at work on both sides? It is inconceivable that we could even begin to think of this problem without the aid of history. And even the most brazenly stupid suggestions for resolving it depend upon knowledge of the past (or what is assumed to be knowledge of the past).

Let us pose this query in still broader terms. If at any one moment we were to destroy all knowledge of the past held by any one group of Americans, we would at the same time be transforming a group of reasonably pert and intelligent human beings (who take for granted the historically-developed science, technology, and social structure with which they live) into a disorganized panic-stricken mass stumbling in terror from surroundings they know not and very probably driven to sudden insanity by the incomprehensible sights of the world about them.

What this suggests, I think, is that knowledge of the past is not only obviously essential to survival (or man would, like the rest of the animal world, have to begin every generation from scratch), but that it is knowledge of the past alone which can provide us with a comprehension, an understanding of the forces, ideas, institutions which shape, condition, and determine our society today. I can think of no idea, no historical force, no societal institution which has ever been created spontaneously—all have their origins in the past and many even stretch back thousands of years.

Now I would say that the reason why it is important for us to understand and know everything we can about the varied forces, ideas, and institutions which make up our world is because these are, as it were, the materials with which we have to work in our efforts to meet the problems and circumstances of life which we continually face in society. The point is that we cannot rise above these materials by ignoring them or assuming that they do not exist just because we don't like them or believe them to be bad or because they appear to be dull and uninteresting. We may believe that excessive nationalism is a menacing force in the world today, but we cannot dissolve the tensions created by nationalism simply by blindly assuming it does not exist. We cannot ignore these materials because we are compelled to work with them, and we cannot work with them— that is, in the sense of facing intelligently up to the problems which confront us—unless we know them. We must understand their nature, the context in which they originated, the circumstances which surrounded their growth, the conditions which play upon and alter them today. . . .

Now, in a general way, it seems to me that we have here a clue to the value and meaning of history. We study the past in order to know, as thoroughly as we can, the social, political, intellectual, economic, cultural materials with which we have to work in our world, and if we know them, then we are better prepared and equipped to handle them and live with them. If we do not know them, then in trying to meet our problems we must depend not upon knowledge and understanding, but solely upon emotion, instinct, intuition. Unhappily, to achieve success by such methods alone means to depend entirely upon luck which is too rare a gift in itself on which to rest the fate of mankind.

I am not saying that knowledge and understanding of the social materials of our world can guarantee us success in meeting our problems, because they cannot—history offers no guarantees, no certainties in this respect. But knowledge and understanding do offer us the best hope of success, and perhaps just as importantly, of dignity in the attempt to achieve it. For we are presented here with the opportunity to use the processes of thought and perception which, after all, distinguish man and his purpose in this world. A great American historian called this "the noble object" of man's efforts and proclaimed that "even though every door be slammed in our faces, still we must knock."

Given this broad and flexible framework of purpose in the study of the past, we are able not only to appreciate the essential richness of knowledge which the study of the past can provide us about the nature of the world in which we live, but also to draw from that knowledge varied and thoughtful generalizations about man which can be equally useful in giving order to our understanding of our world and in determining how best to meet its problems. From time to time, many such generalizations are suggested to us by our continually expanding knowledge of the past, and I would not presume to catalogue them all or to assess their worth. But I would by way of illustration like to indicate three which have generally seemed significant to many historians.

To begin with, even though it is clear that man is a product of the past and hence limited by it, nevertheless it would also seem to be clear that it is possible for man to defy the past—a defiance which may express itself suddenly and violently upon the barricades, or it may take place slowly within the minds of men. History would seem to indicate, in other words, that man possesses an area of originality and freedom of choice which keeps him from being simply the victim of predetermined forces—whether they be supernatural or environmental—and allows him to work within the framework of a destiny which, in its hope of change and betterment, is the one thing which gives the future advantage over the past and the present.

Next, I would say that history suggests that there is a genuine commonality of man. As Boyd Shafer has remarked in a notable address, "Men Are More Alike." All men fall within the same general range of height and weight. All require the same amount of calories and vitamins. All have a facility for conceptual thought and speech as no other animals do. Men everywhere, and in all times, have shared the same basic problems of acquiring food and shelter, establishing social relationships, seeking creativity in the arts, and trying to develop some sort of understanding of the universe and the purpose of life. Of course, there are differences, but too often, for example, we forget that the compelling impulse which prompted that unknown artist of long ago to try his hand on the walls of the caves at Altamira was the same impulse which put the brush in the hand of Picasso.

Finally, I think it would be a safe assumption to draw from history that there is truth in the ancient injunction that man cannot live by bread alone, but that he has deep need of idealism. As Herbert Muller has said so well, men of good will in all ages have valued the human spirit that seeks truth, goodness, and beauty, and every age has made, and must make, its own contributions in this regard. Thus it is not really true to say that the great civilizations of the past have died. Their peoples have died, as all men must, but before doing so they have enriched the great tradition of human values and human dignity—a tradition which must be *known* to be appreciated, protected, and expanded.

These are but a few of the things which a knowledge of the past can give us, and without which we would, indeed, approach the problems, the follies, the pressures of life, with sightless hands and barren minds.

History for the Elementary School Child
Vincent R. Rogers

Seven-, eight-, nine-, and ten-year-old pupils can work with historical source material! Rogers describes three sample experiences, and asks some questions about Jerome Bruner's concept of the structure of a discipline. These questions lead to his outline of major ideas about history. The author does not claim that these ideas express perfectly the structure of history, but he certainly provides the reader with a springboard for formulating his own ideas.

From the *Phi Delta Kappan*, 64:132–135, December, 1962. Used by permission of Phi Delta Kappa, Inc. Dr. Rogers is a professor of education at the University of Minnesota.

DURING THIS YEAR'S summer and fall quarters at the University of Minnesota's demonstration centers one might have observed the following "lessons" being carried out with various groups of elementary school children:

A group of seven-year-olds has just heard Virginia Lee Burton's engaging story, *The Little House,* as a part of their study of the community. The story has to do with a house in the country that is eventually engulfed by the growing city. Roads are built, trains roar by, and skyscrapers appear. Eventually the little house is moved back to the country again, and so ends the story. Following the reading of the story the children list all of the changes they can think of that have happened to them during the last year. They follow this by listing changes on their streets, in their houses, and "down town." When the list is completed the teacher suddenly erases it and asks this question: "Suppose none of these changes had ever taken place— would you like it or not? Would things be better or worse?" There is considerable disagreement, since some of the items on the list are (in the children's eyes) "good," some "bad." This discussion of change continues off and on during the next week, resulting in a collection of pictures on a bulletin board illustrating "good" and "bad" changes in the community, such as the construction of a new theater, the opening of a new busline, and the burning of a nearby school (this last was classified as "bad," incidentally).

A group of eight-year-olds is studying the First Thanksgiving and the coming of the Pilgrims and others to America. The hardships of the first winter here are discussed briefly. The children are then asked to imagine that they are going to make a similar voyage today to an unknown, unsettled wilderness. They would not get any help from anyone "back home" for a year. "What food and clothing would we need in order to live through a year? What should we take along?" A long list is made on the board, including many items that only one living in the 20th century might consider essential. The children are then shown a list of essentials that were actually taken by a group of settlers. The lists are compared and the teacher draws a line through the items on the children's list that do *not* appear on the settlers' list. A number of the children express the view that it would have been very hard to go with just those things; many say they wouldn't have gone had it been up to them. The teacher then suggests that they imagine for a moment that they are living in London at the time the Pilgrims came to America. However, in this case they have no intention of moving—they like things in London. The children are asked to look again at *their* list. What items would not be available in London? They find that most of the items that had been crossed off their lists originally would have to be crossed off again. Life was hard (by 20th century standards), they conclude, both for those who went *and* for those who stayed. It is hard to tell what you would or wouldn't do unless you lived as the people did then.

During a study of the westward movement, a group of ten-year-olds is told to imagine that they are living on a rocky, rather unproductive New England farm during the year 1867. One evening an older brother bursts into the kitchen with a poster clutched in his hand. It says, in effect, that the Union Pacific railroad is offering new lands for sale in Kansas. The land is said to be cheap, abundant, and fertile. Schools and churches have been built and there will be no taxes for six years! The family is gathered around the fire. The poster is read.

Now the class is asked, "What do you suppose the family will do?" The quick and almost universal reaction is, "They'd move west to Kansas!" The teacher then suggests they try acting out the story, with different people in the class playing the roles of various members of the family. Each volunteer is given a 3 × 5 card telling something about his "character." For example, father knew the farm was failing and felt he had little choice. Grandfather had brought his family here from Scotland fifty years ago. His wife was buried here. He had had enough of travel; this was home to him. The oldest son loved adventure and wanted desperately to go, while the sixteen-year-old daughter was in love with the boy on the next farm. When the play is finally dramatized, the decision turns out to be far more difficult than the children had first imagined. In the final analysis the class is evenly divided on the issue of whether the family should go or stay.

Each of the experiences described above is designed to help children understand some element or strand in the "structure" of history. While the descriptions are brief and (of necessity) incomplete, they represent halting first steps in a long overdue attempt to strengthen and improve, to both "beef up" and yet make more meaningful, children's early encounters with history.

Those of us who read the journals of our profession regularly know that we have more than our share of educational diagnosticians, but that we seem to suffer from a serious shortage of therapists. Criticism voiced during the last decade alone would (and does) fill volumes, and programs in elementary school social studies have gotten their share and more. A good deal of this criticism has to do with an almost universally misunderstood and often mishandled area: the teaching of history to elementary school children. Critics have complained that history is generally approached at this level as a precise body of knowledge, proven beyond doubt and ready to be "mastered" by students; the textbook is still the basic teaching tool, and particularly at this level they (the texts) tend to be exceedingly unrealistic, overly idealistic, and often lack the stimulating detail so necessary to give meaning to the broad generalizations they so freely employ. One might add that children in current programs are seldom asked to use thinking processes characterized by Torrance and others as "divergent" (i.e., independent or original work that gives students an opportunity to discover ideas for themselves), or "evaluative" (i.e., work involving critical thinking, judging, selecting and organizing). Unquestionably, the reader may wish to add or perhaps subtract from this list. We are attempting, however, to proceed beyond diagnosis and enter the realm of therapy. . . .

STRUCTURE AND HISTORY

If one accepts Bruner's assumptions that an understanding of the structure of history is of vital importance *and* that structure can be taught to young children, where, then, do we go from here? The first step, of course, is to decide what basic principles comprise history's structure. Apparently the physicists, the biologists, the chemists, and the mathematicians have been able to do this promptly and rather effectively in their areas. We are still waiting, however, for a similar treatment of history. This is, of course, understandable. Man's behavior is a complex thing and exceedingly difficult to classify. Nevertheless, the first steps must be taken, and I offer the following analysis as a possible beginning.

As I read the literature dealing with the nature of history, I find considerable agreement on at least one aspect of its structure. The methodology of history—how the historian works—is generally agreed to be an essential element of the discipline. Some would go so far as to say that the historian's method *is* the structure of his discipline, that once one has mastered the methodology of history one has gained an understanding of history's underlying principles. It seems to me, however, that ideas related to the structure of history tend to cluster around *three* major hubs: first, ideas related to the methodology of history; second, ideas related to the nature and goals of history; and third, ideas related to the content, the people, and events themselves that comprise history. The "sample" ideas stated under each heading below seem to me to represent important principles that form the foundation for a mature understanding of history. I am suggesting that much of this can be taught to and understood by young children. I suggest further that the content chosen to aid in the development of these ideas (a unit on the community, the westward movement, or colonial life, for example) is of secondary importance to the principles themselves.

Ideas Related to Nature, Goals of History

History attempts to delineate, assess, interpret, and give a relative place to the efforts of people, important ideas, and great national achievements.

History is *not* a body of precise, memorizable facts; history is, in a sense, constant controversy. Historians do not always agree.

Historical interpretations change as man examines events at different times and in different places.

History provides us with a series of case histories that may help us deal with contemporary affairs; history does not, however, offer us revealed unchanging laws or patterns of events.

All historical events were, at one time, "open questions," just as today's decisions (which will become tomorrow's history) are similarly open. We may only evaluate the choices made in the past and attempt to find meaningful alternatives or possibilities for today's decisions.

Ideas Related to Content of History (1)

Change has been a universal condition of human society. Change and progress, however, are not necessarily synonymous.

Races, cultures, and civilizations in various historical periods have made contributions to the growth of our present civilizations.

Mankind has been motivated by morals and ideals *and* by material wants and needs.

While physical environments in many places and regions have been altered, human motives or drives have remained nearly the same.

Peaceful cooperation is one of man's worthiest, earliest, and most persistent historical experiences. Conflict and hostility, however, are also within man's experience.

In the contemporary world, historical events affect people and places far beyond the limits of the place of their origin.

Men in every age and place have made use of basic social functions such as educating, transporting, communicating, etc., in adjusting themselves to their world.

Ideas Related to Method of History

The historian works basically with primary sources such as letters, diaries, traveler's logs, newspapers, and magazines. These are the "stuff" of history.

The historian draws conclusions, formulates principles, and makes generalizations on the basis of his study and interpretation of primary sources.

In evaluating sources, the historian is concerned with the authenticity of his material; he recognizes, for example, that the time that elapses between the occurrence of an event and the reporting of an event often affects the accuracy with which the event is reported; he is concerned with the author of the report, his interests, and qualifications, and biases.

The historian recognizes that one's feelings and emotions, his drives and motives, may often affect how one interprets a given event.

The historian looks at historical events with an appropriate perspective. For example, one must gauge the real heartbreak and suffering involved in the Pilgrims' coming to America or the pioneers' moving west in relation to the hardships of life in general at this time.

The historian is aware that advances in historical scholarship, discoveries of new sources of information, may necessitate a re-evaluation of his conclusions and generalizations.

The ideas presented above are undoubtedly incomplete; statements of considerable importance may have been left out while minor points were included. This is, however, a beginning statement or working paper that has proven most useful to us in the development of new materials and techniques in the teaching of history to elementary school children. Each of the experiences described at the beginning of this paper is directly related to one or more of the basic historical principles described above. As new materials and techniques are experimented with, we are of course trying to discover whether children do begin to understand the method of history; whether they are able to apply generalizations to other problems and other content. We are analyzing children's written materials and their discussions, looking for evidence of deductive and evaluative thinking. We are also curious about the types of children who are able to work successfully with these materials. How important is IQ, for example? We wonder, too, whether so-called "average" teachers (with appropriate manuals and guides) will be able to work effectively with these materials. At the moment, precise answers to these questions are not yet available. We are, however, both encouraged with and enthusiastic about current progress and future possibilities.

References

(1) The statements in this section were largely adapted from the *Report of the State Central Committee on the Social Studies* published by the California State Department of Education, Sacramento 14, California.

ᴇ§ Using Source Material With Children
Vincent R. Rogers

A good deal of time, effort, and money has recently gone into projects aimed at developing source materials for use by high school students. Less time, less effort, and less money have been allotted the production of similar material for use in the elementary grades. Rogers' article considers the purposes of using source materials, gives several examples of such materials, and lists a number of books in which the reader can find a wide range of materials.

THE USE OF original sources in the teaching of American history has had, to say the least, a rather stormy past. Some have seen it as a veritable panacea—a cure-all for all of the educational ills of the times. Others have roundly condemned the technique as narrow, arid, and vague (1).

In any event, the use of sources with children *below* the senior high school level seems to have been at best neglected, and at worst, totally ignored even by those who favor the technique. Before we wonder why, it might be wise to think a little about the possible uses of original source material at any age level. Keohane pulls them together for us very effectively, I think (2). Check this list for any additions or deletions you might want to make.

1. Inspirational
2. "Making history live"—giving it warmth, color, and the flavor of the times
3. Reinforcing knowledge about important persons, events, laws, institutions, and problems
4. Gaining firsthand knowledge of significant documents
5. Developing habits of critical reading and thinking
6. Gaining familiarity with some creative ideas in U.S. history through analysis of some classic statements of American social thought.

As one who has taught in the intermediate elementary grades, junior high school *and* senior high school, it seems to me that these "objectives" are both valid and, at least to some degree, achievable at each of these levels. If so, *can* relatively young children use original

Used by permission of the author and the National Council for the Social Studies; from *Social Education*, 24:307–309, November, 1960.

source material to aid in the achievement of these objectives? If you've given a positive answer to this question (as, of course, I have) you'll have to face up immediately to certain harsh realities:

1. Usable sources *are* hard to find—and it takes time to locate, browse and extract.
2. If poorly chosen, original sources can be deader than the deadest text.
3. Sources do not always fit the vocabulary level deemed appropriate for grade by the writers of the basal readers.

The first objection can be overcome by diligence, persistence, and perhaps to some extent, by the brief bibliography which follows this article. Dealing with the second is somewhat more difficult. Overcoming it depends largely upon each teacher's understanding of both his students *and* his subject. The third can be, at least partially, ignored.

Perhaps, then, this is the time to examine some sources which I have used effectively with sixth-, seventh-, and eighth-grade children.

These are excerpts from a letter written by Lewis B. Williams of Orange, Virginia, to his sister, Miss Lucy P. Williams of Richmond, on July 12, 1836. It concerns an unusual slave called Polly.

> . . . On last Monday week, I had to whip Polly for her impudence to me, since which she has continued in a pet, not treating myself or any of the family with the slightest respect, and continually telling me that she did not wish to stay with me as she could not please me and alleging that she was willing to be sold, in fact anxious even to the Southern traders. . . .
>
> . . . She has been now for eight days in a continual ill humor, speaking roughly and rudely to every member of the family and continually throwing it in my teeth, that she could not please me, ever since and altho' I told her that she should never be sold, as long as I was able to keep her, provided she would behave herself and that I would sell her, if she did not, she still tells me that she is perfectly willing to go and that she cares not about staying with me. Upon this I have informed her that she must make up her mind, take her choice to be in a good humor and behave herself or be sold and I am resolved that one or the other must be done. I regret it very much, but there must be one master in a family or there can be no peace. I told her that I did not wish to sell her, and particularly to separate her from her husband, father, mother, and brother, that I was opposed to it except in case of necessity and that she could take her choice. She still persists in saying that she is willing to be sold and that she cannot please me and that she had as soon be sold to the negro traders as to anyone else, and I am satisfied that I will have to sell her in the course of the week. . . .

This seems to me to be a most devastating challenge to a stereotyped concept of the master-to-slave relationship. Here is an impudent Polly, literally sassing her master and the rest of the family, and, what's more (temporarily, at least), getting away with it. Students might be asked to dwell a little on the lines, "I regret it very much, but there must be *one* master in a family or there can be no peace." Children can be asked such questions as: What kind of a person *was* Polly? Why didn't Lewis Williams simply sell her immediately? Why was he so concerned? What was Polly's "status" or "position" in the Williams family? Do you suppose all slaves owned by the Williams were thought of in the same way? Who were the "Negro traders"? Was Polly treated differently from other slaves?

Obviously, this material cannot be used in isolation. Its value depends entirely on what preceded its use and what will follow it. This source can be used most effectively to challenge, to raise questions, and to encourage further study.

Prospective settlers in Jamestown were given advice concerning what equipment was necessary for survival in the New World. Excerpts from a document published in 1622 appear below.

	HOUSEHOLD IMPLEMENTS		TOOLES
For a family of 6 persons	One Iron Pot	*For a family of 6 persons*	Five broad howes
	One kettle		Five narrow howes
	One large frying pan		Two broad Axes
	One gridiron		Five felling Axes
	Two skillets		Two steele hand sawes
	One spit		Two two-hand sawes
	Platters, dishes, spoones of wood		One whip-saw
			Two hammers
	VICTUALL		Three shovels
	Eight bushels of Meale		Two spades
For a whole yeare for one man	Two bushels of pease		Two augers
	Two bushels of Oate-meale		Sixe chissels
	One gallon of Aqua-vite		Two percers stocked
	One gallon of Oyle		Three gimlets
	Two gallons of Vine-gar		Two hatchets
			Two hand bills
			One grindstone
			Nailes of all sorts
			Two pickaxes

Most of us who teach American history are concerned with helping children develop an understanding of the bitter realities of life in the colonies during these trying times. Intelligent use of this document, it seems to me, can contribute a great deal towards developing that understanding. A comparison, for example, of the household implements brought here "for a family of six" with the implements found in the children's own kitchens would certainly be revealing. A comparison of the diets of these early settlers with the diets of contemporary Americans would be equally revealing. Teachers might, before using the document, ask children to make a list of things they thought would be absolutely essential for survival if they were to make a similar voyage. These lists could then be compared with the document.

The settlement of the West was often encouraged by posters like this one, distributed in 1867.

Farms and Homes in Kansas

EMIGRANTS
Look to Your
I N T E R E S T

Farms at $3. Per Acre!
And Not a Foot of Waste Land.
And on Purchase No Portion of the Principal Required!!

LANDS NOT TAXABLE FOR SIX YEARS!
FARMING LANDS IN
EASTERN KANSAS
The Central Branch

UNION PACIFIC RAILROAD CO.,
Offer For Sale Their Lands in the Celebrated

KICKAPOO INDIAN RESERVATION
152,417 acres
Schools and Churches

This was certainly a vivid, dramatic chapter in our history. Intelligent use of this poster may raise such questions as these: "Why did so many people move west?" "Was it mostly a matter of adventure (as many of our TV oriented children must believe) or were there other motivating factors?" "Why did this poster attract settlers?" "How could the Union Pacific Railroad sell lands in the Kickapoo Indian reservation?"

The sinking of the Titanic was, of course, widely reported in the newspapers of that period. This was a portion of the front page of the *New York Evening Sun* for Monday, April 15, 1912.

THE EVENING SUN

New York, Monday, April 15, 1912

ALL SAVED FROM TITANIC AFTER COLLISION

Rescue by Carpathia and Parisian:
Liner is Being Towed to Halifax
After Smashing Into An Iceberg

On Tuesday, April 16, this headline appeared in *The New York Times*:

TITANIC SINKS FOUR HOURS AFTER HITTING ICEBERG,
866 RESCUED BY CARPATHIA, PROBABLY
1250 PERISH
ISMAY SAFE, MRS. ASTOR MAYBE,
NOTED NAMES MISSING

These contrasting headlines can serve as a dramatic introduction to a study of the responsibility of the newspaper as an organ of communication. They may lead children into a discussion of such questions as: Why did the *Times* wait until Tuesday before it published its account of the sinking? What is the responsibility of a newspaper? How can we judge the accuracy and reliability of newspapers?

The sources used in this article were chosen because of their unusually challenging, thought provoking, and dramatic nature. There are, of course, many similar items tucked away in seldom used corners of most libraries. Perhaps the following bibliography will give the reader a start toward beginning his own collection of original source material.

Bibliography

P. ANGLE. *The American Reader*. New York: Rand McNally, 1958.

B. H. BOTKIN, editor. *Lay My Burden Down, A Folk History of Slavery*. Chicago: University of Chicago Press, 1945.

B. CATTON, editor. *American Heritage, The Magazine of History*. New York: American Heritage, Bimonthly.

H. S. COMMAGER. *Blue and Gray: The Story of the Civil Was as Told By Participants*. Indianapolis: Bobbs, 1954.

H. S. COMMAGER. *Documents of American History*. New York: Appleton-Century-Crofts, 1949.

H. S. COMMAGER and A. NEVINS. *The Heritage of America*. Boston, Mass.: Little, Brown, 1947.

M. B. DAVIDSON. *Life in America*. Volumes I, II. Boston, Mass.: Houghton Mifflin, 1951.

H. R. DRIGGS. *The Pony Express Goes Through: An American Saga Told By Its Heroes*. New York: Stokes, 1935.

O. EISENSCHIML and R. NEWMAN. *The American Iliad*. Indianapolis: Bobbs, 1947.

A. B. HART. *American History Told by Contemporaries*. Volumes I–V. New York: Macmillan, 1924.

Log of Christopher Columbus' First Voyage to America in the Year 1492. New York: Scott, 1938.

P. A. ROLLINS. *The Discovery of the Oregon Trail: Robert Stuart's Narratives of His Overland Trip Eastward from Astoria in 1812–1813*. New York: Scribner, 1935.

V. STEFANSSON. *Great Adventures and Explorations*. New York: Dial, 1947.

The reader may also wish to investigate the following:

(a) *The Century Gazette*. This is a new monthly publication which will feature reprints from newspapers of a century ago. Available at Department S, Old Mill, Morrison, Illinois.
(b) The various publications of *The New York Times* Schools Service. Write School Service, *The New York Times*, New York 36, New York, for further information.

References

(1) Robert E. Keohane. "Historical Method and Primary Sources." Chapter 25 in Richard E. Thursfield, editor. *The Study and Teaching of American History*. Seventeenth Yearbook of the National Council for the Social Studies. Washington, D.C.: The Council, 1946.

(2) Robert E. Keohane. "Use of Primary Sources in United States History for High School Pupils." *School Review*. December 1945, p. 580.

◄§ THE NATURE OF GEOGRAPHICAL STUDIES

G. H. Gopsill

Has geography, as a discipline, always contributed to the social studies? Have geographers been able to agree on the nature and scope of their subject? In this selection, Gopsill traces the positions that English geographers have taken on their discipline. The role of Sir Halford Mackinder in stressing the importance of tracing the interaction of man and his environment is noted. His basic definition of geography is then expanded and defended. Gopsill's article provides a general framework within which the subsequent articles on geography can be viewed.

AN AGE IN WHICH the scholars could describe the study of Geography as "merely the study of shapes" or "a compendious description," could hardly be expected to make very much contribution to geographical education. Yet these and other even less flattering descriptions probably represented a perfectly true picture of the nature of geographical studies at that time. In the middle of the nineteenth century geography, if it had any place at all, was regarded as an offshoot from, and entirely at the service of, the study of geology. . . . The natural result of this origin was an altogether undue emphasis on the physical side of geography, and a denial that any other sort of geography was at all possible. This emphasis persisted even when a more liberal interpretation of geographical studies admitted the possibility of a more human approach; the tendency to cling to the original conception of physical geography as a separate study gave rise to a most unfortunate dichotomy—"physical geography" which was regarded as the "real" geography, and "geography" which concerned itself with a rather cursory description of foreign countries, the two subjects being taught separately and having very little in common.

In this, as in all other aspects of human endeavour, we find some few thinkers in advance of their time, and it is from them that a more generous view of the nature of geography originally came. Mary Somerville's *Physical Geography* first appeared in 1848, written in a style rather more readable than is usual in such works, stressing for the first time that physical and human facts are very closely interrelated. "The influence of external circumstances on man," she wrote, "is not greater than his influence on the material world. It is true that he cannot create power . . . but he dexterously avails himself of the powers of nature to subdue nature." (1)

A little while later in 1872 Francis Galton as the president of

Used by permission of Macmillan and Company Ltd.; from "Observing Geography in the Local Environment" by G. H. Gopsill, in *The Teaching of Geography*, London: Macmillan and Co., 1956. (New York: St. Martin's Press) pp. 5–9, 12–15, 24–27. G. H. Gopsill is a lecturer in education at the University of Nottingham.

section E of the British Association announced that "the configuration of every land, its soil, its vegetable covering, its rivers, its climate, its animal and human inhabitants, react upon one another. It is the highest problem of geography to analyse their correlation and to sift the casual from the essential," (2) thus expressing his conviction of the interdependence of the various branches of geographical study, a view which was far from widely held at that time.

Among these prophets before their time there eventually emerged the dominant figure of Sir Halford Mackinder. With lucid expression he soon formulated the ideals of the subject and forecast its pattern. Around these ideals geographical thought really began to crystallise into anything like modern form. Mackinder was still a young man when the vitality of his teaching and the enterprise of his views were first noticed.

When quite by chance in the Christmas vacation of 1885 he happened to pass a wet afternoon visiting an exhibition of "geographical appliances" he there met Scott-Keltie, who in the previous May had submitted his report on the Teaching of Geography to the Royal Geographical Society (3). This chance meeting had far-reaching consequences, for after some discussion with Francis Galton and H. W. Bates, then Secretary of the Royal Geographical Society, Mackinder was invited to address the society. This was arranged, and in 1887 he presented his famous paper on the "Scope and Methods of Geography," (4) in which his liberal views were forcibly expressed. It cannot have been easy for a young man of 25 years to expound an interpretation of geography which he knew to be contrary to that which was commonly accepted, but in spite of the august company, his tone was forthright and the argument sound. The paper and the discussion which followed still make instructive and inspiring reading.

Mackinder here defines geography as the subject whose main function is to trace the interaction of man and his environment. "Environments" can be regarded as regions when they exhibit roughly homogenous characteristics, and on the whole the smaller the region, the greater the number of conditions which are uniform within it. "Communities" of persons inhabit these regions—a community being a group of persons having certain characteristics in common, and again, the smaller the community, the greater tends to be the number of common characteristics. It is in the recognition of such geographical entities, and in the interpretation of the relationships between the physical features of a region on the one hand and the social, historical and cultural features of the community which inhabits it, on the other hand, that we find the proper scope for the geographer's activities. Although we may still argue as to what precisely constitutes a "region" or how we may define it, the basic conception of the regional idea, and the recognition of the fact that regional problems take their shape from the subtle relationship between natural and human forces, originates in the first instance from Mackinder's statement, and has been consolidated by a round half-century of his teaching.

Recent views on the nature of geographical studies have expressed very much the same idea, in various terms.

The *Norwood Report* (5) announces in chapter 6 that geography implies the study of man and his environment, which really does not add very much to what Mackinder told us 57 years before. The late Mr. J. Fairgrieve provides a rather more imaginative definition:

> The function of geography is to train future citizens to imagine accurately the conditions of the great world stage, and so to help them to think sanely about political and social problems in the world around (6).

This is a neat metaphor, of a stage on which the human drama is enacted day by day. And, Mr. Fairgrieve tells us it is our function to give an account of the *conditions* which are to be found upon this stage—presumably the more or less permanent geographical factors of physical structure, composition, distribution, climate and so forth —the many and various factors which go to make up the geographical setting. These are the conditions on the stage, but they are not enough, for there is no specific mention of the actors who play upon it, and it is most important to remember that men are very powerful agents in geographical change; they can both alter the conditions and are themselves in their turn profoundly influenced by them.

Any satisfactory definition of the nature of geography must take full account of this fact. There are many other definitions, as many as there are thinkers who express themselves silently in their books or vocally at their conferences. As an example we may consider one of them.

Professor Frank Debenham has recently marked the close of a long and distinguished career as a geographer by setting down in homely terms his views on the teaching of the subject. He notices that men have been learning at an alarming rate from the vast increase in knowledge of the nineteenth and twentieth centuries. But so far, what has been lacking is a unifying science which could satisfactorily interpret the findings of other sciences in so far as they apply to the surface of the globe on which we live. That, and nothing less, is the full task which Professor Debenham gives to the geographer:

(i)   To interpret the facts of distribution
(ii) To correlate the life of man with his physical environment
(iii) To explain the interaction of human and natural agencies (7).

There seem to me three reasons why this statement is so wholly satisfactory. In the first place, it preserves such a nice balance between the physical and the human aspects of geographical study. There is no emphasis on either of them but there is a simple recognition of the fact that in the synthesis which is geography, each has its appointed place.

Secondly, and arising out of the first point, there is an implied but discreet warning to the specialists to curb the exuberance of their personal enthusiasms, and if they are to remain geographers, not to trespass too far into alien, but allied, fields. It is perhaps pleasant to pursue a topic into geology, into meteorology, or into economics, but an excessive preoccupation with any one science and the department of geography which is closely associated with it, is to lose sight of the unifying purpose which is the principal characteristic of geography itself. Each one of these sciences, and many others, may provide the geographer with information which will help him to "interpret the facts of distribution," or possibly to illuminate some other aspect of geographical knowledge, but there his interest in them should end.

Thirdly, this statement contains a timely and appropriate reminder that the most important duty of the geographer is to *interpret* what he sees. So long as geography consisted of a catalogue of factual knowledge to be memorised, or at the best a mere description of events, then it is not difficult to understand that the scholars at the turn of the century could see very little future for it as an intellectual study. And wherever the teaching of it remains in this form to this day, then it deserves no better treatment than it often receives at the hands of those who are concerned with education. If geography makes any claim at all to the dignity of an intellectual exercise, it is only in so far as it provides its students with opportunity for an intelligent appraisal of its content.

The scope of the subject then concerns the study of the surface of the earth and of the natural and physical forces which take place in it, on it, or around it, and the relationship between these forces and the lives of the men who inhabit it. In dealing with this material, one should be careful to avoid giving disproportionate prominence to any one aspect of it, either physical or human, and to recognise the fact that it is the *relationship* between the facts, rather than the facts themselves, which is the essential part of the study.

References

(1) Mary Somerville, *Physical Geography*, 1848.

(2) Francis Galton, President, *Report of the British Association*, Section E, 1872.

(3) J. Scott-Keltie, "Report on Geographical Education," *Royal Geographical Society Supplementary Papers I*, 1885.

(4) Published in the *Proceedings of the Royal Geographical Society*, Vol. 9, 1887.

(5) "Curriculum and Examinations in Secondary Schools," *The Norwood Report*, 1943.

(6) J. Fairgrieve, *Geography in School*.

(7) Professor Frank Debenham, *The Use of Geography*.

❦ Major Concepts in Geography

Henry J. Warman

Ever since Bruner put his finger on the term structure and pointed out one road to curriculum revision, subject matter specialists have intensified their attempts to settle on the structure of their disciplines. Among those most willing to identify concepts that give structure to geography is Warman. His article specifies nine major concepts of geography. Some are famiilar, some are newer acquaintances—but all nine are exciting concepts that will be increasingly before us as new texts are written and new courses of study are planned.

THE LITERAL MEANINGS of the term "Geo"—earth, and "graph(y)" —writing, were used by Edith Putnam Parker when she stated that, "Man continually writes into the earth." We may go one step beyond and add that "Nature, too, writes into the Earth." It is the geographer's task to read and interpret these earth surface writings. Geography then is born and reborn when one looks and looks again at places, (regions, if you will) and, with techniques to do it, strives to see how mankind has nestled down into the earth. Understandings and concepts are needed to assist and guide him in the doing if he is to read correctly the "earth writings" of both the past and present,

Used by permission of the National Council for Geographic Education; from its *Curriculum Guide to Geographic Education*, 1964, pp. 9–27. Henry J. Warman is a professor of geography at Clark University.

and then make and execute plans for writing new chapters into the earth for posterity to read.

It should be clearly understood at the outset that the concepts which now follow are for administrators, supervisors, teachers,—all those concerned with the dissemination of geography. Only in rare cases and then most probably at the secondary school level should the concept be taught, if a concept is teachable. The preceding sentence was written because the writer believes that a concept is something conceived, born, in the mind. It may, like an organism, grow, multiply, be split up; it may assume a comprehensive quality of idea-gatherings or of intuitive mental collectives. Such idea collections—concepts—naturally are fraught with information content. . . .

The lasting quality of teaching facts and formulating understandings within a conceptual frame has been put into precise sentences by Jerome S. Bruner in his book, *The Process of Education* (1). He states ". . . the curriculum of a subject should be determined by the most fundamental understanding that can be achieved of the underlying principles that give structure to that subject.—The best way to create interest in a subject is to render it worth knowing, which means to make the knowledge gained usable in one's thinking beyond the situation in which the learning has occurred.—Organizing facts in terms of principles and ideas from which they may be inferred is the only known way of reducing the quick rate of loss of human memory."

In the paragraphs that follow, first a concept will be given. In most cases just a word or phrase will be supplied. Then understandings will be suggested that can make great contributions to the concept. No attempt will be made to supply a complete set of understandings; indeed, to do so would defeat the very purpose of presenting the concepts. Suggestions will be made, however, of ways in which the teacher can "let the mind go." . . .

CONCEPT ONE—GLOBALISM

The sphericity of our earthly dwelling place provides geographers with a multitude of facts from which many understandings about location may be drawn. The knowledge, however, of the earth's grid system—a series of circles (parallels of latitude and the intersecting half circles, meridians), is but an introduction to this concept. The "splittings-off" from the Globalism concept take many forms. Distance is one ramification, but this term, too, divides into expressions of measurement of not just how far in degrees, in linear and areal units, but also in how fast. When units of time as a teachable measure of distance enters the conceptual framework of Globalism the spinning of our globe on its axis needs to be understood. The resultant periods of daylight and darkness, hours, minutes, and seconds are perceived in the concept of Globalism.

The development of an understanding of daylight and darkness necessitates the introduction into the discussion of yet another globe —the sun. Thus from the fact of rotation of the earth one moves to the revolution of that spinning earth around the sun. A mental step from this fact reveals that the whirling earth has parts quite exactly located within the latitudinal lines designated above. These parts or latitudinal bands receive varying amounts of sunlight through the orbiting time (365¼ days for one revolution). The inclination of the globe's axis and the parallelism of the axis' positions at all times are additional facts necessary for understanding the seasonal distribution of heat on the earth. These understandings, growing out of the fact of the global shape of our dwelling place, enable one to picture where maximum heat from the sun may be received. Learning about the input of the sun's energy, the outgo of it, the distribution of it through the year over the curved surface of the earth provides fundamental bases for building patterns of climate, zones of vegetation, seasonal activities of groups of people, and to a large degree the broad limits of animals' and mankind's distribution.

The spinning of the globe also gives direction to air and water movements which, when coupled with the location and size of the land and water components of the earth, enable one to plot on the earth grid the flow and hence directional patterns of both wind and water currents. . . .

CONCEPT TWO—THE ROUND EARTH ON FLAT PAPER (2)

This expression is teeming with ideas and problems not the least of which are those encountered when one attempts to develop the curved surface of our globe, in toto or in part, on a plane. Mathematics is required, and if the concept is to emerge fully then plane and solid geometry—perhaps trigonometry are needed. Projections which show, or afford grids for showing, the earth's surface are increasing in number and in fascination. One finds that horizontal and vertical distances—using directions of north, south, east, west, up, and down are essential understandings. Lands "down under" may be shown as lands "on top." Simulated relief maps, really excellent models, introduce the up and down dimensions.

The major phases of cartography are related to the uses to which the maps are to be put. Is one creating a map which shows true shape (a conformal map), or is there major concern for a map which possesses "equal-area" qualities? What compromises are significant?

In reaching these decisions regarding the routes to the finished map product, facts, understandings, and perception all enter. The symbolization must be adjusted and adapted to the projection and scale —and vice versa. The symbols may be of physical or cultural geographic phenomena; but all portrayals, map-wise, are fitted into a plane surface representing part of the "round earth on flat paper."

CONCEPT THREE—THE LIFE-LAYER

It has been said that the most important function of the continents is that they provide a standing place for people. While this fact is clear one needs to recognize that the "standing room" on each continent has within it certain choice spots. Certainly one can say that, broadly speaking, groups of people need the continents—those parts of the lithosphere which jut up visibly through the hydrosphere into the atmosphere. Next, one may proceed to point out the choice spots as comprised of most favorable combinations of earth, water, and air. Where the earth's mantle of soil is coupled with water and air in adequate amounts, and there is periodic regularity in presence of the last two, there one finds "life" and "new life." The "good life," to use the third of the three terms supplied by H. J. Fleure in his paper, "Human Regions," depends upon surpluses in the life-layer, upon cultural advances, and upon realization of "values." (3) In the life-layer, which is fixed quite definitely on our globe, we find animate objects—people, plants and animals, obtaining in varying degrees and amounts their sustenance from each other and from the inanimate factors around them.

The concept of the life-layer may have parallel growth with that of globalism. It also may be depicted with little to great accuracy depending upon the competence and insight one possesses when he tries to depict the choice spots on flat paper. Thus the life-layer concept, while meeting to a large degree the test of independence, does permeate all the others. A geographer assesses the life-layer in its vertical and particularly in its areal intensity and extent. The inhabitability of a place is understood basically in terms of its three fundamental elements—soil, air, water. The great agglomerations of people, in the choice spots of the life-layer reveal these facts of population. There are four great human concentrations; one in Western Europe, one in East Central North America, and the remaining two in Asia wherein well over half the world's total population lives.

A different approach to this concept of the life-layer can be taken by studying first the world's "empty" lands, i.e., where there are fewer than two persons per square mile. When an inventory is made of the assets and liabilities of "empty" spaces certain ideas of what constitutes favorable habitats for people evolve. A progressive study, starting with the sparsely populated and proceeding to the most densely populated lands of the earth, can build this concept of the life-layer, and particularly highlight the "choice spots" of the life-layer.

CONCEPT FOUR—AREAL DISTINCTIONS, DIFFERENCES, AND LIKENESSES

This concept follows quite naturally that of the life-layer, and quite properly could be placed under the regional concept which follows. The understandings leading to full realization of it are based on two simple statements. People differ from place to place. Their environments differ from place to place. The combinations of the different groups of people and the differing environmental complexes seem at first glance to present a hopelessly endless task for geographers who are committed to the study of areal variations and interactions from place to place. Here regions of manageable size, geared to levels of comprehension, enter to make the job easier. One thing, however, becomes remarkably clear to all teachers at the outset of the study. The stages of development in many areas at a given time have a wide range. The arrangement of things and the association of things are peculiarly characteristic to certain selected areas. The singling out of those characteristics which lend distinction to any area or to several areas presents an ever-present challenge as new groups of students tackle the same area, or as the same students study new areas. Likewise, the comparison of similar regions calls for critical appraisals. Areal likenesses and differences need cataloguing, but the listed facts can be used in developing understandings which eventually create a conception of wide diversity within terrestrial, global, unity.

CONCEPT FIVE—THE REGION

The formulation of regions and the development of the technique of regionalizing are paramount in building this concept which is the central one of all geography. Geographers strive to recognize or identify the meaningful aggregations in space. The filling in may be one showing the physical elements or the web of nature, or it may be a pattern revealing man-made categories of cultural matrices. Implicit in the evolution of the regional concept is the selection of significant criteria. While these may be mapped singly, one after the other, the real mental challenge lies in divising the true, functionally interrelated complexes in the so-called region.

This operational concept carries with it the ideas (and the

problems) of scale. The magnitude of the area to be delineated must be proportioned to the number of details desired to be shown. Hence, the quantitative, the measurable elements demand careful selection. The qualitative collectivities to be shown also need sifting and often call for a priority listing. The "materials need to be wedded to the methods."

A vast array of "regions" confronts students of geography. Included in the array are the systematic, the cultural, the physical, the economic, the one-element and the combined-elements regions. There also are those termed nodal, uniform, urban, and rural. One type of region which is most easily delineated but nevertheless fraught with a whole gamut of geographic factors and problems is the nation-state (4). In it one sees areal differentiation as a continuing process. Seen, too, is one type of unity of geographical space. This kind of region, the political geographic unit, possesses agencies which gather meaningful data. Through time these data make possible a study of changes in activity and of movements in fixed, well-defined areas.

Appraisal and reappraisal of regions necessitate training in observation, analysis, synthesis, and presentation in the field and in the literature. The mere dropping of lines around "earth parcels" without justification of what the lines enclose and where the lines fall is totally untenable in the geography discipline. . . .

CONCEPT SIX—RESOURCES CULTURALLY DEFINED

When early man picked up a club to use as a weapon he expanded the immediate area over which he had physical human control. When he tied a stone to the club he had a tool as well as a weapon; his arm was made stronger and longer. Today aircraft and harnessed power do the same for people over a world-wide area. When man tamed a dog he made his hearing more acute and widened his protected area. Today radar does this for him world-wide. When he tamed the donkey, camel, horse, elephant, then worked and rode them he made his legs longer and stronger. Today the automobile, the train, the ocean liners, and astrojets make his travel shorter in time and more efficient.

All the above have not come to all the world's people. There has not been and probably there never will be such a progression as outlined skeletally above for all groups of men. By way of illustration one may point out that coal (anthracite for heating, and bituminous coal for cooking) was here in the United States when the Indians reigned supreme. To them coal was not a resource; their culture had not reached the stage where it was useful to them. When, however,

Europeans whose culture did include this source of heat and power reached the North American continent the vast coal resources became one of the first foundations for industrial greatness. . . .

The . . . substance, clay, can be keyed to man's cultural emergence. Soil enrichment, mud (clay) home construction, vases and urns, tiles for walls and roofing and for drainage of homes and fields, and tablets for record keeping, all attest to man's ingenuity and utilization of clay in civilizations both past and present. In like manner, metallurgy, when treated as a cultural development, may bring out with more meaning for the student the distribution of mineral resources of the nations of the world. With this concept of culturally defined resources the learning of the world's major productions, animate and inanimate, does not become a dead inventory list to be memorized, but a live record of man's innovations at which we can both marvel and draw hope. By viewing resources in the light of people's readiness and constant search for them, reached through time by a slowly accelerating cultural evolution, geographers are able to discard what has too often been a deadly inventory sort of economic geography.

. . . Finally, and probably most important, people also may be regarded as a resource which is "becoming" more and more. As Miss Semple once stated it, the "mantle of humanity is of varied weave and thickness—it is the magic web whereof man is at once woof, warp, and weaver, and the flying shuttle that never rests." (5) Human resources may, in time, be those studied first by other humans assessing regions.

CONCEPT SEVEN—MAN THE CHOOSER

Groups of people in their diverse regions are confronted by opportunities and restraints. They are, nevertheless, the "ecological dominants" of their regions. Through time they have assessed and re-assessed both the physical environment and the cultural milieu in which they live and have their being. What to use, when to use, where to get, and how to control earthly and man-made items have been questions posed by people and which they have tried to answer. In seeking answers, groups of people have organized spatial systems which seem rational to them. The crops they grow, the animals they raise, the minerals underneath the surface and the vegetative cover of the earth are available in varying qualities and amounts from place to place.

People's economic well-being and often their survival are based upon personal, private, and public decision making. Some would say people always operate according to the "law of comparative advantage." With the power of volition, the freedom to choose and follow courses which seem at that time to offer the greatest advantage, mankind has been the most significant factor of the total environment, though Nature in her usually silent way has persistently permeated all. To say that man always has acted rationally would mean that the unfolding of world history would have been logical in the past and predictable for the future. This is not entirely possible. Some of man's actions, often for inexplicable reasons, are irrational to nearly everybody; but more often what seems to be rational behavior to members of one national or cultural group may appear totally irrational to those of others. Understandings of "how people got that way" require intimate knowledge of the circumstances involved, of both place and period. There are political, economic, social, and physical environmental impactors, and people compare, then select those which offer the greatest advantages which in time may be judged "right" or "wrong."

CONCEPT EIGHT—SPATIAL INTERACTION

The connections and movements within and between regions are exemplified in the communication and transportation facilities and routes. The commodities carried and the carriers used are but sets of facts used in developing understandings that are part of the concept of spatial interaction. Other generalizations grow out of the study of the great circulations of goods, men, and ideas. One finds that expressions such as supply and demand, constraints and restraints of trade, periodic pulsations in marketing goods, are all related to this lively geographic concept. The idea of pressures and flows can be applied to air masses, wind systems and storms, just as easily as it can be brought out in the study of exchange of surplus goods, battle front shifts in times of war, and even mass movements of people migrating to new lands or just taking a week-end vacation at the beach or mountains. Less spectacular but more relentless would be the interplay and interdependence of the vegetation and animal life, the throbbing activity in our great conurbations, and especially between the latter.

One may point out that the physical world's dynamic processes are largely interdependent. Large regions of the world, comprised of varied cultural attributes, are being viewed today as interacting parts of a terrestrial unit. From the smallest area (a region) with a family, its home, and garden plot to the greatest international cooperative—the United Nations—spatial interaction enters as a concept which possesses a promise for the future. Such a promise does not call for dull uniformity or just careful inventory. Indeed, to reach its richest fulfillment one must see unity, but unity achieved by interaction of the great diversities present from place to place.

CONCEPT NINE—PERPETUAL TRANSFORMATION

There is a geography for every time. Successive or continuing occupance by groups of people results in changing and changed landscapes. Natural forces, tectonic (vulcanism and diastrophism), coupled with those of gradational character (water, wind, ice, organisms, and gravity) alter the earth's surface, or parts of it. Today's surface is but one frame, however, in the long moving-picture of the earth's story. This earthly surface, constantly being altered by Nature and Men, has been not only the stage but also has provided the properties for the great acts and actors of civilizations. The actors in the scenes are not always the same; new faces appear in creative roles. Often scenes are re-written to include many more persons. The plots, too, are often altered. Some result in happier productions, others in dismal failures, but the play goes on.

One finds evidence that great cultural groups have come and gone; that some were and are able to live side by side; that others have lost original identities through intermingling; that still others have been made layers in superposition or have been swept away. The intensive studies of these peoples in their past and present places, and the significant attributes they have accrued through time provide geographers with an on-going mission. Viewed in the bright light of this concept one can understand that the world *always* has had "developed" and "underdeveloped" areas. Regions which were epitomes of development in some early centuries now may be regarded as underdeveloped even by their own inhabitants. One geographer from a country in Asia put it succinctly when he said, "Our past is our present guide and our future angel,—that is our trouble." Such generalizations need not lead to gestures of despair, but to assurances of betterment in the increased competence of many groups of people as they transformed and were transformed through time. Truly great traditions do not deter progress, but provide springboards for leaps into the future.

This concept, perpetual transformation, implies an "open-end" or "no final answer" aspect to our geography teaching. The world and its parts thus are not wrapped up and tied tightly in neat little packages.

References

(1) Jerome S. Bruner, *The Process of Education*, Harvard University Press, Cambridge, 1960, pp. 31–32.

(2) This concept is the title of a National Geographic Society publication; a monograph issued in 1947, Washington, D. C. Its author is Wellman Chamberlin; drawings are by Charles E. Riddiford. The third chapter presents the concept very well.

(3) H. J. Fleure, "Human Relations," *Scottish Geography Magazine*, 1919.

(4) Much of what is given here has been suggested to the author directly (and indirectly) by Stephen Jones, Political Geographer, Yale University. The interpretations, however, are the author's own.

(5) Ellen Churchill Semple, *Influences of Geographic Environment*, Henry Holt and Company, New York, 1911, p. 79.

❧ THE IMPORTANCE OF DEVELOPING GEOGRAPHIC CONCEPTS   *Zoe A. Thralls*

The earlier article on geography contained a good deal about big ideas and major concepts. But how does a concept develop? What sort of planning can a teacher do to help pupils develop concepts? Thralls provides concrete examples. Her development of the concepts of river *and* latitude *should provide the reader with ideas of how to teach other ideas, such as* continent *and* longitude. *The difference between this mode of teaching and that of requiring memorization produces the difference between concept development and rote recall.*

WHAT IS A CONCEPT?

The term *concept* may be applied to a class or group of objects, occurrences, situations and/or ideas which have certain qualities or characteristics in common. Thus, we have a *concept* when we recognize a group of objects, occurrences, situations and ideas which have a resemblance or common elements. To such a group we give a name or label. The name or label refers to the common elements or characteristics and ignores the details in which the object, the situation, or the idea differ. For instance, the term *river* refers to a large natural flowing stream of water. Specific rivers such as the Congo and the Mississippi differ in details, but both are rivers; that is, both are "large natural flowing streams of water." Both have many characteristics common to all rivers. The term "metal" or "metallic" is the

This article first appeared in the September, 1960 issue of *The Journal of Geography*, 59:279–288. Zoe A. Thralls is a professor emeritus of geography and education at the University of Pittsburgh.

name or label that we may give to all objects which have certain common characteristics, although they may vary from a penny to a stove, or even a mountain of iron. Honesty, interdependence, or conservation are all concepts of certain groups of abstract ideas.

Cronbach, in his *Educational Psychology*, says: "A concept has two aspects. It is, first, a classification or discrimination. The person recognizes what events or objects the concept applies to. Second, it is a set of associations. Once a thing has been classified, we call up many associations about the class. Is the egret a *bird*? If so, then it probably lays eggs, has feathers, makes a nest, follows migration habits and has a mind less keen than a mammal." (1)

In geography, for instance, if a country such as Tibet is a high plateau, we recall the various associations we have with the term "plateau." It is an extensive, nearly-level area of elevated land. It may be surrounded by mountains or bordered by steep scarps on one or more sides. It is probably arid or semi-arid. The population is usually relatively sparse. Some questions also arise in our minds (What type of plateau is it—inter-montane, piedmont, or continental?) as we try to extend our concept of "Tibet as a plateau." The moment that we are able to classify an object, event, or situation, we have a basis for thinking about it and extending its meaning to us. . . .

DEVELOPMENT OF CONCEPTS

The acquisition of concepts in any field is gradual and cumulative because a concept is a complex affair. A child may recognize the word "climate," but may not have much of a concept of "climate." Thus the teaching of concepts requires both time and skill on the part of the teacher—skill in introducing the concept and time filled with numerous appropriate pupil experiences related to the concept. A concept must have meaning and usability before it becomes a part of the learner's thinking. The teacher cannot give meaning to the learner. He can act only as a guide as the learner gradually constructs concepts out of his own experiences. This fact has certain implications for both learning and teaching concepts.

First, the teacher should choose carefully the number of concepts to be taught. Usually the curriculum demands entirely too many in all the subjects. Only those basic concepts essential for understanding in that particular field should be selected. For instance, in geography, concepts of *time, location, weather, climate* and *terrain* are but a few of the essential concepts.

Secondly, the teacher must keep in mind constantly that the process of learning is gradual and cumulative. He cannot expect complete understanding at the time the concept is introduced. The growth in understanding of a concept proceeds step by step in ascending levels of difficulty. This expansion of a concept, or growth in understanding, may be illustrated with some examples. One example, the *river*, is fairly simple; the second concept, *latitude*, is more difficult and complex.

The term river means "a large natural flowing body of water." The learner first becomes acquainted with a specific river, either through actual experience or vicariously through reading and pictures. He learns that it is a large flowing body of water. It has banks, a channel, and a slow or fast current. He may note that man uses the river as a highway.

Next, he has experiences with other rivers and notes their particular characteristics. Some flow rapidly, others slowly. Some have deltas at their mouths, others do not. Some have low, fairly level land for their banks; others flow between high rocky walls. He begins to discriminate between rivers and other large bodies of water. At this stage, he is increasing his general information about rivers. His concept of rivers gradually gains in clarity, specificity, and abstractness. By this time, he recognizes that although rivers differ, they have common characteristics. He has gained the basic meaning of the term, river. He can now use the term with real understanding.

He is ready to acquire a more comprehensive understanding of rivers and to classify rivers in various categories. He also begins to understand how man's activities may be affected by different rivers and how man may use them. He now has a rich and meaningful concept—a part of a system of ideas.

Latitude is a much more difficult concept to acquire. It is an abstract idea to start with and also is dependent upon a background of experience with such concepts as sphere and direction. Latitude is a means of measuring distances by degrees north or south of the equator. Children can memorize that definition, but it will have no meaning to them and they will not be able to use it unless the concept is developed step by step under the teacher's guidance. Furthermore, a certain intellectual maturity is necessary.

First of all, the learner must recognize the difficulty of locating places on a sphere such as the earth. How can that be done? In attempting to solve that problem the necessity of latitude or some means of location and measurement becomes evident.

By questions, the teacher helps the learner to recall the equator and its meaning and the poles. These terms the children should have become acquainted with in the fourth grade. The teacher guides them in recalling how they used such general terms as "half-way to the North Pole," or "near the equator." Now a more exact method of measurement is needed. The teacher introduces and explains latitude and degrees of latitude. In his explanation, he compares the lines of latitude to east-west streets and degrees to the numbers on the houses which help us locate a friend in a city. Some learners are bothered by the fact that the lines of latitude run east-west, yet they measure distance north-south. If this point comes up, the teacher may mark off on the blackboard a series of lines one foot apart up from the chalk tray. Then the learner will see that these parallel lines help one to find the distance *up* from the chalk tray, although the lines run the opposite direction. Exercises that require the learner to find on the globe and on maps cities at various latitudes north and south of the equator should follow this explanation.

The next step is to guide the learner in recalling from his fourth grade experiences the significance of location at different distances north and south of the equator in terms of length of day, sun position, and climatic conditions. Then, in the fifth grade, the child learns how latitude is related to the frost-free season, the crops raised in northern and southern United States, the length and severity of winter, and other everyday items. Thus, in recalling his fourth grade learnings and adding new information, he begins to see the significance of latitude in man's life on earth.

Learning and application activities should follow discussion. The purpose of these activities is to make the concept clearer and more exact. The activities should require the learner to locate a number of places both north and south of the equator by latitude. Then he should be able to tell approximately: 1) the sun position during the summer and during the winter at that place; 2) the length of daylight in the winter and in the summer; 3) the probable length of the frost-free season; and 4) the possible crops if there is sufficient rainfall. Of course other factors affect the crops raised in any area, but latitude is always one vital factor.

Now that is as far into the concept of latitude . . . [as] a fifth grade child is able to go, and some may not be able to reach that level. Not all children can be expected to attain the same level of understanding. In the sixth and seventh grades, the learner may be able to take further steps forward under the teacher's guidance (2).

Thus, the building of concepts in geography is a gradual and cumulative process. It really never ends, but the teacher can be fairly satisfied when the child is able to use the concept to attack new problems. For instance, if the child can use the concept of latitude in attacking such questions as these:

Over how many degrees of latitude does Chile extend? Is it in the north or south latitude? What does the great extent of latitude

(17° S. to 55° S.) suggest concerning climatic conditions in Chile? In what months of the year would crops be harvested in Central Chile? What possible crops might be raised in Central Chile?

Gradually, the child's concept of latitude is extended and he notes certain factors which modify the effects of latitude, such as terrain, location on a west or east coast or in the interior of a continent. He also gains new concepts and modifies or extends the concepts of latitude and climate. He may be able to develop some simple generalizations such as, "The climate of a region is influenced to a large extent by its latitude"; "In the middle latitude lands have four seasons, and the weather varies with the season."

CONCEPTS AND THE CURRICULUM

The main weakness of most geography curriculums and textbooks is that basic geographic concepts have not been identified, introduced, and developed cumulatively throughout the curriculum or the textbook series. As a result, such fundamental concepts as direction, latitude, longitude, weather, plateau, mountain range, river system and many others never become useful tools in the child's intellectual equipment. For instance, latitude is introduced either in the fourth or fifth grade. It is explained and a few activities given. It may be mentioned once or twice later and then dropped. How can one expect the pupil in a high school geography class, in college, or even in later life to be able to use latitude intelligently? The same may be said of longitude and a dozen other basic geography concepts. No amount of real geographic understanding will be attained until, in our textbooks and curriculums, basic geographic concepts are introduced and developed cumulatively from grade to grade and are as familiar to the child as two plus two in arithmetic (3)!

References

(1) Lee J. Cronbach, *Educational Psychology*, Harcourt, Brace & Co., New York, 1954, p. 281.

(2) Some excellent problems in latitude may be found in Lucia Harrison's "Daylight, Twilight, Darkness and Time" published by Silver, Burdett, pp. 199–207. Part I gives many examples of the relation between latitude and human affairs.

(3) For an example of the cumulative development of concepts of weather and climate, see: Zoe A. Thralls, *The Teaching of Geography*, Ch. 11, pp. 305–330, "Teaching Weather and Climate."

✑§ EDUCATION AND POLITICS   *Sir Norman Angell*

> *Politics is the art and science of power. One of the instruments of power is the verbal symbol. Such symbols as socialism, communism, or capitalism often arouse more emotion than intellect. Angell examines some myths of our day and deals with the touchy subjects of sovereignty and internationalism (themselves powerful symbols). He stresses the power of ideas in our government—and thus he sets a tone for the selections on political science. He does not tell us which ideas to teach, but his argument presses home the necessity of political education in a nuclear age.*

PREVALENT MYTHS

The first step to the cure of any disease is diagnosis. Mass opinion as it concerns the relations of states and nations is determined by certain prevailing basic ideas, attitudes, and assumptions. These basic ideas are embodied in watchwords and slogans now current throughout the world and which, by a monstrous irony, are employed very largely by Moscow's College of Propaganda. They voice demands for complete national freedom, absolute independence, self-determination, unqualified state sovereignty, and are particularly articulate in the case of the two score or more new states which have come into being these last ten or fifteen years.

In addition to the assumptions which determine the relations of states to each other, there are other assumptions which usually determine the relations of parties within states. We usually find a doctrine called socialism opposed to another called capitalism; or communism opposed to private ownership of property; or trade union power opposed to employers.

I suggest that these slogans which dominate the mass mind—those in the international field which demand complete national freedom and independence, self-determination, and unqualified state sovereignty and those which within states imply that socialism or

From "Political Education in a Nuclear Age" in *The National Elementary Principal*, 42:6–10, May, 1963. Copyright 1963, Department of Elementary School Principals, National Education Association. All rights reserved. Sir Norman Angell has been a distinguished leader in international affairs during the twentieth century; he was awarded the Nobel Peace Prize in 1933.

communism is something totally incompatible with what is called capitalism or the institution of private property—I suggest that these basic assumptions are at best half-truths and at worst sheer falsehood. Yet they are ideas which even when utterly fallacious have the power to arouse deep emotions. Perhaps their power to arouse emotion is due to the fact that they have no precise meaning, just as martial music which has no specific meaning can deeply stir emotion and a catchy marching song can induce a thousand men to go on marching without even wanting to know their destination.

Let us analyze for a moment some of these slogans. The most powerful of all, perhaps, in the international field is the demand for complete national freedom. Now there are certain freedoms which I, for one, regard as beyond all price, as quite indispensable to the realization of the good life. But if these freedoms are to be preserved, then certain truths about freedom must be taken into account. They are truths quite obvious in the daily life of the world about us: for instance, the fact that if everybody had complete freedom, nobody would have any. If everyone were allowed to drive his motor car as he saw fit, there would not be more freedom on the roads. There would be none, for all would go in danger of sudden death. Traffic freedom must be subject to a traffic code. The time has come in this modern world when we have annihilated distance to establish a traffic code for the relation of states. If every state is to be completely sovereign, then we can surrender any idea of a world sovereignty capable of controlling armaments.

The doctrines upon which party divisions within states are based are often just as incompatible with a stable and workable society, that is to say, with peace. To assume, as in Russia and China it is assumed, that socialism is something completely incompatible with private property, an institution which must be fought to the death; to assume, as it was assumed by a large section of the American public during the McCarthy era, that socialism is a creed or doctrine fatal to a capitalist or a free society—such assumptions constitute a myth. There is no capitalist system in the world that has not adopted and does not go on adopting in greater measure what our grandfathers would have called socialism. And I suggest that it would take the bite out of much communist propaganda if in our public discussions we made it clear that what Moscow calls a capitalist society—the British or, for that matter, the American—has already adopted a lot of socialism and is ready to adopt as much more as will prove workable in practice. Public discussion along those lines would help to break down at least part of the barriers which divide the world.

The habit of dogma making is worsened by another feature of

the public mind: crowd psychology or herd instinct, in which we lose nearly all sense of personal responsibility. A agrees to a course of action because B does and B does because A does. What is the basis of the decision? And this crowd-mindedness or herd instinct can become monstrously evil, as it has at times in America on the occasion of a "lynching bee."

THE TASK FOR EDUCATION

These failures of the public mind are not going to be corrected merely by giving the mass public, the millions, the electorates, more knowledge—more knowledge of history, geography, science, what-have-you. The knowledge which could well have prevented the major errors of our century, the two world wars, was already possessed by those who committed the errors.

It is not lack of knowledge which has caused lynchings. It was not lack of knowledge on the part of the German public as a whole which enabled Hitler to exploit feelings of anti-Semitism. It did not require learning, or erudition, or scholarship to see that such a proposition was errant nonsense.

Yet not all the aspects of the mass mind and mass behavior as revealed in our century are discouraging. In one sphere, there has been very great improvement. It is an improvement emphasized by the fact that the religious wars in the West at least have come to an end and that orthodox and heretic can live peacefully together, which for so long they could not. Indeed, we now seem to be in sight of a Christian unity in which theological differences which for centuries excited the deepest hatred and hostility and were the source of unspeakable cruelties are now fading away. What has been brought about in the religious field must now be brought about in the political field. But more quickly. This great and beneficent change in the attitude of ordinary folk has certainly not been due to any widespread study by the millions of the mountainous literature of theological philosophy.

Reviewers and commentators have been good enough to say that the arguments made and conclusions drawn in my books have been verified by the event. There is not an argument I have made, or a conclusion drawn, which was not made on the basis of facts already known to the reader. I mention this because I think it indicates the lines along which there should perhaps be a reshaping of some of our educational aims and methods. Education should aim more definitely than it does at developing that habit of mind which enables the ordinary man to use in his political decisions the knowledge he already possesses; the truths inherent in the daily life about him. An

American educationalist has put it thus: The real three R's in education should be reality, relatedness, responsibility. Commenting, I have
said that the greatest of these three is relatedness because where there
is no sense of relatedness there can be no sense of responsibility.

Education is not merely what goes on in school and university.
It goes on, or should go on, our lives through—by what we read and
how we discuss. The publicist—journalist, commentator, writer—
should be encouraged to attack more vigorously the myths with which
I have been dealing: the myth that in our age the state can be absolutely sovereign; that a nation's independence must not be touched;
that the welfare of mankind depends upon some particular economic
or political dogma destroying all opposing concepts; that one dogma
must bury its opponents. If such ideas and conceptions dominate
the mass mind, the UN will not succeed and we shall not have peace.

As I look about me in my ninety-first year, it seems to me that
our hopes of a humane and free society depend first upon a more
complete Western unity. We of the West must hang together or
we hang separately. We do not need to change human nature, whatever that may mean, but human behavior; and behavior and feeling
depend on ideas. To achieve improved political behavior, we must
have, first, better understanding of the forces within ourselves; second,
better understanding of the nature of modern society, especially the
interdependence of its economic life; and, third, development of the
habits of mind which enable us to discipline anti-social emotion and
impulse. The education received by the mass of our people does not
achieve these ends as effectively as it might. There is still almost
complete negligence of even elementary economics, though economic
ignorance can lead to social chaos.

It once fell to me, on the eve of a Presidential election, to put to
a class in political science at an American university this question: "If
the vote goes against the President next week, how do you know he
will not refuse to vacate his office?" The burden of the replies was
that it was a damn silly question because the contingency never arose.
I said: "In this Western hemisphere are twenty republics. In nineteen
of them, it is often happening. For over a century, it has been normal
for a president who could depend on his army to stay in office and become dictator. Why not in the United States?"

That it does not happen in the United States proves that power
rests ultimately in ideas, in opinions; in the ideas, for instance, that
military force must be the servant, not the master, of the state and
that a union of states creates more power than can separate sov-
ereignties. Thus, the United States, possessing far less territory, fewer
resources, perhaps even fewer soldiers than Latin America, has im-

mensely more power than all the nineteen republics put together. This surely has a lesson for Western Europe. It is time we learned it.

The major forces which have produced war throughout the ages, and may still produce it, are not obscure. Though belonging in large part to the region of the unconscious, they are discernible enough in the event. The tendency to dislike those who are not of our group —political, social, religious—is as old as the tribal conflicts which have raged throughout history. To dislike those who have the in- sufferable impudence to disagree with us in matters political, social, or religious is natural enough; it is a reflection upon our intelligence. To make a decision in some public problem is often difficult, trouble- some, and it is a relief to get rid of responsibility by going with the herd—to justify ourselves by the fact that "everybody's doing it" and that "everybody" cannot be wrong.

But the biggest defect of all in mass judgment is the failure to apply to the decisions which the citizen as voter must make the knowledge he already possesses, the commonplace truths in the daily life of the world about him—the failure of that sense of relatedness already touched upon.

Both problems—that of group intolerance, the tendency to group animosity; and a lack of a due sense of the connectedness of social and political issues—should figure more largely in our education than in fact they do. The parent can, by the simple example of his attitude toward those of different race, color, or creed, do a great deal to engender tolerance in even very young children. In the later stages of education, the social subjects, particularly history, could be so taught as to develop more than at present the habit of mind, the particular skill, which enables a citizen to grasp the interrelation of social and political phenomena.

Failing such approach to education, political behavior in the largest sense of the term is likely to remain what it always has been. And in that case we perish.

&§ POLITICAL REALITY IN CHILDHOOD

Franklin Patterson

What is citizenship? Do we belong to a political society larger than our government? Does citizenship involve more than politics? Patterson answers these questions and then turns to consider the fact that so many people today do not feel they are part of our political life. What causes this political alienation?

What can teachers do to eliminate past practices that planted the seeds of alienation? The author discusses three answers— and the following article expands one of them.

THE IDEA OF CITIZENSHIP

Before we turn to the problem of educating for effective citizenship, it is important . . . to consider the definitions we use. The prevalence of cant and cliché in defining "citizenship" is matched only by the industry of those who have sought instead to make the term more educationally manageable by dissecting it into detailed "behavioral outcomes." (1) Unfortunately, neither glittering generalities nor a list of molecular "behaviors" will serve as an adequate general guide in thinking about citizenship. Behavioral and operational descriptions are useful in specific curriculum planning and research (2). But we need, first, something that will help us get to the heart of the matter, a definition sufficiently abstract to be at once flexible and accurate.

The idea of citizenship within the Western tradition has been stated with admirable and deceptive simplicity by D. W. Brogan, the British political scientist:

> What is this idea? It seems to me to have two aspects. The first—possibly the most important, certainly the most novel—aspect is the assumption that every citizen has the right to be consulted on the conduct of the political society and the duty of having something to contribute to the general consultation. The second aspect is the converse of the first. The citizen who has a right to be consulted is bound by the results of the consultation. His duties flow from his rights (3).

In understanding Brogan's definition, it is necessary to note that he uses the term "political society" instead of "government." In doing so, he recognizes that government, complex as it is, is only one of many organized and informal structures of power, influence, and relationship in which the citizen finds himself. The individual enters into a political society at many levels and in different roles.

The Detroit Citizenship Education Study led by Stanley E. Dimond was operated under somewhat broader definitions. During the five years, 1945–1950, the Detroit Study involved the faculties

From "Political Reality in Childhood: Dimensions of Education for Citizenship," in *The National Elementary Principal*, 42:18–23, May, 1963. Copyright 1963, Department of Elementary School Principals, National Education Association. All rights reserved. Franklin Patterson is the director of The Lincoln Filene Center for Citizenship and Public Affairs, Tufts University.

and children of eight schools; four of the schools were elementary. No other study of comparable depth in terms of teacher development and child study is available in the civic education field. The Detroit Study held that:

> Citizenship as it relates to school activities has a two-fold meaning. In a narrow sense citizenship includes only legal status in a country and the activities closely related to the political functions— voting, governmental organization, holding of public office, and legal rights and responsibilities. Citizenship, in addition, has also acquired a broad meaning almost synonymous with those desirable personal qualities which are displayed in human associations. . . . For this Study, then, citizenship means the relations of the individual to his government and, in addition, his relations to other members and groups in a democratic society (4).

Implicit in both Brogan's and Dimond's definitions are factors of knowledge, value, and skill which it is the business of education to make explicit. These may be stated in various ways. They need to be articulated in terms of the varying contexts and situations in which the democratic citizen is an actor. The heart of the matter, at whatever level, is what Brogan calls "consultation." It is in this transactional process that democratic citizenship is expressed, whether one is dealing with the political economy of a primary school reading group or an election to the United States Senate. . . .

THE BEST OF TIMES, THE WORST OF TIMES

Writing about our times and the social studies, C. W. Hunnicutt and Jean D. Grambs have remarked that "the chief characteristics of the world in which we teach are *change* and *uncertainty*." (5) Some years ago, Ralph Tyler wrote that our personal lives are affected by a civilization which features increasing mechanization, increasing complexity, increasing commercialization, increasing impersonality, and continuous, chaotic stimulation. Innumerable observations of an analogous sort have been made about the times that we and our children live in. These are, as always, "the best of times and the worst of times," depending on which part of the scene you view and what refraction you use.

Jerome Bruner, for example, is sanguine about man's capacity for handling the increased stimulation which surrounds him in a rapidly changing technological civilization. Bruner argues that people are getting incredibly good at cognitively ordering and dealing with external events (6). John R. Seeley takes a different view, seeing today's individual confronted by gigantic monoliths (big government, big business, big labor, etc.) on the one hand, and an infinitude of unrelated fragments (his life experience) on the other (7). In context, both Bruner and Seeley probably are correct. Considering the present acceleration of change, it is remarkable that men are able to ride the whirlwind as well as they do; our hope must be in Bruner's direction, i.e., that man's cognitive apparatus can keep up with the changes he creates.

At the same time, all too ample evidence exists that there is a widening margin of possible breakdown in human affairs, a gap between our technological brilliance and our handling of the consequences of technology. Old answers for new problems may be as bad as no answers at all. Yet we tend to depend on obsolete solutions for many reasons. Our perceptions of phenomena are apt to be stereotyped. Since behavior is deeply influenced by what we "see" in a situation, and since much of what we "see" is the memory of an earlier perception, our reactions to new situations are often unrealistic. Our times require a conception of problem-solving as a process for developing "solutions to problems for which no man has a ready answer." (8) A productive, flexible approach to problem-solving: (a) includes substantial reliance on the communication and corrective feedback processes of consultation; (b) is difficult to develop after early adolescence; and (c) is more possible to achieve by personalities whose basic needs are adequately met than by those with deep unmet needs (9).

THE PROBLEM OF POLITICAL ALIENATION

There is also evidence that many citizens today do not feel that they are a part of the political process. This feeling, called "political alienation," pervades a proportion of the electorate who view themselves as politically powerless and their vote as meaningless.

> Political powerlessness is the feeling of an individual that his political action has no influence in determining the course of political events. Those who feel politically powerless do not believe that their vote, or for that matter any action they might perform, can determine the broader outcome they desire (10).

Expression of the feeling of political alienation may take any of several forms. One of these is political withdrawal, in which the person removes his interest and activity from politics. A second form of expression is projection, in which the citizen displaces the anger and resentment which arise from political alienation onto some other person or group whom he "blames." Identification with a charismatic leader is a third way a person may attempt to deal with his feelings of political alienation: the individual seeks to gain a feeling of power and meaning by incorporating within himself the attitudes held by a leader he perceives as powerful. . . .

A different level of response to one's feelings of political alienation is rational activism: political action based on a realistic assessment of the political situation. Rational activism is behavior founded on relatively undistorted perception of political reality and on logical reasoning.

Now we come to a basic dilemma in developing programs of education for citizenship. We are committed to a liberal Western definition of citizenship, very much like Brogan's statement of it. Yet this pervasive, ideal definition itself can operate so as to *create* political alienation. . . .

For citizenship education, such a view, if correct, means that we must not instill in children a Utopian image of the citizen and his government. If we do so, we are unwittingly contributing to his later disillusionment when he encounters the political process directly. There will be limits—his own and those externally applied—on the possibilities of consultation. There will be less than human perfection in the political world he grows up into. Politics will be a healthy, earthy part of all government, private and public, and he had best know and accept it in realistic terms.

He will live in times laden with change and uncertainty and remarkable opportunity. He can realize his birthright as a citizen best to the degree that he is helped to achieve political maturity rather than a fantasy about the citizen role and government. To achieve political maturity, he must be helped toward a level of rational activism in which he can "perceive the realities of the political structure, hold political goals which are potentially operational, and attempt to develop institutions through which these goals may be realized." (11) And all of this still within the central values of democratic life, of which the Brogan definition is a clear cut example.

Such a view means that the education of citizens in a modern democracy cannot afford to be mythological in its orientation because the end product, alienation, will erode the system in ultimate practice. It means that a major amount of attention in early and later education must be paid to the building of rational political maturity strong enough to meet the challenges of reality.

ELEMENTS IN CIVIC EDUCATION

At least three emphases suggest themselves as being vital to this mission:

1. Intellectual honesty. Political maturity is apt to begin and grow in childhood if we are straightforward in our treatment of the political facts of life, not deploring all that is less than familiar, congenial, or perfect in our system. Bruner says it well:

> Most important of all, the educational process must be free of intellectual dishonesty and those forms of cheating that explain without providing understanding. I have expressed the conviction elsewhere that any subject can be taught to anybody at any age in some form that is honest. It is not honest to present a fifth-grade social-studies class with an image of town government as if it were a den of cub scouts presided over by a parent figure interpreting the charter— even if the image set forth does happen to mesh with the child's immediate social experience. A lie is still a lie—even if it sounds like familiar truth (12).

Part of our task is to recognize that there are structures of knowledge realistically pertinent to the idea of citizenship at every level of individual learning. Another part is to devise strategies of education which will help children discover these structures and internalize them for use in their own behavior. But neither of these parts of the task can be accomplished without the kind of intellectual honesty of which Bruner speaks. . . .

2. Historical models plus jurisprudential consultation. Out of his work with children, Donald W. Oliver offers an approach to education for citizenship which deserves wide attention and trial. Essentially, Oliver has sought a formula which would enable teachers to help children toward two fundamental kinds of learning: the acquisition of basic values of our culture and the development of capability to dissect and interpret our culture with the tools of rational inquiry. Space does not permit detailed review of Oliver's approach, but in barest outline it has the features noted here.

First, he proposes the use of dramatic narrative history to establish a firm foundation of value models early in the child's life. One illustration of what Oliver means is Sandburg's treatment of the Lincoln family in 1817–1819, when Nancy Hanks Lincoln died and Abe's father remarried. Oliver feels that narrative history, handled in various media, but always with as much power and beauty as possible, can help children to find concrete images of the courage, suffering, adventure, cooperation, and aggressive impulses from which America has sprung. In case one thinks that present materials already do this, it is instructive to compare the selection from *The Prairie Years* with most current elementary textbooks.

Second, Oliver proposes emphasis on a consultation-oriented

approach to what he calls political process values, meaning largely those classes of rights which are the foundation of our freedom: freedom of expression, freedom to evaluate and change governmental leaders, due process of law, etc. Oliver calls this approach *jurisprudential*, focusing "upon the earnest use of free speech and open debate," guided by established rules of evidential proof, for students to determine themselves what man's proper relationship to government is in terms of particular public issues) (13).

(Oliver's jurisprudential approach uses controversy and its resolution through proof and persuasion as a vehicle for giving children experience in personal and group policy decisions. The protocols of Oliver's experimental use of this vehicle reflect a carefully conceived teaching strategy aimed at responsible consultation about meaningful issues, not at producing random-talk democracy. His approach requires the use of narrative background texts, illustrative cases, dilemma cases, argumentative dialogue, persuasive documents, case-play, and the construction of personal briefs.)

3. *Study and practice of self-government.* Much that is sentimental and not a little that is artificial has been written about the uses of self-government as a part of school experience. But in elementary and secondary schools alike one finds little that could honestly go by this name; there is, I suppose, an understandable wariness about the whole subject. . . .

Marion E. Turner's unusual verbatim reports of the conversations of a group of children four to nine years of age who learned to call meetings when some member created a disturbance is a rare record of experimentation with self-government in childhood education (14). Rules, using parliamentary procedures, were made to prevent similar disturbances, and when these rules were broken, the children established their own system of penalties and restraints.

Turner dealt with what are essentially political aspects of interaction in childhood society and sought to use "power factors in children's play" as subject matter. That is, she used conflict and conflict resolution in childhood relations as a means for introducing children to the political process. And from the verbatim reports, it would appear that in her three-year experiment, children gained a notable level of self-control and ease in consultation procedures without adult steering. . . .

TOWARD A REALISTIC VIEW

The emphasis on intellectual honesty about politics and governance, the use of value models based on rich historical narrative, the deliberate involvement of students in jurisprudential study of political process values as exposed in particular issues of real significance, and the utilization of self-government as a conscious educative procedure are far from a panacea. But taken together, they can help to introduce children to a realistic view of their relationship to a democratic culture in which lasting values are to be found and yet unceasingly reinterpreted in the changing context of life.

References

(1) Cf. my discussion of this in Patterson, Franklin. "Citizenship and Schools for the American Future." *Citizenship and a Free Society: Education for the Future.* Thirtieth Yearbook. Washington, D. C.: National Council for the Social Studies, 1960. Chapter 1. pp. 2–5.

(2) Operational definitions of citizenship for research and curriculum planning are dealt with at length in Patterson, Franklin, and others. *The Adolescent Citizen.* Glencoe, Illinois: The Free Press, 1960. 387 pp.

(3) Brogan, D. W. *Citizenship Today: England, France, The United States.* Chapel Hill, North Carolina: University of North Carolina Press, 1960. pp. 4–5.

(4) Dimond, Stanley E. *Schools and the Development of Good Citizens.* Detroit, Michigan: Wayne University Press, 1953. p. 36.

(5) Hunnicutt, C. W., and Grambs, Jean D. "The Social Studies Under Fire." *The Elementary School Journal,* 56: 210; January 1956.

(6) "Minutes of the Planning Committee, February 22, 1963." The Social Studies and Humanities Curriculum Program, American Council of Learned Societies. Cambridge, Massachusetts: Educational Services, Inc., 1963. Mimeo.

(7) Seeley, John R. "The Social Sea Around Us." *The School Review* 67: 429; No. 4, Winter 1959.

(8) Tyler, Ralph W. "We Are Learning More and More About Human Behavior. What Are the Implications for Education?" *NEA Journal* 44: 428; October 1955.

(9) *Ibid.*

(10) Levin, Murray B. *The Alienated Voter: Politics in Boston.* New York: Holt, Rinehart & Winston, Inc., 1960. p. 63.

(11) *Loc. cit.*

(12) Bruner, Jerome S. *On Knowing; Essays for the Left Hand.* Cambridge, Massachusetts: Harvard University Press, 1962. p. 124.

(13) Oliver, Donald W. "Educating for Responsible Individualism, 1960–1980." *Citizenship and a Free Society: Education for the Future.* Thirtieth Yearbook. Washington, D. C.: National Council for the Social Studies, 1960. p. 216.

(14) Turner, Marion E. *The Child Within the Group; An Experiment in Self-Government.* Stanford, California: Stanford University Press, 1957. 93 pp.

✑ CHILDREN, POLITICS, AND ELEMENTARY
SOCIAL STUDIES   *Gloria Cammarota*

*For some time now, political scientists have been interested
in the ways in which, and the extent to which, children view
political phenomena. Although the child's political world is a
reality to him, it is largely a mystery to the teacher. The political scientist uses a special label—political socialization—to
identify the development of attitudes and understandings about
political behavior. Cammarota draws on the work of Easton
and Hess in probing such learning; she then raises some questions about utilizing their findings in elementary schools.*

As A RESULT of research which they are doing in the area of the
political socialization of children, Professor David Easton and Robert
Hess of the University of Chicago make these startling comments,
"Every piece of evidence indicates that the child's political world
begins to take shape well before he even enters elementary school
and it undergoes the most rapid change during these years," and "The
truly formative years of the maturing member of a political system
would seem to be those years between the ages of three and thirteen."

There is little evidence in the social studies curriculum typical of
most elementary schools of the United States to show awareness of
the ideas stated by Easton and Hess. In most cases, the social studies
program of the primary grades (K–3) focuses on the home, family,
and community. In the intermediate grades, children usually study
about their home states, about the United States, about some foreign
countries, and sometimes about the history of the Old World. In
grades seven and eight, geography or community study and study
of the U.S.A. are the general rule. Examination of materials used
throughout these grades, especially in K–4, shows that study of
politics and government, when included, is often incidental rather
than central. If it is true that children form their ideas about the

Used by permission of the author and the National Council for the Social
Studies; from *Social Education*, 27:205–211, April, 1963. Easton and Hess
published their findings in the article, "The Child's Political World," found in
the fall issue, 1962, of the *Midwest Journal of Political Science*. Gloria Cammarota has been an assistant superintendent of schools in Levittown, Pennsylvania.

political world during these years, it would appear that it happens, to a degree at least, in spite of the school rather than because of it. . . .

CHILDREN AND POLITICS

. . . In considering the child's political world, Easton and Hess talk about "political orientations" and "political socializations." They define political orientations as consisting of political knowledge, attitudes, and standards of evaluation. That is, a child's political orientation consists of what he knows and the opinions and values he has about the political world.

Easton and Hess define as political socialization the process through which children acquire their political orientations. In other words, political socialization has to do with the way a child obtains knowledge and develops attitudes and values about the political world. Easton and Hess stress the importance of political socialization: ". . . no system is able to function, much less maintain itself . . . without either intuitively or consciously undertaking to transmit some of its political heritage to the maturing members of the society or to construct a new heritage for them. . . ."

According to Easton and Hess, the three levels of a political system about which members of the system must acquire political orientations (that is, knowledge, attitudes, and values) are: 1) the people in a society who are joined together by a political system, 2) the structure (legal and cultural) through which governmental work is carried out, and 3) the individuals who occupy government roles. From their study of orientations held by children through grade eight, they report findings such as these:

1. Children begin to learn about government and politics even before they enter school. The formative years in politics appear to be those years between the ages of three and 13.   Children learn early that they are Americans. They have positive feelings about this during all their elementary school years. When asked in the primary grades to list best things about America, children mention their "schools, the beauty of their country, its animals and flowers, and the goodness and the cleanliness of its people." They mention freedom but they think of it in nonpolitical terms and interpret it to mean that a person can do whatever he wants to do. In the higher elementary grades, when asked for the same information, children list "democracy, government, voting, and elaborations of freedom to mean freedom of speech, press, religions, and choice of occupation."

An interesting result reported by Easton and Hess is the difficulty young children have in "disentangling God and country." For example, most children when asked to whom they pledge allegiance replied "to flag" or "to country." However, a sizable number responded that they pledge allegiance to God. Easton and Hess hypothesized that it is the similarity between political and religious piety and ritual which exists in the child's world (as they say the Pledge, for example) that accounts for this confusion of political and religious sentiments.

2. Children's political attitudes and values are firmly established by the time they leave the eighth grade. Data shows that children have developed a very favorable attitude about our governmental structure by the time they reach the seventh and eighth grades. They most often have little accurate knowledge about it—but they have strong ties to it. Easton and Hess report that the ties develop on three bases. First, children become aware early of governmental authority outside the home and school. Second, the major representatives for them of this authority are the President and the policeman. Third, emotional rather than rational processes help children to develop their favorable attitudes. Easton and Hess hypothesize that children come to value the entire system as the good feelings about the parts visible to them begin to spread to other parts.

3. During the high school years, youth obtain much knowledge about government and politics, but this knowledge has little effect upon values and attitudes previously formed. Perhaps it is because we assume that political development will occur most logically during the high school years that most work and study of government and politics are done at this level. From data gathered, there is little evidence to show that there are fundamental changes in attitudes and values regarding the political world during those years.

Easton and Hess comment about the unwillingness of adults in the United States to expose children to political realities which they consider inappropriate for them. They write, "The child has to learn as best he can that in politics the stakes are high, passions are strong, motivations may be less than pure and altruistic, conflict is endemic, and men have the capacity to place self, party, or occupation above country." They state that their data suggest that children are capable of facing up to the realities of political life. As an example, they cite presidential electoral campaigns. Children are aware of the bitterness of the campaigns; they know that they (their families) are committed to one party and that other people have different commitments. However, after the election, they have great esteem for the successful candidate and accept completely the idea that he now has authority as President. . . .

IMPLICATIONS FOR CONTENT OF THE ELEMENTARY
SOCIAL STUDIES PROGRAM

The apathy of the vast majority of American citizens is well known. The development of citizens who are active, informed, and interested has long been a goal of citizenship education and an important facet of the social studies program. If children are forming their attitudes during their elementary school years about politics and government, should they not during these years be learning the importance of commitment and participation? How can we teach them what is involved in running for office, in working to help candidates, in making opinions known to governmental leaders—and at the same time impress upon them the importance in a democracy of activities such as these?

If children are developing on an emotional basis attitudes and values about government and politics, should they not at the same time be learning at an intellectual level about government and politics? How can we start from the early grades to give them some understanding of government, of what it does, and of the relationship of the individual to it?

If there are very definite symbols such as the President and the policeman which have strong meaning to children, can these symbols not serve as bridges across which children can be helped to a broader understanding of governmental and political structure? How can we help children to understand what the President does, who other governmental officials are, what their roles are? Building on their understanding of the policeman, how can we help children to some understanding of laws and law enforcement structures at local, state, and national levels?

If a child's school day is to include activities like the Pledge of Allegiance and the singing of patriotic songs, should children not be helped to understanding rather than misunderstanding of what is involved? Many patriotic "rituals" are and should be part of the school day. Many national holidays are discussed and celebrated. How can we help children to accurate understanding of the meaning of each?

In sum, if we are indeed to select new content for the elementary social studies program, is it not essential that we redefine the learnings we consider to be appropriate for children of various ages? Easton and Hess use the term "age appropriate," and make the point that in stressing learnings which can be immediately applied to the child's experience, we ignore areas (like government and politics) in which

children are learning from the time they are infants but in which they
will not have direct experience until they are much older.

✑ THE ECONOMIC WORLD OF THE CHILD
Lawrence Senesh

*Professor Senesh, an economist, has not been content to pre-
scribe remedies in economic education. He has gone into early
grade classrooms and worked with youngsters. In this article he
offers several examples of how the lives of children are related
to the larger world of economics. The first grade teacher, often
working with the major topics of home and school, will find his
examples familiar. Senesh's insistence that children can understand and use economic terms should give confidence to the
teacher who wants to strengthen this part of the social studies.*

THE LAUNCHING OF Sputnik awakened the scientists who awakened
the government who awakened the schools to the necessity of improving the science training of our youth. The unified efforts of
scientists, government, and schools started a new reaction. But scientific progress is not an unmixed blessing. The social scientists, being
mindful of the rapid dislocations which come in the wake of scientific
advances, are urging the improvement of the social science curriculum
in the public schools.

Economics, among all the social sciences, is one of the most
underdeveloped areas of the public school curriculum. Before the
Great Depression, many people looked on the economic system as
a perpetual-motion machine in which balance was assured by the
interaction of consumers and producers. As long as the mechanism
worked smoothly, only a relatively few specialists were curious enough
to study the mechanism; therefore, economics as an organized body
of knowledge was not a part of the school curriculum. Also, curriculum builders had their own notions about the scope of economics.
Some still think that economics is identical with personal money

management. Others think it is simply a matter of value judgment.

Recognizing the need for improvement of economic education in the public schools, the American Economic Association organized in 1960 the National Task Force, which a year later produced a report, "Economic Education in the Schools." The Task Force has alerted the public schools to the existence of an organized body of economic knowledge and urges schools to incorporate this knowledge into the curriculum.

Unfortunately, the Task Force's scope of economics education is too narrow, and therefore useless for curriculum building. Its recommendations are limited to high schools. Having ignored the learnings and intellectual conditioning which do and could take place in the elementary and junior high schools, and having isolated the high-school program from the rest of the curriculum, the National Task Force had no other choice but to limit the objectives of economic education to minimum understandings for citizenship.

Minimum understandings may be adequate today, but will they be sufficient tomorrow as new horizons open, and the economic system is put to new tasks? Minimum economics will not excite youth, will not gain respect for analysis, nor motivate youth to consider careers in the economic world.

Can the economic world be made as exciting as the world of numbers or of atoms? Yes, if the child's experiences are related to the larger economic world, and if children are helped to understand the principles underlying their experiences. A common motif in children's fairy tales is the granting of wishes. The fulfillment of the wishes often leaves the wishers unhappier than before because as humans they can never be satisfied and because they do not know how to make wise choices. The conflict between unlimited wants and limited sources plagues families and nations as well as individuals. Since men cannot have everything, they must learn how to make wise choices.

Simple exercises can help children to appraise available resources and make the best choice. The teacher could use "pretend" situations for practice in choice-making. For example, "Pretend you have cut your finger. What would you want most? Chewing gum? A yo-yo? A Band-Aid?" "Pretend you are in the woods where there are lots of mosquitoes. What would you want most? An electric fan? A storybook? A mosquito net?"

The range of choices depends on man's ability to produce goods and services. The important discovery of the first-grade child is that when men do useful work they are producers. When Mother cooks, she produces goods; when Father drives a truck, he produces a service. Everyone, so long as he does useful work, provides himself or others with goods and services wanted.

First-graders can realize that the faster and better men can produce goods and services, the more wishes and dreams can be fulfilled. They will discover various ways by which goods and services can be produced faster and better. The teacher decides to clean the classroom. She may assign the whole class to clean the chalkboard, then the whole class to sweep the floor, then the whole class to empty the wastebasket. What confusion! Or she may divide the labor among the children. Individuals do certain chores, and if each does his job, the work is done quickly and well.

In one first-grade class, two teams produced gingerbread boys. One team worked on the assembly-line principle—one child rolled the dough; another cut the forms; the third pressed in the candy eyes; the next child put in raisin buttons; the last child put cookies on the cooky pan. In the other team, each child did all the jobs by himself. The waste of material, duplication of equipment, slowness of execution, were obvious. The discovery of the division of labor will help children to understand the advantages of assembly-line production and specialization according to occupations, and the production patterns of the world as they are affected by climatic and geological differences—a basis for comprehending the theory of international trade.

But the division of labor has disadvantages, too. People and nations become interdependent. The children can discuss what would happen to gingerbread-boy production if the child cutting the cookies refused to work, or if, in the cleaning of the classroom, the child assigned to chalkboards would not do the job.

Besides the division of labor, the invention of new and better tools and production methods enables men to produce faster and better. The comparisons of tools used in the past with present-day tools, a class experiment of working with and without tools, the observation of big machines—all these can convince children of the importance of tools in producing goods and services.

Children can be shown that making tools is a roundabout way of producing goods. Time and materials are needed for tools, but once they are made, more can be produced and in shorter time. The years children spend in school are a roundabout way of producing goods and services. Who can deny that more education leads to a higher standard of living? When children understand this, then they will realize why people who live from hand to mouth cannot afford to take time out to go to school or produce tools.

With men needing each other's products, a mechanism had to

be designed by which goods and services could be distributed. The children can experiment with barter. A baker with a toothache might be willing to give five loaves of bread to the dentist to fix his teeth, but since the dentist needs rather a pair of shoes, trade is frustrated. If the children "invent" money, they will discover the importance of price.

To discover how income, price, and tastes determine what people buy, the children might decide which ice cream they would buy if they had ten cents and if vanilla, strawberry, and chocolate all cost ten cents. After children have made their choices, they may be asked what flavor they would choose if the price of chocolate dropped to five cents. Finally, would they spend their dime on an electric train or a coloring book, assuming that the train cost fifty dollars and the coloring book ten cents? The rule can be formulated that people's spending depends on tastes, incomes, and the prices of goods.

Does the economic system function smoothly? Last year, one first-grader said that his father took his piggy-bank savings and promised to repay them if he got his job back. The child asked why his father lost his job and when he would get it back. The teacher had the problem of introducing the employment theory in an understandable form.

A game started with three children going to the "pretend" bank, applying for, and receiving loans for opening new businesses. They bought raw materials, hired labor, purchased tools, and started to produce food, clothing, and houses. After the goods were produced, and wages paid, the wives of the workers purchased all the food, clothing, and houses produced. The businessmen were encouraged to produce again. But now no one bought houses, as they already had them. The construction workers had to look for other jobs, which they eventually found in the clothing industry since the workers' wives bought more clothing than before.

These examples, all related to first-graders' experiences, and the principles abstracted from them represent the fundamental ideas of economic knowledge. These same ideas have to be discovered and re-discovered in succeeding grades, each time with greater depth and complexity. By the time children enter high school, they will be ready, not for minimum understandings, but for sophisticated economic generalizations.

◆§ ECONOMIC EDUCATION: PROBLEMS
AND PROGRAMS   *Harold J. Bienvenu*

*The role of economics in elementary school social studies has
been a strange one. We have had "economic topics" with us for
a long time; community helpers, banking, and transportation
are three common examples. But these units seldom have been
based on economic fact, and have even less often taught children much about the concepts and structure of economics.
Bienvenu gives us some sound examples of what a desirable
economic emphasis would be like.*

IN MATTERS OF curriculum, there is a strong tendency to confuse
words and deeds. If enough economic terms appear in study units—
terms like "community helpers," "banking," "transportation"—it is
easy and comforting to assume that economic education is an effective part of the curriculum.

This complacency often finds expression: "Economic education?
Why, we have units on money, banking, farming, trucking. Goodness! Our curriculum is full of economics!"

And so it is. The elementary-school curriculum is full of
economics. Yet real economic education exists in only a few elementary-school classrooms. Why? Teachers, curriculum leaders and administrators do not know enough about economics to discern the
inadequacy of much that today is accepted as economic education
in the elementary school. . . .

The elementary-school educator's lack of training in economics
is at the root of this special form of complacency. The complacency
may well lead to the belief that, in a unit labeled "Transportation,"
for example, children really learn about transportation, or that, in a
unit labeled "Banking," children actually learn about banking.

Action research carried out in the elementary-school classrooms
of the Cooperating Schools Program of the Joint Council on Economic Education suggests that this commonly held premise cannot
be supported. Studies in the twelve school systems (1) now engaged

Reprinted from "Economic Education: Problems and Programs," by Harold J.
Bienvenu in *The Elementary School Journal*, 59: 97–104. © Copyright November, 1958, by The University of Chicago Press. Used by permission. Dr. Bienvenu is a professor of education at Los Angeles State College.

in this program have led the participants to conclude that the typical elementary-school unit in banking or transportation has little or nothing to do with the economic function of those institutions. Thus, such units contribute little or nothing to economic education.

What is true of banking or transportation is also true of other phases of economic education in the elementary school. Since the entire subject can not be covered here, a few examples must suffice.

What does the child in elementary school learn from a typical banking unit? Primarily, that banks are safe storehouses for money. He also learns that banks perform services for people: checks are convenient for paying bills, and banks will kindly lend you money if you are honest and need the money for a good purpose. To be sure, most children learn that banks pay interest on deposits, and therefore it is not only virtuous but profitable to save money in banks. But the children have only the vaguest notion of why banks pay interest.

The basic economic functions of banking are ignored—not because the children are incapable of understanding the role of banks in the creation of money or in capital formation, but because the teacher does not understand this role and hence cannot effectively guide learning.

In units on transportation, children spend endless hours learning the speed of planes, the capacity of trucks, the power of locomotives. They visit roundhouses, truck terminals, and airports. They build models. The children learn a great deal about trucks, planes, and trains. Unfortunately, they learn almost nothing about transportation.

Teachers seldom present transportation as a process—the movement of persons and goods from one location to another—which has inevitable and demonstrable economic effects. The simple relation of improved transportation to increased specialization and to the subsequent intensification of interdependence is usually overlooked. Rarely are changes in transportation associated with changes in land values, prices, plant location, job opportunities, or community development. In short, most elementary units labeled "Transportation" deal with the material things of transportation—trucks, busses, planes, trains—rather than with transportation itself. Such units cannot qualify as economic education.

The elementary-school teacher's predilection for staying at the "thing" level in economic education, instead of developing principles and basic concepts, is not restricted to the teaching of transportation. This inclination affects other phases of economics and may be attributed to the teacher's inadequate preparation in this field. The function of transportation is lost in a procession of trailer trucks and cabooses. The economic function of banking is forgotten in the fascination of huge vaults and mechanical change-counters. The function of money is ignored in the pleasure of contemplating and computing the value of coins and currency from many lands. And, too often, the economics of international trade dwindles to a study of collections of curious cuckoo clocks, delicate damask, and fragile French figurines.

Along with a tendency to stay at the "thing" level, teachers often show an inclination toward economic moralizing. Community cooperation is extolled as a moral good—the "we should help each other so we will all be happy" approach. Certainly this approach is not objectionable if it supplements more realistic, tougher economic arguments. The point is that community specialization results in interdependence and forces co-operation—willing or unwilling, personal or impersonal. This forced co-operation, in turn, leads to greater efficiency and more goods and services for all. These are the hard, economic facts, devoid of a moral overlay.

In world affairs a moralistic approach may lead a teacher to teach that our foreign-aid program is undertaken almost exclusively as a moral obligation to the poor people of underdeveloped countries. It would seem that the economic motivation, with all its political implications, is unknown or unworthy.

Saving is often taught primarily as a moral virtue. Too many teachers still regard instalment-buying as less than respectable. The fact that our whole economy would collapse without the extensive use of credit seems to concern them not at all. In fact, some teachers may consider such a collapse a fitting end for a system not built on the puritan bedrock of cash-and-carry.

ECONOMICS AND SOCIETY

Another stricture on the typical economic-education program in elementary school is the emphasis placed on personal economics to the virtual exclusion of economics affecting our whole society. There is nothing intrinsically wrong with developing children's concern for sound budgeting, careful saving, wise buying, or adequate and comprehensive insurance programs. The development of this kind of personal economic competence is wholly proper and necessary in any program in economic education.

However, economic education is less than complete if learning is not permitted to rise above this personal level to a consideration, for instance, of the impact on the total economy of millions of free, personal decisions about saving and spending.

If the economic decisions of our nation are to be informed and wise, the schools must help build in each citizen an understanding of the operation of our economic system. In the American economy, the free decisions of free people in the free market act as the major determinant of what shall be produced, how it shall be produced, and how it shall be distributed. Exclusive emphasis on personal economics will never lead to such understandings.

THE ULTIMATE ECONOMIC PROBLEM

Effective economic education at every school level, including the elementary school, must ultimately lead to a consideration of the one basic economic problem: limited human and natural resources versus unlimited needs and desires. If instruction in personal economics does not result in an understanding of the economic problem that confronts all organized societies, neither will perfect teaching of banking, trade, transportation, or any other separate economic institution.

Whatever the institution studied, the stress should be on economic function not on "things." But the sum of the parts—money, banking, trade, transportation—does not equal the whole of economic education.

The entire scope of economics must be used in formulating the integrating theme for economic education in every grade and in every learning situation. The goal? To give every child what Ben Lewis has called, "a genuine sense of 'what it's all about' as far as the economic phases of our lives together are concerned—a 'feel' for economic issues—a rather clear impression of 'having been here before' in the presence of economic situations . . ." (2).

Is this too large an order for the elementary schools? Are the problems of elementary economic education, as some educators and economists contend, insoluble? Must economic education be restricted to the few in college who take courses in economics or to the fewer still who, as juniors or seniors, elect economics in those rare high schools that offer a formal economics course?

The answer is an emphatic "No!" Effective economic education in the elementary schools is feasible, as all the Joint Council Cooperating Schools are demonstrating. The principles and patterns evolving from the program can be used in any school system that is willing to devote the necessary time, energy, and resources.

Notes

(1) Now taking part in the Cooperating Schools Program of the Joint Council on Economic Education are the school systems of: Akron, Ohio; Decatur, Illinois; Indianapolis, Indiana; Kalamazoo, Michigan; Milwaukee, Wisconsin; Minneapolis, Minnesota; New York City, New York; Oklahoma City, Oklahoma;

Palo Alto, California; Portland, Oregon; Ridgewood, New Jersey; and University City, Missouri.

(2) Ben W. Lewis, *Economic Understanding: Why and What*, p. 14. New York: Joint Council on Economic Education, 1956.

ANTHROPOLOGY IN THE SOCIAL STUDIES CURRICULUM *George D. Spindler*

As with each of the other social sciences, there is more to anthropology than can be packed into elementary school social studies. Spindler confines his remarks to cultural anthropology and points out a number of instances in which he feels anthropology can make major contributions. He then suggests several ways that teachers can prepare themselves to translate the subject matter of anthropology into content for the social studies.

ANTHROPOLOGY—A SUBJECT until now studied mainly in colleges—can make an important contribution to the social-studies curriculums of elementary and secondary schools.

One of the reasons for this is that anthropology, with its accumulated knowledge of colorful societies, affords students an opportunity to study both the range of human motivations and the varying solutions that men have devised for the problems of existence. The social-studies teacher who can use this knowledge skillfully will offer his students fresh and stimulating insights into human behavior.

A second reason for using anthropological ideas and knowledge in the curriculum is that it is a synthesizing subject which pulls together seemingly unrelated parts of human behavior. In a complex society, a child may grow up with little understanding of the interrelationships of human groups. He may not understand that what a human group believes about God may have something to do with the way this group handles its economic problems or that the kind of technology a society has is related to the kinds of values motivating the behavior in that society.

Used by permission of the author and the *NEA Journal* from "Anthropology in the Social Studies Curriculum," 47:626–627, December, 1958. Dr. Spindler is a professor of education and anthropology at Stanford University.

The informed use of anthropological studies will help to create social-studies programs that produce these understandings in children.

WHAT is anthropology? As one noted anthropologist put it, "Anthropology is the study of Man—embracing Woman." And indeed, the subject is that comprehensive.

Its divisions include the study of human evolution and the physical similarities among the races of mankind (physical anthropology), the study of material traces of man's past existence (archaeology), the study of human languages (linguistics), the study of the history of human culture (ethnology), and the study of present-day societies and cultures (social, or cultural, anthropology). All these divisions are adaptable for use in elementary and secondary schools. This article deals mainly with cultural anthropology.

What do anthropologists do when they study a present-day society and its culture? The basic purpose of any research in the social sciences is to understand better why people behave as they do. The anthropologist is like any other social scientist in this ultimate goal. His approach differs in many subtle ways, but the major distinction is that his study is comparative, and that he is concerned with the whole of life—even when studying a specialized problem.

The social anthropologist compares the culture he examines to a number of human cultures, not merely to his own. He studies a way of life in order to describe its religion, family life, economics, language, and the like, in such a way as to allow an understanding of the relationships between these factors.

Cultural anthropologists also work on special problems. Some are interested in the ways in which cultural values affect behavior; some in the ways in which language forms thought and how language and thought are related to other dimensions of behavior. Others are interested in the ways in which cultures change and how the change affects values and psychological adjustment. One group of anthropologists studies the ways in which education develops and how it is affected by culture.

SINCE anthropology can be useful in the social-studies program, educators responsible for these programs will want to know how to integrate anthropological materials and concepts into the curriculum.

Many specialists in elementary education suggest that intercultural experiences and concepts be introduced at very early grade levels. I feel that a very early introduction of intercultural concepts to children can be confusing to them unless the teacher is exceptionally skilled in building realistic bridges of experience from the child's world to the very different words in other cultures.

My recommendation is that any serious introduction to anthropological thinking be reserved for approximately grades 5 and 6. In many schools, geography receives special attention during this period. In connection with this subject, simple notions of cultural diversity can be presented, with descriptions of ways of life ranging from the hunting and gathering societies to settled peasant societies.

Ways of getting and distributing food and other necessities, the use of tools and weapons, the kinds of things made and used by human hands, the part magic plays in the beliefs and behavior of peoples, and perhaps family life and childhood—all these can be examined. Realism can be afforded by films and slides, by music, by using simple materials and utensils, and perhaps by dramatic role-playing.

IN THE sophomore and junior years of high school, more complex understandings of the nature of cultural values and the way in which they motivate different kinds of behavior can be developed in the social-studies program. Students at this age can grasp the meaning of cultural integration—how the parts of a culture work in relation to each other, and how they support the values of the society.

At this level, it also becomes more feasible to present students with an analysis of the ways in which various social institutions, such as the family, the institutions of social control, and religious bodies, work in different societies to serve the same basic purposes. High-school students can grasp what younger children probably cannot: that although cultures and societies are highly diverse, the same parts exist in each of them, and basically for the same reasons.

During the high-school years, the horizons of young people expand rapidly; these students can be introduced to the idea of cultural change, particularly to changes in the world areas where the impact of America and Europe has been the greatest.

IN TEACHING anthropology at either the elementary or high-school level, the teacher will have to seek and adapt materials for class use. Books written by anthropologists are often exciting in their descriptions of the exotic and diverse ways of man's life, but they are often too difficult for either elementary or secondary students.

The teacher will have to read these books and pass the information on to students. He can also help his students by preparing simplified written materials about anthropology and by using films and slides in the classroom.

Studying the many available books on anthropology will also give the teacher more than a perfunctory knowledge of the subject.

It is most important that he be well informed before he begins teaching anthropology, for only then can he present this subject without inadvertently adding his own viewpoints and prejudices.

In the hands of a partially informed teacher, another people's religion becomes superstition, and their earth lodges become hovels, because the teacher sees these things from his own cultural experience, and not from the necessary crosscultural point of view.

Merely reading books on anthropology will not be enough; the teacher will need special training if he is to present this subject capably. At least one full semester of work is needed, beginning with broad courses that combine introductions to the various divisions of the field. Intermediate-level courses should then be taken, such as culture change, prehistory, comparative social organization, primitive religion and art, language and culture, and world ethnography.

An ideal approach is for a group of social-studies teachers to form a special study class in a university. This group, with the guidance of an interested anthropologist, can select materials and plan studies both for classroom use and for their own instruction.

Teachers may at first find it difficult to use anthropological knowledge in their teaching, and many have trouble acquiring the needed new materials. But the pioneering effort will be worth the struggle. Our children will be the winners when well-informed teachers are able to offer them learning opportunities in social studies enriched by the contributions from anthropology.

✍§ New Viewpoints in Sociology

E. Merle Adams, Jr.

This selection provides a perspective on sociology as a discipline and insight into a number of topics commonly taught within that discipline. Structure, process, institutions, culture—these are but a few of the intellectual tools of the sociologist. Adams identifies eight institutions necessary to the functioning of a local community. His explanation of these institutions suggests a number of possible roles they could play in the teaching of the social studies.

THE STUDY OF PATTERNS OF BEHAVIOR

Single sentence definitions are of doubtful utility; nevertheless, sociology may be defined briefly as the empirical scientific study of the structure and process of systems of interaction among humans ("social actors," as many sociologists tend now to call them). On the most general level, this means that the sociologist observes the consistencies or patterns of behavior which humans manifest as they are oriented to each other and as they share common values. These patterns of interaction may be analyzed as *systems;* that is, sociologists are better able to understand and, to a certain degree, predict behavior if they regard it as made up of units or "parts" all of which are interrelated. Thus a society is analyzed as a system made up of units which, at the appropriate levels, are institutions, groups or "collectivities," ecological complexes, and status-roles. More will be said about the idea of "system" shortly; the important point is that sociologists tend to look at any specific pattern of social interaction as part of a larger whole.

When the sociologist is engaged in studying the units or parts of a system of action, it is said that he is analyzing its *structure.* For example, in the analysis of a family system, the structural aspect involves a description of the status-roles of its members, their responsibilities, rights, and rewards. When he proceeds to the analysis of *process*, the sociologist studies the relationships among these status-roles in the family and their modification through time. . . .

It is also important to note that the behavior which the sociologist observes is patterned in part because it is *value-oriented*. The values to which the members of an action system are oriented are to some degree shared, are always learned through experience, and are to some degree passed on to the succeeding generation. That is, the value-orientations constitute a *culture*. . . .

THE LEVEL OF THE LOCAL COMMUNITY

Although all . . . areas in the field of sociology are potentially of interest to the teacher of social studies, some have a more direct bearing on his professional functions than others. In focusing on a

Used by permission of the author and the National Council for the Social Studies; from its Twenty-Eighth Yearbook, *New Viewpoints in the Social Sciences*, 1958, pp. 97–103. E. Merle Adams, Jr. is an associate professor of sociology at the University of North Dakota.

few of the new viewpoints in sociology which are most pertinent—
in order to make the most headway and avoid randomness—a particular level for discussion should be selected. It seems that the level
of the *local community* will be the most useful for purposes here,
especially when the strong links between the public schools and the
community are considered. . . .

We shall approach the community as a local system of action
made up of certain basic institutions. This analysis will apply primarily to "urbanized" communities, since, with 64 percent of our
population living in such communities, they have become a most
significant phenomenon. According to the Bureau of Census, an
"urbanized area consists of one or more cities of 50,000 or more and
all the nearby closely settled suburban territory, or urban fringe." (1)
This is a new definition of "urban" population and reflects the
necessity to adjust the classification of population data so that
recognition can be given to the rapid growth of settled areas surrounding cities. Increasingly, our population has become not so much
city dwellers as "suburban dwellers" and the prospect for the future
is that this trend will continue (2).

Analyzing the community as a local system of action does not
imply that it is an isolated or self-subsistent entity. It must be recognized that there are numerous relationships between the institutions
of a given community and those of other communities. There are
significant governmental, economic, and cultural relationships among
communities. Further, there is considerable movement of population
between communities although the extent is only recently becoming
known. Actually, the local community should also be analyzed as a
sub-system within a larger regional or national system. Nevertheless,
the local urbanized community contains enough of the essential life
activities of its members to constitute a meaningful unit of study.

Before listing the basic institutions essential to the functioning
of a community as a system, we need to consider briefly what is
meant by the term "institution": First, an institution is a pattern of
behavior which has a certain probability of occurrence; that is, the
behavior in question occurs over and over again given the appropriate
conditions. For example, young people in our communities "leave
home" when they become socially mature; they nearly always marry
and/or take jobs and set up a place of residence apart from their
original family. Although this is not legally compulsory, it is consistent enough to be considered a significant part of the institutional
structure of the family.

Second, institutionalized behavior is, as Parsons points out,
"legitimately expected," that is, it is considered morally right and
members of an action system have a right to expect the behavior

to be forthcoming (3). Thus, in the example of the family, we say that young people have a right to "get out on their own" and have their own family, and that their parents and others may expect this of them.

Third, institutionalized behavior is behavior which has become a matter of self-expectation. This means that the social actor not only feels the pressure of others' expectations of him but that he also expects it of himself. It has become a part of the controlling mechanisms of his personality, of his "super-ego" in psychoanalytic terms. Thus, in the example of the family, the young person who does not achieve some independence from the family in which he grew up will, unless there are special conditions such as the necessity of care for an invalid parent, suffer from internal pressures.

Fourth, the pattern of behavior may be considered an institution if it is a significant part of the structure of the local community system; that is, the functioning of the rest of the institutions in the system would be seriously disturbed if the pattern in question were to disappear or be materially altered. Thus, to return again to the example of the family, if young people did not "get on their own" and establish their own families, it is doubtful whether they would be able to achieve the degree of job mobility which seems to be demanded by our occupational structure. This would be a serious consequence for our industrial system.

THE EIGHT INSTITUTIONS OF A LOCAL COMMUNITY SYSTEM

We may consider a local community system to be made up of the following eight institutions which are necessary to its functioning:

1. kinship (or family)
2. occupation
3. exchange
4. property
5. authority
6. stratification
7. education
8. religion

These institutions are defined in terms of the functions which they serve for the community; each institution solves certain basic problems which must be faced if the community system is to exist and grow. Thus the institution of *kinship* or family takes account of the basic human factors of age, sex, biological relatedness, and the considerable care necessitated by the helplessness and plasticity of the newborn child. Our kinship system is distinctive by reason of the small size and independence of its basic unit, the "conjugal" or "nuclear" family, consisting of father, mother, and immature children.

The institution of *occupation* refers to the organization of work or "job" roles in the community. The occupational structure in

American communities is characterized by a high degree of division of labor, elaborate specializations, and a complex organizational structure. *Exchange* as an institution represents the manner in which things of value are regularly transferred from one individual or group to another. Our institution of exchange is characterized by a market system and media of exchange which make for easy transfer of goods and services. *Property* refers to the way in which individuals or groups hold and exercise rights in things of value. Three types of property rights should be distinguished: control, use, and disposal. With respect to any given item of property, these rights may be vested in one person or group as in the classical case of "private property," or distributed among different persons and groups as in the case of modern "corporate property." The three institutions of occupation, exchange, and property are often grouped together by sociologists under the heading of "economic institutions." There is considerable basis for such grouping since they are in fact always closely inter-related. However, the use of the term "occupation" here is somewhat broader than that usually implied by the label "economic organization." As herein defined, work roles in the areas of business and industry, education, government and even religion would be considered occupations if the division of labor is carried to the point where the holder of the role devotes a major portion of his time to it and relies upon it for his "living."

Authority as an institution in the community refers to the recognized right exercised by certain individuals in controlling or influencing the behavior of other individuals. If it is to be stable and effective, authority must be recognized as legitimate by those subject to it. Control which is effective but not recognized as legitimate or "right" may be termed "power." The institutionalized patterns of authority include not only those formally structured arrangements which are usually subsumed under "government," but also those informal patterns of control and influence which are not legally or officially designated. Our communities characteristically show an informal pattern of authority of broad scope while, at the same time, formal structures have been greatly elaborated. *Stratification* refers to the differential distribution of prestige among persons in the community. Some persons and families are always ranked higher than others on a scale of relative evaluation. The criteria upon which such ranking is based always involve both "ascribed" and "achieved" elements in varying degrees. Family background and inherited wealth and position are the principal elements of ascription; they involve an evaluation of the person on the basis of "who" he is rather than what he can do and how well. Achieved elements include any evaluation of the person based on his performance which can be altered through effort; the principal modern example is that of ranking based on occupational performance. Our communities show a stratification pattern in which considerable stress is placed upon occupational achievement and social mobility, "being a success and rising in the community," although family background and differential opportunities, particularly in education, play a large part in the rank which any given person enjoys.

The institution of *education* is the pattern of deliberate and systematic facilitation of the learning process beyond that provided in the kinship structure and in general participations in the community. Here the meaning of the term is somewhat more restricted than is often the case in common usage which would include under "education" all learning, whatever the conditions. However, some restriction is necessary if we are to distinguish adequately between institutional structures and the vastly differing conditions for learning which they provide. Education in the present sense refers to systematic training provided in a separate organizational context, for example, a school in which the teacher as an occupational specialist functions. Many communities, particularly those which are primitive, limited in size and changing very slowly, have managed to get along with a minimum of such educational structure. Our modern communities, however, show a high degree of development of formal educational organization and we expect a wide variety of functions to be handled by such procedures.

Finally, *religion* as an institution refers to the pattern of beliefs and rites to which community members adhere. The beliefs define the ultimate nature of the world and man's place in it; they define what the social order should be and why it is right. They provide interpretations of the basic crises of life, such as birth and death; in short, they provide answers to fundamental moral questions which underlie the institutional structure of the community. The rites, or religious ceremonies and observances, are standardized behavior on special occasions which express the moral and ideological commitments contained in the religious beliefs. Our communities manifest a large number of religious sects and denominations representing a wide variety of organizational types; yet, there is a relatively low level of religious conflict.

References

(1) U. S. Bureau of the Census. *1950 Census of Population* (Vol. I.) Washington, D.C.: Superintendent of Documents, Government Printing Office, 1953.

(2) For a discussion of this trend see Bogue, Donald J. *Population Growth in Standard Metropolitan Areas.* U. S. Housing and Home Finance Agency, Washington, D.C.: Superintendent of Documents, Government Printing Office, 1953. See also Bogue, Donald J. *Metropolitan Decentralization: A Study of Differential Growth,* 1950.

Bogue, Donald J. "Urbanism in the United States." *American Journal of Sociology,* 60:471–86; March 1955.

(3) Parsons, Talcott. *Essays in Sociological Theory Pure and Applied.* Glencoe, Ill.: Free Press, 1949. p. 276.

❧ SOCIAL PSYCHOLOGY
Wilbur G. Miller and *Joel E. Greene*

Miller and Greene provide a rationale for the discipline of social psychology and specify the concept of interaction *as a key to understanding the behavior of man. The primary teacher readily recognizes the major role that interaction plays in the usual content of the early grades. The teacher in the upper elementary grades could well make more use of this concept as she guides pupils through the events of history or the relationships among peoples today.*

IN MANY EDUCATIONAL systems the social studies teacher is by choice or by force placed in situations where he must assume the role of a social psychologist. To be sure, psychology may not be formally listed in the unit or lesson plan in use by the teacher at the moment, but it would be a strange class indeed that could discuss in any meaningful fashion many of the issues typically covered in the social studies area without considering, to some extent, the individual and how he interacts with his environment. It is very common in the classroom for questions to be raised related to social issues involving conflicts between nations, between communities, between political parties, and perhaps, even between neighbors. It is a misleading teacher who discusses these issues totally in terms of external environmental factors such as economical and geographical variables; most teachers at one time or another have found it necessary to bring into the discussion the characteristics of the persons involved in these social issues.

Used by permission of the authors and the National Council for the Social Studies; from its Twenty-Eighth Yearbook, *New Viewpoints in the Social Sciences,* 1958, pp. 144–147. Both authors are associate professors of psychology at the University of Denver.

To neglect a consideration of the human individual with all of his intellect, emotions, desires, prejudices, previous learning experiences, and motivations is to ignore extremely important aspects of the social issues themselves. In discussing these factors related to the interaction of the individual and his environment the social studies teacher is approaching the areas of interest of social psychologists. . . .

What differentiates social psychology from the other branches of social science? For that matter, what differences are there between social psychology and other areas of psychology? These questions are not easily answered; no one subject matter has exclusive claim to the many-faceted problems of individuals and society. There are, however, different ways of attacking these problems and, also, diverse levels at which scientific explanation can be attempted. It is with a consideration of these two factors that social psychology comes into its own. More than any other social science, social psychology is concerned with the study of the individual person. Where areas such as sociology and cultural anthropology are most commonly concerned with the analysis and description of social and cultural systems, social psychology is more concerned with the individual and how these social stimuli affect him. Of course, a knowledge of both the social system and the individual is important to a total understanding of the problems of society and hence there is a great overlap and interchange between all of the social sciences. It is the intense interest in and concentration on the behavior of the individual, however, that differentiates social psychology from the other social science areas.

All areas of psychology are concerned with the study of the individual. What, then, differentiates social psychology from other branches of psychology? Social psychology seems to be differentiated in terms of the nature of the problems investigated. General psychology with its emphasis on research related to basic psychological processes and its history of experimental laboratory work serves as a foundation for research in social psychology. When we become interested in the individual in a social setting, however, and when we become concerned with how the reactions of an organism are influenced by other members of a group, we are getting into the realm of social psychology. Obviously, there cannot be, nor should there be, sharp distinctions between the various areas of psychology. Specialization has occurred in psychology just as in most other sciences and it has become traditional to place many of the more socially oriented psychological problems, for example, group influences and interaction, prejudice, attitudes, leadership, propaganda, and the like, under the heading of social psychology.

Considering the preceding discussion then, social psychology could be defined as *the scientific investigation of the behavior of individuals in relation to their social environment.* The two terms behavior and social environment in the definition are used quite generically. The word behavior is used to include any measurable effect of stimuli impinging upon the organism. Some authors would speak of the study of an individual's feelings, or thoughts, or experiences rather than or perhaps in addition to behavior. While all of these terms are perfectly acceptable in the terminology of psychology, the word behavior is used here as the inclusive term in order to emphasize the necessity for observing some identifiable and measurable aspects of the human being. We can only infer experiences and thought processes of the individual through some type of measurable reaction or activity. Social environment as used in the definition would include stimuli which we ordinarily identify with society and culture, as well as those resulting from the actual or implied presence of other individuals. One of the main goals of social psychology is to understand how the behavior of an individual is influenced by other human beings.

In studying behavior in the social situation one must be careful not to imply a cause and effect relationship, an assumption that the type of environment necessarily determines the type of behavior. This is mentioned because many of the present day social studies teachers were reared in the early behavioristic tradition which accounted for the actions of individuals in terms of analyses and descriptions of the environment. Historically, explanatory concepts in psychology have shifted back and forth in emphasis between the individual and the environment. On the one hand was the approach that much of the behavior of humans could be explained in terms of physical structure and instinct and, to a great extent, our external environment was merely a result of the fulfillment of these instincts. At the other extreme was the idea that the behavior of individuals was the complete and total result of the particular environment and hence an understanding of environment would bring about an understanding of behavior. Today psychologists realize that explanatory principles must come from a study of the *interaction* of the individual and his environment. It should be made clear that this emphasis on interaction does not minimize the importance of knowledge or study about either the environment or the individual. It does indicate, however, that as we have gained more facts and information about each, we have become aware of the futility of employing only one of them in our explanations of behavior. It is this concept of interaction which must be used as a frame of reference in understanding human behavior.

The Multidisciplinary Nature of the Social Studies

ACADEMIC SPECIALIZATION marks research and writing within every social science discipline. Specialization tends to foster division within a subject, with the result that the interdisciplinary nature of the social sciences is often overlooked. But although each academic discipline has its framework for studying man, sooner or later, as an idea is pursued within that framework, each discipline comes into contact with other disciplines. History not only draws on data from every social science but dips into the humanities and science; so it is with each of the social sciences. And just as the social sciences are interdisciplinary, so the social studies are multidisciplinary.

John Jarolimek makes a clear case for drawing on many disciplines in selecting social studies content. Bruce R. Joyce provides a reasoned study of the relationships among ideas—ideas that transcend disciplinary boundaries—and Hanna and Lee list a series of generalizations that clearly cannot be thought of as drawn from any single discipline.

Two approaches to citizenship education are described in Oliver's article, and the second approach is illustrated with the sort of source material that should be used more than it is. Muessig and Rogers take up that persistent question of patriotism and provide us with a logically and psychologically sound approach to its solution. The Williamstown Workshop report brings out a number of methods of studying the Bill of Rights which are useful for the elementary and junior high grades.

No one can be informed by reading only history books—all of us need to keep up with the news. William J. Shorrock makes a reasonable case for the use of periodicals in the classroom, and J. D. McAulay illustrates the use of current events in social studies programs. And as we read the news, we are aware of many controversial issues embedded in contemporary events; to comprehend these issues, we must draw on our knowledge of many subjects. John P. Lunstrum reviews the sources and nature of controversy; and Robert L. Brackenbury builds on Lunstrum, making a case for utilizing controversy in elementary grade classrooms.

Social studies is more than the study of man in local, state, and national communities. The study of other peoples and their ways of life are being increasingly stressed in all grades. One serious problem in studying others has been our tendency to settle for stereotypes. Leonard S. Kenworthy not only strikes hard at this tendency, but suggests an appealing pattern for studying other countries. Preston focuses on a number of educational tasks required to build a comprehensive and balanced study of the peoples of the world. Merrill F. Hartshorn reports on the efforts of a school district to build a social studies program that gives specific and conscious attention to the study of world affairs.

✎§ CURRICULUM CONTENT AND THE CHILD IN THE ELEMENTARY SCHOOL   John Jarolimek

As academic specialization has increased in the social sciences, investigators have found themselves borrowing ideas and tools of analysis usually associated with related disciplines. For example, descriptive and interpretive geography uses data from history, economics, political science, anthropology, and sociology. Political science, in turn, draws content and methods of analysis from sociology, anthropology, and social psychology in dealing with the idea of social organization. One result of this trend has been an increased synthesis of subject matter from several disciplines in developing social studies programs. Jarolimek provides a number of illustrations of the interdisciplinary nature of elementary school social studies topics.

WITH SO MUCH to learn and so little time to learn it, one would think that we would set priorities for ourselves in working with children in the social studies. Part of our problem relating to content selection is that many of us have not established priorities; we have not put first things first. We have, in fact, set out to do things in our social studies programs which are simply impossible to accomplish. We set goals which more properly encompass the total life of the

Used by permission of the author and the National Council for the Social Studies; from *Social Education*, 26:58–62, 117–120, February, 1962. John Jarolimek is a professor of education at the University of Washington.

child—in his home, church, neighborhood—rather than focusing upon those which are in some way unique to the social studies. We add new topics to our programs as freely as though we did not already have enough with which to concern ourselves. Elementary social studies cannot continue to be an academic museum for the collection of topics which do not seem to fit into the curriculum anywhere else. The idea that any topic which provides opportunities for social experiences for children is legitimate content for the social studies is unsound and should be discarded. As long as socializing experiences are accepted as the unifying theme of the social studies, the content will not occupy the position of importance which it deserves. The unifying theme in social studies units should properly be the development of some key idea—a concept, a principle, or a generalization—related to some problem of significance in the lives of the pupils, rather than socializing experiences, *per se.* . . .

It has been said that science and social studies have much in common because they both employ problem-solving procedures. Arithmetic also utilizes problem-solving procedures. All of them utilize reading and language. On this basis anything and everything becomes social studies. Consequently, the term "social studies" is stripped of any specialized meaning. If the social studies consist of everything in general, they become nothing in particular. This subversion of the social studies makes it nearly impossible for this area of the curriculum to contribute in a unique way to the education of pupils. The question we need to ask ourselves is not *whether* something can be related and incorporated in the social studies, but rather, *should it?* And the answer to that question is that it should *not* if by so doing we emasculate the legitimate content of the social studies.

It seems odd that such confusion has developed regarding the source of social studies content. If the activities of man are a proper area of concern for the social studies, then their content should be drawn from those organized bodies of knowledge which deal with basic social activities of man. As we study man's ways of living, we are immediately struck with the intimate relationship between man and his surroundings. His ways of living are conditioned by his physical environment. We can call this "earth-man relationships" if we choose, but it is really geography. Content from geography should play an important part in a well-designed elementary social studies program.

Similarly, history provides us with much content for our social studies. Here we have the story of man's successes and failures in his attempt to achieve those goals and values which he associates with the good life. In history the child can learn of the forces which have brought him to this precise moment in time. And as he, himself, blazes trails into the future, he can secure confidence and direction from the pathways of the past.

Nothing will affect the life of our young citizen more directly than the satisfaction of his needs and wants. Thousands of times in his lifetime it will be necessary for him to make decisions on economic matters, both in his personal life and as a member of society. He needs to be equipped with an understanding of how his life is enmeshed in the complex economic system in which he lives. Here we have a vast and largely untapped source of content for our elementary social studies programs.

Sociology and anthropology also provide us with content which can lead the child to important learnings in the social studies. Content from these disciplines helps the pupil develop an understanding of group life in society. Problems of group living centering on the home and family, the school, the neighborhood and community provide important areas of study and investigation for the elementary school child.

The group life of man must necessarily be one governed by some system of law and order. From the dawn of history man has been developing ways to insure orderly processes in human relations. Pupils should develop a deep appreciation of the struggle which man has made in order to implement the concept that governments derive their just power from the consent of the governed. A thorough knowledge of our system of government, the responsibilities which it exacts, and a complete commitment to freedom on the part of individual citizens is prerequisite to the proper functioning of our system of government. . . .

It is not necessary for us to go shopping about for new sources of content for the social studies. What we really need to do is to learn more about these organized bodies of knowledge called the social sciences. We need to know the major conclusions which have been achieved by these disciplines. We need to know the unique way each of them studies the problems of man and arrives at conclusions. We need to know how we can translate and adapt the rich and interesting content with which each of them provides us, to the language, life, and experiences of young children.

At the elementary level we are, of course, concerned with general education. We are not concerned with the preparation of historians, geographers, economists, sociologists, political scientists, or anthropologists. Nor are we interested in designing programs merely to have children learn these subjects. Instead, we would hope that the pupils would develop a familiarity with some of the basic and elementary knowledge of these disciplines in order that they might better understand the social problems of the world in which they live.

At this point a most difficult problem presents itself. That is, what content from the social sciences should be included in the elementary program? In the social studies we have never devised any really satisfactory way of selecting important ideas for our programs nor validating them once they are selected. Teachers and curriculum builders are not the best persons to make these choices since they obviously could not be thoroughly and equally competent in all of these fields. Social scientists, on the other hand, know their disciplines but lack an understanding of young children. It would seem that the only sensible way to proceed is to have social scientists and elementary educators work together on content selection. Each of the disciplines should be asked to answer this question: What are the basic, fundamental, key ideas from your discipline which ought to be a part of the general education of all citizens, no matter who they are or what they do? . . .

Once the key ideas from each of the disciplines are identified and analyzed, it becomes possible for the curriculum specialist to translate them into expectancies representing varying levels of difficulty. These can then be arranged in a sequential, spiraling pattern appropriate to varying levels of maturity. Thus, throughout the grades of the elementary school one could easily discern a systematic development of key ideas from the various social sciences. In this program one would see all of the external evidences of good social studies instruction. There would be a proper concern for the development of attitudes and social skills. At the same time, the program would be rich in content, thoughtfully and sequentially planned, moving pupils ever onward toward a higher level of understanding of the problems of man. The essential point here is that the basic ideas from the social sciences would be so carefully identified and thoroughly analyzed that all instruction at all grade levels would point in the direction of achieving some one or more of these important understandings.

Under the arrangement just described, we would not need to be too concerned about the actual topics selected for study. These could be allowed to vary, since the major learnings with which we are concerned transcend any specific topic. Fundamentally, topics selected for unit study should be considered as models or exemplars rather than being highly important in and of themselves. This seems absolutely essential since it is utterly impossible for the pupil to study all human societies, past and present, even in several lifetimes, let alone the few years he has in school. The teacher must, of necessity, use selected specific topics to get across basic learnings which can be widely applied in situations yet to be encountered by the pupil. . . .

In selecting topics for use as models, we need to be a great deal more imaginative than we have been in the past. In the preceding 20 years a great many significant developments have taken place in the world. New geographical areas have gained in importance. International relations have become a dominant concern of the United States. Transportation and communication systems have been fantastically improved over what they were 20 years ago. Children have many more opportunities to learn about the world than they once did. We could make an almost endless list of developments of this type. Yet we do not often see these developments reflected in the selection of social studies topics to any marked degree.

But even the traditional topics could stand some up-dating. To cite just one example, let us take units on the home and family in grade one. Today many American children come from homes in which there is only one parent, not two. In many families the mother not only makes the beds, does the cooking, and does all the other things that mothers are supposed to do, but also is employed full time outside the home. A great many children would find it difficult to visit grandfather's farm on a week-end because their grandfather lives halfway across the country. Not all first graders are the oldest children in their families as we like to teach, and some may have parents who are as old as the grandparents of some of their classmates. In spite of the many changes which have occurred in family living, we often present the traditional picture of family life. All topics selected for study at all grade levels should be examined critically to make sure they represent present-day situations accurately. One of the things we cannot afford to do is to give twentieth-century pupils nineteenth-century concepts of the world.

✑§ CONTENT FOR ELEMENTARY SOCIAL STUDIES
Bruce R. Joyce

Perhaps no one has stirred the pedagogical world during the past few years quite as Jerome Bruner has. His writings on

structure and his thoughts about the function of relationships
among ideas have found expression in several new proposals
for restructuring the social studies. Among the best of the ex-
pansions of Bruner's ideas is this article by Joyce. He analyzes
relationships especially well in identifying three major functions of structural ideas.

Not only should his comments be useful in planning for
children, but they should be helpful in studying the social
sciences.

SCHOLARLY KNOWLEDGE has reached the point where complete factual knowledge of any field has become an impossibility even for the
advanced scholar. More than ever before in the history of education,
we need to devise a method of analysis which will enable us to sort
out the truly important and organize it in such a way that the relatively few things we are able to teach will have maximum educational
effect.

THE NOTION OF STRUCTURE

For a good many years educators have worked for an arrangement
whereby the central ideas used in the various scholarly fields be
identified by practicing scholars and translated into a form which
would assure that even the younger pupil be taught up-to-date ideas
and ways of thinking. Chapter XIV of Dewey's *Democracy and
Education* deals with the "Nature of Subject Matter" and suggests
that the logical arrangements of a discipline consist in an organization of the major ideas of that field (1). . . .

Charles Hubbard Judd similarly proposed: "Let a specialist in a
given field indicate those lines of thought which his special study
has shown him to be significant and worthy of attention on the part
of pupils in schools. Then let some teacher who understands the way
in which ideas should be presented to immature minds organize a
teaching unit based on the material furnished by the specialist (2).

Alfred North Whitehead, speaking of the problem of selection
from available content, made the suggestion in a little different form
when he suggested that few especially illuminating ideas be identified
and that these be introduced early and reiterated until the learner can

Used by permission of the author and the National Council for the Social
Studies; from *Social Education*, 28:84–87 and 103, February, 1964. Bruce R.
Joyce is an assistant professor of education at the University of Chicago.

use their power. "Let the main ideas which are introduced into a child's education be few and important, and let them be thrown into every combination possible. The child should make them his own, and should understand their application here and now in the circumstances of his actual life. From the very beginning of his education, the child should experience the joy of discovery. The discovery which he has to make is that general ideas give an understanding of that stream of events which pours through his life, which is his life." (3)

Recently, Jerome Bruner has restated and popularized this approach to the analysis of subject matter (4). Bruner's formulation rests on the contention that the product of scholarly endeavor is a series of major ideas or relationships which explain the findings of the field. The scholar collects facts and thinks about them. The relationships he sees or thinks he sees among them are the heart of his knowledge, for it is in the light of these relationships that the facts are explained. These relationships Bruner refers to as elements of the *structure* of the discipline. . . .

The potential utility of structural ideas in education is very great. Since they are the part of a discipline which has the greatest "explaining power" the learner who masters them will be able to understand information much more coherently. Also, since they are relatively few in number, they are more manageable than the masses of data from which they are drawn—they are a kind of map of the fields of raw data—and the child who is introduced to them will have at his command the most powerful scholarly ideas which we possess.

Bruner has provided us with a series of hypotheses concerning the application of structure to education.

1. The major structural ideas of scholarly disciplines are essentially very simple.
2. These ideas can be developed in a form that even young children can discover (in childish terms, at first, and progressively in more sophisticated forms).
3. Structural ideas can be utilized as organizing themes in curriculums, being reiterated and rediscovered in more complex and adequate terms.
4. The child who is taught in such a way that he discovers the structural ideas in discipline will be advantaged in that:
   a. Structure facilitates memeory. Learning how things are related makes it easier to remember facts.
   b. Structure provides intellectual power by ensuring greater comprehension of the area concerned.
   c. Structure facilitates transfer of learning to new situations and problems.

d. Structure is the language of the scholar. By learning structure the learner is brought closer to the leading edge of the discipline. He learns to think with the most advanced minds in the field (5).

These hypotheses are so tantalizing that one might ask why we don't immediately proceed to select those structures which appear to help us best accomplish our objective of social education and proceed to the experiments we will need to test these hypotheses. . . .

When one concentrates on the mathematics curriculum, he can call together mathematicians and educators, and they can concentrate their attention on the structure of a single discipline. Furthermore, it is clear that a portion of the curriculum will be focused on mathematical content alone. The political scientist, asked to contribute to a discussion of the social studies, knows that the content from his discipline will be mixed with that of several others. His ideas have to be placed in context with those of the economist, historian, and so on. What may be a more serious problem in the examination of the social sciences is that the older ones have not had a tradition of quantitative methods. Their structures have, therefore, not been expressed in the terms of mathematical logic which so helps us sort out the content of the natural sciences. The new social sciences, while they have been built on a tradition of quantitative approaches, have the problem of newness. Their content is emerging and developing at such a rate that their taxonomies, terms, and methods are less discrete and definite than are those of the older disciplines. A third problem is that the social world itself is so elusive, so much in flux, and holds still for study so less readily than does the physical world. For example, social psychology defines attitudes in several ways, and attitudes manifest themselves in many ways and vary enormously according to numerous conditions. This uncertainty in the social sciences is reflected in the relatively different statistical levels of confidence which are utilized in the social and the natural sciences. The psychologist will accept a proposition at the 5 percent level. Imagine a physicist who reported that we could accept his observation that day is brighter than night, with the probability that he could be correct 19 out of 20 times! But that is the relative uncertainty with which we live in the social sciences.

Eventually, any approach to the determination of the social sciences to find their structures will have to take the form of a long-term effort by scholars representing the several social sciences and educators who combine both acquaintance with behavioral sciences and sophistication in translating ideas into operational constructs which can be approached by children. . . .

STRUCTURE AND CERTAINTY

Let us turn again to the question "What is structure?" Bruner explains that it is "the way things are related." What he means, really, is that structure is the way we think things are related. He gives the example of an inchworm crawling up graph paper held at various inclinations. The inchworm varies his angle of progression across the graph paper so that his angle of climb does not exceed a certain proportion. We have discovered a *relation* between slope and climb. Now, one may ask how the identification of that relationship helps us select content for the child to learn. It doesn't, very much, but before we make a hasty conclusion, let us examine some other living organisms to see if they control their movements in patterns analogous to those of the inchworm. We can look, for example, at movements of the sunflower plant. Lo and behold, we find that the sunflower reacts to direction and intensity of illumination, turning its blossom to face the light source. We could examine further examples, but the point is clear. We have discovered what we presently call tropism, an innate tendency to react to a stimulus in a definite way. Now, the tropistic relationship between organisms and stimuli becomes a structural idea in those sciences which study the behavior of living things. A person who discovers the idea of tropism is prepared to investigate many behaviors in living things.

Bruner suggests that if we can identify major ideas like these we will have identified the organization of the discipline concerned. By teaching these structural ideas, or by introducing them to the child, we will help him to identify an organization for the things he learns, an organization which will be in accord with the way the scholar organizes the information from his discipline. If we follow these structural ideas, says Bruner, we will avoid teaching fragmented bits of knowledge from a field, because the structural ideas are themselves of relationships which have been at least tentatively established. The child will thus have better comprehension of the field and an easier time remembering what he has learned, and his learning will be much closer to the front-line thinking in the field. Further, since learning which stresses structural relationships within a field emphasizes the identification of relationships, a program of instruction which is centered around structures will emphasize the discovery of relationships by the child and hence prepare him to be an independent thinker. Bruner rather carefully stresses that the structural idea which the child forms need not be the same form as the idea possessed by the scholar. The child should discover the structures in a form which he can handle, and then rediscover more and more complex and adequate forms of the structure as he proceeds through the curriculum. This practice in revising ideas will teach him to hold them tentatively and prevent him from developing the erroneous notion that present knowledge will last for all time. . . .

We are now in a position to make a tentative statement of the function of structural ideas.

First of all, they are expressions of generalizations concerning the data of a field. They are the ideas which show how things are related in any given sphere of enquiry.

Second, they are the basis for organizing knowledge in a field. Facts are classified according to the way they relate to other facts. In the example of tropism, for example, the behavior of certain animals and plants would be classified together because of their similarity.

Third, structure guides the search for future knowledge. It does this in two ways. Sometimes knowledge is looked for because a relationship has been discovered in another place. . . . At other times, the awareness that a structural idea is inadequate gives rise to research. . . . As the guide for research, structure serves as a kind of "strategy" for a discipline, a tactical guide to use when venturing into previously unexplored territory. . . .

Let us assume that we will be able to identify structures in the social sciences. What will be some of our tasks before they will be useful in education?

First, we will have to be satisfied that they can be discovered in a form which will be useful in citizenship education. The learner has to have potential use for the ideas or they will wither and be of little good to him. Insofar as is possible, we want the ideas we present to become part of his permanent intellectual equipment, available as he needs it to attack new problems. The ideas should be ones which will serve one or more of the following functions:

1. Illuminate his study of some topic, such as American history, which he will meet many times in school and life. If the idea can illuminate an area which will recur, then it will have much opportunity for exercise.
2. Be applicable to the study of social and personal problems which will make up part of the curriculum. It should help the child as he studies contemporary affairs, or local government structures and functions, or problems of democratic organization in his classroom. The study of economic relations in his own community should, if properly conducted, result in the development of some structural ideas which the child can apply to the study of economic relations in other nations, or in colonial times, for example.

In other words, even as the structure of a discipline provides the scholar with a strategy which he can use to approach the acquisition of knowledge, so the learning of structural ideas should provide the child with a systematic method of attack on areas where he seeks new knowledge. If he learns how rainfall and land use are related in the United States, he should use that relationship as he looks at either land use or climate in Austria. If he learns that political beliefs were related to economic interests in Revolutionary times, he should seek to find if the same relationship holds true today. In other words, if structural ideas are to be useful educationally, it will be because we have found a method for helping children learn to use them as they pursue research on their own.

In this writer's opinion, structural strategies will be useful in all aspects of the social studies curriculum, especially in terms of our view of social education as preparing the child with the modes of thought necessary to effective citizenship. Topics for study in social studies curriculum might be thought of as coming from four sources. These are: topics dealing with past times, topics from contemporary cultures, topics centered around contemporary affairs as they happen, and topics centered around the conduct of the classroom. Let us examine very briefly the possible application of structural ideas to topics drawn from these four sources.

All the social sciences bear on the study of the community, one of the topics dealing with contemporary society. The very young child can find economic functions in his community that he can apply to the study of other communities. A six-year-old I know classified several communities which she knows according to available consumer goods. "This one you can buy gas and some groceries. That one has more, you can buy shoes and some clothes, and they have a movie. The next one has almost everything, just like Newark does, but they're not like the city, which has even more."

All the social sciences apply to the study of history. Sociology, for instance, can supply the idea of values to the study of the ancient Greek society, to American Colonial and Revolutionary times, and to the Civil War. Contemporary affairs in the community can illustrate how land use has become important to city government, as in the case of the second graders who studied the need for a park in their town, or a third grade which found that there were laws which prevented building a factory in the center of town. The classroom provides a perfect laboratory with which to experiment with ideas about the political behavior of men.

Identification of teachable forms of social science structures will not solve all the problems of social studies content. It should, however, aid in the identification of themes which can focus and strengthen elementary social studies instruction and provide the basis for content continuity with secondary education. It also will enable the testing of Bruner's exciting hypotheses concerning the benefits of teaching structures and strategies for children's thinking.

Further, although most social studies curriculums do not reflect it, there exists much basic scholarship in the area. I refer specifically to Hanna's work at Stanford, which certainly can and should be extended in terms of structures and strategies (6).

References

(1) John Dewey. *Democracy and Education*. New York: The Macmillan Company, 1916. Especially Chapters 13 and 14.

(2) Charles Hubbard Judd. *Education and Social Progress*. New York: Harcourt, Brace and Company, 1934. p. 263.

(3) Alfred North Whitehead. *The Aims of Education and Other Essays*. New York: The Macmillan Company, 1929. p. 3.

(4) Jerome Bruner. *The Process of Education*. Cambridge: Harvard University Press, 1960.

(5) Bruner, *op. cit.*

(6) Paul R. Hanna and John R. Lee. "Generalizations from the Social Sciences." Section one of Chapter III, "Content in the Social Studies" of the Thirty-Second Yearbook of the National Council for the Social Studies. John U. Michaelis, editor. *Social Studies in Elementary Schools*. Washington, D.C.: National Education Association, 1962.

∾Ⴤ Generalizations from the Social Sciences
Paul R. Hanna and *John R. Lee*

At Stanford University a number of professors and graduate students have been at work for some years in an effort to identify generalizations from the social sciences that might be used in selecting and organizing content for social studies programs. This article by Hanna and Lee reports only a few sample items from ten studies. As the section included here is only a fraction of the original work done by several researchers, the reader is referred to the original NCSS article for information on the methods used and for copies of the original documents.

Used by permission of the authors and the National Council for the Social Studies; from its Thirty-Second Yearbook, *Social Studies in Elementary Schools*, 1962, pp. 62–88.

[A] TEAM OF ADVANCED graduate students had the counsel of many Stanford faculty members drawn from the School of Humanities and Sciences and from the School of Education. From time to time the entire team of students and faculty met as a group to discuss purposes, assumptions, research design, specific techniques, and to review progress.

The team arrived at seven basic assumptions concerning the studies:

1. Significant literature from the various social science disciplines provides one of several sources of social studies content.
2. The identification and classification of generalizations from the various social science disciplines will represent a contribution to social studies programming and instruction.
3. Generalizations, as differentiated from concepts, literal facts, and opinions have value as end products or "anticipated outcomes" of the learning process in the social studies.
4. The judgments of selected specialists in each of the social science disciplines can be accepted concerning the selection of basic literature for use in these studies.
5. The researchers in these studies are competent to apply the established criteria for the identification of generalizations from the selected research literature.
6. The criteria set forth by the researchers for the identification are such that a high degree of consistency can be achieved among the members of the research team.
7. The categorization of generalizations within a scope comprising 10 basic human activities common to all cultures and societies is of greater functional utility to school systems than methods of categorization used by researchers previous to these studies. The method used is selected because of its inclusiveness and its utility for purposes of this series of studies.

The team further stated four delimitations for the series of 10 studies:

1. The six selected social science disciplines of anthropology, economics, geography, political science, social psychology, and sociology, and the cross-disciplinary field of each basic human activity will constitute the source material from which generalizations for these studies will be derived.
2. Because each of the six social science disciplines enumerated above has its own historical dimension, history texts (per se) were not included; but generalizations having historical content were sought and recorded in abundance in each basic human activity.
3. The identification and organization of generalizations from the various social science disciplines will be in terms of 10 basic human activities common to all cultures and societies.

4. While these studies deal only with the identification and classification of generalizations according to 10 basic human activities common to all cultures and societies, the researchers assume that these classified generalizations will be the springboard for further investigations. . . .

The team sought help from faculty in selecting the basic literature which would form the core for all 10 researches. The detailed method of final election is given in the second chapter of each study, together with the titles of the literature studied. In addition to this list of 36 volumes (six books in each of six social science disciplines), each researcher had an extended list of references for his own basic human activity that usually doubled the final list he used.

The team developed systems for identifying generalizations, uniformly recording them, coding, building a classification framework, verifying, synthesizing, and editing—all of which are described fully in the dissertations.

The team arrived at an operational definition of a generalization: for the purposes of this series of studies *a generalization is a universally applicable statement at the highest level of abstraction relevant to all time or stated times about man past and/or present, engaging in a basic human activity.*

In accord with this definition, the following statements must be made explicit:

1. The stated generalization, or the context within which it appears, shows that the author believes that there are no known exceptions.
2. The stated generalization is not limited by reference to specific geographic or cultural boundaries.
3. The facts upon which a generalization is based are not in themselves generalizations.
4. Neither a concept nor a definition is here considered to be a generalization and can appear only in the context of an otherwise acceptable generalization.
5. Opinions are not considered to be generalizations unless the specialist also reports that the opinion as a hypothesis has been tested and found to have no known exceptions.
6. Generalization must have applicability to all places in all times, or be applicable to all places within a stated period of time.
7. Generalization can be either primary, statistical, or functional.
8. Generalization must deal with man in a societal orientation, not as an isolated individual.
9. Generalization must be applicable to man at the highest level of abstraction rather than to specific men or communities.

. . . In the samplings of generalizations from the 10 studies which follow, an attempt was made to show the range of content from many different parts of each study. . . . The reader will have to obtain the dissertation or its microfilm for the more complete view of the structure of ideas for each of the 10 dissertations.

A sampling follows of the 541 generalizations found in the James Runge study which focused on *Producing, Exchanging, Distributing, and Food, Clothing, Shelter, and Other Consumer Goods and Services.*

   1. "There is no society without methods of production, distribution, consumption, and some form of exchange. . . ."
  37. "While people are supporting themselves with hunting, fishing, and wild food-gathering, the area will support only a thin population. . . ."
 117. "With their present specialization of effort and numerous wants, civilized populations are dependent on many and often distant regions for a considerable part of their food, clothing, and other requirements. . . ."
 197. "Power-driven machinery multiplied many times the specialized production per man and greatly increased total volume of goods to be exchanged. . . ."
 479. "When a great many men specialize and exchange their products, greater production brings a higher living standard. . . ."

A sampling follows of the 423 generalizations found in the John Rambeau study which focused on *Transporting People and Goods.* . . .

  56. "The most important trade routes center on those regions where high productivity and dense population combine to produce a surplus of goods."
  94. "Transportation charges are part of the costs of production, must be included in the price of the goods, and must be borne by the consumer. . . ."
 108. "A society with a very simple technology and lacking any means of transportation save human carriers is confined to the resources of a single area and may achieve only a bare subsistence. . . ."
 354. "The growth of large cities in a modern, industrial society results from the territorial division of labor, large-scale production, and exchange of goods which cheap and efficient transportation makes possible. . . ."

A sampling follows of the 488 generalizations found in the George Rusteika study which focused on *Communicating Facts, Ideas, and Feelings.* . . .

  62. "Prestige is wielded in the modern world through control over or access to the formal channels of mass communication—press, radio, film, and in another respect, church and school."
  89. "Regional specialization in production has promoted the develop-

ment of communication nets of various degrees of complexity. . . ."

206. ". . . the greater the degree to which members of one group perceive the behavior of members of another as being hostile, the more communication between the two groups will be reduced."

209. "In modern communication across language barriers the parties concerned are notably at the mercy of their interpreters. . . ."

239. "Travel and the communication inventions . . . break down differences in dialect, in customs and in manners. . . ."

Following is a sampling of the 268 generalizations found in the Owen Geer study which focused on *Protecting and Conserving Human and Natural Resources.*

1.3.2 "Where water is scarce enough to jeopardize the well-being of a community, its control [(conservation)] becomes a matter of public concern. . . ."

1.7.12 "Over wide areas men have overstepped the limits of stable, permanent production and in many cases have destroyed the very soil on which they depend."

1.8.1 "[Since]mineral resources are exhaustible, . . . only thru wise and careful use can the supply be maintained for use. . . ."

2.2.2 "When forests are protected from fire, insects, disease, and overgrazing of animals, they serve to preserve soil, hold underground water, shelter wildlife, supply material for man's use, add beauty to the landscape, and regulate climatic conditions. . . ."

A sampling follows of 268 generalizations found in the Vinton Stratton study which focused on *Providing Education.* . . .

46. "Whenever the functions of a society become differentiated or specialized, there is an increase in the formal aspects of its organization, and this is as true of education as it is of community life in general. . . ."

112. "The individual is a living member of the human whole, deriving his life from it through social and hereditary transmission; the transmission of the cultural heritage from one generation to another is a universal purpose of education."

121. "What individuals do and what they learn vary for two different cultures even though the natural environment is the same for both, for the cultural environment clearly has more effect on learning than does the natural environment."

129. "Though culture is a major force in molding the personality, no society succeeds in reducing all its members to a single personality type; individuals have distinctive cultural experiences and develop dissimilar personality traits. . . ."

A sampling follows of the 196 generalizations found in the Harold Emmerson study which focused on *Providing Recreation.* . . .

15. "Recreation patterns vary from country to country and from region to region within a country."

18. "With the occasional appearance of creative minds, new play methods are invented or improvements made in the old methods. . . ."

45. "The difference in recreational patterns is an outcome of the cultural conditions under which a people live, with the play forms of the group tending to become the play forms of the individual. . . ."

82. "As work becomes routinized and mechanized, recreation . . . becomes more and more important as fulfilling a cultural need. . . ."

Following is a sampling of 254 generalizations found in the Clay Andrews study which focused on *Organizing and Governing*. . . .

72. "In a complex society, associations tend to be specialized so that each stands for a particular type of interest or interest complex. . . ."

81. "In all the countries where political associations are prohibited, civil associations are rare. . . ."

207. "When private property rights are a recognized means to personal security and happiness, men will organize governments to protect these rights. . . ."

252. ". . . individuals and groups oppose vigorously government regulation of their activities, and support vigorously government activities that directly benefit them. . . ."

A sampling follows of the 267 generalizations found in the John Lee study which focused on *Expressing Religious Impulses*. . . .

154. ". . . in the history of the founded religions, increase in membership stimulates development in religious thought, activities, and organization. . . ."

253. ". . . when the pressure of whites upon aborigines reaches a certain point there will be a revival of the ancient religion or a partially new cult of messianic type will arise."

258. "The more advanced the process of social and cultural differentiation, the more diversified are the forms of religious expression."

259. ". . . subjective religion has at all times proved enough to unite and integrate people who are otherwise widely separated by differences in descent, profession, wealth or rank."

Following is a sampling of the 282 generalizations found in the A. Daniel Peck study which focused on *Expressing and Satisfying Esthetic Needs and Impulses*.

6. "There are no societies which lack artistic activities altogether."

54. "In all arts . . . [techniques] change to some extent with the growth of science, and with the change of styles in the product, necessitating new techniques to fit them."

58. "Changes in art forms are rarely sudden, but occur along with changes in religion, government, and social ideals."
59. "Innovation in the arts must win its way against the association of sentiment with old forms."
108. "Tradition, adherence to existing forms, accepted patterns and conventions inhibit change in art forms. . . ."

A sampling of the 285 generalizations found in the John Hofstrand study which focused on *Creating New Tools, Technics, and Social Arrangements.* . . .

40. ". . . the simpler a culture is, the fewer are the materials and the narrower is the range of knowledge of which the inventor can be possessed, so that as a consequence the possibilities of invention are more limited. . . ."
120. "National emergencies and conditions of social disruption provide special incentive to invent new techniques, and to strike out boldly for solutions to practical and social problems."
136. "Technological invention and industrial expansion rapidly develop some industries and destroy others; they demand new skills and discard old ones. . . ."
284. "Modern technology is changing at a rapid rate and creating important social changes, with which our social institutions have not yet caught up."

THE USES AND LIMITATIONS OF THE GENERALIZATIONS

Obviously, this small sample of generalizations selected from various studies does not constitute an organized social studies program. Nor is there any inference here that the content of these combined studies constitutes a program or a curriculum. The assertion is rather that the generalizations contained in this series of studies provide a rich source from which teachers, administrators, and particularly curriculum workers may draw in giving substance, direction, and much needed balance to their social studies programs.

ఆ EDUCATING CITIZENS FOR RESPONSIBLE INDIVIDUALISM, 1960–1980 *Donald W. Oliver*

The American has always been interested in his freedom, yet he must give up a part of that freedom in order to be an American. How do we help youngsters to think and act as individuals, while at the same time accepting the major beliefs that hold our nation together? Oliver suggests a well-thought-out approach.

*The limitation of space prevents a thorough presentation of his
ideas, but a fuller discussion can be found in the original source.*

AN APPROACH TO CITIZENSHIP EDUCATION TO PROVIDE FOR BOTH DIVERSITY AND CONFORMITY IN THE AMERICAN VALUE SYSTEM

. . . A dual approach to citizenship education will now be considered
which would not only allow for but encourage the expression of individual values, yet which would teach at least minimal conformity to
certain areas of belief which foster social cohesion. The key to this
approach is the theory that symbols of unity and cohesion can be
taught on a very different level from the process of free inquiry which
we commonly associate with individualism.

The first, or symbolic, level requires only that the student be
taught to verbalize the general values in the American Creed and
to experience a sense of identification with the nation that holds these
values. Most of us acquire this sense of national identification very
early in the elementary grades. We learn the legends about Columbus, the Pilgrims, the Revolution, the Founding Fathers, the explorers of the West, and the Civil War. We learn that these events
symbolize suffering and achievement, courage and killing, equality
for all men, freedom for all men. Understanding and appreciating
these legends requires no translation of the Creed into contemporary
personal experience. There is a spontaneous projection of personal
values into historical symbols, which give the Creed flesh and bones
and reality. Understanding at this level is more emotional and symbolic than intellectual and literal.

The second or objective level of understanding is based on
reasoned self-interest. It requires that the individual understand the
system of government and law under which he lives, the broad
concept of government by consent as well as supporting concepts
that have been associated with it, such as federalism, checks and
balances, an independent judiciary. This level involves a deeper
understanding of the rationale for our particular system of government, including an understanding of the importance of applying
one's own substantive values to the discussion and judgment of larger
political, economic, and social issues; an awareness of the fact that
one's own values influence decisions on political issues; and finally

Used by permission of the author and the National Council for the Social
Studies; from its Thirtieth Yearbook, *Citizenship and a Free Society: Education
for the Future,* 1960, pp. 211–217. Donald W. Oliver is an associate professor
of education in the Harvard Graduate School of Education.

an awareness that both the right to have value commitments and the right to make choices which flow from them are only protected in so far as there is a political system which will ensure this protection.

The first level of understanding results in an emotional allegiance to a highly dramatic and personalized historical image of the nation; the second level results in enlightened self-interest within a multi-value society.

Teaching the first level of understanding. Teaching children to believe in the Creed without requiring that they translate it into a particular set of personal actions, as suggested above, may sound impossible. It can be done only by assuming that the individual can "understand" the world on more than one level of "reality." Myths, legends, symbols, the whole superstructure of religion, provide examples of truth at a level of consciousness in which scientific verification is not a relevant issue. Anthropologists, among others, call this level projective rather than objective reality.

The correctness of projective truth depends upon the extent to which the symbols that describe and explain reality serve both the internal emotional needs of individuals and the cohesive requirements of the society as a whole. Projective truths are set forth in order to allow people to translate their own internal needs, frustrations, aggressions, and sexual impulses into symbols which can transcend petty hedonism and which can be seen and understood by the culture as a whole. These symbols can then bind the culture together through apparently common methods of handling the problems of socialization and survival which everyone in society faces.

Teaching projective truth or projective conformity tends to develop an historical image of greatness in our children. This image of greatness focuses upon the problem of cultural integration and probably could best be taught in the elementary school. It does not demand that children act out a creed of literal equality and interpersonal harmony, as do some citizenship education programs. Rather, it instills cultural cohesion at the symbolic or projective level and allows the whole gamut of human emotions to find expression: love, dependence, aggression, courage. In short, it builds an image of individual and cultural greatness. It further allows the individual to internalize selectively those facets of a symbol which are most consistent with his own temperament and values.

The content of a great-image curriculum should be a moving personalized narrative history of America, written by literary artists.

Such a history would be punctuated by dramatic ceremonials that would emphasize the highlights of the narrative. Perhaps great-image teaching can best be explained with an illustration.

Two of the mysteries and problems with which any society must deal are courtship and death. Societies develop a variety of ways of handling these problems. The commonness of such experiences within a single culture undoubtedly has much to do with cultural integration and cohesion. Carl Sandburg describes these experiences in the Lincoln family in the following way:

> A wagon one day late in 1817 brought into the Lincoln clearing their good Kentucky neighbors Tom and Betsy Sparrow and the odd quizzical seventeen-year-old Dennis Friend Hanks. For some years Dennis would be a chum of Abe's. . . . The Sparrows were to live in the Lincoln pole shed till they could locate land and settle. Hardly a year had passed, however, when Tom and Betsy Sparrow were taken down with the "milk sick," beginning with a whitish coat on the tongue, resulting, it was supposed, from cows eating white snakeroot or other growths that poisoned their milk. Tom and Betsy Sparrow died and were buried in September on a little hill in a clearing in the timbers nearby.
>
> Soon after, there came to Nancy Hanks Lincoln that white coating of the tongue; her vitals burned; the tongue turned brownish; her feet and hands grew cold and colder, her pulse slow and slower. She knew she was dying, called for her children, and spoke to them her last dim choking words. Death came October 5, 1818, the banners of autumn flaming their crimsons over tall oaks and quiet maples. . . . The body of Nancy Hanks Lincoln lay in peace, the eyelids closed down in unbroken rest. . . . The children . . . tiptoed in, stood still, cried their tears of want and longing, whispered and heard only their own whispers answering. . . .
>
> Tom Lincoln took a log . . . , and he and Dennis Hanks whipsawed it into planks, planed the planks smooth, and made . . . a box to bury the dead wife and mother in. Little Abe, with a jackknife, whittled pine-wood pegs. And while Dennis and Abe held the planks, Tom bored holes and stuck the whittled pegs through the holes. This was the coffin they carried next day to the little timber clearing nearby. . . .
>
> So Nancy Hanks Lincoln died, 34 years old, a pioneer sacrifice, with memories of monotonous, endless everyday chores, . . . of blue wistful hills and a summer when the crab-apple blossoms flamed white and she carried a boy child into the world. . . .
>
> Lonesome days came for Abe and Sarah in November [the next year] when their father went away, promising to come back. He headed for Elizabethtown, Kentucky, through woods and across the Ohio River, to the house of the widow Sarah Bush Johnston. They

said he argued straight-out: "I have no wife and you no husband.
I came a-purpose to marry you. I knowed you from a gal and you
knowed me from a boy. I've no time to lose; and if you're willin' let
it be done straight off." She answered, "I got a few little debts," gave
him a list and he paid them; and they were married December 2,
1819 (1).

The elements of greatness that one can select from this particular
passage are numerous. The selection can be made in terms of the
special values of the individual reader. The tender-hearted romanticist
can see the tiptoed footsteps, the tears of want and longing, the
wistful hills, and the crab-apple blossoms. The more practical-
minded may see the whipsawed planks and homemade coffin and the
brief, frank courtship between Tom and Sarah. The passage contains
elements of courage particularly characteristic of our pioneering culture. As obvious as the deeper symbolic message contained in the
passage, moreover, is its stylistic quality: the concrete, dramatic
narrative which could provide all children with a somewhat common
conception of the American heritage.

The conflict between scientificism and the image-of-greatness
idea may make this approach repugnant to some teachers in the
elementary school who feel a responsibility for teaching a realistic
view of contemporary culture. The question may be raised: Why not
teach an explicit contract theory of society from the beginning? We
give allegiance to society, and in return for this allegiance we get
services and, to some extent, the protection of our liberties.

The most important reason for teaching the great image as a
crucial initial step in citizenship training is the need to provide a
common, concrete basis for our dynamic faith in a truly liberal
society. Otherwise there is the real possibility that some men may
never be trained to see the world beyond their own petty personal
interests. We must commit our children so completely to a system
of government which protects constructive nonconformity that day-
by-day contact with the hazards and realities of the system will not
tarnish the ideals for which the system stands.

The hope is that later these same children will gain a self-
conscious awareness of their own values and a realization that the
right to apply those values in daily conduct is only protected by the
allegiance they give to the system of government and of law in which
they live. For some, then, the earlier historical or projective concept
of America will no longer be required. For some, reality is not too rich
a diet for idealism. Some will be able to see the limits of man's
tolerance, his natural tendency toward prejudgment, the mutual
suspicion among men that develops within a pluralistic, multivalue

society. Within this context, they cannot help but feel a deep respect for the wisdom behind the basic political institutions on which this country is founded. The crucial question, of course, is how many persons are capable of actually understanding this view of reality. For those who cannot, better the projective image of greatness than a total lack of idealism.

The problem of cultural cohesion is difficult enough in a society of free men. It is even more difficult in a culture that idolizes scientific rationalism. It is suggested here that a "reality" of historical imagery symbolizing our own liberal tradition should be provided to children to lay the basis for cultural commonalty until or unless a deeper appreciation of liberty comes with the self-conscious awareness that a variety of personal values—especially substantive religious and political values—is important and requires political protection.

Teaching the second level of understanding: a jurisprudential approach to citizenship education. A projective view of America based on dramatic narrative history has been discussed. A second, and perhaps a deeper, foundation of loyalty can be based on a much more objective model of American society.

Freedom inevitably involves controversy. In a society governed by principles of constitutionalism, this controversy is expressed not in physical violence or intimidation but in words. The object of political life is not coercion, but persuasion. As Justice Douglas has said, "The function of free speech under our system of government is to invite dispute."

Much of the dispute centers upon the establishment of man's power relationship to his government: the definition of his rights and the restrictions upon his liberties. There is continuous controversy and redefinition of the words which describe these liberties, as well as the words which justify their restriction. All should have a right to "equal opportunity," "security," "a decent standard of living," "justice," "freedom," and "progress." But the government may restrict these rights "to provide for the general health and welfare of the community," "to prevent crime and disorder," "to provide for the common defense," "to prevent individuals or groups from being exploited," and "to penalize lazy, stupid, or incompetent people." These are the kinds of words we use in our political discussions. The definition of these words which describe our rights and their restrictions evolves through open discussion and application to particular situations and to particular problems.

This process of interpretation and intelligent application of words is not easy. Different people apply different meanings to the same rights. A Negro, for example, may say that it is his basic right to eat in a restaurant with whites. Some white people may say it is their natural right to associate with whomever they please, and this does not include Negroes. The white owner of the restaurant may say he has a right to control who will eat in his restaurant. Both Negro and white claim it is their right to have freedom, but the word has a different meaning for the two groups.

Often one right seems to conflict with another. One man wants to be free to see that his children get a better start in life than he had. If he has enough money, he will hire special teachers to give them a good education and use his influence to see that they get good jobs. Another who has less money may say that his children deserve equal opportunity. He wants his children to have as good an education as anyone else and to have the same chance to find a good job. The freedom of one may interfere with the equal opportunity of another.

Although we probably never shall solve the problem of defining basic rights to the point of universal consensus, through the process of free debate we continually define and redefine these rights and carry them into public policy. Each time a law is passed or a judicial decision is made, that law or decision defines the rights of people. By encouraging individuals and groups to debate and to work out conflicting definitions of basic rights, we come to conform to, if not to accept, restrictions upon these rights. We rationalize these restrictions by asserting that the government must have certain "police powers" in order to protect health, morals, safety, and the welfare of the community.

One of the most important jobs of a citizen is to reflect upon what he thinks these rights mean when applied to particular public issues. The citizen must constantly act as a judge interpreting the words which describe general moral and legal principles to see whether public action, and hence restriction of liberty, is warranted in a particular situation.

The strategy for teaching such a model of American society might be to build a curriculum—call it a "jurisprudential curriculum" —which would focus upon the earnest use of free speech and open debate for the students to determine what is man's proper relationship to his government. The question would be: To what extent should the government protect or restrict basic rights. The debate should not be carried on in an atmosphere of academic calm, but rather in the midst of that heat and pressure which characterize fundamental societal disputes.

Such a curriculum would focus upon a series of related questions:

1. What is an adequate description of the objective situation which causes the dispute? This refers to empirical, testable questions, though the evidence at hand may, in fact, be scarce. For example, how many labor unions really are corrupt? Exactly what is the nature of the dishonest acts in which some labor leaders engage?
2. To what extent is the situation so pressing that the government can justifiably use its police powers to restrict personal liberty? Will whites and Negroes, for example, corrupt each other's cultures so that "separate but equal" is a reasonable standard for legislation?
3. To what extent do the rights which we wish to restrict by laws have constitutional guarantees?
4. To what extent do specific checks within the American constitutional system adequately reduce or unreasonably restrict governmental power?

The jurisprudential curriculum would clarify these questions by teaching specific skills and content directed at them. This content would include:

1. Concepts relating to the process of proof
   For example:
   a. distinction and relationships among definitional, empirical, and ethical problems.
   b. the process of proof and use of evidence for these different kinds of problems
   c. distinction between inductive and deductive types of proof
2. Concepts relating to the American form of government
   a. constitutional checks and safeguards; e.g., rule of law, federalism, separation of powers, checks and balances, judicial review
   b. constitutional rights; e.g., free conscience and expression, substantive and procedural due process, equal protection under the law, property and contract rights
   c. rationale for police power; e.g., provide for the general health and welfare, prevent crime and disorder, provide for the common defense, protect groups or individuals from being exploited
3. Concepts and facts necessary to describe disputes or problem areas. Selection of facts depends largely on problem area being described. Concepts, however, might run across several problem areas. Concepts such as "culture" and "social class" would certainly apply to many problem areas.

The essential skill which would come out of this program is the application of the content characterized as critical thinking and concepts of constitutional theory to actual conflicts and disputes within a free society.

References

(1) Sandburg, Carl. *Abraham Lincoln: The Prairie Years and The War Years* (One-Volume Edition, copyright 1939 by Harcourt, Brace and Company, Inc.; copyright 1954 by Carl Sandburg). New York: Harcourt, Brace and Company, Inc., 1954, p. 11–12. Reprinted by permission of the publishers.

❧ TEACHING PATRIOTISM AT HIGHER CONCEPTUAL LEVELS
Raymond H. Muessig and *Vincent R. Rogers*

The question of how to develop patriotic attitudes and behaviors remains a difficult one for the teacher of the social studies. Some people believe that all efforts to teach patriotism are desirable, while some others doubt the value of any attempt by the schools to develop loyalty. Still others feel the only patriotism worthy of the name is their particular brand. A teacher must somehow avoid excesses and guide youngsters toward a reasoned loyalty to what the United States has been, is, and can become. Muessig and Rogers not only discuss the need for teaching patriotism, but give a number of examples of what they consider competent development of this important goal.

As WITH NUMEROUS other important, all-embracing terms and concepts, "patriotism" can connote different things to various people. At a superficial level, most persons would agree with the "love of country" definition commonly found in dictionaries. Consensus dissolves quickly, however, when an effort is made to enlarge upon what love of country can and should signify operationally. "Love" is regarded generally as a word carrying positive overtones; but misdirected love—as in the case of some warped parent-child relationships—can misshape the object of affection almost beyond recognition. . . .

What *should* the schools do about patriotism? Is there a way of dealing with the love of country which is neither over-saturated

Used by permission of the author and the National Council for the Social Studies; from *Social Education*, 28:266–270, May, 1964. Raymond H. Muessig is a professor of education at Ohio State University.

with indigestible chauvinism nor totally void of intellectual, moral, and emotional sustenance? Is there a respect for one's homeland which transcends frantic shouting on the one hand or apathetic ritualism on the other? Is there a substance in patriotism which can be identified and broken down into components like facts, concepts, generalizations, skills, attitudes, and appreciations? Can dimensions of patriotism be taught and caught, grasped firmly and then transferred to a multitude of situations in these anxious, troubled times? Is there a unique essence to democratic patriotism unlike the love of country conveyed in a fascistic or communistic state? If we become more and more like the powers which threaten to engulf us what will we have saved? Can we afford to ignore the need for an intelligent look at patriotism?

Perhaps the following ideas will stimulate some thought on the part of school administrators, teachers, parents, and others interested in the teaching of patriotism to our children and youth. Each of the statements below is derived from the fundamental definition of patriotism as love of country, but it is neither expected nor anticipated that each will be accepted uncritically by all individuals and groups. Each can stand alone as a basic, significant belief related to democratic behavior. Yet each is inevitably related to the other. The five points offered here are by no means exhaustive. The authors identified others at one stage in the preparation of this manuscript, but space limitations make it impossible to treat so many ingredients. Hence, representative points have been used and what space remains has been devoted to examples of methods teachers might employ to achieve these types of objectives.

A patriotic American should have a balanced love of country. In democratic patriotism there should be a degree of symmetry with respect to both cognitive and affective—or mental and emotional—elements. Americans should be both rational and capable of deep feeling, informed and devoted, sensible and sensitive. There is something in the human organism which responds emotionally to the strains of martial or laudatory music, to the sight of a flag fluttering in the breeze or dramatized by a spotlight in a darkened assembly hall, to speeches with soul-stirring phrases, to hallowed monuments, statues, and places, and to yellowed documents which have shaped the course of men's lives. Man cannot deny his sentiments, nor should he. He would be inhuman if he did not experience an occasional lump in the throat, the swelling of tears, a feeling of pride and dedication. Yet the democratic citizen's emotional impulses cannot carry him from a real world into a dreamland from which there is no return, from lucidity to blind irrationality. Although he is justifiably proud of America's strengths and achievements, he must be aware too of its weaknesses and failures. Otherwise, he cannot assume a responsible, enlightened role in improving conditions in this country. Further, while loving the United States and the noble attributes in living which it represents, he can perceive values in other cultures as well though he may not accept them as his own; identify with people in other lands as fellow human beings with at least some needs and aspirations similar to his; and understand the patriotism of others as a natural phenomenon and a potential source of positive and negative properties depending upon its interpretation and application.

A fifth-grade teacher asked her charges to write the name of the best school in their city on a slip of paper and to hide their responses until everyone was finished. After collecting the papers and going through them, the teacher announced that every child had chosen *his own* school. The teacher then discussed with the youngsters *why* they liked their school better than others and made a list of suggested items on the chalkboard. She then asked whether anyone had ever attended or visited another school in their city. No one had. (This school was situated in a suburban . . . community with low geographic mobility. A few children had attended schools in other cities, but all had remained in this school after their arrival in this area.) The class was silent for a minute. Suddenly hands went up, and several children blurted out that they only *thought* their school was better than others but that they did not *know*. A girl observed that some of the things on the board *might* even be true of *other* schools. A boy remarked gingerly that other schools could be *better* in some ways. A classmate in front of him agreed but added that other schools could be *worse* too—and that he would still like his school more than others, no matter what. Many heads nodded affirmatively after this comment. It was time for another "Why?" from the teacher, and she received several reactions. Children pointed out that they usually grew to like the close and the familiar; that they became fond of people who were good to them and of places associated with various kinds of satisfactions (such as "learning new things in school and getting to play too"); and that they were expected to be loyal to their families, friends, schools, churches, and *country*. Other things were discussed, but eventually the teacher focused the attention of her pupils upon their feeling about nations in the world. Her questions paralleled the previous ones she had asked about schools, but the children were less positive about their statements. The teacher beamed when a girl said, "Schools in one place and countries all over the place aren't quite the same thing. It's a lot harder to talk about countries."

The children slowly composed a list of several questions which the teacher wrote quickly on a fluid duplicator master. A boy left to have copies run off for everyone. Another boy offered to contact the building librarian for books that would assist the class. A girl said she was going to ask the questions of her parents, and other pupils indicated that they would follow suit. The teacher said that some class time could be made available for class study and individual help. There was agreement that further discussion should be postponed until the following Monday.

During the three days following the class discussion the teacher encouraged her pupils to try to pull their thinking together. With her help the children were able to formulate generalizations like the following:

Most people love the country where they were born or where they have lived a long time.

Every country must have good things about it. Every country has problems too. People are proud of the good things.

Sometimes they work together to solve problems.

Many nice things happen to us because we live in America. Americans get to do and have things that people in some other countries cannot do or have. (Numerous examples appeared after this statement.)

It would be hard now for any country to get along all by itself. Countries get ideas, ways of saying and doing things, and products from each other. An invention by a man in one country may be used by many other countries. America has learned things and received help from other countries. As a leader in the world, it gives different kinds of help to many nations.

The citizens of each nation believe certain things. If we know people's important beliefs sometimes we can understand better the way they live. Countries agree and disagree on beliefs. When they agree they may get along well and even work together. When they disagree they may not like each other and may even fight each other. Americans share some big ideas. (Representative ideas were listed here.) Some nations think these are good ideas. Others do not. In the past Americans have had to stick up for their beliefs. They must be strong today too so they will not lose their freedom and rights. We should understand American ideas so we can be better citizens. . . .

A patriotic American should understand the underlying meaning of national ceremonies and symbols. Every nation—whatever its social ideology—has its rituals, emblems, traditions, celebrations, folklore, and legendary personages. It is the rationale behind practices and tokens which distinguishes free people from those under the totalitarian yoke. In a democratic environment it is not enough to engage in rote observations for their own sake. There is a significant difference between the "indivisible" nation described in our stirring "Pledge of Allegiance" and the "invisible" one which so many children identify daily and cannot comprehend, between a lush "fruited *plain*" as envisioned in "America the Beautiful," and the jet *plane* festooned with grapes, bananas, apples, etc., which the little boy drew to portray these words in the song. While the "Gettysburg Address" has *ear* appeal, especially as read by one of our great American actors, it must reach the intellect and the soul as well through discussion and contemplation. A year or so before Congress changed Armistice Day to Veterans Day in 1954, one of the authors was a spectator during the period of silence at 11:00 A.M. His thoughts had just turned to a close friend killed in World War II when he heard a loud "Shhhhh!" next to him. A mother was silencing her little boy. Naturally, the little boy asked why he was supposed to be quiet. His mother said she did not know but that he should be still anyway. This lack of understanding permeates too many patriotic observances.

Children should both know the story and grasp the philosophy in back of given patriotic actions, should delve into the meaning of words used in songs and ceremonies, and should see reasons for the reaffirmation of the democratic faith through continued observances. There is a lesson to be learned during the period just prior to a presidential election and following the inauguration of our Chief Executive. Young people can marvel at the intense rivalries that often exist before a vote is cast and the respect freely and sincerely given to the newly installed president. Children ought to discover that this regard for the head of state is not diminished by the informed criticism which citizens offer of specific executive decisions and actions.

A sixth-grade teacher wanted his pupils to understand more fully the commitment they were making each morning when they pledged allegiance to their flag and country. To establish a foundation for discussion at a higher level, he read three "pledges" aloud to the class, leaving time after the reading for questions and comments. The first was the "Boy Scout Oath" which was familiar to most of the children. Next the class listened to portions of the "Hippocratic Oath." The teacher did most of the talking this time because words like "discernment" and "regimen" were unknown to his charges. The *idea* of the oath was clear, however, and the children were intrigued by the thought that their own doctors had repeated this pledge in medical school. Finally, the oath taken by a prospective Athenian soldier-citizen was examined. The children were impressed by the fact that this pledge was administered only once and taken with real seriousness. The sentence, "I will hand on my fatherland greater and better than I found it," seemed particularly important to many children. Pledging allegiance from that time on carried both greater depth of understanding and feeling. . . .

A patriotic American should realize that democratic means must be used to achieve democratic ends in this society. The implications of this point should be self-evident today, for this inescapable philosophical insight has been with us for a long time. However, the consonant relationship between means and ends has still escaped many people—among them the militant chauvinists. The man who shouts, "They'll have democracy if I have to shove it down their throats!" expresses the means-ends schism that is still present in some circles. No matter how involved emotionally an individual may become in the love of his country, he cannot violate rational, moral, ethical, legal, aesthetic, and mannerly democratic canons to win others to his form of patriotism. When democratic tenets and modes of behavior are ignored in the name of patriotism, the end result is the weakening or destruction of fundamental ideals from which a love of country should have emerged. . . .

A patriotic American should grasp the import of "diversity" and "pluralism" as democratic concepts. The observation that all people are different and capable of countless patterns of living is obvious and time-worn. What one does about variations in human beings is another matter. One can choose to ignore individual and cultural diversities in the naive hope that they will "go away." Or he can acknowledge their presence and do everything possible to obscure, reduce, overrule, or eliminate multiformities in values, feelings, capabilities, wants, and actions. Still a third alternative—the one which seems most compatible in an open society—is to enjoy, prize, foster, and protect distinctness in man. Each person should be viewed as a bundle of possibilities, a one-of-a-kind character who may make the good life better through his unique insights, perceptions, and methods of approaching or solving individual and societal problems. How many Americans would agree that there should be only one type of artist, musician, playwright, architect, engineer, teacher, doctor, or elected representative in our pluralistic country? Hopefully, no citizen of the United States seeks a monotonous uniformity. Yet too often some groups seem to operate on the postulate that there is only one kind of patriot acceptable in America. Patriotism in this wonderfully variegated homeland of ours should be a many-splendored thing. Oliver H. Perry, Walt Whitman, Susan B. Anthony, Clara Barton, Joyce Kilmer, Jane Addams, Will Rogers, Clarence Darrow, and W. K. Kellogg were all patriots—

though in different ways. Our children must discover that there are many ways to love and serve America.

A fourth-grade teacher reproduced brief excerpts dealing with the lives of four famous American patriots: Samuel Adams, Patrick Henry, Paul Revere, and Nathan Hale. The highlights of their careers were discussed and their differing roles in the movement for independence emphasized. Each biographical sketch also touched, however, on the man's background, education, vocation, interests, religion, and physical appearance. The class began by discussing the love of country that served as a common bond to unite these four men. They concluded by listing and comparing the obvious differences in their backgrounds, arriving after some time at the position that "patriots" can come from many walks of life and that here is no one mold in which all must be formed.

A patriotic American should internalize a deep, abiding, and selfless respect for the rights of others. He cannot afford, nor does he want to be a religious, political, and philosophical neuter. He must have a functional, consistent, durable frame of reference, hammered out of broad and varied experience, study, consideration, and reconsideration. He possesses virile convictions, but they do not prevent him from reading and listening to the tenable positions of others. He realizes that to have intellectual and social freedom for himself he must protect fundamental rights of others. There is a kind of self-interest that leads one to do for others, to share with them, and to protect their rights and freedoms because this form of behavior protects his own integrity and contributes to a more livable life for him and others at the same time. He does not, then, disrupt a meeting of a group whose opinions he cannot accept, nor does he prevent another individual from being heard because he cannot share that man's views. He does not maintain the naive, unrealistic stand that one man's views on general concerns are innately just as good as any others, *ipso facto*—informed or not, tested or not, moral or not, etc. But he is convinced that the roads to learning, understanding, agreement, consensus, and improvement are not paved with inquisitions, pogroms, witch hunts, fratricide, and genocide. He hopes that the truth will out with time if men seek it individually and together in an open, faithful, permissive manner. While he sometimes gets disillusioned and discouraged with mankind past and present, he never forgets his stake in humanity. He feels that some of his efforts to secure and hold rights for himself and others today may be a rich legacy for his children or grandchildren. . . .

While years of research by skilled social and behavioral scientists have been devoted to attitude formation and change, we still know very little about this complex phenomenon. Many studies lead one to observe that it is extremely hard to deal with attitudes, let alone change them. Some pieces of research appear to indicate that the school has relatively little impact attitudinally when compared with the home, the peer group, and the media of mass communication. While the teacher is regarded by sociologists, anthropologists, social psychologists, and psychologists as a "significant other" who *may* shape some attitudes, there is evidence that the teacher is not always an ideal model for identification for a variety of reasons.

One might conclude "logically" that the schools should stick to nothing but hard and fast facts which have been around a long time and seem to be accepted with a minimum of friction from a variety of quarters. Certainly, dealing with patriotism in a more penetrating way is not an easy thing, might be a bit risky in some communities, and could be ineffectual as far as producing a change in behavior is concerned. Again, one might reach the "logical" position that concerns of this nature could be deferred. The primary teacher could pass the buck to the intermediate teacher and so on all the way up to, or beyond, the college professor. A fair question, however, is whether we can afford to lay aside this vital problem on an indefinite basis. Perhaps we will not bring about a complete, lasting renaissance in the patriotic behavior of Americans through what is said and done in public schools. On the other hand, we may surprise researchers and ourselves if we grapple systematically with democratic attitudes related to patriotism and if we try out methods tailored to those predispositions. Doing nothing or yielding to groups which make the loudest noise is certainly no solution. Why not "give it a go," as the English put it?

◄§ On a New Approach to Bill of
Rights Teaching   *The Williamstown Workshop*

We must teach politics to survive as a nation. Muessig and Rogers have suggested some elements necessary for successful teaching of patriotism; Oliver has presented two possible levels of approach. In this brief extract on teaching our Bill of Rights a number of other methods are mentioned. Although none is developed into an example, the suggestions illustrate the range of procedures available beyond the too familiar assignment-reading-recitation triad.

We need to develop effective, responsible adult citizens, aware of their own and others' rights, concerned with their exercise. Our students are not born with such desirable attitudes nor do they necessarily come with growth. No matter what the direction our students' lives may take in the future, we can be certain that they will function in the matter of rights. It falls to us to provide the basis for responsible action rather than apathetic or irrational response. This is a large assignment. How do we do it?

First, with knowledge. The American history course approach that provides the chronological development, the documents, events, institutions, processes of our heritage of freedom, is the foundation of knowledge in the Bill of Rights area. The Bill of Rights may be used as a core for understanding our legal system and the nature of our judicial process. Presented as such, it is a necessary part of the knowledge students must receive to become responsible citizens. Other aspects of the theory and practice of individual rights in our free society also involve matters of fact and knowledge. The discrepancies between particular rights and the difficulty of harmonizing them must be acknowledged. Otherwise, students are confused between the real world they observe and the education they receive. Where can they put their trust?

Methods, also, can help the teacher personalize and dramatize individual rights, can deepen understanding, heighten responsibility and good citizenship. The teaching of individual rights is a complex matter because our society is rich with human conflicts, pressures and uncertainties.

Rights can be of interest and understood by students when they see them as conflicts or issues which must be decided by an "umpire" or as problems that need to be solved. Through this orientation, they can come to appreciate the nature, scope and limitations of our rights.

The case method offers a stimulating and valid approach to the controversy inherent in every issue of rights. The dramatic human situations appeal to students. The subject matter becomes personalized and has a sense if immediacy which captures and in-

From *A Program for Improving Bill of Rights Teaching in High Schools*, Civil Liberties Educational Foundation, Inc., 1962, 13–15. Distributed by the National Assembly on Teaching the Principles of the Bill of Rights, under whose auspices the Workshop was held.

volves most students. Law and judicial decisions become alive. Students learn from leading majority and minority decisions how learned and intelligent men weigh the relationship between the individual's right to liberty and society's need for an orderly community. They can also see the dynamics of value change as minority opinion at times becomes majority decision. They are pitched into the heart of the process of decision-making and conflicts—often between cherished rights and the need for order.

The problem-solving technique promotes competence in reflective thinking. It is ideally suited to the subject matter of individual rights. The skillful teacher maneuvers to a starting point of interest by raising a problem. The process of problem-solving requires that information be gathered and organized. Students are actively working or thinking the matter through to a conclusion. The solution of a given problem results from the logical organization of materials of study and consideration of values and alternatives. As a learner progresses, step by step, his outlook broadens and deepens with the addition of new insights and the modification of old ones. But the teacher must see that with the additions and modifications of insight, each learner also continually considers how well the new and the old agree. Failure to agree may require modification of the old or of the new, or perhaps both. The question of consistency of total outlook should be an important consideration at every step of the way. Consistency is the essence of logical organization. It permits the learner to act rather than remain apathetic as a result of conflict and confusion. This approach permits the learner to go from practical problems to theoretical working out of principles. This results in new practical solutions through the reaching of broader and higher levels of insight. It is the essence of intellectual creativity and independence.

A reasoned, objective method of thinking about individual rights is required for responsible citizenship. It should be a part of the teacher's method. The process of rational and reflective thinking is a necessary tool that students should develop for themselves while they are in school if they are to cope responsibly with the real issues they will meet as adults. The untrained thought processes that lead to emotional and unreasoned judgments must be exposed for the danger they hold for a free society. Rational thinking, or degrees of it, is, of course, involved in all decision-making. In all curriculum areas it needs to be encouraged and developed. It is central, however, to our consideration of training students for the responsible practice of rights.

There are five steps to rational choice that leads to the responsible exercise of rights. First, *what is the right involved* and what is the issue? Second, with the general goal always of finding the best balance between the liberty of the individual and society's need for order, *what is the specific statement of the goal at issue* here? Third, we must consider the *alternative courses of choice* that are available to all the parties involved. Fourth, we need to consider *the consequences of each alternative course* in the light of the democratic goal. Fifth, *decision on which action is best,* all things considered.

While this is oversimplified, it suggests how this approach to thinking about questions of individual rights and responsibilities in a free society can be applied to most questions and provide the necessary training which students can carry over to adult life.

Socio-drama is also an effective teaching technique in the Bill of Rights field. Here, actual cases and conflicts can be acted out by students as they project themselves into the experiences of those who have been involved in an issue of rights. Use of the real case or situation provides students with the actual substance of action, defense of a position, understanding the rights and positions of others, decision-making, and balancing the rights of the individual with the interests of an orderly society. Role-playing enables many a student to learn with insight subject matter which he might otherwise encounter ineffectually.

Actually, there is nothing unique about the approach we recommend. Many teachers have long been using the case-method, the problem-solving approach and socio-drama. Many have been keyed for many years to teaching that develops analytical and reflective thinking.

The substance of our recommendation is that this approach be more universally adopted. We believe teaching cannot be really effective without a student experiencing the quality of learning that these techniques make possible.

The classroom, the school and the community become the workshop for this approach. The classroom teacher pursuing a reasoned, objective method of thinking about rights serves not only as a model but becomes meaningfully related to his students in the process of learning and decision-making. The atmosphere he engenders of respect for the democratic process and the rights of others, individual differences of opinion, respect for dissent, is communicated to his students. They sense its validity as the environment which esteems individual rights. They flourish and are strengthened in their search for workable answers. Their decisions and opinions are scrutinized by their classmates for the facts and values on which they are based and all gain experience in the analytical process and the rational development of position and its defense.

The school, too, is part of the student's training in rights. The student council that really has an area of authority in which it can make and enforce decisions is a valuable learning experience for the entire student body. The administrator who in his day-to-day dealings with students evidences his commitment to the esteem of individual rights contributes to the learning experience in inestimable proportion.

The community that cooperates with the school to encourage and provide the opportunities for student involvement and expression about its affairs offers students the live workshop in which to cut their teeth.

✎§ A Case for the Classroom Periodical
William J. Shorrock

> *Although Shorrock's article refers specifically to junior and senior high classes, most of his comments apply equally to the primary and middle grades. Each year, the elementary teacher faces the question of whether to use one of the widely available classroom periodicals. Careful consideration of Shorrock's comments should help a reader make up his mind on this question.*

In our generation people do not have to be taught to be concerned about current history. From teen-agers on up, men and women *do* live in the present and *do* spend a good part of their time trying to predict the future. Like it or not, we are part of the larger world. The home, the neighborhood, the village and town are still important to us, but our future is irrevocably tied in with the future of peoples whose existence we were not even aware of a generation or more ago. The obligation which American citizenship imposes today requires that youth, and their elders as well, "gain an understanding of the moving forces of our time and of the workings

Used by permission of the author and the National Council for the Social Studies; from *Social Education*, 23:260–262, October, 1959. William J. Shorrock is a social studies editor at the Houghton Mifflin Publishing Company.

of our political, economic, and social institutions, and that they gain such an understanding of the world that they will not be lost in it, or be so baffled that they seek to escape from it. Herein lies today's imperative." (1)

For this reason the systematic study of current affairs has become an essential part of the school curriculum, and it is safe to predict that it will continue to play an ever-growing role in the total school program. The prevailing national pattern of approximately one class period per week devoted to the study of current history could profitably be expanded to two, three, or more periods per week if we gave due consideration to the enormity of the problems confronting our own and all other peoples of the world today. Nevertheless, the fact remains that the typical history or social studies course in junior and senior high schools allots but one period per week to current history.

BASIC TEXT MOST IMPORTANT

Let's accept that fact for the time being and move on to consider an implication of it: *The crucial importance of the study of current history and the limited amount of attention given it in the schools today requires that teachers use the utmost care in the selection of text materials.* The best possible use must be made of the limited time available in the classroom; the most effective, most efficient text materials available must be employed.

Webster defines the word "textbook" as "a book containing a presentation of the principles of a subject, intended to be studied by the pupil and used as a basis of instruction by the teacher." Relating this definition specifically to the current history course, we may list the minimum requirements of an appropriate "text." The basic text for the current history course should (a) focus on what is pertinent to an understanding of the contemporary scene; (b) present in understandable terms the current problems on which the citizens of a democracy must make decisions and form policies; (c) define and present problem areas objectively; (d) provide the factual historical background of all problems considered; (e) summarize proposed solutions to problems; (f) present leading viewpoints on proposed alternatives—both majority and minority opinions; (g) encourage students to reach *their own* conclusions on problems in the light of available evidence; and (h) show how young people may bring their influence to bear in the formulation of public policy.

The teacher of current history has a wealth of information sources available, among which are daily newspapers, weekly or monthly periodicals of fact and opinion, the public affairs programs of radio and TV, motion pictures and filmstrips, leaflets and pamphlets from a wide range of sources, both governmental and nongovernmental. He will want to make use of some of these resources from time to time, and it should be his obligation to acquaint students with *all* of them. An important goal of current history study is attaining an understanding use of a wide variety of information sources.

However, such materials, while extremely useful for supplementary reading and extended reference, are less than adequate as *basic texts* for the current history course. Why? For the same reasons that primary and contemporary sources are inadequate as basic texts for the junior and senior high school courses in United States History, Modern European History, World History, Citizenship, Civics, or Modern Problems. Such sources are, for the most part, too fragmentary or too inclusive or too unorganized or too diffuse or too unobjective or too bulky for practical classroom use. They lack organization, synthesis, focus, and interpretation.

QUALITIES OF THE BASIC TEXT

For these reasons, the vast majority of teachers rely on specially-prepared classroom periodicals (2) as the *pièce de résistance* of their current history study. The specially-prepared current history periodical (which we shall label "the current history text" from this point onward), like any other good textbook, is specifically adapted to meet the particular needs of classroom instruction. All such texts are written and edited by highly skilled staffs of teachers and journalists who know how to present vital and timely information in a form that meets today's classroom needs. All of them are continuously scrutinized by editorial advisory boards consisting of classroom teachers, curriculum specialists, school administrators, and well-known historians. The publishers of these periodicals expect their products to be subjected to the same rigorous examination applied to any other texts used as basic teaching tools.

We should like to direct attention to several unique characteristics of these current history texts—characteristics which, over the years, have qualified them eminently as *basic texts* for current history classes:

They are compact. They offer a condensed view of current events and problems. Through close to a half century of school experience, these publications have developed the art of dealing with a number of issues succinctly yet understandably. They are brief enough so that all the members of a class may read them in their entirety, thereby acquiring a common body of information so essential for carrying on intelligent discussion. Yet these publications are full enough in presentation so that each week all the members of a class may gain an accurate picture of the more important events and problems of the week.

They are selective. Many publications dealing with the current scene are unspecialized, offer a great quantity of material of all kinds, much of which, at best, may be merely diverting or amusing, or, at worst, confusing or demoralizing to the immature reader. Frequently such publications make no clear distinction between what is truly important and what is merely sensational or shocking. It is one of the functions of a publication prepared especially for students to make this distinction and to present for study the more important and significant of current problems.

They are objective. The current history texts, when presenting controversial issues, maintain an approach which is entirely impartial. The first obligation of the teacher is to see to it that students have a completely objective explanation of the issue. The admitted facts must first be presented. Then there must follow an impartial examination of the different points of view. Students should not be influenced by teacher or text to follow one opinion or another.

The impartial approach *at the very outset* is especially important. If an issue is first examined through a publication offering a one-sided presentation, the opinions of students may unconsciously become permanently biased in the same direction. Even though they later read other publications with differing points of view, the arguments with which they became familiar at the outset, whether right or wrong, may carry greater weight. The *impartial* approach is followed scrupulously by the weekly current history texts prepared especially for school use.

They link the past to the present. A strong point of the current history texts is their emphasis upon cause and effect. They treat current history as a continuation of past history and provide bridges between the major course textbook and the contemporary scene. They carefully delineate the backgrounds to current problems, thereby providing the necessary base for an understanding analysis of today's issues.

They organize and grade content carefully. The current history text takes over the task of winnowing, analyzing, and interpreting the vast bulk of news, thereby saving the already overburdened classroom teacher an enormous amount of work each week. Teachers should not be expected to undertake an additional full-time job of collecting facts and opinions from the nation's best news services, newspapers and magazines, TV and radio programs, and other sources.

Moreover, why should they, when the job has already been done for them by the weekly current history text? These publications present current news and issues in systematic form. Their organization, scope, vocabulary level, and manner of treatment are determined by classroom needs. For teachers, they offer suggestions on points of emphasis, historical parallels, developmental relationships, concepts, emerging trends, and teaching devices. For students, they provide a controlled vocabulary, study guides, activities suggestions, and lists of periodicals, books, and newspapers for extended reference work.

They incorporate selected visual aids. Major articles and news features appearing in the weekly current history texts are carefully illustrated with appropriate visual aids—charts, maps, cartoons, diagrams, and the best news pictures available from all parts of the world. Such aids are closely integrated with the textual content in order to provide an efficient and effective teaching tool. At the same time, such illustrations reinforce the development of essential study skills—map reading, graph interpretation, cartoon techniques, and critical thinking.

They offer supplementary services. The special needs of both teachers and students are taken into account in supplementary service programs provided by the publishers of weekly current history texts. Maps; charts; handbooks of information on geography, government, politics, and economics; study guides; weekly, monthly, and semester tests—all these are available either free or at a nominal cost.

All these publishers offer teachers' editions of their various weekly texts containing suggestions on the teaching of current history—useful classroom projects and procedures; lesson plans; organized units of work; extensive reading bibliographies on specific topics; notes on worthwhile TV and radio programs, appropriate motion pictures, filmstrips, and recordings; announcements of useful publications issued by state, national, and international governmental agencies, private organizations, and foundations; and reviews of current books in the areas of education and public affairs.

A FINAL WORD

Nothing which we have said should be interpreted as a denial of the usefulness or importance of other information media. All current history classes should be called upon to expand their basic studies by reading newspapers, magazines, and books, and by following the public affairs programs of radio and TV. As students proceed with their work, they will encounter problems requiring more extended study. With their interest aroused, they may easily be induced to turn to the vast array of supplementary materials.

The study of current affairs is in the curriculum to stay. There will probably be more of it, not less, in the future. Carried on half-heartedly or inexpertly, with little or no attempt to make it part of the larger whole, it can leave the student confused and discouraged. Organized, correlated, and integrated with history and the other social studies, it can be an enlightening and liberating activity. It is the task of the specialized current history text to help make it so.

References

(1) American Association of School Administrators. *Education for American Citizenship*. Washington: The Association, 1954. p. 25–26.

(2) Among the best known and most widely accepted of the classroom current history texts for junior and senior high schools are the offerings of (1) Civic Education Service, 1733 K Street, N.W., Washington 6, D.C.— *American Observer, Weekly News Review, Junior Review*; (2) Scholastic Magazines, 33 West 42nd Street, New York 36—*Senior Scholastic, World Week, Junior Scholastic*; (3) American Education Publications, 1250 Fairwood Avenue, Columbus 16, Ohio—*Our Times, Every Week, Current Events*.

✒ CURRENT AFFAIRS AND THE SOCIAL STUDIES

J. D. McAulay

Have the news media so saturated our lives that current events can play no effective role in the social studies? Professor McAulay gives a sound answer to this question and then identifies three criteria for teaching current events. He next illustrates the use of current affairs in social studies in the primary and middle grades. His suggestions for reporting current affairs should be helpful, for scarcely anything is more deadly than the dreary, daily recitation of headlines.

Used by permission of the author and the National Council for the Social Studies; from *Social Education*, 23:21–22, January, 1959. Dr. McAulay is a professor of elementary education at Pennsylvania State University and a frequent writer on elementary social studies.

WITH NEWS POURING from the radio and television in an ever-swelling flood, many teachers have concluded that it is no longer important to discuss contemporary affairs in the social studies classroom. Why, they ask should we take up valuable class time rehashing what almost every child already knows?

There is a positive answer to this question. The social studies curriculum has a major responsibility for relating the present to the past. The social studies, perhaps more than any other subject in the curriculum, should provide a living link with the society in which the child moves and has his being. For this reason, it is difficult to see how current affairs in the community, in the state, in the nation, and in the world at large can be excluded from the social studies program.

As far as current affairs are concerned, the social studies should seek to develop: 1) a continuing interest on the part of the pupil in what is going on in the world around him; 2) the ability to sift and sort the news in an effort to arrive at the truth; and 3) a sense of values that will enable him to separate the trivial from the important.

EXAMPLES OF USES OF CURRENT AFFAIRS

If there is any validity in what we are saying, the study of current affairs should be carried at every grade level, starting with the primary grades. In the primary grades, for example, an item of news from the local community can be used as a subject for discussion in the "share" or "experience" period. Let us suppose a new fire hall has just been opened. The local television and radio stations have featured the event. Although "The Fireman" may not be the unit of study at the moment, the teacher can use a discussion of this timely topic to review the unit already completed or to preview a unit yet to come. The teacher can also encourage the children to gather additional information, thus setting their feet on the first rung of the ladder of research. Moreover, with this information the class can begin to construct its own reading chart—"We have a new fire station. Our fire station has four engines . . ." etc. The point is that an alert teacher can bring local news into everyday class discussions and, in so doing, help to stimulate the children's interest in the larger life of the community.

It is important at all grade levels to integrate the discussion of current affairs with other subjects in the curriculum—the language arts, science, and the social studies. If, for instance, pupils in the intermediate grades are studying a unit on Canada, they can be encouraged to set up a separate bulletin board with items clipped from newspapers and magazines—items about Canada's elections, recent discoveries of gold and other minerals, or any other current information about Canada. One way to organize such an activity is to set up a special committee and give it the responsibility for gathering and displaying current materials on Canada. This committee can be asked to organize its material into a permanent collection. The committee may, with the help of other members of the class, paste the pictures and news items it has gathered on large sheets of butcher paper, which, when filled, may be formed into a booklet.

Another way for the committee on Canada to present its material is for one member of the group to give an oral summary. A summary of this kind can be given at the beginning of each class period or it can be given once or twice a week. Moreover, the student giving the summary may present the "news" by speaking into a microphone (a perforated tin can will serve nicely) while standing before a "television camera" (made of a cardboard box and broom handles). If the "newscaster" has prepared a written summary, it can be pasted on the bulletin board. This bulletin board, or "News Chart," will serve as a handy reference for all members of the class.

The completion of a unit should not end the gathering of current information about a particular subject. News items collected after the unit has been completed should be added to the section of the "News Book" reserved for that particular unit. In the process, the unit will again be brought to mind, and in many instances a review of one unit may dovetail very nicely with the unit currently in progress. This joining of units does much to overcome a too frequent weakness of the social studies—the dispensing of "packaged information."

CURRENT AFFAIRS AS A CONTINUING PROJECT

Current affairs enterprises should, of course, involve more than the mere collecting of news for a particular unit. The current affairs class itself should engage in a continuing project extending throughout the entire year. A sixth-grade class, for example, might concern itself throughout the year with news of the United Nations; another class might follow the progress of the St. Lawrence Seaway project. The clippings and news items dealing with the continuing project should be kept in a separate area of the bulletin board, and separate "News Books" should be compiled. The reviews, or summaries, of the continuing topics need not be as frequent as those given in connection with the individual units, but they are important for they serve to keep the complete picture before the class and to keep interest alive.

A good current affairs topic is one that is in some way related to some problem or interest of the class itself. The progress of the Yankees' Baseball team, for instance, has little value unless the class has a high interest in baseball and a team of its own. The collecting of political cartoons is only valuable if the class is interested in drawing cartoons and has some knowledge of and interest in political problems. Many classroom current affairs bulletin boards are covered with neatly and attractively displayed clippings. On inquiry, however, it is often found that the children have no idea why the particular items were chosen. In fact, one ten-year-old chairman of a current affairs committee reported that she had asked the members of her group to cut out *big* headlines, the more quickly to cover the space on the board allotted to her committee's particular project.

A field trip to a newspaper printing establishment or to a radio station can be of great value to a current affairs class. The children should be given specific instructions before the trip is taken to look for methods and procedures in the gathering of news as well as in the process of reporting it. A visit to the classroom by a newspaper reporter or a radio newscaster who would discuss with the class the techniques of collecting and reporting news, might serve as an introduction to, or the culminating feature of, a field trip.

Having had such a close look into the business of securing accurate reports and presenting them in an interesting manner, the class should now undertake some reporting on its own. For example, a committee of students might visit the headquarters of the Community Chest Drive on the last evening of its campaign. The committee would secure facts and figures and report on the degree of success achieved by the campaign. The following day, the class could compare the committee's report with the one given by the press and radio. Such an exercise would give the class a better appreciation and understanding of current affairs and, perhaps more particularly, of the human factor behind the collecting and composition of the news.

There are many ways of presenting current affairs, and the class should be encouraged to use as much variety as possible. One week they can present their news by means of a "television broadcast." Another week a dramatization can be arranged. Pictorial representation through blackboard charts or murals can be utilized. The news can be mimeographed and copies distributed to all class members. Headlines can be printed and attached to the bulletin boards, with ribbons leading to detailed accounts of the headline event.

Source materials for current affairs may be simple or elaborate. A small portable radio in a corner of the classroom might be used by the group responsible for the collection of current affairs. The radio can be tuned quietly to the mid-morning newscast, and the children will record only that news that they consider important. Newspapers and magazines used need not be those printed that day. Those already read at home and brought to school by the children the following day, or even the following week, may prove useful. A special table or shelf should be set aside for these source materials.

However current affairs may be taught, there must be some provision for periodic testing. The form of the testing may vary. It may take the form of a radio quiz, a crossword puzzle, a completion test, or an interpretive essay. Guided by the results of such tests, the teacher can determine the content and methods that best meet the interests and ability of the class.

The study of current affairs should help to bridge the gap between the classroom and the outside world. Good teaching can make the study of current affairs alive and meaningful.

✌️ CONTROVERSIAL ISSUES *John P. Lunstrum*

This article reviews the nature and sources of controversy about controversy. Lunstrum carefully reports divergent views of social studies specialists, examines the social foundations of controversy, and considers different ideas about the proper relationship between the school and the society that supports it. The material included here is taken from a longer two-part article that gives considerable attention to the problems of creating school policies on the teaching of controversial issues. Interested readers will find the original articles, as well as those mentioned in the footnotes, valuable.

RECENT ACCOUNTS IN the press and reports from teachers suggest increasing activity on the part of extremist organizations who are apparently bent on making the school and teachers instruments of

Used by permission of the author and the National Council for the Social Studies; from "Controversial Issues, School Policies and Reflective Thinking," by John P. Lunstrum, in *Social Education,* 26:189–192, April, 1962, and 26:244–246+, May, 1962. John P. Lunstrum is an associate professor of education and coordinator for school social studies at Indiana University.

their own policies. The concern of some NCSS teachers is reflected in the passage by the members of the Indiana Council for the Social Studies on April 15, 1961, of a vigorous resolution asserting in part that "such efforts to use the schools as tools of blatant indoctrination are more representative of the Totalitarian than the Democratic tradition." The unanimous endorsement of a similar resolution by the NCSS during its 1961 convention suggests that teachers in many states are deeply troubled by what an executive secretary of one Midwestern state teachers association has called the "Vigilante impulse." (1) . . .

BACKGROUND OF THE PROBLEM

The significant publications of professional and academic organizations during the last three decades have continuously emphasized the legitimate position of controversial issues in the secondary school curriculum and the freedom of teachers to deal with such topics particularly in social studies classes. Despite the sanction of such organizations as the American Historical Association, the Mississippi Valley Historical Society, the National Council for the Social Studies, and the Educational Policies Commission of the NEA, there is increasing evidence that teachers lack a clear understanding of their proper role insofar as the treatment of controversial issues is concerned. Investigations made concerning teacher attitudes on this subject in several states indicate that many teachers lack insight into the nature of a genuinely controversial issue; these studies also suggest that a substantial number of teachers have no conception of a defensible theory with which they could support the introduction of controversial topics or materials into the classroom (2).

FACTORS UNDERLYING CONFUSION

When questioned specifically on their freedom or willingness to express opinions on controversial topics teachers revealed uncertainty and confusion. For example, in two inquiries conducted in 1953 and 1957 in Ohio and Virginia, teachers were apparently willing to endorse the utilization of controversy on an abstract level, but when confronted with the need for a specific application of this principle, they tended to acquiesce in certain limitations or taboos (3).

Confusion over method. These comments are in no way offered in disparagement of classroom teachers or administrators. That educators have made great gains in public recognition with the assistance of their professional organizations is clearly evident. The difficulties they face in trying to place into practice the ideals of intellectual freedom may be viewed in part as a reflection of the conflicts in values in American education. One has only to examine a number of social studies methods texts to illustrate this point. Some authors advocate extreme caution, particularly with reference to the expression of opinion by the teacher. Emphasis is placed on "presenting facts as they really are," (4) and the teacher's role is seen as one of "neutrality" (5). The author of a pamphlet published by the NCSS entitled, "How to Handle Controversial Issues," advises teachers to avoid stating their beliefs in order to encourage pupils to do their own thinking. These points of view are challenged by other methodologists and social scientists who contend that it is impossible for a teacher to exemplify reflective thinking in a classroom and conceal his own opinions (6).

On the subject of the instructor's qualifications to explore the realms of controversy, some writers insist that the teacher must first possess a high degree of scholarship and a mastery of the pertinent facts (7); others urge the teacher to assume the position of a "learner among learners." (8) To the question as to how much emphasis to assign to the study of controversial topics, there is an equally contradictory array of answers. Only a "few topics" in current events are likely to be controversial according to one ruling (9) while other claims are made that the study of controversial materials is implicit in the social studies (10) and that controversial topics should be deliberately and frequently introduced into class discussion and study (11).

Social foundations of controversy. This conflict in education seems to be part of a larger problem, for there is a growing body of evidence accumulated by social scientists and other students of society that American society is confronted today by a cultural crisis of increasing dimensions (12). Various symptoms frequently cited as evidence include: 1) confusion and contradiction in values, 2) decline in communication, 3) personal disorganization, 4) discontent of the intellectuals, and 5) an irrationality expressed in the cultivation of myths, absolutes, and a "two-valued" semantic orientation based upon simple "good" and "bad" distinctions.

The rapidity and nature of social change have been advanced as reasonable explanations for current tensions and contradictions. This view is reinforced by Mannheim's concept of a "transitional era" (13) or a period of change between two forms of social organization. More specifically, it now is held by a number of scholars that the rapid development of science, democracy, and technology has provided new conditions of life and new functions for existing social institutions which clash with the rules and values operating in an agrarian or pre-industrial society.

Although the limitations of space do not provide sufficient room for a thorough analysis of the thesis of cultural crisis, some examples drawn from significant areas of human affairs may point up the problem. Reflecting uncertainty in the basic rules of American society has been the tendency in international affairs for American symbolism to assume parochial characteristics (14). This specifically refers to the eagerness of many to identify Democracy with America. Eventually this could lead to the definition that Democracy is whatever America does. Writing in this vein, author Clarence Manion (whose work was distributed to Indiana teachers by a patriotic organization) finds the only hope for a prosperous free world is the acceptance ultimately by all peoples of American principles (15). On the other hand, Quincy Wright points out that there might be fewer neutral nations on matters of security, democracy, and justice provided Americans could develop the habit of viewing justice in terms of the Universal Declaration of Human Rights in the United Nations Charter (16). To this might also be added the hope in the light of recent events that citizens learn the dangers of equating Democracy with Anti-Communism.

In the realm of economics the strife between opposing values appears to be increasing, particularly with reference to the perennial issue of "individualism vs. collectivism." On this issue, there is evidence of a definite opposition between social classes (17). Business owners, managers, professional and small businessmen generally cling to the concept of government as an impartial guarantor of opportunities for individual initiative. Workingmen, on the other hand, display a so-called "collectivist" viewpoint when they sanction the government's role as a guardian of the citizen's economic welfare.

A folklore containing myths and fallacies has also appeared in discussions of the American economic system. "Free enterprise" and "full employment" as honorific and somewhat ambiguous terms are highly desirable although they are logically incompatible (18). In view of the apparently unavoidable tendency of the state to intervene in economic matters there is a nostalgic yearning on the part of many persons for a return to a laissez-faire or agrarian economy (19). This attitude, of course, constitutes a refusal to acknowledge that the very socio-economic restrictions causing concern stemmed from the results of large-scale industrial organization within the framework of capitalism.

Race and minority group problems reflect important tensions

of American society (20). The position of the American Negro poses a dilemma in conflicting valuations between the prescribed rules of Christian and American behavior on one general plane with those rules on specific planes which are distortions of social reality as they purport to rationalize fallacious theories about the Negro and his role in society (21).

There is undoubtedly a close relationship between the tensions and contradictions previously described and the increasing inability of groups to comprehend opposing views even when they share common values (22). This difficulty in communication introduces the topic of semantics or the study of the types of responses directed by people to signs and symbols which confront them. Students of semantics have noted that symptoms of semantic malfunctioning occur when emotionally-charged labels are used indiscriminately to categorize ideas or persons displaying some similar characteristics (23). Despite the warning of a distinguished authority in semantics that " 'out there' there are no absolute identities," (24) there are indications that we are increasingly plagued with dangerous forms of semantic malfunctioning. For example, a book supposedly exposing communism was sent anonymously to the senior class president of an urban Indiana high school. Among other things, students were urged to detect "left-wing slanting" in textbooks and lectures (25). "Socialists," "centralized planners," "communists," and "home-made materialism" are all perceived together as enemies of "free enterprise." (26)

SCHOOL AND SOCIETY

Underlying a discussion of this problem are undoubtedly a number of differing assumptions about the proper relationship between the school and the society it serves (27). Some educators may feel strongly that the school is simply an instrument of culture yet powerless to act upon culture; hence the formal educational process under these conditions becomes primarily concerned with preparing the student to make successful adaptation to existing social conditions. Others may agree with Russell Kirk when he insists that "what the twentieth century needs is the check-rein not the goad." (28) If this viewpoint is influential in schools, it means renewed emphasis on the school's function in the conservation and transmission of the cultural heritage and the introduction of controversial topics into the curriculum seems to interfere with the inculcation of basic virtues. Still another interpretation of the social role of the school stresses its operation not only as a means of assimilating traditions but also as a creative force in shaping individuals and modifying beliefs and institutions (29). The latter view is more compatible with the deliberate introduction of disputed subjects into the course of study.

References

(1) Robert H. Wyatt. "The Vigilante Impulse." *The Indiana Teacher.* 106:159–161; December 1961. . . .

(2) Calvin Deam. *Opinions of Virginia Schoolmen Concerning the Treatment of Controversial Issues.* Indiana University, 1958. 357 p.; T. L. Hall. *A Study of the Teaching of Controversial Issues in the Secondary Schools of the State of Ohio.* Ohio State University, 1953. 250 p.; M. J. Felsinger. *Investigation of the Study of Controversial Issues of American Democracy in Certain High Schools in Oklahoma.* University of Oklahoma, 1952. 167 p. All three of these studies were completed as doctoral theses.

(3) *Ibid.*

(4) Arthur C. Bining and H. David. *Teaching the Social Studies in Secondary Schools.* New York: McGraw-Hill Book Company, 1952. p. 323.

(5) *Ibid.*

(6) Maurice P. Hunt and Lawrence E. Metcalf. *Teaching High School Social Studies.* New York: Harper and Brothers, 1955. p. 439; Earl S. Johnson. *Theory and Practice of the Social Studies.* New York: The Macmillan Company, 1956. p. 50–51.

(7) Edgar B. Wesley. *Teaching the Social Studies in High School.* Boston: D. C. Heath and Company, 1950. p. 16–17.

(8) Richard E. Gross. "How to Handle Controversial Issues." No. 14 of the How To Do It Series. Washington, D.C.: The National Council for the Social Studies, 1958.

(9) Maurice P. Moffatt. *Social Studies Instruction.* Englewood Cliffs, N.J.: Prentice-Hall, 1954. p. 348.

(10) Earl S. Johnson. *Theory and Practice of the Social Studies.* New York: The Macmillan Company, 1956. p. 145.

(11) Hunt and Metcalf, *op. cit.*, p. 21.

(12) W. O. Stanley. *Education and Social Integration.* New York: Columbia University Press, 1953. p. 116; Clyde Kluckholm. *Mirror for Man.* New York: McGraw-Hill Book Company, 1949. p. 244; Gunnar Myrdal. *An American Dilemma.* Vol. I. New York: Harper and Brothers, 1944. p. 306; J. H. Randall. *Our Changing Civilization.* New York: Stokes, 1934. p. 203–204; David Bidney. "The Concept of Cultural Crisis." *American Anthropologist* 48:534–552; October-December 1946.

(13) Karl Mannheim. *Diagnosis of Our Time.* London: Routledge and Kegan, Paul, Ltd., 1943. p. 1–4.

(14) P. Lerner. "Strategy of Truth: Symbol and Act in World Propaganda," in Lyman Bryson and others, editors. *Symbols and Values: An Initial Study.* New York: Harper and Brothers, 1954. p. 371–382.

(15) Clarence Manion. *The Key to Peace.* Chicago: Heritage Foundation, Inc., 1951. p. 76.

(16) P. Lerner, *op. cit.*, p. 382. (Comments by Wright are in reference to Lerner's paper.)

(17) R. Centers. *The Psychology of Social Classes.* Princeton, N.J.: Princeton University Press, 1949. p. 64.

(18) Henry P. Fairchild. "Free Enterprise and Full Employment." *American Sociological Review* 11:271–277; June 1946.

(19) Sidney Hook, *The Hero in History.* New York: John Day and Company, 1943. p. 264.

(20) Gunnar Myrdal, *op. cit.*

(21) *Ibid.,* Vol. I, p. xlii–xlv, 209.

(22) W. O. Stanley, *op. cit.,* p. 160–165.

(23) S. I. Hayakawa. "How Words Change Our Lives," in Richard Thruelsen and John Kobler, editors. *Adventures of the Mind.* New York: Vintage Books, 1960. p. 260–262.

(24) *Ibid.,* p. 261.

(25) W. L. Skousen. *The Naked Communist.* Salt Lake City, Utah: Ensign Publishing Company, 1961. p. 280.

(26) *Ibid.,* p. 276, 277, 327–328, 361–362.

(27) R. F. Butts and L. A. Cremin. *A History of Education in American Culture.* Holt and Company, 1953, pp. 542–543.

(28) Russell Kirk. "Conservative vs. Liberal: A Debate." *New York Times Magazine.* March 4, 1956.

(29) National Education Association Educational Policies Commission. *Policies for Education in American Democracy.* Washington, D.C.: The Association, 1946. p. 128.

⊷§ A Case for Controversy

Robert L. Brackenbury

Is controversy necessary? Don't all Americans believe in the same basic principles? Brackenbury provides historical perspective on these questions. Should we deal with controversy in the social studies in the elementary grades? The author reasons persuasively that the answer to each of these questions is yes. Is the role of the teacher neutrality or objectivity? Brackenbury takes a definite position on this question, and then expands his comments to deal with the limits of controversy and with the appropriateness of indoctrination in a democracy.

From *The National Elementary Principal,* 42:14–19, April, 1963. Copyright 1963, Department of Elementary School Principals, National Education Association. All rights reserved. Robert L. Brackenbury is a professor of education at the University of Southern California.

CONTROVERSY IN THE ELEMENTARY SCHOOLS

The controversial issues that divide Americans are almost without number. And nearly all such issues, in one way or another, eventually get into the classrooms, even at the elementary level. . . .

In recent years, there have been strong and frequently violent differences over how patriotism should be taught. There are those who hold that love of country can best be taught by acquainting students with the American heritage, by glorifying the lives of American heroes with little or no debunking of the founding fathers, and by familiarizing students with the famous documents that have given shape to our basic democratic institutions. On the other hand, there are others who believe that patriotism can best be taught by developing in children an understanding of the way Americans have resolved their differences and by helping students realize that the founding fathers were great men, but nonetheless human beings with faults along with their virtues.

The thinking of the two groups may well grow out of fundamental ideological differences, with the former subscribing to a belief in absolutes, self-evident truths, and a social contract theory of government, while the latter hold to beliefs of a more recent and relativistic vintage. Be that as it may, the former usually want the elementary school to stress flag salutes with recitations of the Pledge of Allegiance, with the singing of the National Anthem, and with assembly programs glorifying the American heritage. The latter group, however, while not against such activities, doubt that they do much to develop love of country. A man may stand erect, salute Old Glory smartly, recite the Pledge flawlessly, and sing the National Anthem with gusto and still cheat on his income tax and attempt to get a traffic ticket fixed. Flag salutes, the latter group hold, are occasions for the expression of a person's love for his country, not a cause thereof.

The unfortunate thing about controversies such as this is not that differences of opinion exist. The unfortunate thing is that all too often so many on both sides fail to understand the real nature of the differences. In the case at hand, too many people on both sides cast aspersions on the loyalty of those who disagree with them. Loyalty is not involved. Both groups are composed of good Americans who differ not in their love for their country but in their beliefs about the best means to promote that love in the oncoming generation. There exist in this country contrasting conceptions of democracy which may or may not have equal validity but which certainly have equal claim to being democratic. One of the central tasks of the social studies is to develop an awareness of such differences in children. . . .

If we are to teach children to think, it is not enough to teach them to regurgitate our words. Children need to learn how to explore an idea. They need to examine it, to dig out hidden assumptions underlying it, to perceive its implications for action, and to determine its compatibility with other ideas that they hold. They also need the example of a teacher who himself holds firm convictions about vital issues and who is unafraid to state them.

PARTIALITY OR IMPOTENCY?

For far too long a misconception has been in vogue concerning how impartiality is best achieved. Impotency, not impartiality, is achieved by the teacher who keeps his own convictions hidden. The teacher who presents all sides of a controversial issue and then says, "Now, children, make up your own minds where you stand," is perhaps nobly motivated. But he is sadly misguided. Can his students be blamed for concluding that perhaps it does not make any difference which side they take or whether they take any side at all? . . .

Far sounder is the approach of the teacher who, while attempting to encourage his students to explore all sides of a controversial issue, does state his own position. It is doubtful that any teacher can keep his convictions completely out of his teaching, anyway, try as he will. The tone of his voice or the way he states the problem may give him away, or he may even lean over too far backwards in the attempt to be fair to a point of view with which he disagrees. In any case, it would be far better for a teacher to state where he stands but to state his position in the interest of objectivity rather than in the attempt to make converts. In this case, students can discount their teacher's biases for they know exactly what they are.

The argument most frequently raised against a teacher's stating his position openly is that the students will be indoctrinated. But indoctrination, at least the vicious variety, is teaching a set of beliefs in such a way that their validity seems beyond question. The teacher who has thought through his position does not feel threatened when it is challenged. Indeed, he can discuss his convictions without becoming too emotionally involved. He believes that his convictions have been derived logically from sound basic assumptions, and he is willing to expose his thinking to public scrutiny. If his students subscribe to different basic assumptions or if they reason differently, such differences can be recognized and respected. History teaches us that men of unquestioned moral integrity can have honest differences of opinion.

THE LIMITS OF CONTROVERSY

. . . The United States did not become great because all its citizens always thought alike. Quite the opposite is true. From its very beginning, our nation was composed of people who thought quite differently from one another. Coming from different countries with different cultural and religious backgrounds, the early settlers lived constantly with controversy. . . . Throughout our history, differences of opinion have been a source of strength.

Of course, it might not have been so. Indeed, at times its appeared that the differences that divided Americans might bring about the downfall of the nation. But somehow, some way, our forefathers resolved their controversies, divisive as they were. And the priceless heritage they left us consists not so much in the solutions they reached as in the methods they devised to settle their differences. At heart, democracy is a process that enables men to resolve the problems that confront them, and such a process cannot be learned in a school that supresses controversy.

If future differences are not to bring about America's demise, we must learn the process that is democracy and learn it well. There are rules of the game that must not be violated. Belief in the various freedoms that make up our civil liberties, belief in majority rule with minority rights, and belief that every man's vote should count as one and no more than one—such beliefs are essential to democracy. These beliefs can be questioned and they can even be modified slightly, but any major change could destroy democracy as we have known it. The rules of any game can be changed slightly and it will be recognized as the same game. A radical change, however, will likely bring into existence a new game.

INDOCTRINATION IN DEMOCRACY?

Enough has been said to suggest an answer to the perennial question, "Should the schools indoctrinate children in democracy?" If indoctrination is regarded simply as the teaching of a doctrine, the answer is "yes." Certainly, the schools in any social order can be expected to perpetuate the nature of the social order that created them. Schools in a democracy will teach democracy, and this includes imposing the democratic "rules of the game" upon children. Imposition simply cannot be avoided. By their choices of textbooks, subject matter to be studied, and even such simple matters as room decorations, teachers impose upon students. If imposition, then, is unavoidable, does it not seem defensible to impose the best that is known? Thus, majority rule, respect for the individual, and all the other elements of democracy we impose upon children.

However, the democratic rules of the game may be discussed, examined, and debated. Indeed, it would be most undesirable if they were taught in such a way that their validity seemed beyond question because to do so would be to contradict the rules themselves. Thus, it is impossible to indoctrinate in democracy, if by indoctrination we mean the teaching of any set of beliefs in such a way that their validity seems beyond doubt. For by insuring free speech, the democratic process itself provides for self-criticism. . . .

ADMINISTRATORS AND CONTROVERSY

. . . Teachers ought to hold firm convictions on social issues and they should feel free to express them when appropriate. But convictions should be expressed in the interest of objectivity, not for the purpose of winning converts or making disciples. Whether the student holds the same values as the teacher has nothing to do with his competency as a scholar, and his marks or grades should never be at issue.

The social studies teacher who is attacked by the community because he deals with controversial issues needs to know that he will be firmly supported by the administration so long as he strives for objectivity, strives to be fair—in brief, so long as he strives to teach rather than preach. It might be added that tact and good judgment are also essential equipment for those who seek to develop critical thinking in the young. When community feeling runs high on a particular issue because some current incident or occurrence has incited an emotional outburst, the time may not be ripe to commence a discussion of the issue. This is not cowardice; it is merely common sense. Critical thinking is not developed in a climate in which emotions are out of hand. This does not mean that a teacher should not stand up and be counted. But in a community crisis, his convictions might better find expression outside the school than in the classroom. When emotions have cooled down, the issue can then be considered and explored.

All this is not to say that current issues should not be considered in a social studies class. Most assuredly they should be, for we should take advantage of interest in current events. It is only suggested that the consideration of an issue be postponed when students are directly, personally, and passionately involved because of a community incident. . . .

We live at a time when international tensions run high. The

foreign policies of the major powers have been characterized as consisting of a "balance of terror." Mankind may well be running a fever that could lead to his demise. In times such as these, it would hardly seem that much of a case could be made for controversy. Yet, ironically, the need for concern for the fundamental issues that divide men and nations is even greater than ever. And such concern cannot be brought about if controversy is avoided. It is possible for men to learn to discuss without discounting the motives of their adversaries, to disagree without being disagreeable, and to differ without doubting the integrity of their fellow men. To teach these skills remains the abiding task of the social studies.

❧ Studying Other Countries

Leonard S. Kenworthy

How does the busy elementary teacher lead her pupils to effective study of the many nations of today's world? What does she do to avoid the pitfalls of stereotyping, of chauvinism, of misrepresenting national characteristics? Kenworthy examines these questions and provides examples of a number of ways students can study other nations without falling into the usual pitfalls. He further suggests a pattern for study that many teachers may find appealing.

SOME PEOPLE SAY that the world is growing smaller, and in a sense that is true. But in another sense the world is constantly growing larger. At the close of World War II there were approximately 75 countries on our globe. Since that time 25 new nations have been formed, bringing the number of nations in the world today to around 100.

This means that the effective social studies teacher must be able to move quickly and competently from Chile to Ceylon to the Central African Federation, or from Guatemala to Germany to Ghana, or from Mexico to Morocco to Malaya.

With so many countries to study now and with the expectation that there will be more within a few years, it is more important than

Used by permission of the author and the National Council for the Social Studies; from *Social Education*, 23:159–162, April, 1959. Dr. Kenworthy is a professor of education at Brooklyn College and author of many articles on world affairs.

ever before for teachers to consider effective ways of studying other countries, to start or to enlarge their small libraries of books and their files of current materials on the various nations of the world, and to reflect on the criteria by which countries should be selected for study.

This article singles out the problem of how to study the many nations of the world, leaving the reader to explore other writings on the materials available for the study of other lands and peoples, and the criteria by which countries should be selected for study (1).

SOME PITFALLS TO AVOID

Unconsciously and without malice towards other lands and peoples, most of us have fallen into ways of studying other countries which do a great injustice to their citizens and give a distorted view of them to our students. It might be well for all of us to examine our current practices to see if we have fallen into such traps.

One pitfall is to present other countries as they existed yesterday, but not as they exist today. For example, we still picture the Mexican, with his serape, sleeping in the sun, with his sombrero at his side or tilted over his eyes. Or we portray Africans as naked, drum-beating savages living in mud-huts in hot, wet lands. We forget or we fail to stress the fact that all Mexicans never fitted that stereotype or that all Africans did not live as we have said. Furthermore, we tend to forget the vast changes which have taken place in these and other parts of the world, with the industrialization of so many nations and the development of large metropolitan areas like Mexico City, Casablanca, Leopoldville, Johannesburg, and other urban centers.

Or we devote two or three days to a country, treating it hurriedly and superficially, content that we have "covered" that part of the syllabus, little realizing that the residue of our study will be a few unrelated and probably unimportant facts. Like the men in the fable of the blind men and the elephant, our students will have discovered the trunk or the ears or the tail and not the whole animal—or country.

In our desire to arouse interest on the part of pupils, we often fall into the pitfall of stressing the bizarre and the colorful rather than the realistic, especially at the elementary school level. Hence we teach about the igloos of Alaska and the windmills of The Netherlands, leaving lasting misimpressions about these and other parts of the world.

Or we teach about a country as if all the people in it dressed alike, thought alike, and acted alike. We talk about *The French, The Japanese,* or *The Brazilians,* failing to stress the infinite variety within countries as well as between them. How can one gain a complete and accurate picture today, for instance, of Malaya without taking into account the large numbers of Chinese, Indians, and Pakistani as well as the larger group of Malays? Or how can one study Guatemala without stressing the large percentage of Indians as well as the Spanish and mestizos?

Then again, we may like a country very much and present only the best aspects of it—or conversely, dislike it and present only the worst phases of it.

As historians and social scientists we need to have a single rather than a double standard for studying countries. This is especially true of countries like Russia and China. One result of presenting only their weaknesses has been the tailspin into which the American public has been thrown by its recent realization that Russians, like the peoples of other countries, do some things uncommonly well.

Another pitfall into which we often fall is that of judging others by our standards. Thus we condemn India, Burma, Ceylon, and other nations for being "independent" in their foreign policies, rather than trying to understand why they have taken such a stand. Or we ridicule the French because their plumbing is not as good as ours, often overlooking or minimizing the areas of life in which the people of France may equal or surpass us.

Finally, we often tend to equate knowledge about a nation with respect for it or an understanding of it. We amass an enormous number of facts, hoping thereby to promote an understanding of that country. As a result we produce, or try to produce, little walking World Almanacs or National Geographics rather than competent, well-informed, understanding world-minded Americans.

THE MANY WAYS OF STUDYING COUNTRIES

There are scores of ways of studying other countries, from which competent teachers can select the ones most appropriate to their classes or the ones which they are able to handle. The combined use of many of these approaches in the study of any nation can enrich the understanding of it and provide a variety of methods for building and maintaining interest on the part of pupils.

On a recent nine-months trip to the new nations of Africa, the Middle East, and Asia, the author of this article tried out several of these approaches and found them exciting and revealing. For example, one can enter a village or city and listen for all the sounds that he hears, tape recording them for future use. In this way the dimension of sound is added to that of sight to develop a well-rounded view of a country.

Or one can stand on the side of a major highway and learn

much about a nation. In Pakistan, for example, the writer saw 12 different modes of transportation on one street corner, ranging from rubber-tired camel carts carrying cotton bales to the modern limousine of the Pakistan Airways.

A view of the hats of a country can help one to understand it, for they represent history, position, religion, rank, economics, and politics. A count, for example, of the number of old men wearing the fez in Morocco as opposed to the number of young men wearing . . . [it] reveals the tremendous cleavage between generations in their acceptance of innovations, for the fez is still a symbol there of the old regime.

For those competent in music, the songs of a country can tell much about its philosophy and history. In a student group at Penn State University recently a highly qualified musician was playing a piece of Indian music. When she stopped playing, one of the students asked her if she had completed the song for it sounded unfinished to him. To this question she replied, "Does life always complete itself? Does one always return to *do?*" The group stopped and thought, and through the incident gained a much deeper insight into India and Indian philosophy than lectures and books had previously revealed.

Similarly, the study of literature, of language, of movies and plays, of holidays, of children's drawings, and of a host of other subjects and activities can help us as teachers and through us our students to get inside other countries and cultures (2).

Taken alone, these methods may give a distorted view of a country; taken together they should give as broad and deep a view as is possible without close contact with the people themselves.

What is needed today in the study of any country or culture is a multidimensional, interdisciplinary approach, drawing upon the insights of history, geography, sociology, social psychology, economics, anthropology, government, psychology, psychiatry, literature and language, religion and philosophy, and the arts. As social studies teachers or social scientists, we should draw upon the many disciplines in our own broad field as well as upon many related disciplines.

A POSSIBLE PATTERN FOR STUDYING COUNTRIES

There are always dangers in suggesting "patterns," for they may be meaningful to the person who has developed them and not prove useful to others. Or they may become merely "patterns" rather than teaching devices for better understanding. Over a period of several years the writer has experimented with the chart or pattern for study-

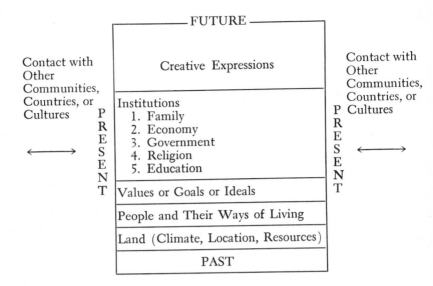

ing communities, countries, and cultures which appears at the top of this page. It is hoped that this pattern will suggest to both teachers and students a logical way of looking at any country. Even after much of the mass of detailed information has been forgotten they may still have a method by which they can re-examine countries which they once studied in school or new nations which they have never studied. Or they can use this pattern to look at a new community or state into which they have moved in this period of high mobility in the United States.

The best point for starting any study of a country is usually with its geographic base. This is the stage on which the drama of human history takes place and it is of vital importance to any nation.

A look at the geographic base of Norway should reveal the mountainous terrain of that country and explain quickly why the Norwegians have settled largely in small communities along the fjords; have taken their livestock up into the cleared patches in the mountains; have gone to sea; or have emigrated to other parts of the world. Or an examination of Libya or Jordan's geographic bases will soon show why their economies are not viable. The use of polar projection maps will explain to students why Russia feels surrounded by the various pacts of the Western World or why Cambodia and Laos and other Southeast Asia nations are cautious in their relations with China and Russia.

Then come the people—the actors on the stage which has just been examined. They cannot be portrayed in one simple tableau, for there is always an infinite variety within any given country, whether it be Kenya in East Africa, with its large African population, its small but economically and politically dominant white group, and its large number of Indians and Pakistani; or Brazil, a melting pot of Italians, Spaniards, Portuguese, Germans, Russians, Japanese, and others.

There is almost always an infinite variety in ways of living, too, within countries. This is far more true of the economically underdeveloped nations than it is of the countries of the Western World. But there is variety even in a country like France, with vast differences between the lives of the French farmers and the residents of Paris, Lyons, or Marseilles, making it ridiculous to study France by concentrating on Paris, as is so often done. How much greater are the differences in a nation like India, with the range of human activities covering the span from the most primitive life in an isolated village to the highly sophisticated existence of upper-middle class citizens in a city like New Delhi.

In moving from the geographic base to the people, it is important in every country to see the relationships between these two factors, and to understand how the land has affected the people and in turn how the people have affected the land.

The values or beliefs of the people of any country are not easily understood by an outsider, but they are central to the study of every nation. How can one understand the institutions which have been created in any part of the world without knowing why these institutions developed? How can one understand the actions of any group of people without some knowledge of their values? Lacking such knowledge, the student will judge others by his own standards—a grievous mistake in the study of any country.

Thus any study of Southeast Asia must include at least an elementary knowledge of Buddhism, or any study of the Middle East a passing acquaintance at least with Islam. Students should also understand the belief in the importance of the larger family in most parts of the world today and of the values of tribalism in large parts of Africa. Any understanding of the Union of South Africa today must be predicated on at least some stress on the rigid, orthodox interpretation of Christianity on the part of most whites in that country, and any understanding of Russia must be based on at least an elementary knowledge of dialectic materialism, even if that phrase must be interpreted in the most elementary ways.

In every country in the world today there are deep rifts and conflicts between value systems which must be understood in order to appreciate current events in any country. Thus, in Ghana, one can only appreciate the political struggle if it is set within the frame of a titanic struggle between the tribal chiefs and the representatives of modernization and westernization, or between the various economic forces within the country. Similarly, one must appreciate the views of the zamindars in West Pakistan and of the mullahs as representing the power of Islam in order to probe below the surface of unrest in that part of the world.

In the [foregoing] chart the section on values or beliefs precedes that on institutions because it is the beliefs of any group of people which have largely effected the institutions which they have created.

In all or almost all societies there are five basic institutions which people have developed. These are the family, the economy, the religion, the government, and the educational system—whether it is formally or informally organized. Some attention needs to be given to each of these major forms of human organization, even at the elementary or junior high school level of instruction.

In the future it may be necessary to add other institutions, such as the mass media, but the five we have mentioned here are central today in all societies.

In studying each of these human institutions it is important for students to know that there are problems connected with them in each country. These range from the problem of internal security in Burma, Malaya, and Vietnam to that of governmental organization in France and Italy.

As an integral part of the study of any country, students should learn about the creative expressions of that part of the world. Students need to learn that people everywhere have created in the past and are still creating. And students need to understand that the future vitality of any nation or people is dependent in large part upon its creativity.

Such creativity may yield simple and beautiful products such as the kente cloth togas for the men in Ghana or the simple wooden stools in the homes of Kenya Africans, with colored beads attractively embedded in patterns in the soft wood. Or creativity may mean the development of new ideas such as the growth of parliamentary democracy in England or the public school system in the United States.

The emphasis in most studies of other lands and peoples should be upon the present, but the present cannot be understood without reference to the past. And no study of a country will be adequate without a look at its future. People everywhere are proud of their history; people in many parts of the world are pulled today by their hopes for the future. This pull of the future is especially apparent in the new and emerging nations of the world.

Finally, it is important to see that no country today is isolated. Each has its contacts with other parts of the world and affects and in turn is affected by other nations.

To include all these aspects of life in our studies of other countries means that we will need to study fewer countries, but to examine those few nations with far greater depth and with far greater breadth than we have usually done in the past.

References

(1) For material on the other two topics not treated here, see the writer's volume on *Introducing Children to the World in Elementary and Junior High Schools* (Harper, 1956) and his two chapters in Ralph C. Preston's *Teaching World Understanding* (Prentice-Hall, 1955).

(2) For a provocative study of many of these techniques, see Margaret Mead and Rhoda Metraux. *The Study of Culture at a Distance* (University of Chicago Press, 1953).

Introducing Children to the World

Ralph C. Preston

Preston, in his usual penetrating manner, cuts quickly to the core of problems involved in introducing children to their world. He focuses on nine educational tasks, each dependent upon the others, and all necessary to a balanced, comprehensive understanding of the world that exists beyond the boundaries of our nation. His suggestions are practical. His examples are clear. His ideas should result in improved teaching of topics on our world and its affairs.

I INVITE YOU TO explore with me nine educational tasks which, in my opinion, require our attention if we are to introduce children to the world in a manner calculated to develop on their part an intimate

Used by permission of the author and the National School Board Association; from its 1960 Convention Proceedings, *Education for World Leadership*, pp. 125–131.

acquaintance, a penetrating understanding, and a lasting desire to help preserve its good features and correct its shortcomings. I shall not take them up in the order of their importance. They probably are of more or less equal importance and are dependent upon one another.

First, in our hierarchy of educational aims, social literacy should be accorded the importance which it deserves. Social literacy is no less important than literacy with respect to the printed or written language. I am speaking now of sheer, minimum social literacy—not of mastery of the intricacies, subtleties, and refinements of the various disciplines of the social sciences. In our conversations with children and in our teaching, we should attach prestige to having a good stock of precise information. We might not agree on all the particulars of information which should be taught, but we would probably agree that, say at the conclusion of grade six, a child of average ability should be able to point to Greece and Spain on a map of Western Europe, even if Gallup found that his parents can't; know that the Revolutionary War occurred before the Civil War; know that it is not true, as one high school student wrote on a college entrance examination, that Budapest is simply the modern way to spell Bucharest; etc. We are interested in particulars of information known by the child, not only because such knowledge is often important in and of itself, but chiefly because it is a by-product and a correlate of the knowledge of significant generalizations, such as those which explain how contrasting peoples are affected by their environments and traditions, and why nations today are interdependent.

One way to promote the role of social literacy is to fortify the social studies program in the primary grades, where it is often thin, and to improve social studies teaching in the intermediate grades, which is often weak.

Second, let's turn at once to the primary grades, that is, grades one to three. The need here is for more substantial content. Many social studies courses of study and textbooks at this level do not provide enough challenge for the child. They offer pablum when the child's condition calls for meat. McAulay and others have reported how badly we tend to underestimate the young child's background; that from television, family trips, and other experiences, children acquire content which exceeds the content of their social studies in both depth and scope. The idea that the child's first-grade program, for example, should be confined to concepts centering around home, school, and neighborhood is no longer valid. The "expanding environment" theory, which has dominated the social studies curriculum for the past generation, needs modification. According to this theory, the child starts out studying the home; then, as he advances in school, he studies consecutively an ever larger unit of the environment—the neighborhood, the community, the state, the nation, the hemisphere, and the world. While this scheme is in part valid, as Fraser points out, "there are some questions to be raised. . . . do not most [children] push out the frontiers of their experience irregularly, jumping via television, radio, and other experiences from home to foreign lands and back to distant parts of their own nation, perhaps before they ever go to school? . . . These and many other factors in our fast-moving, modern world cause a child's horizons to be considerably wider and to expand in directions unthought of a generation or two ago." Thus, our clinging to a too-pat armchair theory of child development can obstruct educational progress. The need today is for widespread experimentation at the primary level with new and more challenging content in the social studies field.

Third, consider with me the intermediate grades, that is, grades four through six, or, in some schools, grades four through eight. The task here is to cut sharply the immense volume of content which is covered in most schools. The overload of concepts and generalizations in most published programs is excessive. Because of this, teachers are inclined to push their classes at a more rapid rate than is psychologically defensible, for the sake of getting to the end of the book by June. The result is superficiality, empty concepts, misconceptions, and unnecessary boredom with the subject. You can prove this to yourself by taking a typical intermediate-grade textbook and reading a passage on a subject with which you are familiar. I did this the other day, reading a passage on Philadelphia, a city which I think I know well. The passage starts out by saying that Philadelphia is a Quaker City, but its citizens welcome people of all denominations and backgrounds. In view of the fact that today only a tiny fraction of one per cent of Philadelphians are Quakers, this statement is wholly misleading. The passage contains a number of statements such as, "Philadelphia has many fine stores," which could be said of virtually any city—Chicago, Tulsa, Emporia, London, Düsseldorf, or Warsaw.

All textbooks are highly condensed, even when accurate and cogent. They lack the space for meaningful, colorful detail that will give to a region or culture or historical period its authentic savor, its vivid reality. If a teacher is going to help pupils delve deeply, he will have to move at a leisurely pace and supply detail that it is not possible to place in a textbook. After all, it is the detail that makes a subject realistic and interesting. It is not facts that are dry; rather the lack of the right kind of supporting facts. Alfred North Whitehead, the late and great American philosopher, once wrote, "Do not teach too much . . . What you teach, teach thoroughly." This wisdom has been taught by sages throughout history. The passion of school people to cover ground is perhaps the greatest evil in our schools today. Teachers should be given the necessary encouragement and freedom to cover less ground and to uncover more. The result would be better mastery of content and a desire on the part of more students to continue their study of man and society, not only during their school years but so long as they may live.

Fourth, we need to overcome the provincialism into which it is so easy for adults, no less than children, to slip. Provincialism is often amusing. The city boy was visiting his farmer relatives. Upon being served honey at breakfast, he said, "I see you keep a bee." When Pszczyna, Poland, suffered an earthquake, a correspondent of an American newspaper cabled his editor: "Pszczyna damaged by earthquake." The editor cabled back: "How was it spelled before the earthquake?"

In today's world, provincialism is a luxury which we cannot afford. Our children must learn that foreigners who differ from ourselves in looks, language, customs, or dress are not to be regarded as strange. The world has shrunk considerably since Robert Louis Stevenson wrote the stanza:

> Little Indian, Sioux or Crow,
> Little frosty Eskimo,
> Little Turk or Japanee,
> Oh don't you wish that you were me!

Such arrogance toward others will only block the understanding and appreciation of other peoples, without which the future of mankind is bleak indeed. Our task here is two-fold. First, we must enable children to find in the strange ways of other people a source of world enrichment. The world is more interesting because of its cultural diversity. Second, children should be presented with data which will reveal that the world is rapidly changing, and traditional stereotypes of other peoples need re-examination.

An example of the lag of our concepts was seen when an Eskimo girl came to my university to study. Newspaper reporters congregated at her dormitory upon her arrival. You can guess their first question: "Do you live at home in an igloo?" She replied that neither she nor any of her friends lived in igloos, and that she had never even seen one. Even the dignified and sophisticated *New York Times* ran a headline next day: "Eskimo Student Never Saw Igloo."

Another, less humorous, situation can be cited. We as a nation are disliked in many parts of the world because our generation has been slow to recognize the factor of change. South American countries, for example, resent our ignorance of their industrialization, of their contemporary developments in the arts, of their literary and scientific work, and of their history.

In their own interest, our children must learn that the whites are a minority race in today's world; that the majority of people in the world are non-Christian; that the majority of people live in Asia and do not speak English; and that the majority of the world's governments and economic systems are distinctly to the "left" of ours. This knowledge should not be taught in order to spawn defeatism; quite the contrary. Children must learn these hard facts in order that they will know what the score is, so that they will have time to plan a strategy that will enable us to forward freedom and the other human and social values which our country stands for. As our children develop world understanding, they will no doubt discover that some of these differences are no cause for alarm; that in all parts of the world are men and women who, despite superficial external differences, share our ideals; and that others, who may not share our ideals, are not *all* bent on imposing their preferences on us.

Fifth, even as we introduce children to the world, we must develop their love of their community and their homeland. It would, in fact, be futile to try to build world understanding if love of one's own country were not well rooted first. Dorothy Thompson has pointed out that patriotism is actually the basis of internationalism; that it is only those who love their own country who can appreciate and respect the love of others for their countries. Miss Thompson reminds us that those who have achieved world-wide acclaim in literature—such as Shakespeare in England, Dante in Italy, Goethe in Germany, Dostoevski in Russia, and Mark Twain in the United States—are precisely those who are most deeply rooted and immersed in their *own* cultures.

Sixth, as children are introduced to the world, they become increasingly aware of conflicting points of view in the adult world. Few social issues are beyond the reach of controversy. Some issues have no final answers. Different observers of a single event may have divergent reports. To complicate the situation further, legend and fact often become intertwined. What can we do to help children handle the conflicting data and the lack of definiteness which they inevitably encounter in the social studies? It seems to me that these situations provide a perfect opportunity to encourage children to maintain open-mindedness and to make a habit of searching for facts. I am not proposing that they should be taught to defer decisions and action until all data are in. That would be folly; we have to act on our best present knowledge. But it would be an even greater folly to gloss over the conflicts that exist in society. To prepare children for participation in a free society, we must encourage them to see how new facts often make it necessary to modify old ideas, to learn to listen courteously and attentively to points of view differing from their own, and unceasingly to ask themselves, "What are the facts? What is the evidence?" In this way they can be protected against those who would falsely influence and manipulate them through the dazzle of authority or power.

Seventh, we should see to it that children are introduced to the real world and not to the fairy-tale world which is presented in many a textbook. Such books depict men and women of the workaday world as possessing uniformly cheerful miens, serene dispositions, and out-reaching personalities. One of these textbooks contains a picture with a "Keep Out" sign at the entrance of private property which reads, "Please (sic) Keep Out." Historical content in intermediate-grade books often converts heroes of fascinating and robust character into rather wooden stereotypes of virtue. When the world is thus euphemistically and evasively presented, the content of social studies becomes insipid and uninviting.

　　Whether we like it or not, it appears that many children, far from rejecting anti-social behavior, eagerly assimilate it from their outside environment and, to quote Murphy, "in a form which dissolves our sugar-coated doses of social science into nothing." We might better face the fact that our society is based to a considerable extent on conflict, force, and competition, and that to label them, in our teaching, sweepingly as "bad" is futile and often false. Introducing the child to the world honestly and frankly increases his respect for the teacher and heightens his attention.

Eighth, a good introduction to the world requires classroom and school libraries supplied with an abundance of supplementary social-studies teaching aids—reference books, biography, fiction with authentic historical or regional setting, films, and filmstrips. In schools not so equipped, a conscientious teacher must devote a disproportionate share of his spare time looking for supplementary materials. Not only should these materials be readily available to teachers and children, but they should be marked and catalogued topically in standard library form. It is regrettable that in this prosperous country only ten per cent of our elementary schools have rooms set aside for libraries staffed with librarians.

Ninth, and finally, nothing makes for a more felicitous introduction of the child to the world than a teacher who is an expert in a certain field and whose enthusiasm for it is contagious. Much of teaching fails to "take" because of the indifference of the teacher. Each teacher should be encouraged to teach one short unit a year on a topic of his own choosing, a topic which he can present authoritatively and with enthusiasm. Society is the loser when school administrations are so wedded to a course of study or a textbook that they neglect utilizing special interests and talents of teachers. From the perspective of my knowledge of European schools, I feel strongly that the American teacher is handicapped by over-supervision and over-regulation. I fear we are not apt to attract larger numbers of superior persons to the teaching profession until we recognize that teaching is an art and become accustomed to trusting teachers with greater freedom in curriculum matters than many teachers now have.

In this paper, I have suggested nine points which I believe should be kept in mind if we wish to improve the effectiveness of our introduction of children to the world. At certain places I have mentioned that parents as well as teachers have a responsibility in this area of education. This I believe firmly. It is difficult for teachers alone to interest their pupils in other peoples and to further their pupils' understanding of the world and its problems if they learn materialism at home and if they view education not so much as an adventure but as a means of getting ahead. If intellectual, academic, and cultural affairs are indifferently prized at home, it is difficult for the teacher to promote them successfully at school. I read recently that the dog-food industry of this country yields a higher annual income than the book-publishing industry. I have nothing against dogs, but this is symptomatic of a situation which disturbs me. Our schools can exercise their full potential impact in developing world leadership only when they are aided and abetted by the home, and by an earnest, dedicated society.

✌❦ THE GLENS FALLS STORY   *Merrill F. Hartshorn*

Every once in a while a school district moves out on its own to approach a problem in social studies in a dramatic manner. Hartshorn tells of the efforts of the citizens and faculty of Glens Falls, New York, to develop new materials and approaches to the study of world affairs. This selection provides an idea of the procedures used and the persons involved.

MAN HAS ONLY begun to reach for a stable world order through the education of youth. What could happen if we really made an all-out effort to achieve such a goal?

It occurred to a small group of educators thinking about this problem that one of the failures of today's violent world was a partial failure of education. They wondered what would happen if a deliberate effort were made in education, starting with the kindergarten, to educate people to understand one another better. If such a program proved successful, and if it were tried in many communities, perhaps the path to eventual world peace would be made smoother. . . .

To help provide some knowledge on how to direct education towards the goals suggested a pioneer program was launched six years ago in the public school system of Glens Falls, New York.

PURPOSE OF THE PROJECT

The importance of providing sound instruction in elementary and secondary schools about other peoples and their cultures and about this country's role in world affairs is obvious. Pupils must acquire an understanding about the complexities of the world in which they live. They should practice methods of inquiry and become expert in the use of various sources of information. The ability of citizens, young and old, to think clearly and constructively about the role of the United States in world affairs is prerequisite to the development and implementation of wise national policies. This is vital to our own national interest and perhaps also to the survival of mankind.

Used by permission of the author and the National Council for the Social Studies; from its Bulletin No. 35, *Improving the Teaching of World Affairs*, 1964, pp. 1–9. Merrill F. Hartshorn is the executive secretary of the National Council for the Social Studies.

American citizens must become sensitive to other cultures, conscious of the complexities of intercultural relations, humane in their outlook. They must feel a deep sense of personal obligation for the general welfare. Schools should use all available resources in an effort to achieve these outcomes. This country's future, indeed its very existence, may well depend on our success or failure in helping pupils learn the dimensions of world problems and what this country can and should do about them. . . .

Some educational efforts in this area have been bitterly attacked by pressure groups. In some communities programs have had to be abandoned because citizens generally had little knowledge of what the schools were trying to do and why. Community support and understanding must be an integral part of any realistic program designed to further an understanding of world affairs in our schools. . . .

NATURE OF THE PROJECT

This project called for a full-scale effort in one selected school system to improve education about world affairs. This was to be done through the involvement of teachers in every aspect of the school program at both the elementary and secondary school levels. The first step, naturally, was to identify an appropriate school system —a small city system in which there existed good educational leadership and happy school-community relations—a system able and willing to cooperate in a three-year program to improve the teaching of world affairs. While the policy direction of the study was to be entrusted to a special NCSS committee, and funds for its partial support administered by the Council, the full and hearty cooperation of the selected school system was essential. Local school authorities were always in control and no steps were taken without their full approval. In reality the project was developed and carried out by Glens Falls school personnel.

Having selected a school system, arrangements were completed by which an outstanding social studies teacher in that system was made Project Director. It was considered desirable that the Director be well known in the school system and have the support and confidence of the school administration, teachers, and the citizens of the community. He was released from most of his teaching in order to give major attention to the project. In cooperation with teachers, supervisors, administrators, and the sponsoring NCSS committee he was given the responsibility to: (a) evaluate the understanding of world affairs possessed by students at various grade levels, (b) assume responsibility for securing (and give direction to the preparation of) materials needed for instruction and evaluation, (c) develop, with the assistance of teachers and consultants, ways in which the teaching of world affairs could be incorporated into the school curriculum at each grade level in all subject matter areas, and in extracurricular activities, and (d) make continuing formal and informal efforts to appraise the results. The techniques and materials utilized were designed so that once their value had been established they could be adapted for use in other school systems. This last point is important since it insures that other school systems could profit from the experience of the pilot school system.

The project continued over a three-year period, and was developed in a coordinated fashion, systematically improved through experimentation, continuously evaluated in a variety of ways. Thus the project could prove to be the first major action-research program designed to explore the ways and means whereby a school can improve instruction about world affairs. The project should be of direct and enduring value to the school system concerned, and it is hoped that this report will stimulate and prove helpful to other schools and teacher training institutions seeking to improve the teaching of world affairs.

The program developed within the Glens Falls school system involved all appropriate subjects, teachers, and school services. The Director secured the cooperation of many outside agencies offering consultation, materials, or services related to the subject of the experiment. This description of the Glens Falls program provides useful insight into how to identify and make use of the available resources in a project of this kind.

One outcome of the Glens Falls Project was the production of such teaching aids and units as the following: other peoples and other lands—their history, institutions, value systems, and ways of life; United States foreign policy and the forces which helped shape it; causes of war; international organizations and the machinery for peace; the United States as a democratic nation in a world setting; conflicting ideologies in today's world. Among other approaches were activities focused on: the comparative study of student art from schools in several countries; comparative business methods, merchandising and office practices in other countries; foods and families of the world; health and disease problems of the world; the literature and culture of other countries in English and foreign language classes; mathematics as a means of international communication; music of Western and non-Western cultures; physical education, games, and recreation in other lands; and the technology of business and industry in other nations. Bibliographies that include both audio-visual and printed materials were prepared for the use of teachers. A service was established to coordinate the use of classroom periodicals, radio, television, news magazines and newspapers in the several schools.

Foreign visitors and government officials were used as resource persons. So were special consultants on curriculum and evaluation, and persons who were experts on topics of special interest to teachers. Such activities as pen pal correspondence, stamp collections, school-wide assembly programs, speaking before community groups, making arrangements for foreign guests, planning model assemblies of the United Nations, and others were used to further the goal of improving the understanding of world affairs throughout the total school program.

The production of tests and means of evaluating the outcomes of the program was a vital part of the project. There is a great need to discover what techniques and materials are effective in teaching about world affairs. In this facet of the project specialists in evaluation played significant roles.

It is expected that a more sophisticated awareness among students of the realities of international life—both hopeful and discouraging aspects, whether positive or negative—will be a result of such a program of teaching world affairs. It is important that citizens learn of the difficulties of developing a world in which nations cooperate in a responsible fashion, and of the specific obstacles and threats to peace. It is important that they learn to think clearly about solutions to world problems. This is precisely why such a program designed to improve the teaching of world affairs is so necessary. Without such education in our schools we run the grave risk of naive, volatile and immature public response to the dangerous challenges that confront us. . . .

It is becoming increasingly clear that if education is to play the vital role envisioned for it, a new dimension of knowledge about world affairs must be made part of every school program. It is also important for us to recognize that such a program must inevitably lead to a better understanding of ourselves, and to deeper insights into the nature of our own country—its values and beliefs. It is of paramount importance that we first of all understand our own nation and have a deep commitment to the values of our society before we seek to understand other nations and their cultures.

OVERVIEW OF OUTCOMES

. . . To provide an overview of the entire report, we shall list and answer briefly a few questions most often asked by teachers, administrators, and laymen who have written or visited Glens Falls to learn more about the experiment.

1. What role did the Board of Education and the school administration play in the program? The Board of Education formally approved the guiding principles developed for the project and also its budget. After the completion of the three years of the experiment, the Board absorbed some of the costs earlier met from outside sources and continued arrangements to insure that the emphasis on the teaching of world affairs would continue. Individual members of the Board in a great variety of ways demonstrated their interest in ITWA.

The Superintendent formally gave his approval to the project and gave invaluable advice for its implementation. He named the Director of ITWA to the Curriculum Council, and the Director later became chairman of a subcommittee which included teachers from several subject fields at various grade levels. The Curriculum Council has the Superintendent as chairman and includes all principals and at least one teacher from each school and deals with all curricular problems that require attention.

2. Were teachers of various subjects at various grade levels receptive to suggestions that more of the teaching and classroom time be devoted to teaching an understanding of world affairs? In many cases it was not a matter of giving more time but of using time differently. In general teachers appreciated suggestions with respect to materials and methods, and the scheduling of films and resource persons, including visitors from overseas. Members of the faculty who were not teaching social studies were enthusiastic about showing contributions which could be made by their subject fields. Teachers willingly gave their time to conferences and workshops.

In general, it was easier for elementary than for high school teachers to make adjustments in teaching programs. And, of course, there were differences among teachers at any grade level. The fact remains that teachers from all grade levels and all subject fields contributed to the success of the program.

3. What was the attitude of the community toward the program? There was a high degree of community support, involving a variety of organizations and agencies, and a great number of individuals.

The support of the press, churches, luncheon and patriotic groups is noteworthy. So, also, is the way in which families opened their homes to foreign visitors who came to Glens Falls.

Community support manifested itself not only in attendance at related school and community functions, but also through financial contributions to help support ITWA activities.

4. Did this program call for a large expenditure of funds? About $15,000 per year in outside funds were made available for three years to support ITWA. But it does not follow that a school system cannot improve the teaching of world affairs unless it receives this amount of outside support. In a typical situation, changes may be made more gradually. Quite possibly many of the items for which funds are needed will already be included in the school budget. Among such items are: books, periodicals, films, supplies; travel funds for teachers and funds to bring consultants to the community; budgeted time and funds for curriculum and evaluation committees; budgeted time and funds for the in-service education of teachers—workshops, conferences, school visitation, travel.

5. What was the effect of the program on the general scholastic achievement in all subject matter areas? Doubtless the thought of being involved in an experiment and doing something new and different inspires students and teachers to greater effort.

Students in all subject fields did well in terms of performance on conventional achievement tests. There was no suggestion that ITWA interfered with "regular teaching." Indeed ITWA was enthusiastically accepted as an essential ingredient in, and enrichment of, the total school program.

6. Could this type of program be carried out readily in other communities? The answer is "Yes." It should be noted, however, that ITWA involved cooperation between school and community, faculty and administration, the local system and nearby educational institutions and agencies. ITWA's success also depended on the "know-how" demonstrated by the Director and members of the school administration in identifying and using a variety of resources. It should be added that Glens Falls had been resourceful along these lines before ITWA was established.

7. What were some of the significant experiences that resulted in improving instruction? The visits of teachers and students from overseas—often at no cost to the school—helped immeasurably in introducing new points of view and in motivating students to learn about other cultures. At the same time the teachers discovered that the more students learned about other peoples, cultures, and nations the greater was their desire for a better understanding of our own nation and culture. So far as the teachers were concerned the opportunities for in-service education about world affairs, and for information about geographic regions concerning which they knew little were greatly appreciated. The special conferences and workshops were a means of making teachers better informed and, therefore, more secure in their pioneering efforts. Once the teachers had the information at hand they showed great ingenuity and creativity in teaching procedures.

Methods, Techniques, Procedures, and Activities

DESPITE THE ABUSES and widespread criticism of instructional method, it remains the central element of teaching. Method consists of stimulating, guiding, directing, showing, informing, and creating. Thus the act of teaching is composed of method. Truly, method is highly personal, intangible, and elusive. But the difference between the teacher's knowing, believing, or being able to, and his success in leading others toward knowledge, belief, or skill, clearly lies in method. Thus, any serious consideration of instruction in social studies must devote significant attention to method.

The readings in this part explore various aspects of method. The first section analyzes some of the basic elements of and related to method, while it concentrates on the means of developing pupils' study and work techniques, and their practical skills in social studies.

The second section shifts attention to methods of teaching pupils who are distinctly above or below average in ability. The articles identify pertinent characteristics of, and suggest special techniques for, working with both gifted and retarded children in social studies.

The third section considers both the planning and teaching of units and lessons. The popular, almost universal, unit organization of instruction in social studies deserves continuing efforts by teachers to improve its effectiveness.

Concluding this part is a section of readings on the evaluation of pupils' learning. While progress in this phase of instruction has been slow, and the problems are many, some guides to meaningful and pertinent means of appraisal appear in the selections.

SKILLS FOR DEMOCRATIC CITIZENSHIP IN THE 1960's — Helen McCracken Carpenter

As the social studies serve to uphold the democratic society that supports them, it is important that we consider skills to be

261

developed in social studies on social as well as on pedagogical grounds. This author does just that in the following selection. She suggests answers to questions about society's need for and utilization of skills that its youthful citizens may acquire. What kinds of skills does our democracy demand of its prospective participants? What in the nature of democracy points toward skills thought desirable for its citizens? How has the developing conception of democracy modified the need for skills of social significance and civic value?

BOTH THE NEEDS and the conditions for the functioning of citizens in our democracy derive from the characteristics of American life. What are the implications for responsible citizenship . . . ?

The virility of the American ideal of democracy. Although the nature of political democracy . . . and the attributes of democratic citizenship are necessarily related, the concept of one has attracted the attention of articulate Americans more than has the meaning of the other. When allowance is made for the fact that wording varies with the time, many expressions reveal surprising agreement in viewpoint on the bases, purposes, and functioning of democracy. . . . Here are . . . the principles that constitute the essence of the American ideal: government by consent which implies participation of citizens in the process of government; the maintenance of civil and political rights or liberties; and the supreme importance of the individual.

Utterances of modern-day Americans attest the continuing virility of these tenets. Franklin Roosevelt made them the heart of his famous "four freedoms" speech. Senator Estes Kefauver in the opening line of the 1951 NCSS Yearbook writes, "By political democracy I mean a form of government based upon the consent of the governed in which the will of the majority of qualified citizens rules." (1) And again, Henry M. Wriston affirms the ideal with an emphasis reflecting a concern of the sixties, "The acid test of successful democratic government is the degree of effective liberty it makes available to the individual." (2) The various aspects of the classic ideal have been interpreted according to the needs and insights of differ-

Used by permission of the author and the National Council for the Social Studies, a department of the National Education Association, Washington, D.C.; from its Thirty-Third Yearbook, *Skill Development in Social Studies*, 1963, pp. 7–16. Dr. Carpenter is a professor of history at Trenton State College, New Jersey.

ent eras but the tenets have remained the criteria for the examination of our society.

The changing view of democratic citizenship. Americans have not addressed themselves with equal vigor to consideration of the qualities of democratic citizenship. The expressions which have been made tend to be minutely analytical of behavioral characteristics rather than broadly philosophical. Some of this accrues, perhaps, from the nature of citizenship. Fundamentally, citizenship is the means of denoting the legal status of an individual and hence signifies membership in a political society. It implies the reciprocal obligations of allegiance owed by the individual and of protection assumed by the government.

Interpretations of even this elemental concept of citizenship have varied. What constitutes evidence of allegiance, for example, has been subject to differing opinions. In the days when loyalty oaths were not as generally demanded as they are today by government at all levels, most citizens born in the United States had no occasion to attest their fidelity by repeating the official oath of allegiance required of naturalized citizens. One accepted manner of expressing loyalty to the country was through the salute to the flag and the repeating of the pledge of allegiance. These acts became almost standard practice in classrooms across the nation until the right of parents to forbid their children to participate in the observance for religious reasons created a legal controversy. The Supreme Court at first upheld boards in excluding from public schools children who did not comply. Later, however, the Court declared invalid a West Virginia statute requiring the salute on penalty of expulsion. As the matter now stands, a school child may or may not salute the flag depending on his conscience or that of his parents. Such observance is not today considered evidence of the allegiance of a citizen, young or old.

The connotations of citizenship beyond the narrow legal sense have always been and continue to be yet more nebulous. The broad meaning of citizenship is constantly subject not only to shifting judicial and legislative interpretations but to changing popular ones as well.

Americans for decades, even centuries, thought of the rights and responsibilities of citizenship primarily in terms of activities related to political functions. The right to be represented in government, to hold public office, to vote for men and measures of one's own choosing were considered inherent characteristics of democracy. . . .

And so the story of the struggle to achieve the hallmarks of citizenship might be traced through the pages of America's history.

First it was a struggle to secure full political citizenship for some men, then for all men and finally for women. This early interpretation of citizenship as related chiefly to political functions rested on basic civil rights. Although a complete enumeration of the civil rights of a citizen at any time in the nation's history would be impossible, the first ten amendments to the United States Constitution have been considered a fundamental statement of these classic civil liberties.

Concurrently with the development of the idea of citizenship in terms of political rights and civil liberties went the concept of civic duties. In a government in which sovereignty resides in the people, it has been assumed that rights must be accompanied by responsibilities for those enjoying them. Thus a good citizen, as first understood, was a person who considered the privilege of voting a serious matter and cast his ballot thoughtfully; who deserved the right to equal protection of the laws by obeying the laws; who earned the precious freedoms of speech, press, and religion by not abusing them nor interfering with the enjoyment of these rights by others; who merited the protection of the government against evildoers at home and aggressors from abroad by paying taxes and giving service, if necessary, to police and military forces; who warranted the benefit of the processes of justice by his willingness to assist in law enforcement and jury duty. The criteria of democratic citizenship still include all of the obligations just mentioned. Today, however, the concept of what constitutes a good citizen in a democracy has so broadened that these characteristics alone are insufficient.

The widening view of democratic citizenship evident by the middle decades of the twentieth century has resulted from a variety of factors, some of which are interrelated. By the turn of the century America had changed from an agricultural to an industrial nation. This fact together with the advance of technology made possible a life of greater physical comfort for many Americans but one attended by increasing social and economic tensions. In addition, the status and responsibilities of Americans have been affected in the last 40 years by the steady rise of this nation to a position of world leadership. The same decades have been marked likewise by a growing consciousness of human relations and of the need to focus on them in school and in society. Although full political democracy has not yet been attained in fact for all citizens, gradually the horizon of Americans has widened enough to make clear that the goals of democracy must be social and economic as well as political.

From the combined effect of all these forces an expanded concept of democratic citizenship has emerged. The need for the individual to assume greater responsibility in political citizenship is acknowledged. Progress toward realization of the latent social and economic phases of citizenship can be discerned. Definitions of the effective citizen today often include those qualities desirable in the personal relationships of daily living. At all points there is recognition of the importance of action if a democratic citizen is to be effective. . . .

The paradoxes of theory and reality. . . . The classic concepts prevailing in our society derive chiefly, as has been indicated, from the era of the Enlightenment which was a far different world from ours. The strength of democracy was predicated on government by consent of an informed, interested, active citizenry. The chief justification for the establishment and expansion of public education has been, and still is, the provision of a means for equipping citizens with the knowledge, attitudes, and skills necessary to the maintenance of democratic government. The theory still holds; it is the concept of the functioning of the theory which needs revision.

Wherever the citizen turns today he is confronted with the need to cope with bigness. The rapidity of change has, by this decade, accelerated and compounded aspects of this phenomenon which has been present in our society since the advent of industrialization. . . .

Bigness brings impersonality and robs some people of a sense of individual identity with constructive effort. There is the tendency to depreciate individual worth and to lose faith in the efficacy of social action. . . .

What of the great majority of Americans who do not lose their perspective on the obligations of citizenship? For the citizen with a strong sense of purpose and the will to act responsibly, the current situation presents obstacles as well. Bigness implies complexity which, coupled with multiplicity and rapidity of change, makes necessary the services of the expert. The magnitude and ramifications of the issues of government—political, economic, and social; national, international, and interplanetary—require the combined talents of experts from many fields. No one citizen can be expected to know enough to determine public policy today, even in matters of local concern. Furthermore, the direct involvement at the core of the governmental process can be the experience of only a relative few. Most Americans must depend on the decisions and abilities of experts in the various areas of mass communication for any information about the course of events in which he, as Mr. Citizen, is theoretically an active participant. In an age with better distribution of news than ever before, there exists the paradox of knowing more which amounts, against the sum total of knowledge, actually to knowing less. . . . The world of the individual citizen is not shrinking today; instead it is getting larger and larger.

MacIver sees in this growing specialization of function another peril to democracy. With the tendency and necessity to focus on less and less in the process of earning a living, there is the possibility that Americans may lose a view of the whole. He fears the rise of competition among specialized groups and the diverting of the loyalty of individuals from the general welfare to the special interest. MacIver labels this "the peril of group anarchy." (3)

How can the functioning of democratic citizenship be reconciled with the realities of government and society today? This is the supreme challenge of the social studies teacher. . . .

Defining the role of the citizen in democracy today. . . . One of the needs in social studies education is for teachers to examine realistically what the citizen does and does not do as a participant in the governmental process today. The next step is to help students understand the role of the citizen as a guide for intelligent action. A realistic approach can also help to allay feelings of individual futility about participation in directing the course of public affairs. It is essential for every citizen to feel that he is taking part in important political decisions that affect his life but he needs also to be aware of how this is done.

An understanding of the related roles of the people, the elected officials of government, and the experts is important. Today, the specialists determine how to carry out the broad policy decided upon by officials in whom the people have expressed their confidence by election to public office. Rarely today does the voter decide directly through referendum any matter of policy or even the goals to be achieved.

In this connection Evron M. Kirkpatrick, Executive Director of the American Political Science Association has observed, "It is important to recognize our dependence on experts, and to disabuse ourselves and our students of the notion that good citizenship requires omnicompetence concerning public policy and the institutions and processes by which it is made." In fact, Dr. Kirkpatrick sees in such disabuse implications for the quality of citizenship expression in life and of social studies instruction in school. Continuing, he says:

> Knowing what one does not know is a most important part of self-knowledge. It is a kind of self-knowledge that has important im-

plications for citizenship. Decent humility about complicated substantive questions of public policy should reduce the dogmatism, demagoguery, and violence that characterize the discussion of so many public issues (4). . . .

Perhaps the most penetrating analysis of the role of the citizen in government today has been offered by Elmer E. Schattschneider in his *The Semisovereign People; A Realist's View of Democracy in America*. He too feels that an understanding of the limitations of the people in government, as well as their powers, is essential to effective citizenship participation. The crux of his viewpoint supplies the clue to the next consideration, "Democracy is a competitive political system in which competing leaders and organizations define the alternatives of public policy in such a way that the public can participate in the decision-making process." (5)

Identifying the skills of decision making. The viewpoint of citizen responsibility presented here in no way eliminates the necessity for arriving at decisions. In fact, the decisions made by individuals in judging officials and the effectiveness of their policies is the essence of government by consent. The tempo of our era puts a premium on the skills necessary in judging and arriving at conclusions in the midst of competing forces. The exact nature of the issues which lie ahead are unknown. However, it is certain that the problems of the future are going to be many and difficult and will appear in accelerating succession. Consequently, citizens in the future will need to have the skills for dealing with very difficult, problematic situations quickly.

Another certainty of the unknown future is that it will mean an increasing battle for men's minds and emotions. Future citizens must be made aware of all forms of persuasion and must know how to find facts and draw valid conclusions despite many forms of subtle suggestion. They will need to distinguish between emotional persuasion and intellectual reason. Again, logic and logical thinking are basic.

For effective social studies education, it would be helpful to know a great deal more about problem-solving skills, about logical and critical thinking, and about those conditions of life that hinder skillful thought processes. However, the skills which seem basic to decision making at this time are those of gathering information through reading and listening; of interpreting information by organizing logically and evaluating accurately; and of communicating information through speaking effectively and writing lucidly. Another group of skills necessary to decision making in responsible citizenship constitutes techniques in group participation. One of the hopeful signs testifying to the virility of democracy in this country is the prevalence of public debate over questions involving government at all levels. To maintain perspective in an expanding world, it is important, also, for citizens to be oriented in both time and place. In the development of these skills the social studies have unique and sole responsibility.

Deepening and broadening the concept of social studies skill. Today, theories about skill development in the social studies are based primarily on the experience of teachers who appear to be successful. In only one area, that of developing a sense of time and chronology, is it possible to base some conclusions on what can be considered scholarly research. This was the situation in 1953; regrettably it is still the situation in 1963. It is to be hoped that this gap will soon begin to be closed.

Social studies educators are increasingly conscious of the need to draw more heavily on other areas of the social sciences, in addition to history, geography, and political science, for curriculum content than has been done in the past. A corollary need is to incorporate into the program of skill development in social studies an understanding and opportunity to develop some competence in use of the methods employed by scholars in arriving at knowledge in these fields. Skills in the use of the historical method and of regional analysis, for reasons that are apparent, are the most likely to be developed, although this probability cannot be depended on. There should be opportunity also to explore the possibilities of such methods as the case study, model building, and various kinds of statistical approaches.

Today the word "skills" is often in the forefront of public consciousness. The skills may be those necessary to maintain physical fitness; or they may be those of technical competence. Often they are the mental ones involved in critical thinking and decision making. Increasingly there is recognition of the relation of these skills to the maintenance of a healthy democracy and of the responsibility of the social studies program within our nation's schools for the development of these skills.

References

(1) "The Vitality in Political Democracy." *Education for Democratic Citizenship,* Twenty-Second Yearbook. Washington, D.C.: National Council for the Social Studies, a department of the National Education Association, 1952. p. 1.

(2) Commission on National Goals. *Goals for Americans.* p. 48.

(3) MacIver. *The Ramparts We Guard*. Chapter 9, "The Peril of Group Anarchy."

(4) Kirkpatrick, Evron M., and Kirkpatrick, Jeane J. "Political Science" in *High School Social Studies Perspectives*. Boston: Houghton Mifflin Co., 1962. p. 102.

(5) New York: Holt, Rinehart & Winston, 1960. p. 141.

THE PSYCHOLOGY OF SKILL DEVELOPMENT
John Jarolimek

What are the psychological ideas underlying skill development in the social studies? The author of this selection analyzes and illustrates three major psychological elements undergirding the learning of skills in relation to the study of human relationships. First, he identifies key factors that bear on the learning of social studies skills. Next, he dissects the anatomies of various types of learners in order to uncover which of their characteristics affect acquisition of social studies skills. Finally, he stresses the sequential development of social studies skills essential to a desirable school program.

THE NATURE OF SOCIAL STUDIES SKILLS

. . . . It is because of the kinship of social studies learnings that skills emerge as being fundamental and necessary. Skills are the basic tools of learning. They help the pupil learn. Inadequately developed skills foreshorten the opportunity to continue learning and lead inevitably to poor achievement in the social studies. It is simply impossible for a student to be deficient in skills and to excel in social studies.

There has been a tendency to associate the word skill with behavior which is somewhat habitual and mechanical in nature. Perhaps this is because skills are often identified with physical-motor behavior. When this narrow interpretation of skills is applied, responses are expected to be more or less automatic to certain stimuli, without the need for conscious mental activity. The performance of a skill by one who is expert in executing it does give the appearance of action without active thought or intention. It looks decep-

Used by permission of the author and the National Council for the Social Studies; from its Thirty-Third Yearbook, *Skill Development in Social Studies*, NCSS, 1963, pp. 18–33.

tively simple to the neophyte. The common belief is that practice makes perfect. Consequently, skills teaching has relied heavily upon drill techniques; and the abuses of drill procedures are so well known that the word itself has come to connote something in the way of malpractice in teaching. Educators today prefer to talk of practice and application—terms suggesting a functional use of drill.

For the most part, social studies skills are much more complex than such motor skills as handwriting, typing, throwing a ball, or jumping rope. In almost all cases, social studies skills are intellectual in nature and call for the use of cognitive processes. When the pupil is reading a map, for example, he should be thinking about what the map represents. When he is discussing a problem with his classmates, he is listening to and thinking about what others have to say and is reacting to it. If he is doing problem solving, he is thinking critically about various alternative procedures which might be employed in finding a solution. If he is writing a report or preparing to give one orally, he is thinking about what it is that he is going to say. To think of these skills as an accumulation of habitual responses is to misunderstand their nature and their complexity. Rather, effectively developed social studies skills are demonstrated in highly organized and integrated patterns of behavior.

To be skillful means that one is able to do something with proficiency in repeated performances. The standard of proficiency is determined by how well others can perform the same task. In other words, the measure of competency in a skill is the norm of the population of which the person is a part. We may, for example, properly say that a fourth-grader has demonstrated skill in preparing a report for social studies. The same level of performance by an eighth-grader or by a high school senior, on the other hand, would probably not be regarded as a skillful one.

Complex skills, such as those associated with the social studies, consist of several component elements or subskills. For example, the reading skill used by a high school sophomore in social studies calls into play many subskills related to the reading process. Early in the elementary school he learned how to recognize words and how to read selections with short sentences and simple words. Later he sharpened his reading-comprehension skills. He learned how to skim for a main idea and how to read intensively for details. Still later, perhaps in junior high school, he learned how to interpret a written passage to detect an author's bias. Somewhere along the line he should have learned to read creatively, that is, to react intellectually to the content by testing his own ideas against those presented by the author. Through the years his teachers have worked carefully with him so that he is now equipped with a vast array of reading subskills which have been integrated into a single act which is called a reading skill. The student is now able to approach a variety of reading tasks comfortably. Moreover, he will continue to extend his repertory of reading subskills each time he encounters a reading task which demands some variation in those already at his command. He will also learn to apply the ones he has with greater facility as he practices using them. This process continues not only throughout his years in high school but, indeed, throughout his lifetime.

Somewhat the same process applies to other skills as well. Map reading begins with simple, three-dimensional layouts and pictorial symbols in the primary grades and leads to the use of complex map reading and interpretive skills in high school. Group-process skills begin with simple parallel play and lead later to cooperative behavior and high-level intellectual interaction with others. In the case of these complex skills, it is apparent that the learner does not master them once and for all time but rather moves to more mature, more proficient, and more advanced variations of them. . . . In explaining the meaning of a skill or in demonstrating it, the teacher should present a more advanced variation of the skill than the one with which the learner is presently familiar, yet the advanced variation should not be too far beyond the present stage of the learner. If it is, the explanation or demonstration is likely to overwhelm the learner and will not serve to motivate and help him in refining goals. In fact, it is likely to have the reverse effect. Models used at all stages of skill instruction should represent performances which are attainable by the learner.

In order to make skills meaningful to pupils, many authors have stressed the need to teach skills in their functional contexts. In general, the more closely the skill can be taught and related to the situation involving its actual use, the better. However, it is easy to misapply or misunderstand this principle. Teaching skills in their functional settings is one thing; expecting to have them emerge incidentally without systematic instruction is quite another. Students who prepare reports; do reference work; use maps, charts, and graphs; or are engaged in small-group enterprises should be given instruction and guidance in the skills which inhere in those activities. If they are not given such guidance and instruction, the likelihood is great that learners will be getting firsthand experiences in performing skills incorrectly or, at best, in a slipshod manner. Whenever possible, teachers should avoid giving pupils an opportunity to reinforce incorrect responses.

However important it is for the learner to know the meaning of a skill, no amount of meaningful teaching will make him proficient in it unless the teaching is accompanied by practice with intent to improve. Practice makes it possible for the learner to become more discriminating in his responses; to perform them with greater ease and confidence. Practice in and of itself does not insure improvement—it merely provides the opportunity for the improvement of performance. . . .

Practice is one of the most essential aspects of skill development, and learners will not develop facility in skills without it. But if practice is to be effective, it must be performed under certain conditions. For example, halfhearted practice, without a desire to improve, is self-defeating. Since the learner is not achieving success by improving his performance, there follows a deterioration in motivation to do the practice which is needed to learn the skill. If such a set of circumstances is allowed to persist over a period of time, the learner is likely to reject practice entirely and avoid situations where the skill is needed.

The purpose of practice is to improve performance. This is, of course, obvious, but it is nonetheless frequently overlooked in teaching and learning skills. Improvement occurs when the learner becomes conscious of the results of performing the skill. The teacher provides guidance to help the student discriminate between faulty performance and effective performance. . . .

Initial practice of a skill should be done under close teacher guidance and direction. This allows the teacher to clarify any points not understood by the learner. It also insures that the pupil is responding correctly. Careful supervision is important at this stage because if the learner practices the response incorrectly, he must unlearn the incorrect response before he can proceed with the correct one. This would constitute an unnecessary obstacle to learning. Immediately following the presentation and initial practice under close teacher supervision, frequent practice periods should be planned. Short, spaced practice periods seem to be more effective than those of longer duration but occurring less frequently. The practice sessions should be highly motivated in order to avoid having them seem like drudgery to the learner. The heavy loading of practice following closely the presentation will bring the skill up to a functional level for the pupil. Henceforth, less frequent practice periods will be needed but are nevertheless necessary in order to maintain and improve the skill.

Knowledge of success or failure is important in making progress in learning skills. Information concerning his success which the learner receives from any source is referred to as *feedback*. Feedback can be provided by the teacher, by classmates, by some mechanical device, or by the learner himself as he analyzes his responses. Feedback serves as a reinforcing agent, and as such has positive or negative values. Negative feedback tells the learner what he is doing wrong and what he should avoid; positive feedback tells him what is right about his responses and reminds him of his successes. . . .

Feedback gives direction to the learner, steers him away from unproductive responses, and lets him know when he is on the right track. Without feedback the learner probably could not improve. If improvement is sought in such skills as reporting to the class, organizing information, participating in a discussion, or working together in a small group, learners must have their performances evaluated. In general, feedback is most effective in contributing to improved skill learning when specific and given during or immediately following the performance.

INDIVIDUAL DIFFERENCES IN SKILL DEVELOPMENT

Successful teaching of social studies skills cannot be achieved until the teacher comes to grips realistically with the problem of the wide range of abilities, interests, and backgrounds which exist among learners. These differences are often obscured by the practice of placing and keeping learners of similar chronological ages together in the same class. As the teacher faces his class, therefore, there is little to remind him that while he may be teaching a skill to a *class*, the skill is not learned by the class but by *individuals* within that class. Clearly, he will have to devise ways of helping individual students to learn through the use of group-teaching procedures much of the time.

Perhaps the most difficult concept of all to accept in teaching is that learners differ widely one from the other and that these differences are unavoidable. Teachers cling to the hope that all learners can do average work if they work hard enough at it and if they develop good habits of study. The tendency to look at effects of, rather than to seek causes for, poor achievement sometimes makes the learner the object of criticism by his teacher. Too often the teacher appears to think that his students have the same motivations, interests, ideals, and ambitions that he does. . . .

In dealing with the preparedness of learners for skill learning, there are three ways by which the teacher may proceed: First, he may defer teaching the skill until such time as the learners have developed sufficient maturity to handle it or have gained adequate life experience. Second, he may build into his teaching those experiences for learners which will hasten their maturity or provide them with background they will need to master the skill. Finally, he may present a simpler variation of the skill.

Deferring skills teaching until learners develop a preparedness for it on their own has both advantages and limitations. It is not economical from the standpoint of instructional time to labor the teaching of a skill which could be taught easily and in a much shorter time a few years later. On the other hand, if the teacher simply waits for the learner to mature or to gain background experience, the skill may never be taught. Where there is a gross lack of readiness for learning a skill, the teaching of it should be deferred. Along with such postponement, the teacher should take steps which will hasten the time when the learners will be ready for the skill. That is, the role of the teacher in such cases is not simply a matter of waiting passively for the learner to ready himself. For example, pupils may not be equipped to locate and gather information from a variety of references and incorporate such data into a polished oral or written report. They can, nonetheless, begin by using one or two books to supplement information obtained from their textbook and by contributing those ideas to class discussions. Or if pupils have been accustomed to formal question-and-answer procedures based on the textbook, the teacher can acquaint them with other ways of learning by planning a field trip, which will stimulate problem solving and critical thinking in a simple and concrete way. When primary grade teachers find pupils not ready for successful small-group enterprises, they can give pupil-committees minor responsibilities for housekeeping tasks about the room, leading gradually into small-group work in the instructional program, and thus preparing the pupils to do productive and responsible work in small groups in the middle and higher grades. . . .

There are two sequences which must be observed in teaching skills: One is the logical sequence which inheres in the skill itself. In map reading, for example, a pupil learns that symbols on a map stand for real things on the earth before he learns that color is a special map symbol which can be used to represent elevation. The logical sequence is one which the learner must follow as he moves from one level of complexity of the skill to the next. The other sequence is psychological and is peculiar to individual learners. It has to do with what should be the next step in the learning *for the individual* in terms of his total background, experience, prior learning, and general maturity. It is obvious that a teacher following a strictly logical sequence of skills teaching may be offering experiences which are out of sequence for individual learners. The particular point from which further learning is to proceed is a highly individual matter. The teacher's task, therefore, is to synchronize the logical and psychological sequences for individual pupils in order that learning may progress in an expeditious manner.

PROMOTING GROWTH IN SKILLS

Wherever one sees a good program of skill development in operation, he will find that the teachers regard skills teaching as an essential and important part of the total social studies instructional effort. The teaching of skills cannot be handled in an incidental or peripheral manner if good results are anticipated. Rather, it must be considered as one of the central purposes of social studies instruction. Often skills do not get the attention that they should because they are not identified carefully enough for the teacher. It is frequently assumed that every teacher knows what skills need attention and that every teacher will include instruction on them. Such an arrangement rarely works well in practice, because teachers often feel that their chief responsibility is to present the factual content which is designated for the grade or for the course rather than to emphasize skill development. Therefore, while everyone teaches skills to some extent, there is no real sequential program in operation for the development of skills. It would be hard to think of a situation which is less likely to produce learners who are competent in skills. The chance that important skills will be neglected or omitted entirely under this random scheme is very great indeed.

In order to attach some degree of importance to skills teaching, schools must identify specific skills which are to receive attention. The program of instruction at each grade, throughout the total 12 years of school, should clearly indicate what the teacher's responsibilities are toward maintaining and extending social studies skills. Pupil expectancies need to be spelled out and should, of course, be consistent with variations in learner abilities.

Finally, frequent and regular appraisals of skill growth need to be made, and a record should be kept of the progress of individual pupils. This should include test score data on progress in reading; in the use of maps, graphs, and references; and in communications skills for which standardized tests are available. It should also include teacher comments on and appraisals of the growth in group processes, human relations, problem solving, and study skills, for which informal evaluative procedures are more appropriate. Pupil progress in learning skills should be noted annually and kept as a permanent part of the learner's school record.

The necessity for direct teaching of skills needs to be emphasized. Because skills are associated with learning activities, it is often assumed that pupils will learn them simply by doing them. . . .

While it is true that pupils must perform skills if they hope to learn them, the learning can be more fruitful and efficient if the pupils are taught how to do them well. Perhaps the strongest programs are those which provide for instruction in skills within the functional framework of the topic studied. Thus the learner's attention is called to the need for the skill. He must learn the skill if he is to solve the problem which confronts him. The need for the skill is a real rather than an imaginary one. If the teacher utilizes such strategic moments of pupil need to give systematic instruction in skills, many opportunities for skill development exist in connection with on-going activities. . . .

Since learners vary to the extent that they do, a sound approach to skills teaching will allow for a wide range in the performance of skills. When expectancies are established, they should serve as guides to the teacher rather than as standards to be attained by all learners. In the lower grades there is a tendency to restrict the pupils' opportunities to move to more advanced levels of skills, while in the secondary school the inclination is to set unrealistic goals for low-achieving students. Pupils in the third, fourth, and fifth grades who are able to move rapidly on such skills as map reading, locating and gathering information, preparing reports, reading complex materials, and doing critical thinking should be encouraged and helped to do so. Sometimes teachers avoid the introduction of such skills because the course of study calls for their presentation in a later grade. There is little to justify this practice if teachers are well informed on the nature and extent of individual differences among pupils. Courses of study should not be so inflexible as to make adjustments in terms of individual learners impossible. The goal for the skills program should be continual growth for all learners. This means that skills performance can be expected to be variable rather than to show a rigid and fixed pattern. For some pupils, any progress, however small, is a mark of outstanding achievement.

A well-established principle in teaching is to ascertain what the learner already knows about whatever is to be taught, and to continue his instruction from that point. This being the case, teachers need to make careful appraisals of the status of skills learning of individual pupils before instruction is planned. A careful diagnosis of the skills-learning status of pupils will make it possible for the teacher to be more effective in properly gearing the instruction to the appropriate level of individuals within a class. A diagnostic approach to the teaching of social studies skills is essential if psychologically sound sequences are to be maintained.

A diagnostic approach to skills teaching underscores the continuous nature of skills growth. The complete learning of skills is not achieved in any one grade or set of grades. All teachers throughout the full 12-year program share the responsibility to introduce new skills or variations of skills; to maintain those which have been taught earlier and to reteach them if necessary; and to provide adequate practice and use of skills in order that they may be refined by the pupils. The teacher cannot fulfill his responsibilities along these lines unless he has a fairly complete and detailed knowledge of the learner's present level of proficiency. Schools need to explore ways of helping teachers get such information easily and quickly. More work needs to be done in the whole area of determining the existing status of learners with respect to social studies skills. . . .

The school not only provides instruction in important learnings but also serves as a proving ground for the application of these learnings. Within the school environment, problem-solving and decision-making situations can be carefully controlled. Errors in judgment or wrong decisions rarely have disastrous consequences. In life outside the school, however, decision making and problem solving are much more critical. The skills needed to resolve many of the problems encountered in life are the ones with which the social studies deal. Consequently, the school seeks to bring the student's skill development to a level that will make it possible for him to do creative problem solving on his own throughout his lifetime. Perhaps much of what the pupil learns in the social studies will wear thin or become obsolete. But skills learned in school continue to be functional indefinitely, or for so long as they are used. Skills are among the most permanent of the learnings.

✒ Experiments in Method   *Findlay C. Penix*

A dominant movement in contemporary education is directed toward earlier and more extensive development by pupils of their rational powers, intellectual capabilities, or cognitive skills. This selection is particularly timely, then, since it reports some interesting findings from recent research on children's acquisition of thinking abilities applied to social studies content.

> *Readers who are interested in the results of research on the
> other areas of children's social learning mentioned below will
> find it profitable to consult the original article.*

AFTER REVIEWING MORE than 80 articles published since 1959 on
various aspects of method, it must be concluded that much of the
literature in this area consists of opinion, personal experience, or description of classroom practices. Although such reports may be useful in suggesting techniques, they provide no evidence upon which
to determine effective procedures. Gross and Badger (1960) reached
similar conclusions in their review of research in teaching methods
for a 10-year period when they commented that much that was
being tried in techniques or advocated as effective procedure was
not based upon research.

The most significant studies were those which attempted to
identify various stages in children's growth of concepts, attitudes,
and skills and specific or implied methods that might be used in
teaching these concepts, attitudes, and skills. These studies reflected
a growing realization of the need for change in elementary social
studies curriculum and method based upon a great deal more evidence than is now available. Although several of the studies were in
the realm of curriculum, implications for both curriculum and
method were strong ones. The studies are reviewed under the following headings: time and chronology, government and politics, knowledge and thinking, and economic education. . . .

GOVERNMENT AND POLITICS

Typically, an informal approach to teaching and reinforcing attitudes
toward law and government (citizenship) has been practiced in the
elementary grades with emphasis on national holidays and heroes,
patriotic events, pledge of allegiance to the flag, and attention to
election processes during an election year. Specific instruction has
been delayed until the junior and senior high school years. It is
apparent, however, that attitudes and ideas concerning law, government, and the political world have their beginnings at a much
earlier age.

Estvan (1962) reported a study of teaching of government in
the Wisconsin elementary schools. Major attention was centered on
goals, learning experiences, materials of instruction, evaluation, and

Used by permission of the *Bulletin* of the School of Education, Indiana University, from its March, 1964, issue, 40:31–40. Dr. Penix is a member of the
faculty in teacher education at the University of Michigan.

organization. Data for the study were collected from a 12-page questionnaire returned by 369 of the 432 teachers selected for the study through the use of a stratified sampling approach.

The most important goals reported by the teachers were concerned with the development of an understanding about government and the cultivation of desirable attitudes and values of democratic governing processes. Methods used to realize these goals were largely verbal—reading, writing, discussion—along with audio-visual experiences and pupil participation through teacher-pupil planning. Books and audio-visual resources were most useful for carrying out experiences. Evaluation stressed knowledge and understanding, with less emphasis placed on attitudes, critical thinking, work-study skills, and group processes; in over half the cases assessment of growth was made through observation and group discussion.

The study revealed no clear-cut pattern for organizing instruction and no plan of sequence or continuity; instruction was incidental about as often as it was a part of a current events period. It was introduced even less frequently in special programs or extra-class activities. More attention was paid to government as children moved through the grades. Experiences in the primary grades dealt with individual responsibilities, symbols, and services. More emphasis was placed on organization, representatives, democracy, and history in the intermediate grades. Teachers at all grade levels reported the usefulness of materials covering many facets of government.

In an earlier study (1959) Estvan concluded that boys and girls enter school with little conception of government and that, although the grasp of governmental processes increases by sixth grade, ideas and attitudes about government are slow to appear and mature. Among the suggestions made for continued efforts to improve government education at the elementary school level were 1) the development of an abundance of readily available teaching resources on different ability levels, and 2) the identification of various stages in children's growth of concepts, attitudes, and skills related to government.

Easton and Hess (1960, 1962) attempted to discover the nature of children's political orientation—the concepts, attitudes, and values held about the political world. The study involved 12,000 elementary school children from grade 1 through grade 8. Research is continuing, but present data are sufficiently strong to provide new insights in this area. Thus far data appear to support the following major findings: 1) The child's political world begins to take shape prior to his entrance into elementary school and is subject to rapid change. Many basic political attitudes and values have become firmly established by the time the child has completed the elementary grades. 2) The child's basic political orientation to regime and community undergoes little change during the high school years, and there is little evidence that fundamental attitudes and values toward regime and political community are any different at the beginning than at the end of high school. 3) The years between the ages of 3 and 13 seem to be the most formative years in political maturation.

Cammarota (1963), in a review of the Easton and Hess study, used the findings to draw a number of implications relating to content and organization of the elementary social studies program. She stated that if new content is to be selected there is need to redefine the learnings considered appropriate for children of various ages; for example, areas such as government and politics have been largely ignored even though children are learning about them from a very early age. She suggested that concepts and content from political science be placed in a spiral framework; thus, study about government might begin in the first grade and continue each year through the elementary school. Subject matter would be different at each grade level, but underlying principles would remain the same. This type of organization would build upon and extend the knowledge children acquire outside of school and would help to put facts and ideas into a conceptual framework.

These studies stop short of method other than suggesting development of appropriate instructional resources (Estvan). If findings from investigations such as those conducted by Easton and Hess are to be incorporated into the elementary social studies curriculum, appropriate methods must be found which will help children clarify and refine understandings. Techniques which would utilize children's experiences from their immediate environment along with a strong emphasis on related current affairs would appear to be one approach.

KNOWLEDGE AND THINKING

Mugge (1962) assessed the social studies information of 180 beginning second grade children (90 boys and 90 girls) from rural, urban, and suburban areas in Pennsylvania. Data were obtained from four instruments: an information test based upon seven generally used social studies textbooks; an experience questionnaire; a short test of information beyond the immediate environment; and a definition questionnaire. The investigator found that these second grade children knew 37 per cent of the items on the tests, with no significant differences between rural, urban, and suburban children's information; that boys responded correctly to more items than did girls; and that there was a significant relationship between the variety of experiences which children had had and the scores on the social studies information test. Mugge concluded that second grade children do have social studies information on many topics but they lack the ability to make precise responses. Help in organizing present and newly acquired information into meaningful patterns is needed by these children.

Beaubier (1962) designed a study which involved the deliberate presentation of social studies material of greater complexity than is usually taught to sixth-graders. The experiment covered an eight-week period, with 228 students from eight classrooms participating. Data were gathered from control and experimental groups by a pre-test, a post-test, and tape-recorded individual interviews. Beaubier concluded that the experimental groups achieved greater understanding in all areas studied, regardless of I.Q., with the greatest differences apparent in economics and anthropology. The use of many instructional materials facilitated the development of understandings. Data supported the over-all conclusion that sixth grade children can learn more than is typically expected of them.

The purpose of a study by Maw (1959) was to determine whether critical thinking ability of children in the fourth, fifth, and sixth grades could be improved by using prepared exercises to teach selected skills of critical thinking. Twenty-one experimental and 21 control classes from upper-middle and middle class suburban communities were used in the eight-week study. Critical thinking skills tested were those of selecting relevant facts, judging reliability of data, making generalizations and inferences, recognizing situations in which evidence is insufficient for a conclusion, determining cause and effect, and evaluating arguments. Twenty-four prepared lessons—three per week—were used with the experimental group. Data were obtained from the Davis-Eells Games, and a test of critical thinking was devised by the investigator. In addition, teachers in the experimental classes used check lists for evaluation of individual lessons and made reports of the general effectiveness of the lessons.

Maw found that the mean gain of the experimental classes exceeded the mean gain of the control classes on both tests. The difference on the test of critical thinking was highly significant, but was not significant for the Davis-Eells test. Differences in mean gains among grades, among ability groups, and between the sexes were found to be insignificant. There was a strong indication of the effectiveness of the lessons in improving the thinking skills required by the test of critical thinking. Teachers of the experimental classes reported that the students showed improvement in the thoughtful consideration of problems, the tendency to suspend judgment, and a desire to obtain evidence prior to forming conclusions.

Crabtree (1962) investigated the productiveness of children's thinking. The study was designed to determine whether different approaches to structure—"organization imposed upon the learning situation"—would effect differences in children's predisposition to thinking and to measure the effects of different approaches to structure on children's participation patterns. The six-week study was conducted with 24 second grade children in a single classroom. The subjects were pre-tested for creativity of thinking on the Torrence Product Improvement Task, paired and randomly assigned to one of two groups. Both groups received, in alternate sequence, two experimental programs (Program A and Program B) which used different teaching methods. Each program utilized a harbor and an airport study as content.

Program A was of emergent structure, with children's interests furnishing cues for sequence and pacing of discussions. Subject-matter resources and teaching aids were withheld until relevancy was established by the children's cues. The teacher's role was that of supporting children's ideas, helping in the development of purposes, encouraging identification and definition of interests and problems within content areas, and adding depth to discussions. The establishment of a classroom climate which supported independence and initiative in thinking was the teacher's responsibility. Program B was predetermined in structure, with discussion topics teacher-selected. The teacher-structured discussions were directive and commanding, held children to systematic, logical lines of deductive reasoning, and were evaluated for conceptual accuracy against norms of an adult world.

A discussion period began study in both programs, followed by a play period in a dramatic play center. No limitations were placed upon play; differences which occurred were a function of the type of structuring which had taken place in the discussion period. Teachers became non-participating observers. The play environment in Program A was unarranged and consisted of ambiguous materials; in Program B it was pre-arranged with high realism materials organized to invite certain patterns of response. Data were gathered from scales developed for the measurement of children's thinking and involvement in play. Independent teams of observers obtained both quantitative and descriptive data by point-time sampling and anecdotal recording techniques.

Crabtree found that divergent thinking as characterized by originality, spontaneity, and flexibility of response reached a mean of 48 per cent of the observed thinking responses in Program A; in Program B the mean was 18 per cent. The difference was significant at the .001 per cent level. Convergent thinking as characterized by the degree to which it was conceptually accurate and logically deductive and to which it led to the correct but restricted conclusions that a well-defined situation was intended to invoke totaled a mean of 54 per cent in Program B as compared with 21 per cent in Program A. This difference was significant at the .001 per cent level. The investigator concluded that Program A, which withheld teacher-structuring and encouraged exploration of the ideas initiated by the children, established predispositions to thinking which were maintained in the play periods following discussion and that an immediate, high involvement in play was encouraged. In addition, there was a higher incidence of imaginative, constructive play in the non-structured program which resulted in sequences incorporating real information. . . .

CONCLUSIONS

Research in the methods of teaching social studies in elementary schools during the past five years tentatively suggests 1) that young children have more knowledge related to social studies, even though unorganized, than is generally believed to be true; 2) that this knowledge can be translated into understandable basic concepts; and 3) that methods can be developed and used which will increase children's understanding of and ability to apply basic concepts.

Several of the studies reviewed here only imply method. Identification of the stages of children's growth in concepts, attitudes, and skills is the first step; the next step must be that of developing ways in which children can be helped to progress in the understanding and application of these concepts, attitudes, and skills. The need for further research in method is obvious.

Bibliography

BEAUBIER, EDWARD W., *Capacity of Sixth Grade Children to Understand Social Science Generalizations*, Doctor's thesis, University of Southern California, Los Angeles, 1962.

CAMMAROTA, GLORIA, "Children, Politics, and Elementary Social Studies," *Social Education* 27:205–207, 211, April, 1963.

CRABTREE, CHARLOTTE A., *Effects of Structuring on Productiveness of Children's Thinking: A Study of Second Grade Dramatic Play Patterns Centered in Harbor and Airport Activities Under Two Types of Teacher Structuring*, Doctor's thesis, Stanford University, Stanford University, Calif., 1962.

EASTON, DAVID, and HESS, ROBERT, "The Child's Image of the President," *Public Opinion Quarterly* 24:632–644, Winter, 1960.
"The Child's Political World," *Midwest Journal of Political Science* 6:227–246, August, 1962.

ESTVAN, FRANK J., "Teaching Government in Elementary Schools," *Elementary School Journal* 62:291–297, March, 1962.

ESTVAN, FRANK J., and ESTVAN, ELIZABETH W., *The Child's World: His Social Perception*, G. P. Putnam's Sons, New York, 1959.

GROSS, R. E., and BADGER, W. V., "Social Studies," in *Encyclopedia of Educational Research*, pp. 1296–1319, edited by Chester W. Harris, The Macmillan Co., New York, 1960.

HESS, ROBERT, and EASTON, DAVID, "Role of the Elementary School in Political Socialization," *School Review* 70:257–265, Autumn, 1962.

MAW, ETHEL W., *An Experiment in Teaching Critical Thinking in the Intermediate Grades*, Doctor's thesis, University of Pennsylvania, Philadelphia, 1959.

MUGGE, DOROTHY, *Social Studies Information of Beginning Second Grade Children*, Doctor's thesis, Columbia University, New York, 1962.

⤚§ GROUP WORK SKILLS   *Kenneth Rehage*

A great deal has been spoken and written about group work skills in social studies. Indeed, some educators go so far as to place preponderant—if not exclusive—emphasis in elementary social studies on the development of such skills. It is both heartening and helpful, therefore, to find an author who blends well both the practical and theoretical elements of group work. This writer also balances advocacy of emphasis on group work in the social studies with recognition of both 1) wide-spread opportunities for group work throughout the elementary curriculum and 2) a need for individual and class activities to complement work in small groups.

THE BASIC RATIONALE for developing skill in group work derives from the idea that the successful achievement of many purposes, both in school and outside school, demands cooperative action of several in-

Used by permission of the author and National Council for the Social Studies; from its Thirty-Second Yearbook, *Social Studies in the Elementary Schools*, 1962, pp. 187–196. Dr. Rehage is former director of the elementary education program at the University of Chicago.

dividuals. Cooperative action that is successful in turn depends upon a variety of skills on the part of participating individuals. Such skills, like other skills, are learned through practice. The school is a particularly appropriate place to get the needed practice. Some of the school subjects, like the social studies, can provide situations which are particularly well suited for practice in the application of group work skills.

It is also important to note that instruction in the social studies, as in other elementary school subjects, occurs in a group setting. Recent studies have emphasized that the effectiveness of learning depends in no small measure upon the climate of the group. This appears to be the case even when the class is working on a task that is not essentially a group task. In a setting where pupils give to and receive from each other support and encouragement in their efforts to master certain learning tasks, the learning is apt to be appreciably greater than in cases where pupils are indifferent toward each other's achievement.

When a class is engaged in a task that is a genuine group task, opportunities are provided for nurturing individual development. For example, an individual who becomes deeply involved in a significant group enterprise, and who contributes to that enterprise, gains confidence in himself because of his contribution. He achieves a kind of psychological identification with the group. He senses the extent to which the group depends upon him, and finds in this fact a source of motivation to accept and discharge his responsibility as a group member. At the same time, he has an opportunity to develop respect for other members of the group whose work helps the group to progress. Through a series of such experiences a pupil can assess his own strengths and weaknesses, find new roles for himself, and at the same time recognize the roles that others can perform in a group enterprise.

It is clear that the learning of group skills has value both for the class as a whole and for the individuals in the class. But this learning can hardly be justified as an end in itself. It is valued primarily because it can contribute to larger goals, to goals which will be achieved more effectively through group action than through individual action alone. Emphasis on group activities in the social studies classroom should reflect their usefulness as means to reach goals which cannot be attained as well through other means. . . .

PROBLEM SOLVING IN GROUP SITUATIONS

. . . . Underlying all of this discussion is the general notion that such groups will be concerned with some kind of problem. The activities of the group, then, will in a large measure be problem solving activities. It becomes appropriate to inquire, therefore, about the nature of problem solving activities that take place in group work.

Problem solving behavior in group situations is not essentially different from such behavior when performed by individuals. Perhaps the most important aspect of group problem solving occurs in the planning stage, for here the group maps out its general approach to the problem in hand. A second stage is one which involves the execution of the plans, and at this point the group may be working together or each of the members may be working quite independently on an assigned task. A third stage in group work occurs when the work of all members is brought together in such a way as to complete the assignment. Finally, a group may engage in some effort to appraise its own work.

Among the skills required in effective planning, whether individually or in groups, are the ability to see the various aspects of the problem at hand and to define the problem clearly. One of the distinct advantages in a group approach to working on a given problem is that the various members of the group will often see different aspects of the problem. Some will be able to define it only in a limited way, while others can see the problem in a much broader context. In this manner, the experience of all members of the group can be brought to bear on the problem in the planning stage. A second skill involved in planning is the ability to see alternative courses of action to take with respect to the problem as defined. Here again the advantage of the group is that it often can identify more possible courses of action than one individual would identify. A third skill related to planning is closely related to the second, for it invokes the ability to anticipate probable consequences of any given alternative course of action. Finally, in the planning stage the group must select the course or courses of action most likely to accomplish the goal of the group.

In a group situation these skills related to planning must be applied in a context that presents problems of a somewhat different sort than when the planning is done individually. Members of a group must develop a disposition to listen to the suggestions of others, to recognize the merits as well as the limitations of such suggestions, to identify precise points of conflict when conflict arises, to effect a compromise between opposing views, and to accept such compromises so that the group can proceed. All these behaviors call for a considerable measure of objectivity. In this respect pupils are likely to differ from each other as widely as in other characteristics. Some pupils exhibit striking talents for resolving differences within a group while others neither display such ability nor seem concerned about the problems created when conflict arises.

Planning also involves identification of sub-problems which then need to be distributed among various members of the group for action. This calls for a willingness to assume particular responsibilities, even though the one assigned by the group may not have been the member's first choice. In short, there are many occasions in the planning stage of a group enterprise where the individual needs to subordinate his own desires to those of the group. Likewise, there are frequently occasions when one needs to press his own point of view on a given issue because the logic of the case is on his side. These situations are the prototypes of many others that young people will often face in school and in life. To handle them well requires respect for others and concern for the group enterprise.

When the planning phase of a group project has been completed, the group can turn to activities involved in the execution of the plans. In some instances each member's task can be undertaken independently, with only the requirement that he accept the responsibility of completing his assignment within agreed upon time limits. This is very likely to be the case where a committee has been asked to report to the class as a whole on various phases of a particular subject. In other instances the carrying out of one's responsibility involves working closely with one or more other persons. . . .

Regardless of the requirements for the execution of a particular set of plans, there are certain responsibilities that each group member needs to accept and discharge. Where materials are needed for his work he must see that they are available. He must discipline himself to stay with the task until it is completed. He must use his time with maximum effectiveness, not only for the sake of finishing his own task but because the progress of the entire group project is dependent upon the fulfillment of each individual commitment. It is again evident in the execution of a group project, as in the planning, that an individual must be mindful to the group responsibility, not merely of his own.

At some point it is usually necessary for members of a group to bring together the results of their labor, to organize their material for some kind of presentation to the class as a whole, or to engage in some other kind of activity which in essence marks the formal conclusion of the group enterprise. Here again the job should be defined in such a way as to make it possible for each member of the group to share in this concluding phase of the work. Problems frequently arise at this point. Some pupils may make very significant contributions to a group task but they have neither the skill nor disposition to participate effectively in any form of reporting of their work. Others may have contributed little but are perfectly willing to accept the recognition that comes from reporting on behalf of the entire group. In such situations it is important for the teacher to be guided by the major objectives of the class work and by the interpretations of those objectives that the teacher believes appropriate for each child. If the major purpose of the group work is to get certain information to the entire class, the teacher would normally work with the group to see that the presentation was as effective as it could be. If, on the other hand, the group task is one where the teacher can afford to be less concerned with the substance of the report and more concerned with the pupils' skill in making oral presentations the likelihood is that each student should have some part in the proceedings in order to get needed practice.

In the evaluation phase of a group enterprise the essential question is "Did the group accomplish its major purposes?" This kind of question often leads to a further consideration of how the group might have done a more satisfactory job. At the conclusion of any group work, whether in school or out, group members engage in some kind of appraisal. This may be done privately to oneself, or perhaps publicly to a few close friends. This kind of appraisal, as informal as it tends to be, is likely not to be very useful in helping individual members of a group to become more effective in group work. On the other hand, a realistic appraisal by group members of their achievements will reveal strengths in their results, in which all can take pride, and opportunities for improvement, which constitute a challenge for the next group task. Obviously, the attempts to make some kind of evaluation should be systematic rather than perfunctory, and it is best carried out when the results can be checked against previously determined standards for group work. The skill required here is that of being able to view the work of the group and individual members with detachment, so that the process of evaluation can itself be a useful learning experience.

THE ROLE OF THE TEACHER

If these skills in group work are regarded as important educational objectives, it is essential that appropriate learning experiences be planned to achieve them. As in the case of other objectives, one does not expect appreciable gains in group skills merely by chance. It is at this point that the teacher's role becomes increasingly important.

In the first place, the teacher must make some assessment of the kind and amount of emphasis given to group work in earlier grades. . . .

Secondly, the teacher must ascertain what possibilities for group work are presented within the school program. . . . These opportunities in the social studies are frequent. . . .

A third task for the teacher is to assist the pupils in identifying the skills needed for effective group work. This is most advantageously done immediately prior to an occasion when group work is to be used. . . .

A fourth responsibility of the teacher is to structure the assignment for the group in such a way that the task is quite clear. Once having done this the teacher in effect delegates to the group the responsibility for performing the task. . . .

A fifth responsibility of the teacher is to make certain that the management of the group enterprises proceeds as smoothly as possible, so that a minimum of time is lost in assigning pupils to groups, in the selecting of chairmen, and in similar activities. It is possible for the pupils to become so preoccupied with these matters that they have little time or energy to devote to the task the group is expected to accomplish. . . . It is well to remember, however, that a good bit of the success a group experiences comes from learning how to handle intra-group problems of management as well as how to perform the work for which it was formed.

A sixth kind of responsibility facing the teacher is related to the planning of group work in such a way as to facilitate the maximum development of group skills in the course of the year's work. This calls for beginning the work with tasks that are well within the competence of the pupils at the beginning of the year, and gradually increasing the difficulty and complexity of the assignments as the year progresses. . . .

Finally, as in the case with all instruction, the teacher must make some appraisal of the effectiveness of the activities designed to promote skill in group work. Some of the evidence he needs can come from the group's own evaluation of its work. But there are things which the teacher can note which might not normally come to light in the pupils' evaluation. Was the group task too difficult, or too simple? Were the materials needed available? Were the sub-groups too large or too small? Were the tasks formulated in such a way that each member of the group could make a contribution? As the pupils gain more experience do they tend to use up less time with activities that are not central to the task at hand? Do the pupils seem to be better able to exhibit respect for each other? Does group work, as carried on in this class, facilitate desired learnings at least as effectively as other means which might be used?

On this latter question there has been relatively little research, and what there is presents conflicting evidence. The term "group work" represents different things to different people. It is therefore difficult to draw general conclusions from investigations that deal with various kinds of group activities, in various settings, with children of various ages. We do know that it is possible to describe a classroom group in terms of the kind of "climate" that prevails. We know that one of the primary factors, if not the most important factor, in classroom climate is the teacher. We have reason to believe that the classroom climate has a significant effect upon learning. It becomes increasingly apparent that a teacher, sensitive to the forces at work in his class group and its many sub-groups, can encourage the use of group problem solving as a means of fostering group and individual inquiry. But this requires at least the meeting of some of the conditions outlined earlier in this section, and it falls largely to the teacher to see that such conditions are met.

Group work is, therefore, no panacea for the ills that beset education in general, or elementary social studies in particular. It has a great deal to offer, and undoubtedly will become even more productive as our knowledge of group phenomena broadens and deepens. As has always been true with various methods of instruction, results depend more upon the discriminating and wise use of the method than upon the method itself.

ᓚᗧ A Neglected Skill   *Haverly O. Moyer*

It is easy to oversimplify the idea of skill in observing when people are the object of observation. Moyer calls for specific and extensive attention to the development of observational skills in the social studies. He offers illustrative answers to some pertinent questions. What are some tangible elements in the social environment of children? What are some practical ways for pupils to look for evidence of such elements? In what sequence do levels of purposeful development of observational skill emerge? His article should stir readers to find other elements to observe and to develop additional techniques for such observation.

IF YOU LOOK THROUGH curriculum bulletins and texts on teaching social studies, you will find specific skills related to listening, to

Used by permission of The Social Studies; from *The Social Studies*, March, 1960, 51:94–96. Dr. Moyer is on the faculty of State University Teachers College, Plattsburg, N. Y.

reading, to writing and to reporting. All of these are very important and rightly should be of great concern to the teacher. But isn't there another skill which should be of equal concern that is somewhat if not entirely neglected in many classrooms?

For example, let's think about *observation.* Isn't observation a *social studies* skill? If the teacher thinks of social studies in its full meaning, he should have as one objective: to help children to become aware of and sensitive to the feelings of others. If that is an accepted objective then the teacher needs to think of social observation as an essential social studies skill and include practice in social observation as a definite, conscious aspect of the social studies teaching.

Let's consider some of the things the teacher may help the children to observe better than they would without direct guidance. What are some of the observations that socially competent adults have learned to make by trial and error procedures? Can children be helped to make these observations more effectively through direct teaching?

It seems that much trial and error could be eliminated through direct teaching and that there is an obvious need for it. For instance, let's start with the beginning of the school day. How many of the children observe their classmates when they arrive in the mornings? Do they see their classmates and greet them? For that matter, does the teacher see and greet each child?

It seems probable that the children could be helped to develop better understanding and higher respect for each other if they were taught to observe each other and include in their morning greeting some simple statement of approval or appreciation, to observe the work of individuals in their grade and discover those qualities which deserve commendation and follow through with appropriate complimentary remarks. If visitations were made in many of the classrooms of America it is very probable that a great lack of willingness, awareness and competence on the part of the children to observe each other's good personal qualities, good academic strengths and good social abilities and to recognize them through an appropriate form of complimentary remark would be discovered.

Following the development of the observation of personal appearance, the somewhat more difficult observation of academic ability and the even more difficult observation of personal qualities, might come the most difficult observation of personal mood and in later years the observation of group mood. Doesn't it seem possible that we can teach children to recognize mood? Quite young children learn through trial and error to recognize the level of exasperation beyond which they know their parents may not be pushed with safety. Couldn't we introduce a program for increasing skill in the observation of mood in our social studies classes? For example we might make some observations of animals and their ways of showing approval and disapproval, then lead those observations toward a study of the ways people show approval or disapproval. We might apply it to increased understanding of the class mood that may develop under differing circumstances.

Perhaps the children could be led to see the way people use "name-calling" as a means of showing like or dislike for others. It seems probable that the ability to recognize "name-calling" for what it is, and the understanding of its real meaning, would help children to be more capable of dealing with those who use the device.

For instance, if children can be helped to discover that the statement, "Ricky is crazy," is a revelation of the speaker's state of mind and not necessarily a revelation of the facts, then they will find it easier to deal with "name-calling" without emotion, and, no doubt, will become less likely to use the name-calling device themselves.

In later grades it seems important to teach children to observe the judgments which their peers and adults make. If for example, a pupil says, "This is a good book," then what are his classmates to think? His remark, they may observe, is a judgment presumably based on a number of previously observed facts. If the pupils have been led in their observations to recognize this statement as a judgment, they may be taught to use it wisely; otherwise it will probably stop their thinking cold. Unless the children are led to recognize judgment statements and are given help in knowing how to question the person who made the judgment, tactfully, critical thinking is not likely to emerge.

As soon as children have been led to recognize judgments for what they are, an application of this skill can be made to the pupils' own reports. They can be helped to give reports that have a minimum of personal judgment, and on the other hand they can be led to recognize implied judgments in the oral or written reports of others.

If this skill is directly developed by teachers throughout the elementary school social studies program, many of the children should acquire an acute sense for observing the difference between fact and judgment or between facts and inferences. That ability would certainly help the adolescent and young adult to deal more intelligently with social problems. They would be less susceptible to emotionalized propaganda and less likely to form conclusions on the basis of judgments unsupported by facts.

It would seem that social studies teachers might well accept the responsibility for helping children improve the skill of social observation, proceeding from very simple observations of easily recognized qualities in the primary grades to the more complex observations of opinion, judgment or bias in the later grades or high school. If the children are to be taught to become democratic persons whose behavior is guided by democratic values, it seems essential that they be given direct, conscious guidance in this skill of social observation.

❧ TEACHING SOCIAL SCIENCE AS METHOD

Melvin Tumin

Perhaps too often activities to develop pupils' skills in the methodology of social scientists have been marred by either of two extremes. One is rank oversimplification, misleadingly calling "research" what are merely traditional study procedures. The other consists of trying to have pupils use rather fully the research techniques of mature and skillful social scientists, which they are unequipped to do. The social scientist who wrote this selection recognizes these difficulties and proposes here examples of techniques that are significant, valid in reflecting research methodology, and adaptable to pupils who inevitably lack a high degree of research skill.

THE FIRST, FOREMOST, and most despair-producing problem I see is that of getting across a solid appreciation of how difficult it is to get to know anything with any degree of assurance of its truth. Everywhere it is assumed that reliable knowledge is easy to come by. Even worse, it is everywhere assumed that *systematic*, reliable knowledge is easy to come by. The fact of the matter, of course, as we all know, is that such knowledge even about the most apparently simple dimensions or aspects of human behavior is painfully hard to come by. The question, then, is how can we get a wider appreciation of this fact.

I know of only one way that has a high degree of probability of success, and that is to require everyone concerned to try to answer any one single problem about human affairs by producing reliable, rele-

Used by permission of the author and the National Council for the Social Studies; from its Research Bulletin No. 1, *Needed Research in the Teaching of the Social Studies*, 1964, pp. 52–54. Dr. Tumin is a professor of sociology at Princeton University.

vant data. This means, unavoidably, that all those for whom this appreciation of the difficulty of securing knowledge is important must themselves engage in research projects, no matter how small in conception, trivial in population size studied, or insignificant in the total 'bulk of human behavior.

There are many perplexing problems about how best to organize such research projects. There are numerous advantages and disadvantages to every method I have ever tried or know that others have tried. In any event, it would pay us all a good deal of profit to consider at some length how best to produce that indispensable appreciation of the difficulty of securing systematic, reliable knowledge about social affairs.

Apropos of this, one sure thing is that neither school children nor anyone else can get an appreciation of how difficult it is to get reliable information by turning to their encyclopedias for that information. To be sure one can get a lot of information from encyclopedias, and, if they are good encyclopedias, the information is often reliable. But one does not and cannot thereby begin to appreciate what has been required to establish that information as reliable. If it has proven possible in courses in physical science to have children perform simple experiments in order to come closer to understanding the method of science, I see no conceivable reason why this can't be done in social science. Even simple exercises in systematic social observation would do a lot more to bring home to children what is involved in social science than the more usual techniques currently practiced of sending them to the library to index the warehouse of codified information.

The actual involvement in a research project commends itself on grounds other than those stated but implied by them. I think principally of two such grounds. The first concerns the notion of objectivity. The second has to do with the idea of multiple causation.

The desideratum in science, of course, is perfect and total objectivity of the investigator. We all are familiar with a number of the ways in which we fail to achieve this blessed state. There is one path toward objectivity, however, that is open, and that is perhaps not used as often as it could be. This involves that state of mind implied in the words "critical doubt." The cultivation of this state of mind is, of course, indispensable for the *general* education of anyone in a free society. But it is also specifically relevant in the training in science which necessarily involves an unwillingness easily to accept anything as given until there are pretty good evidential grounds for doing so. The task of encouraging this approach in the classroom encounters two primary difficulties. The first is the fact that the schools are charged, as probably they should be, with the inculcation of basic values—at least some values—along with the training of minds and the

transferring of skills. Values being what they are, it is extremely difficult to inculcate them and at the same time encourage systematic
critical doubt as a general approach of mind. It is, of course, much
easier simply to require children to accept things as given to them.
With the great power the formal position of the teacher gives to her,
it is no trick to have nominal verbal conformity to the teacher's expressed value preferences. It is quite a trick, however, to get a common value base established and, at the same time, communicate a
genuine and sincere interest in the manifestation of the critical mind
at work. But this is what must be done. And on this, then, we need a
good deal of inquiry as to how best we can do it. For critical doubt is
the better part of objectivity, just as, in turn, going around the circle,
objectivity is the better part of critical doubt. Just how a teacher can
maximize both her mandate to inculcate values regarding democracy
and the like, and, at the same time, just as deeply institutionalize a
critical turn of mind and a constant pressure toward objective dispassionate search for evidence is a very perplexing problem.

The second implied value of engaging in research projects referred to the idea of multiple causation. Earlier in this paper we
noted how the untrained mind runs easily toward the simple-minded
explanation, which turns out to be no explanation at all. Nor is it
enough to shift attention off the biologistic causal thinking on to
environmental influences. The further problem is present of getting
an appreciation of how complex are the causal patterns connected
with any simple behavior pattern. For instance, do boys and girls
begin to differ radically in their behavior early in American life? In
what ways? Why? And why are they similar in some respects, nevertheless? Since nearly every public school class has both boys and girls
who are likely to differ in some patterned ways and resemble each
other in other patterned ways, there is a natural matrix of experimental evidence to be researched right in the classroom—if the
teacher is up to it. Even a rudimentary inquiry into the similarities
and differences among boys and girls would involve the class from
the very outset in appreciating that, in addition to the genetic factors
that might be at work, there are a host of other cultural variables
which make their contribution. This realization of 1) the multiple
causation of this everyday fact, 2) the importance of cultural patterns,
and 3) the unsatisfactoriness of the "hereditarian" explanation that
says "that's the way boys and girls are by nature," might begin to
open up a world of understanding that would be extremely valuable.

Two other important social science lessons could be developed
out of the consideration of the differences and similarities in the behavior of boys and girls. First, the skillful teacher could go on to help
the children discover that these patterned and learned differences

have a mixed set of advantages and disadvantages for everyone concerned; neither the boys nor the girls enjoy *all* the results of the sharply different expectations regarding their behavior. From this realization, the teacher could move to the general lesson that is implicit, namely, that *all* events have multiple consequences, and that these are mixed—positive and negative—in their effects upon those who are involved.

Second, an analysis of boy-girl differences in the United States would call naturally for a look at these differences in other culture patterns. The *relativity* of our patterns, the fact that they represent but one of many ways in which male-female relationships can.be organized, and the fact that each culture has its own intrinsic logic or illogic—these are crucial ingredients in the development of a genuinely intelligent and sound appreciation of the nature of human nature and of human society.

I have specified some of these examples at length in order to show what must be obvious to most but needs to be made obvious to all, namely, that we have some very basic scientific truths at our command and that these can serve as general guides to observation and thinking about human social affairs, and that, finally, these can be translated into workable, understandable and enjoyable features of the curriculum of our schools even at the most elementary levels.

ᴈ Developing Social-Civic Behavior

W. Linwood Chase

> *While study or schoolwork skills are more easily taught and learned, the ultimate value of the social studies lies in its contribution to the behavior of children in human relationships beyond, as well as in, the classroom and the school. Admittedly the social studies, and indeed the entire school program, will not alone determine the child's behavior in relation to others. But the problem appears to be mainly that the social studies has little, if any, measurable influence on children's behavior. Can more be accomplished? The author of this selection thinks so, and he suggests some guidelines for approaching the problem.*

Used by permission of the National Society for the Study of Education, from "Individual Differences in Classroom Learning," in its Fifty-Sixth Yearbook, Part Two, *Social Studies in the Elementary School*, 1957, pp. 182–186.

IF THE CHILDREN of a selected group are checked at any specific time—third grade, fifth grade, or even more than once during a school year—there will be as wide individual differences among them in social-civic behavior as in any other aspect of social education, including subject-matter achievement. Whether we concern ourselves with the relationships of a child to his peer group in his classroom in all the various aspects of school living and working or to his social-civic behavior in other community institutions and in community life, we know that growth must start at the point where he is. This calls for understanding the status of each child.

What a child thinks of himself in relationship to others in the group and to standards set up by the group is very important. Teachers committed to a program of democratic teaching through democratic living and learning understand the necessity for instruction in many kinds of skills and techniques required for democratic action.

By the end of the sixth grade, a child should have a certain degree of ability in skills and techniques required as a member of a group, such as sharing intelligently in discussion, participating in group thinking, co-operating with others in work and play, cultivating attitudes of good will and service, abiding by the decisions of the majority, contributing to group enterprises, choosing leaders wisely, participating in the government of the school, serving as a leader, following a leader, adjusting differences with others in a democratic and peaceful fashion, living in friendly relationship with his fellows, serving efficiently on committees, working with others in solving school and community problems, maintaining an open-minded attitude in discussion, recognizing rights and property of others, working for the common good, developing social sensitivity, appreciating the contribution of others to personal and group living, co-operating with those who are older and those who are younger, and using simple parliamentary procedures.

There are also such skills and techniques required in self-control and self-direction as discovering certain tasks to be done, having respect for one's self and others, assuming personal responsibility, exercising initiative, respecting the opinions of others, making plans alone and with a group, carrying plans through to realization, learning how to insist on rights, surrendering privileges as occasion demands, having respect for authority, accepting suggestions, putting one's self in the other person's place, and accepting civic duties.

Also by the end of the sixth grade, a child should have some degree of ability in certain intellectual skills and techniques related to democratic action, such as acting on the basis of carefully weighed judgments; analyzing rumor and identifying propaganda; making decisions and evaluating them; understanding democratic obligations as well as privileges; analyzing democratic techniques used in community, state, nation, and student government; establishing criteria for standards of achievement; evaluating what has been done in terms of standards set up; understanding one's responsibility to school, home, community, and country; thinking critically; and recognizing increasing interdependency of individuals, communities, and nations.

To illustrate further the significance of individual differences for social-civic behavior, the writer has chosen three studies completed at Boston University in recent years.

Claffey (1) conducted a study of the attitudes of fifth-grade children regarding respect for rights and property by setting up twenty situations to which the children were asked to respond, using multiple-choice answers. Here is an illustration:

> Robert borrowed a book from school. His baby sister, Kathleen, marked the book with crayons.
> What should Robert do?

(a) Try to repair the damage.
(b) Tell the teacher.
(c) Say it was that way when he borrowed it.

What do you think Robert did?

(a) Tried to repair the damage.
(b) Told the teacher.
(c) Said it was that way when he borrowed it.

Many of the children did not know the correct response (the socially acceptable response). There was no significant difference between boys and girls. Intelligence or economic status of the family were not important factors in the decisions made by the children. What was important, however, was the difference between what the children thought *should* be done in a situation and what they thought *was* done. The mean of the 268 pupils on the twenty situations as to what they thought *should* be done was 14.15 compared with 9.45 as to what they thought *was* done. The difference between the two means is statistically significant.

Herlihy (2) used the same research pattern with 253 sixth-grade children in setting up twenty-four situations to reveal initiative or leadership in personal contacts, emerging situations, organization of groups, and associations within groups. Again, there were no significant differences between boys and girls, and intelligence and occupation of father did not seem important. But, there was a statistically significant difference between the mean of 15.77 for the socially acceptable responses in the "should" category and the mean of 11.11 for the responses in the "did" category. Both the Claffey and the Herlihy studies were seeking to find out if a child knew the right response to a situation and if he would expect another child to act according to that knowledge. That he does not always know the right response and does not always expect others to make what he thinks is the right response should be of serious concern to all those who work with children. These findings are particularly disturbing because preliminary investigation indicated that children responded to what they thought *was* done in the way they themselves would have acted.

In a study by Cotter (3), concerned with the qualities nine-year-olds wanted to find in their leaders, 512 of them were given a paired-preference check list. The terms used to describe the qualities were evolved in a school which cultivated pupil leadership and democratic planning. In order of preference, the qualities were rated: (1) good sport; (2) helpful; (3) fair and square; (4) kind; (5) polite; (6) generous; (7) good ideas; (8) neat; (9) full of pep; and (10) strict. There was a significant difference between the frequency of mention of the first three and the frequency of mention of 5, 6, and 7; and the frequency of mention of 5, 6, and 7 was significantly different from the frequency of mention of 8, 9, and 10.

The following questions, although not all-inclusive in considering the characteristics of social-civic behavior, may be helpful to the teacher. As he asks himself these questions about the entire group of children, he will immediately become aware of the individual needs to be met.

1. Are pupils developing abilities for the conduct of calm and intelligent discussion?
2. Do citizenship qualities function as habits of action in pupils?
3. Do pupils develop concern for the common welfare and then do something about it?
4. Do the pupils initiate and analyze their own activities to find out what qualities are needed for effective co-operation?
5. Are pupils developing their own criteria for standards of achievement as citizens?
6. Have pupils observed, analyzed, and evaluated the benefits of democratic action in a specific experience of school or community life?

A child's chief concern is getting along with other children and with adults. His consciousness of person-to-person relationships is constantly increasing as he becomes successively a member of larger social groups. Studies in educational method show increased learning when instruction is adjusted to the individual. This means that every classroom teacher must have specific objectives for each individual child.

References

(1) Rose Claffey, "A Study in the Attitudes of Fifth-Grade Children Regarding Respect for Rights and Property." Unpublished Ed.M. thesis, Boston University, 1947.

(2) Jane M. Herlihy, "A Study of Some Phases of Initiative and Leadership of Sixth-Grade Children." Unpublished Ed.M. thesis, Boston University, 1947.

(3) Margaret E. Cotter, "The Quality of Leadership Preferred by the Nine-Year-Old." Unpublished Ed.M. thesis, Boston University, 1950.

ᴥᔆ Helping the Less Able Reader

Robert V. Duffey

Well-recognized by teachers as a major handicap in working with slow learners in social studies is the tendency of the slow learner to be a poor reader. This writer frankly acknowledges and squarely faces the problem. He offers several suggestions specifically aimed at aiding the teacher in identifying and using reading materials that are adaptable to pupils of limited reading ability.

A QUESTION BEING RAISED increasingly often by teachers at all levels is, "What can I do to help my pupils who cannot read our social studies textbook?" This paper is directed to some suggested answers to this question. A limitation which the writer has placed upon the answers is that they must include reading; that is, they must not consist of non-reading activities.

Two basic assumptions would seem to be worth mentioning. First, social studies should not be considered a mere handmaiden to reading. . . . Actually, success in reading and success in social studies achievement tend to go hand in hand: reading helps the pupil in social studies, and what he learns in social studies helps him to read better (1). Our concern with reading in this present instance is its use as a means to an end in social studies.

Second, the raising of the question is an encouraging sign that many teachers are increasingly concerned with individual differences

Used by permission of the author and the National Council for the Social Studies; from *Social Education*, 25:182–184, April, 1961. Dr. Duffey is professor and head of the Department of Early Childhood, Elementary Education, at the University of Maryland.

in achievement. In his "House Divided Against Itself" speech Lincoln said, "If we could first know where we are and whither we are tending, we could better judge what we do and how to do it." It would appear that many teachers have come to the place of "how to do it."

"Vagueness," Bernard de Voto said, "should not be invoked when a precise answer is possible"; but pat answers to educational questions are usually not readily found. The suggested answers to our particular problem are not advertised herewith as anything beyond possible answers, helps to be used with professional discretion.

TEXTBOOKS AT LOWER LEVELS OF READABILITY

This most obvious suggestion is not so easy as it may sound. For one thing, content coverage varies from level to level. Further, treatment of the same content differs from author to author, albeit for good reasons, compounding the instructional task. Students in the upper grades tend to shun texts designated for lower grades. Authorities disagree on the advisability of using multiple texts at the elementary level (2).

The suggestion is made, nevertheless, in the knowledge that it will prove workable in some instances. Its use will be greater where the possibilities of its use are better known. A master inventory of the contents—titles of chapters, stories, poems, and pictures—of all the books in a school, with grade levels indicated and arranged according to unit topics or broad topical headings (for example, "Westward Movement," "Mexican Life," "George Washington") is an excellent stimulant. Compiling and maintaining such an inventory and doing the necessary librarian work are the kinds of service projects with which gifted pupils may be entrusted. . . .

TRADE BOOKS, OR CHILDREN'S LITERATURE

In brief, pertinent juvenile literature is available as never before. It has always been coveted in social studies because it provides the depth and detail which textbooks cannot provide.

A service of great merit is rendered to teachers at all levels in their efforts to keep abreast of this avalanche of material by the *Bulletin* of the Center for Children's Books (3). This publication critically reviews current juvenile books, pointing out each volume's relative importance, its strengths and weaknesses, its general content, its specific usefulness, and its reading level. Valuable information is also available from publishing houses, school and public librarians, and the curriculum offices of large city school systems.

A matter of great importance in winning over the less able

reader to the reading of a whole book is the size of the book. He must be able to see the end of the job from the time he starts. The teacher must constantly be on the prowl for shorter presentations (4).

JUNIOR NEWS PUBLICATIONS

These newspapers and news magazines (5) provide tremendous coverage. Just how true this statement is can be learned best by anyone who will take the time and trouble to clip the articles (at least two copies of each issue will be needed) of a year's subscription and file them under appropriate headings. Doing this faithfully for all the issues of all the papers at the different grade levels will result in a veritable library. Because the publishers treat the same subject sometimes on different levels, and often follow up a topic in subsequent issues, a file of clipped articles can soon become a rich repository of information on a surprising array of topics.

Special features, supplements, and tests add appeal for students. Excellent background material and suggestions for teachers can often work together to help keep the presentations informal.

MATERIAL RE-WRITTEN BY THE TEACHER

There is evidence to the effect that simplification of vocabulary and other structural elements aids achievement of meaning; however, this procedure has limitations (6). Anyone using this technique must bear in mind the danger of mistaking an "easier" (shorter, less complex, more common) word or expression for an easier meaning. Seegers put it this way:

> A word is difficult or easy to a child not in proportion to the incidence of its general use, but according to the amount and type of association the child has had with the concept for which the word stands. Words are not difficult. Ideas are (7).

In other words, an explanation of the principle of "No taxation without representation" re-written in words of one syllable cannot be expected to replace the necessity of understanding the basic elements of the situation.

Social studies teachers, along with their colleagues who teach literature and with librarians and with well-intentioned but ill-informed writers in popular magazines, sometimes raise another objection. They say—and entirely correctly—that a teacher's re-written version of any classic—a letter or a speech by Lincoln, for instance—loses its original quality. (We could mention that our school editions of Shakespeare are not pure Shakespeare: certain earthy Elizabethan expressions are carefully expurgated.) We admit that this is so; we regret the loss; but we are willing to pay this price in order to enable perhaps another one-fourth of our pupils to get the basic ideas *through reading.* An important part of this fourth suggestion is that all the pupils should *hear* the original so as to appreciate something of its classical beauty.

To supplement the teacher's judgment on suitability of vocabulary, there are the usual lists of "new" words in the back of basal readers and the normative listings like Rinsland's (8). To help him devise interesting formats there are works like Dunfee's and Merritt's (9).

MATERIAL RE-WRITTEN BY OTHER PUPILS

The "other pupils" are those who can and do read the text and are able, in addition, to summarize in their own words their understanding of what they read. This writing, edited by the teacher only as absolutely necessary, often communicates very nicely to less able readers the gist of the text. The more child-like the re-writing remains, the better. Reading is facilitated when the reader's re-thinking of the author's thoughts is made easier.

EXPERIENCE CHARTS

Taking this last-mentioned thought to its logical conclusion leads to the writing of experience records or charts. This technique, widely used in the primary grades, has great applicability all the way up the line. It consists very simply of the pupils dictating to the teacher material that they have learned—from an excursion, a filmstrip, a television program, a resource visitor, etc.—and the teacher writing it down, usually on the blackboard. After editing, it is put into permanent form on chart paper and perhaps also on mimeograph. If the products of these last three suggestions—re-writing by teacher and by pupils, and experience record—are collected, along with illustrations and comprehension checks, notebook style, each pupil will have a book of his own that he can read and understand.

The time element in this suggestion is a matter of much concern, for the content, unlike that of any of the other proposals, must be obtained in school from the pupils. One possibility is that of using members of the "Future Teachers of America" club in the local high school to take the original dictation.

When teachers make a point of re-writing just one passage a month, of guiding the better readers to summarize in writing some material each month, they are much gratified with the results in quantity of material and improvement of achievement.

STUDY GUIDES

. . . This technique consists of series of questions matching the text paragraphs, with answers provided on the right-hand side of the paper so that they may be folded back out of sight until checking time. With each slower reader, or perhaps with two, is an achieving reader to help as a pupil-teacher. Variations on the number, kind, length, and specificity of the questions are possible, as are also the methods of using them.

PUPIL SPECIALTIES

"Specialties" is another term for special assignments. The idea is to guide students into special assignments and to encourage them to become "experts" on these specific topics so that they will be resource persons in the classroom (10). These specialties may be short-term (for example, an election, a trip by the President, a biography). Or they may be continuing projects (keeping a scrapbook of Queen Elizabeth, collecting stamps on a specific person, place, or event, being a radio "ham"). This technique influences reading in terms of motivation. Children sometimes read remarkably better, and more, when they are enthusiastic about the reason for it. A child's specialty can vest him with new importance. It can assure him an audience. He will know more about his topic than anyone else in his class. His peers will acknowledge his report as a genuine contribution.

The last word in educational method has not yet been written. Teachers worth their salt are always looking for new and better ways to teach. Usually the new and better has its base in something old and good. Any of the foregoing eight suggestions will be an improvement only as its classroom use is based on the fundamentally sound procedure for directing reading activities in all curricular areas with pupils at all levels of achievement.

References

(1) Ralph C. Preston. *Teaching Social Studies in the Elementary Schools.* Revised Edition. New York: Rinehart and Company, 1958. p. 251, 252.

(2) Alvina Treut Burrows. "Reading, Research, and Reporting in the Social Studies." *Social Studies in the Elementary School. op. cit.,* p. 196, 197. Also Ralph C. Preston, *op. cit.,* p. 263.

(3) University of Chicago Press, 5750 Ellis Avenue, Chicago 37, Illinois.

(4) For example: *American Heroes Series,* by Beals and Ballard. Harr Wagner Publishing Company, 609 Mission St., San Francisco, California. Five 40-page booklets, each describing in narrative form the lives and deeds of four heroes in American history: "Discoverers of America," "Real Adventure With the Pilgrim Settlers," "American Patriots," "American Pathfinders," and "American Plainsmen." Reading level, 5. 64 cents.

Chronicles of Americans. Americana Press, 2038 Pennsylvania Ave., Madison 10, Wisconsin. Twelve colorful booklets: "The American Realm," "The Supreme Court," "Early Rails," "The Civil War at a Glance," "What 'Corporation' Means," "The American School," "The Great Westward Trek," "Great Presidents," "Ouisconsin," "Documents of Freedom," "America's Success Story," and "Early American Recipes." Reading level, 7+. 18 cents.

Fathers of Industry Series. Mercer Publishing Company, 16 East 52nd St., New York 22. Twenty-three booklets, each treating an inventor or captain of industry. Reading level, 7+. 20 cents.

Little Wonder Books. Charles E. Merrill, Inc., 1300 Alum Creek Drive, Columbus 16, Ohio. Sixty booklets. Reading levels, 1 through 6. 21 cents.

(5) Among the best known and most widely accepted of the classroom periodicals are the offerings of: American Education Publications, 1250 Fairwood Ave., Columbus 16, Ohio (issues at all levels, K–12); Civic Education Service, Inc., 1733 K. Street, N.W., Washington 6, D.C. (intermediate grades and upward); *Scholastic* Magazines, 33 West 42nd St., New York 36 (intermediate grades and upward).

(6) Ernest Horn. "Language and Meaning" in The National Society for the Study of Education. *The Psychology of Learning.* Forty-first Yearbook, Part II. Chicago, Ill.: University of Chicago Press, 1942. p. 399.

(7) J. Conrad Seegers. "Recent Research in Vocabulary." *Elementary English* 23:67; February 1946.

(8) Henry D. Rinsland. *A Basic Vocabulary of Elementary School Children.* New York: The Macmillan Company, 1945.

(9) Maxine M. Dunfee. "An Evaluation of Social Studies Source Materials by Fifth and Sixth Grade Children." Doctoral Dissertation, Indiana University, Bloomington, 1949. See also by the same author, "The Stamp of Reality." *NEA Journal* 41:227; April 1952.

James W. Merritt. "A Study of Sixth Graders' Comprehension of Specially Prepared Materials on Broad Social Conflicts." Doctoral Dissertation, Harvard University, Cambridge, Massachusetts, 1951. See also, "Children Can Understand Social Conflicts." *Educational Leadership* 10:298; February 1953.

(10) Donald D. Durrell and Leonard J. Savignano. "Classroom Enrichment Through Pupil Specialties." *Journal of Education* 137:1; February 1956.

❧ ELEMENTARY SCHOOL PROGRAMS FOR THE SOCIAL EDUCATION OF THE ACADEMICALLY TALENTED
Merle R. Bolton and *Henry J. Otto*

As Bolton and Otto point out, there are relatively few school practices or plans, and fewer professional reports, involving social studies for rapid learners. Enough reports are at hand, however, to justify the synthesis presented here. These authors provide specific material that furnishes tangible examples of special social studies instruction for the gifted. Doubtless a number of school programs and some research have appeared since this analysis. But knowledge of social studies programs for the gifted has advanced little beyond that indicated here.

THE LITERATURE DEALING with the education of gifted children at the elementary level does not isolate social education from general provisions for these children. At present it is probably correct to say that there are no elementary school programs especially designed to foster the social education of rapid learners. Such attention as is given to social education finds expression within the more general arrangements.

As the present writers corresponded with individuals in school systems in different parts of the country it became increasingly evident that it was practically impossible to obtain materials which dealt primarily with the social education of rapid learners. Most of the available information dealt with general arrangements or special work in such areas as science, music, art, foreign language, and mathematics. Most of the material available did not even mention the area of social education. It was almost equally difficult to get examples of enrichment in the social studies. The broader concept of social education was missing almost entirely, yet the writers feel certain that those working with rapid learners do manifest much concern for the wholesome social development of these pupils.

The lack of materials dealing with the social education of rapid learners probably means that the complexity of the area has defied definitive attention during these early years of more concerted attention to gifted children. Also, social education is a more difficult area in which to work than science or foreign language. The paucity of present materials and programs suggests an urgent need for aggressive attention in the future, but it also leaves the present writers in a dilemma. The pros and cons of accelerated grade placement and part-time and full-time placement in special classes or schools have been debated at length in available sources. . . .

ENRICHMENT IN THE SOCIAL STUDIES

Teaching the social studies in ways that will hold taut the intellectual reins of rapid learners is much more than a method, although method is the vehicle whereby the adaptation is accomplished. As the teacher of a heterogeneous class strives to meet the intellectual demands of rapid learners, he must at the same time make appropriate provision

Used by permission of the authors and the National Council for the Social Studies; from *The Social Education of the Academically Talented*, Curriculum Series No. 10, 1958, pp. 25–32. Dr. Bolton is superintendent of schools in Hastings, Nebraska. Dr. Otto is a professor of elementary education at the University of Texas.

for the average and slower learners. Any effort at enrichment for rapid learners in regular classes automatically requires an across-the-board procedure for adapting instruction to individual differences. Classroom method carefully designed to meet the needs of all pupils is basic, therefore, to meeting the needs of rapid learners. But method alone is not enough. There must also be recognition on the part of the teacher that rapid learners have the right to progress as far as their capabilities will permit. . . .

In the materials reviewed, six different avenues for enrichment were evident. First, all of the bulletins, sample units, and memoranda recognized the fact that the academically talented require quantities of reading materials. The importance of a large reservoir of many kinds of material of varying degrees of difficulty was evident. All the bulletins recognized the need for reading materials more difficult than those usually recommended for elementary school use. Such items as high school textbooks, the *World Almanac*, a standard high school encyclopedia, fiction and nonfiction books written for the general reader, and current magazines like *Life* and *Current History* were mentioned. Frequently current magazines can be brought from home by the pupils. Daily papers can also be brought from home and should be among the resources used regularly by rapid learners.

A second avenue recognized by most workers in this field is the rapid learner's need for reading experiences which will broaden, sharpen, and deepen his insights. Among the specific suggestions were: (a) wide reading to get different points of view; (b) critical reading to find inaccuracies or to learn how and why different sources disagree on basic facts; (c) reading for the purpose of preparing an oral or written report on a special topic, such as the history of map making, the advantages and disadvantages of different kinds of map projection, why map making developed into a highly skilled profession, and methods for making accurate maps.

A third avenue consists of first-hand experiences, which are very important for all learners but especially for rapid learners, since their ability to verbalize tends to outrun their experience. Field trips are an important means of enlarging children's experience. A good film or filmstrip or sometimes a well-chosen broadcast or recording serves the same purpose. A speaker who talks about a subject he knows at firsthand is another teaching resource by which pupils obtain meaningful vicarious experience.

The fourth avenue of enrichment commonly used in the social studies consists of giving rapid learners many leadership roles. Teachers like to have committees led by capable and responsible pupils. Frequently small committees work by themselves in another part of the school or carry out neighborhood missions, as in collecting information on local history. Other leadership roles are present in dramatizations, the preparation of murals and exhibits, demonstrations, and other classroom activities.

The fifth enrichment avenue draws on the creative talents of rapid learners. The materials sent us contained such examples as preparing and giving a mock-radio quiz program, making a neighborhood map, making a globe out of papier-mâché, planning a playhouse or a classroom center, developing creative dances or rhythms, writing original plays or stories, and writing editorials for the school paper or even the local newspaper.

The sixth avenue for enrichment in the social studies provides rapid learners with opportunities for self-evaluation. Since the rapid learner generally displays a keen interest in his proficiencies and limitations and may have a tendency to view himself too critically, opportunity for self-evaluation will provide him with much satisfaction. A suggestion for accomplishing this is given below (1).

SELF-EVALUATION OF SOCIAL SKILLS AND ATTITUDES

	SEL-DOM	SOME-TIMES	ALMOST ALWAYS
1. Participated actively in all group planning.			
2. Listened politely.			
3. Cooperated with:			
a. My chairman			
b. Other members of my group and the class			
c. The teacher.			
4. When chairman, assumed my responsibilities of leadership.			
5. Worked to help members of my group attain group goals planned.			
6. Worked to help class attain goals planned for entire unit.			
7. Worked independently to achieve goal I set for myself.			
8. Used my time wisely.			
9. Completed all assignments at designated time.			
10. Followed group instructions.			
11. Attempted to rely on myself as much as possible; asked for help only when it was necessary.			
12. Was dependable and reliable when I accepted responsibility.			
13. Showed consideration for members of my class, my teacher, and visitors.			
14. Was treated kindly by my classmates and received help from them when it was needed.			
15. Was willing to alter my desires to help solve the problems of others.			

EXAMPLE OF ENRICHMENT POSSIBILITIES IN A SECOND GRADE UNIT

The illustration below shows how the needs of the gifted may be met by an extension of the regular classroom activities in social studies. To the left of the chart are the objectives and activities for the entire class. To the right are the additional objectives and enrichment activities for the gifted.

The fireman—a community helper: In most second grades the social studies work centers about "Our Community," and includes a study of community helpers. The activities developed below are concerned with but one part of this work. The descriptions are devoted to "The Fireman—A Community Helper" as they might be used to enhance the experiences of a gifted child above and beyond the activities in which he would participate as a member of a regular second grade group (2).

Objectives for All Children	Additional Objectives for the Gifted Child
To learn about the fire department and how it operates.	To learn to make simple oral and written reports of reading, experiments, and observations.
To understand the fireman's job as a protector of our homes and our lives.	To learn to read about and prepare simple experiments for presentation to a group.
To develop the ability to use the telephone correctly and to give accurate information	To learn to use a card file.
To develop an understanding of the interrelationships between community helpers.	To learn to make inquiries and arrangements by telephone.
To develop an understanding of the responsibility of each individual in the welfare of his community.	To learn some simplified methods of organizing materials and information.
To learn what to do in case of fire.	To encourage the child to make independent excursions to gather more information.
To learn and be able to write his full name, address, and telephone number in case he needs to give this information in an emergency.	To learn some of the sources through which information can be obtained.
To develop an understanding of the democratic principle of majority rule.	
To learn to write letters using the proper form.	

To develop the ability to follow written directions.

To put his knowledge to use in creative activities related to class projects.

To develop the ability to spell.

To further develop the ability to plan group activities.

LEARNING ACTIVITIES FOR ALL CHILDREN	ADDITIONAL ACTIVITIES FOR THE GIFTED CHILD

Write a letter to each parent asking permission to take a trip to the firehouse.

Collect pictures of firemen and plan bulletin board displays.

Plan field trip. Discuss and list the safety factors involved and things to see.

Prepare a list of questions for interview with the fireman when he visits the room.

Send a thank-you letter to the fire station and to the fireman who visited.

Make a mural to illustrate what happens from the time a fire alarm is turned in to the time the firemen return to the fire station.

Locate on a neighborhood map the exact locations of firehouses and fireboxes in the district.

Dramatic play:
1. Safety measures in fire protection.
2. Assisting a fireman in case of fire.
3. Dramatize the fireman's duties.
4. Reporting a fire.

Make a "fire-engine" from covered orange crates which can be used in dramatic play.

Learn how to report a fire by telephone and the proper number to call.

Write a letter to the central fire station asking permission for the group to visit.

Assume the responsibility of calling several mothers to assist on the field trip to the fire station.

Write a letter and arrange for a fireman to visit the room.

Make a "ticker" to show what happens when a fire alarm is recorded from a firebox.

Read more difficult material and report the findings to the group.

Assume the responsibility of collecting information concerning fire stations outside of the school district and record this information on the corners of the neighborhood map according to the direction in which they are located—north of the school, south, east, or west.

To illustrate how we can help to prevent fires, the gifted child can locate in the Science File a demonstration of the different types of matches, their properties and uses and present this material to the class.

The value of fire-extinguishers can be illustrated by using some experiments found in the Science File concerning fire and air. This demonstration can be developed further by showing what to do if one's clothing catches afire and emphasiz-

Compile a vocabulary list which can be used when writing stories, poems and riddles.

Make booklets of group and individual stories, poems and pictures.

See films, filmstrips, and slides of the fireman and his work.

Make a miniature toy community and as the work proceeds add appropriate materials as each new "helper" is studied.

Plan and make a simple "box movie."

Practice writing full names, addresses, and telephone numbers to be put into a class directory.

Elect a room fire chief and assistant to see that fire drills are carried out effectively.

ing the fact that one should never run when on fire.

Make a pop-up book of the visit to the fire station and send it with a letter of thanks prepared by the group.

Aid the teacher by planning a demonstration of the use of the telephone in reporting fires.

Make a list of the things a fireman does which would prove that he must be a strong and healthy person.

Prepare a dramatization to show what the policeman does to help the fireman, including directing traffic, putting up blockades, and keeping people out of the way of the fireman.

Make a diorama depicting the fireman at work.

Take riddles written by the group and organize them for a mock-radio quiz program to be presented as a culminating activity.

Present to a lower grade or another second grade some of the experiments related to fire which he has performed successfully.

Compile children's names, and other information, in a class directory. Children may wish to include photographs.

Act as chairman of the balloting committee in election of fire chief and be responsible for giving an accurate accounting of the results. In announcing the results, he could present winners with a fire chief's hat and badges.

Evaluate his work.

References

(1) Reprinted by special permission from Henry J. Otto, ed., *Curriculum Enrichment for Gifted Elementary Children in Regular Classes.* University of Texas Press, 1955.

(2) *Ibid.*

✒ HANDLING INTAKE AND OUTPUT OF IDEAS

W. Linwood Chase

Desirable social studies instruction goes beyond the facts to deal with related and significant ideas. But communication of ideas, perhaps even more than of facts, requires words. Thus verbal skill becomes even more essential to learning. The author of this selection presents a lucid analysis of the problem and some suggested lines of solution.

GOOD COMPREHENSION and recall are not automatically achieved through vocabulary instruction alone. Even though the child knows every word in the selection, he may still have difficulty in the intake and output of ideas. Commonly found handicaps are the following: (*a*) the child may have attention difficulties in reading, (*b*) he may not see the relationships between ideas, and (*c*) he may lack the ability to express ideas, even though he has good comprehension. All three handicaps may be overcome through the use of study guides.

Every adult reader knows the attention difficulties which appear in his own reading. He may find his eyes perceiving words at the bottom of the page and discover that his mind has left off several paragraphs back. Children have the same difficulty, especially in reading abstract or remote material; their minds may "leave off" at the beginning of the first sentence. They may continue looking at words throughout the lesson without discovering that they are not attending to ideas.

The second difficulty—seeing the relationships between ideas—is essential to understanding and recall. This involves the observation of structure of the presentation, particularly of paragraph patterns. This enables the child to see the facts as part of a whole, not as a series of unrelated items. It is difficult to remember unrelated fragments; it is much easier to recall closely related ideas which are part of a pattern. Outlining is a device for calling attention to structure, but it is often cumbersome and is generally disliked by children. Paragraph patterns may be taught by effective methods which are more acceptable to children: selecting the best title from three, with

Used by permission of the National Society for the Study of Education, from its Fifty-Sixth Yearbook, Part Two, *Social Studies in the Elementary School*, 1957, pp. 177–182.

the rejected titles being too broad or too narrow to fit the material; providing general questions which the paragraph answers, with study teams of two or three pupils listing the facts which answer the general question. Usually a two-step outline is sufficient for comprehension and recall; the more complex outline may be presented, but it is usually more helpful in composition planning than in reading.

Difficulties in recall may still remain when attention and comprehension are assured. Even when the ideas are in the child's mind, they still may not be readily available in all types of recall. He may be able to identify correct responses in a multiple-choice situation but quite unable to answer short-answer questions and still less able to give an oral or written summary. Abilities in recall may be easily studied by asking the child to write or tell what he can remember of a day's lesson, then providing him with a set of multiple-choice or short-answer questions. He will often know many answers in the latter types of recall but his unaided recall may be inaccurate, disordered, and fragmentary. The task of organization, subordination, and selection of ideas is eliminated by the multiple-choice or short-answer questions. Correlations between written or oral recall with multiple-choice recall seldom rise above .40; this is consistent with the often noted discrepancy between standardized test scores and classroom performance. Is the ability to identify answers adequate for independent use of social-studies material in discussion and thinking? Probably not. Clear expression and development of ideas are required in both speaking and writing.

The use of study guides with teams of two or three pupils may prove to be effective in overcoming all three difficulties of comprehension and recall: inattention, organization of ideas, and fluency in expression. Two levels of study guides are usually adequate. The first consists of a series of short-answer questions for each paragraph of the lesson, with answers provided at the right-hand side of the guide so that they may be folded back when they are not to be seen immediately by the child. The second study guide is made up of general questions for each paragraph, followed by a listing of the facts which are related to the question. These two study guides may be used by pupil teams to provide for several levels of need in comprehension and recall.

Pupils very low in attention and reading ability may use the study guide which provides detailed questions. It may be used in various ways, depending upon the level of need of the pupils. It provides the greatest aid when it is used with teams of two or three poor readers, by a pupil-teacher who is a good reader. Each question is asked orally; the pupils find the answers and give them orally, with each checking the other for correctness. Since the questions may contain many of the difficult words of the paragraph, the vocabulary burden is greatly eased for the readers. Pupils somewhat more advanced in reading may work in pairs, first reading the paragraph, then uncovering the questions to see if they know the answers, and finally checking them with the answer sheet. Pupils still more competent may read several paragraphs before uncovering the questions, may write answers upon which they agree, then check the answers. Since the detailed-question study guide carries the burden of organization, its usefulness is primarily for maintaining attention and assuring comprehension. It requires every pupil to "recite" every essential fact of the lesson and provides much more practice than the one-at-a-time recitation following class reading of a lesson.

Well-organized oral recall may be attained through the use of the study guide which contains general questions with listed answers. This, too, is used with pupil teams and may be presented in varying levels of difficulty. It aids the pupils most when the team first uncovers the general question for a paragraph, then reads silently, makes a list of the answers co-operatively, then checks the answers with the list of ideas in the study guide. It requires more effort when the pupils read one or more paragraphs, then attempt to list the essential ideas before uncovering either the general questions or the answers. Complete unaided recall may be required by superior readers who read the entire selection, then attempt to recall the content orally while another pupil checks against the study guide. Faults in sequence, omissions, and inaccuracies are then evident.

Study guides used with pupil teams take advantage of many of the preferences of pupils, yet provide constantly developing disciplines. They allow pupils to work together, which is preferred to working alone. Teachers who use pupil teams find that the only "disciplining" necessary is the suggestion that "tomorrow you will work by yourself." The study guides assure success and security; the child checks the accuracy of his knowledge immediately. They utilize oral work more than writing, and oral work is preferred by pupils. However, research in paired practice in oral recall demonstrates that written recall is also improved by the practice. Most important, every child responds to every question, and the groundwork is laid for the discussion which follows the retention of facts. When used in proper sequence, study guides provide constant growth in the intake and output of ideas.

The language skills of the social studies are obviously not fully served by the time the child can read and recall the facts presented in the textbook. Skill in the use of knowledge is more important than its mere possession. Meaning and significance must be lent to the facts through activities which require elaborative thinking. Relationships must be established between the newly acquired facts and other knowledge possessed by the child. This requires specific planning on the part of the teacher. It is not assured by high intelligence as demonstrated by low correlations between intelligence and tests of higher mental processes.

Elaborative thinking is especially suitable for co-operative work in teams of five. Group discussion appears to stimulate elaborative thinking, and five pupils working together will usually provide a much richer list of associations than five pupils working separately. Larger groups diminish individual responsibility; smaller ones fail to yield the rich harvest of ideas.

Some of the suggestions for stimulating elaborative thinking are the following: finding ways to illustrate or dramatize the facts of the story; planning an exhibit or an assembly program; planning an interview with people who have more information about the subject; preparing a letter of inquiry; comparing the information with similar or different situations; listing questions not answered by the selection; drawing lists of generalizations from the selection; listing special topics for further inquiry; finding personal relationships with the materials; planning a field trip.

Critical thinking is a complex of abilities; it is usually concerned with evaluation of material against various types of standards or for particular purposes. While it is usually identified with more advanced abilities in the social studies, especially in controversial areas, some experience in critical thinking may be given in the elementary school. Practice in critical thinking may be provided by activities such as the following: selecting material which is pertinent to a topic as contrasted with material not pertinent; evaluating material for its suitability for a particular audience or occasion; making suggestions for improving a plan or presentation; distinguishing fact from opinion; finding differences in points of view; noting overstatements and unfounded claims; evaluating the dependability of a statement. . . .

The development of language and thinking abilities may best be undertaken through small-group instruction. However, the size of the group depends upon the objective sought. The acquiring of skills in intake and output of ideas is essentially an individual matter; but individual work is usually limited to silent reading and writing. In these activities, the child often finds learning lonesome and insecure. Oral work requires a listener, but if only one child may speak while all others listen, the amount of individual language practice is very limited. Working in pairs, threes, or fives makes learning more secure, more sociable, and provides far more individual practice. However, pupil-team study and independent small-group work require specific planning by the teacher; ill-defined, unimportant, or unsuitable tasks invite trouble. When the teacher is unable to find time to prepare study guides or to set suitable tasks, he may provide extra language practice through three-pupil recitation teams. Children are divided into groups of three, with the middle child being secretary for the group. Questions are presented by the teacher; each secretary writes the answers agreed upon by the groups. If social studies are to be "social" they must include practice in co-operative effort; the social-development objectives are hard to attain in unsocial, competitive classrooms.

Many of the tasks in the intake of ideas may be done with the entire group sharing the experience. When oral, visual, or multi-sensory presentations are used, how much an individual pupil learns is not dependent upon the size of the audience. Types of activities which may be used effectively in whole-class activities are those which involve demonstrations, field trips, exhibits, displays, motion pictures, listening to poetry, plays and dramatizations, choral reading, appreciation lessons, recordings, radio or television programs, group reports on units, class planning, and listening to explanations and directions. The sharing of common experiences in a noncompetitive situation adds important values to the social integration of the class.

❧ VARIETIES OF UNIT PLANS AND INSTRUCTION
Wilhelmina Hill

For about a generation, various forms of unit organization have played a strong role in social studies instruction. It is, therefore, time to review the nature and value of unit teaching in the social studies. This report was taken from a recent survey by a national leader in elementary school social studies. It provides an inclusive summary of the nature of instructional units, of varying types of units, and of the flexibility that has characterized unit organization from its inception. Such a report helps to

From *Unit Planning and Teaching in Elementary Social Studies,* United States Office of Education, Bulletin No. 23, 1963, pp. 4–14. Dr. Hill is specialist in social science in the U.S. Office of Education.

overcome the limited view evidenced by those who designate their way as the way of planning or teaching a unit.

MANY KINDS AND varieties of unit plans and unit teaching can be found in American elementary schools. These variations are due to differences in the children, teachers, educational philosophy, curriculum, community, cultural environment, and part of the country in which the schools involved are located. Some of the major types of units will be identified and described . . . in ways that may assist teachers and others in planning and teaching units of quality in our elementary schools.

TYPES OF UNIT PLANS

Resource units are planned for use with any group of children of appropriate age and grade levels. They usually contain a wealth of material, ideas, and suggestions from which a teacher may select when working with a given group of pupils. Some units may be prepared by a teacher or a committee. They may become part of a course of study, or be published or used separately as a piece of curriculum material. They may be used by one teacher or by many teachers. Resource units are usually prepared before a unit is taught.

Teaching units are planned for use with a specific group of children in mind. The objectives, content, activities, and materials included are intended to meet the special concerns, interests, and abilities of these pupils. Sufficient flexibilty is provided to permit opportunities for pupil participation in the planning, development, and the evaluation of a unit experience. A teaching unit is usually prepared by one teacher prior to introducing the unit with a class. He must be willing to make changes in this unit plan as the unit progresses, as new and challenging aspects emerge during the course of the unit.

Daily unit plans are prepared by most teachers during the various phases of unit development. They must be flexible, allowing for pupil-teacher planning and encouraging creativity. But they should indicate the kind of learning experience, objectives, content, activities, materials, to be carried on for a given day. Weekly unit plans are also valuable in attaining continuity and direction in the development of a unit.

Descriptive units are often written by teachers to share the unit experiences of one teacher and class with other teachers and supervisors. Photographs of pupil activities may be taken during various phases of the unit. Descriptive units can be written only when the children and teacher have completed the unit experience. Many times these descriptive units are published or mimeographed so that other educators may learn about the outcomes and possibilities of the unit.

KINDS OF SUBJECT MATTER TREATMENT

In American elementary schools, where the unit method is widely used, there is a strong trend toward integration of subject matter, in varying degrees. Most units cut across social studies, science, language arts, fine arts, and other areas. But the main difference lies in how the unit is centered. Its main objectives and emphases are usually in some one subject field. Then other subjects are included as appropriate. For example, in any social studies or science centered unit, there is a good deal of language arts (reading, discussion, written expression) and often of fine arts (music, art, drama, dance). Brief accounts of how subject matter is included in some of the major types of curriculum units follow:

Integrated units. In some schools an integrated type of unit teaching is favored. Appropriate learnings from several subject fields, such as social studies, science, language arts, health, and fine arts are included. Sometimes the units are social studies based, as with units on community life, the Westward movement, or Brazil. They are often science centered as with units on astronomy or wildlife. Again they may focus on both social studies and science which is true with units on conservation, aviation, or communication. Occasionally integrated units may have a language arts or fine arts center of interest, as happens in units about children's writers or music and musicians.

Usually where integrated units occupy a central position in the curriculum and in the daily learning experiences of the children, special time is allocated for the unit in the daily schedule. Often two hours or so are indicated for the *unit,* and on the daily schedule the subjects involved are identified specifically. Often part of the unit block of time is divided into two sections, one in the morning and one in the afternoon. The unit might appear on the daily schedule as: *Unit (social studies, science, language arts, fine arts).* Then at other times during the day, time may be scheduled for developmental work in such subjects as mathematics, music, spelling, and reading, as needed. In other words, not everything in a school day must relate to the integrated unit. Some of the work-type reading will be done in the unit experience. Other reading skills and appreciations must be provided for at another time. The same may be said for other subjects of the elementary curriculum.

Social studies units. The majority of elementary social studies courses and guides contain units or recommend unit planning and teaching. Possibly the most widely taught units in elementary schools are those which are social studies centered. This is because so much of the elementary curriculum revolves around social education in its various aspects. While social studies units deal with some area of social studies such as "Homes Here and Around the World," (1), or "Living in South America in an Air Age," (2), still they draw content, skills, and activities from other curriculum fields, including language arts, science, music, and art. These units are usually broad in scope; sometimes they involve study in depth. From 4 to 6 weeks is usually required for their development and a depth study may take longer.

Social studies units are usually characterized by problem solving and research reading and study. Emphasis is placed upon the development of concepts, map and study skills, and socializing experiences through which the child may develop cooperation, acceptance of responsibility, and consideration of the rights of others as a way of life. Preparation for citizenship, as a child and in future years, and an understanding of his world—local, state, national, international—are significant purposes and outcomes of social studies unit experiences for children in elementary schools. . . .

HOW UNITS ARE DEVELOPED

Units may be experience, activity, or subject-matter centered depending upon the needs of the children and their community, and upon the philosophy of learning held by the teachers and supervisors. There are many variations and shades of difference between an experience unit and a subject matter unit. Some of these will be indicated in this section.

Experience units. When a unit of study is developed around some broad area of living of the children, about which they are aware, interested, and concerned, it may be described as an *experience unit*. It grows out of the children's many experiences and is developed through direct as well as vicarious experiences. The unit usually involves problem solving, the problems being actual concerns of the children themselves who not only study about the problems but take steps toward their solution. They work toward goals that are real and meaningful to them. Such units may be about problems related to their clothing, communication, safety, or conservation of natural resources in their own vicinity or region.

Activity units. Some units involve a variety of learning activities during the course of their development, yet the topic for study may be further removed from the felt concerns of the children than is true of an experience unit. For convenience, such units may be called activity units. They may be about such topics as Brazil, Japan, the Congo, or pioneer life. The children will learn about the subject through wide reading, map and globe study, interviewing people, trips to museums, viewing films, correspondence, construction work, using art and music media, or other learning activities appropriate to each unit.

Subject matter units.   Some unit plans and teaching concentrate on the acquisition of subject matter to a greater degree than others. Most of the learning activities tend to be verbal, with reading, discussion, writing, and testing comprising the main means of learning. There is seldom time or provision for direct learning experiences, such as planting trees and shrubs, meeting someone from another country, or solving a safety problem. Often the subject matter unit is textbook centered, though this is not necessarily so. Many units of the subject matter type follow the organization of a single textbook which has been adopted for a school or school system. There is great variation in such units concerning the degree of wide reading and use of audiovisual aids included in the plans and the teaching and learning.

Unit studies in depth.   One of the promising new developments in unit planning and teaching is the occasional development of a unit study in depth. Rather than skimming over the surface of a large area, such as a continent, throughout a series of units undertaken or planned for a year, time is taken occasionally to study a country or a topic more thoroughly and deeply than when wider coverage is attempted. While depth studies cannot be made of every country or every topic in such fields as social studies and science, still pupils can attain considerable insight about certain unit topics chosen because of their significance. Such study will enrich and give a degree of depth to their learning and understanding not attainable by other means. One example of what is meant was observed in Wilmette, Illinois, where pupils of a class were studying about Africa and its many nations. First they studied the continent as a whole and its various regions. Then the pupils chose four different countries for study in depth and divided into four groups for this concentrated study. Later the four groups shared their learning with each other. It would have been impossible to have studied each of the more than forty nations of Africa in depth. Through careful selection, such study was made possible for four of the African nations which pupils and teacher found most significant. Though the overall unit was about Africa, four parts of it were developed in depth.

Sometimes a class, school, or school system will undertake a depth study of a single country or topic which has special value to its children. On one occasion, 28 San Francisco schools chose to make a depth study of Pakistan which was related to sending a child ambassador to that country. The study was organized as units and resulted in greatly enriched learning on the part of the children.

Contemporary event units. At times, classes may develop an on-the-spot unit because of some significant happening in the world which holds special interest for them. Such units are usually selected and planned through pupils and teacher working together and they deal with problems and questions related to some outstanding contemporary happening such as:

> Presidential election
> Glenn's orbiting of the earth
> Coronation of a queen or king
> International conference

References

(1) *Teaching Guide, Social Studies, Grades I, II, and III*. Providence (R.I.) Public Schools. Providence: The Public Schools, 1957. pp. 36–45.

(2) *Living in South America in an Air Age*. California School Supervisors' Association. San Francisco: The Association (193 Sutter Street), 1958. 95 pp.

⇜§ Looking Critically at Unit Teaching
Gilbert M. Wilson

Widespread acceptance of unit instruction in elementary schooling, particularly in the social studies, has resulted in abuses as well as effective use. Ideals advocated by proponents of the unit approach have not always worked out well in practice. It is helpful, therefore, for teachers to recognize the dangers and difficulties, as well as values, of unit teaching. By suggesting answers to a few pertinent questions, the author of this selection provides aids to better unit teaching. How can realistically appropriate objectives for units be developed? What is the nature of desirable learning activity in units? How can pupils' learning in unit study be soundly and practically evaluated?

UNIT TEACHING MEANS many things to many people and because of this there is great confusion regarding it. Nearly everyone reacts positively to unit teaching, but there is little agreement on what is meant by the term which we hear so often. Perhaps a critical look is in order.

Historically, the idea may be traced from the writings of Herbert and his followers through Charles McMurry, Dewey, Kilpatrick, Morrison, and others. Each had slightly different views, but was concerned with some modifications of the behavior of the learner. Each dealt with unifying learning in such a way that the separate parts became a part of the whole. Each assumed that isolated learnings were not desirable or effective in the total learning process and, in a sense, rejected the prevailing idea of storing up knowledge.

A unit is an organized body of information and experiences designed to effect significant learnings. The teacher must know what *understandings, skills,* and *attitudes* she is trying to develop and then choose appropriate content, design activities of worth, decide on valid evaluation procedures, and select adequate learning materials.

If the teacher cannot state the *understanding* clearly in complete declarative sentences, it is unlikely that she can teach it. For example, we might take a poor statement, "To understand farming in the North Central States," as opposed to a well stated understanding, "The farmers of the North Central States produce more food and food products than they can use. Therefore, they help supply the rest of the United States with these products." The second statement points directly to appropriate content and accompanying activities which will help develop the understanding. The first statement is vague.

The fact load of most social studies textbooks will convince the teacher of the futility of having students learn all the facts. Only those which are necessary in developing the desired understanding should be chosen.

Skills should be stated as specifically as possible while realizing that mastery does not come as the result of any one activity. A statement, "To develop map and globe skills," is almost useless. On the other hand we can see activities more clearly in this statement, "To develop facility in using the graphic scale in measuring distance on maps and globes."

Developing *attitudes* and *appreciations* is a more complex matter than can be fully treated here. Suffice it to say that if we list an attitude such as "Developing open-mindedness," the idea should be evident in the atmosphere of the classroom. This kind of objective does not lend itself to exact measurement, but can be appraised by means of behavioral charts. Thus, we would describe open-mindedness in a series of statements and check the youngster's behavior accordingly:

1. Accepts suggestions of others
2. Uses information rather than emotion
3. Reaches conclusions on the basis of facts
4. Recognizes the worth of others

Activities should be designed with objectives and evaluation procedures in mind. Teachers often confuse the terms *activity* and *unit teaching*, and in fact use them interchangeably. A common misconception is that any activity is good. An activity is good only to the extent that it helps us reach a stated goal. Activities embrace any experiences that children engage in, from textbook reading to building a model of Whitney's cotton gin, from comparing different maps of the same region to learning a native dance. Activities should be chosen by such criteria as social significance, skill development, contribution to desirable human relationships—to mention only a few.

Since unit teaching implies provisions for individual differences, it follows that the worth of uniform assignments, such as a field trip, viewing slides, or seeing a film, should be carefully scrutinized. To take care of differences in intelligence, reading ability, and experience background, a variety of activities and assignments are needed.

Evaluation is of critical importance and many teachers have difficulty coping with it adequately. It should be considered in terms of the objectives, but too often it is concerned only with recall and recognition of factual content. In addition to behavioral charts, teachers find that observation, anecdotal records, conferences, and essays on problem situations are quite useful in determining depth of understanding.

The experience of a fifth-grade teacher and her class may serve to illustrate one way of evaluating the degree to which an understanding has been developed. The class was studying New England. One understanding the teacher wished to develop was, "Southern New England is more urbanized and more highly industrialized than Northern New England." The students, working individually and in small groups, gathered information on the two regions: population figures and density, types of employment, miles of telephone cable, industrial income, railroad and truck tonnage, industrial production, farm production, and miles of highways, including superhighways. Then, the students compiled tables and drew maps to illustrate statistics. These were used in a discussion of comparisons and contrasts. The children were then asked to write on the question, "What is a major difference between Northern and Southern New England." Analysis of their answers indicated that a majority had gained the desired understanding.

Unit teaching is more complex than many people realize and there are many misconceptions prevalent. If success in unit teaching is to be achieved there must be careful planning and execution. Its effectiveness is probably no greater than the understanding the teacher has of the procedure.

✍️ TEACHING SOCIAL STUDIES UNITS

Wilhelmina Hill

This summary of major steps in the selection and teaching of units constitutes a useful overview or review for the teacher. It also furnishes a reminder that each major facet of instruction is involved in the teaching of units. The article provides cues to answering such questions as: What are the chief factors involved in deciding which units to teach? What is the general nature of teacher preparation for conducting a unit of study? How are units usually initiated? What kinds of learning activity predominate in unit study? What is the role of instructional materials and resources in unit study? Throughout this selection the author blends reported and recommended practices in the teaching of social studies units.

SELECTION OF UNITS

Most social studies curricula indicate the broad scope or area which should be studied at each grade level. Usually a number of units are suggested or recommended for each. Sometimes certain units are required. On the whole there is some flexibility so that teachers working closely with a group of children during a given year may select one or more units of special concern to them. And in many school sys-

Used by permission of the author and the National Council for the Social Studies; from its *Selected Resources Units in Elementary Social Studies: Kindergarten–Grade Six*, Curriculum Series No. 11, 1961, pp. 1–4.

tems, some or all of the units are selected through pupils and teachers working together.

While there is considerable variation in the scope indicated for each grade in different parts of the country, still there are some similarities among social studies curricula. Some of the most commonly suggested content areas for the various grades are: ⁵

KINDERGARTEN.	Becoming Acquainted with the Environment
GRADE 1.	Living in the Home, School, and Other Places
GRADE 2.	Living in the Neighborhood and Community
GRADE 3.	Expanding Community Life
GRADE 4.	Life in Other Communities
	and/or
	Life in Our State
GRADE 5.	Living in the United States
	or
	Living in the Americas
GRADE 6.	Our American Neighbors
	or
	Life on Other Continents

Such a sequence as indicated above is usually a guide to be considered in selecting units at a given grade level. On the other hand, pupils and teachers may select a unit outside of the usual framework, in accord with special problems, interests, events, or the increased expansion of the child's world in these times. Examples are where children of primary levels choose a unit about aviation, conservation, travel, or some aspect of life in other parts of the world because television, aerospace developments, and population mobility have helped to create an interest and prepare them for such study. Of course it is important to develop these units in appropriate ways for young children.

In many social studies curriculum guides and courses of study, units are included for children of the kindergarten level. These are most informal, but provide a unifying framework for some of their early experiences. Such informal unit experiences in the kindergarten program can reduce some tendencies to move along from one thing to another on a daily basis with little direction. It cannot be emphasized too much that social studies units in the kindergarten should be simple and informal. Probably the term "unit" is not used with the children. They are simply getting acquainted with their school, or studying about home and family living through their play-house activities.

In other social studies guides, there is considerable provision for experiences in social living when children are in the kindergarten.

These provisions are often similar to unit plans or activities but are not labeled "units." Again the social living guide for kindergarten may suggest a good many seasonal and holiday items, without any provision for learning experiences of larger scope.

PREPARATION FOR TEACHING A UNIT

If a teacher knows far enough in advance that he will be teaching a given unit, there are many things that he can do in preparation. Collecting materials, reading, taking a trip, making a survey, taking a course, or participation in a workshop are some of the kinds of things he might do. . . . In general, it can be said that the more a teacher can learn about the unit area and the more experiences he can have in relation to it, the more understanding and enrichment he can bring to his pupils.

INITIATING THE UNIT

In preparing his classroom for the beginning of a social studies unit, the teacher may wish to set the stage. He may wish to arrange a bulletin board with pictures and maps. He may place art objects and other realia on shelves and tables. He will probably have a variety of reading materials available for the children.

With another unit, the teacher may use the "bare stage" technique and give the class the major responsibility of collecting materials and arranging the classroom for the unit.

Again he may use a combination of the two methods mentioned above and encourage the children to cooperate with him in collecting the materials and arranging the room for the new social studies unit. Probably this combined approach is most commonly used, with teachers and pupils working together.

Pupil-teacher planning. During the initial stages of a unit, it is most important that pupils and teachers plan together. The teacher often gets this planning under way by asking such questions as:

> What can we do as we study this unit?
> What do we want to find out?
> Where can we find information?
> How shall we organize for study?

As such matters as the above are discussed, the teacher or a pupil may make lists on the chalkboard. Another pupil may make a record on paper for future reference. . . .

Collecting and arranging materials. During the initial stages of a unit, pupils and teacher collect materials related to the unit from many different sources. They search for these materials at home, in libraries, and in other likely places in the community. Often they write letters for free and inexpensive materials.

As the materials are assembled in the classroom, a pupil librarian or a library committee arranges them on shelves or tables where they will be convenient for study. Sometimes a chart, bearing the children's names, is posted near the books and bibliography, where the children may keep track of their reading. . . .

Other approach activities. Most of the activities in which pupils and teachers engage in the initial stages of a unit are planning, organizing or orientation in character. The teacher is helping the pupils gain an overall view of the unit and its potentialities.

During this stage of learning, the use of audio-visual aids is especially effective. Pupils view pictures and posters, study maps, and see films or television programs to find out as much as they can about their unit area. They take trips and make direct observations; they interview people.

DEVELOPING THE UNIT

After the unit has gotten under way, pupils are likely to carry out a good many study activities. At first they will be busy gaining information, studying ways to solve problems, and developing understandings and appreciations. Reading, map study, experimenting, vocabulary building, and observation are among the most significant *informational activities* at this stage of the unit.

When children have begun to acquire adequate information and have gained sufficient concepts, they begin to engage increasingly in *expressional activities.* They discuss what they have learned. They write short accounts or creative pieces and make illustrations for class booklets or newspapers.

Soon they begin to develop some large project for their unit. This may result in a post office for their classroom or a conservation-nature trail for their school grounds. It might be a mural, a small weather station, or it could be an exhibit about a foreign country.

Evaluation activities should be carried out throughout the unit. At the end of an activity or study period, each group or committee should usually be led daily to evaluate its progress and its problems. Sometimes this must be done on an individual basis, by informal discussion, or by written means as appropriate. . . .

Many *culminating activities* are evaluational in nature. They usually consist of some large activity which causes the pupils to summarize what they have learned, round off their study, and share it with others. Often parents or other pupils and teachers are invited to the culmination of the unit. This might be a dramatic presentation of what has been learned; it might be an exhibit or a fair; it might be a program or an informal party such as a tea. Often it is a combination of some of the above, as the children present what they have learned in an interesting manner to parents or other children of their school.

Throughout the unit, it is important that the teacher lead the children to have a good balance in their activities. This means balance between oral and written, active and quiet, informational and expressional, and provision for appropriate fine arts activities in each social studies unit.

MATERIALS AND RESOURCES

Unit teaching is usually characterized by the use of a wide range of instructional materials. Textbooks are not only used, but often several textbooks by various authors and a good many supplementary books are available for the pupils. Not only do the children use those books supplied by the school, but they find other volumes about their unit topics at their homes or libraries. Reference books, such as encyclopedias and atlases, are widely used as sources of accurate information. . . .

In addition to books, pupils and teachers today use many pamphlets, posters, and maps which are secured from appropriate sources for each unit. Transportation companies, industries, consulates or embassies of foreign countries, and government agencies are among sources of free and inexpensive materials which may be secured for use in unit study.

Of course films, television, and other audio-visual aids are excellent in unit teaching. And let us not forget photography; teachers and pupils can secure excellent photographs of value in their units, using whatever equipment they have available.

Some of the finest resources for unit study are often in the community where the children live and in the surrounding territory. Here children and teachers can find people to interview, places to visit, processes to observe, and problems to explore on a wide range of unit topics.

Most important of all are the children themselves as resources in social studies units. They can contribute much to many units from their own experiences and observations. Not only do they know a great deal about various facets of life in their own community, but many have taken one or more trips to more distant places, even foreign countries.

✌ BRIDGING THE GAP BETWEEN TEXTBOOK TEACHING AND UNIT TEACHING *Raymond H. Muessig*

Is unit teaching incompatible with and unadaptable to text-book-centered teaching? Professor Muessig contends that the answer to this question is "not necessarily so." He discusses both unique and common characteristics of textbook teaching and unit instruction; and in refreshing manner, he spells out a specific guide to utilizing textbooks as a central strand from which unit activities flow. Some readers may question how practical it is to expect a teacher to devote as much time to planning as is suggested here. The good teacher knows that time spent in planning is well spent—and, as Muessig points out, the recommended procedures are intended to lead the teacher into unit work. As soon as the teacher has a feel for units, he will find that the time required for planning is not excessive.

THE APPROACH WHICH I am going to outline very briefly is not a panacea. It must be considered as tentative, subject to error, open to revision and improvement. As a matter of fact it is proposed as a *temporary* measure to aid teachers in getting a feeling for unit teaching. Once this feeling has been grasped, I hope that this idea will be discarded and new operational levels sought. I worked out this procedure initially to help a group of experienced teachers, used to single textbook teaching, move into unit work. They reported that the idea "worked." Whether this suggestion is good, right, new, or old, it is at least "pragmatic."

. . . . What do I mean by "textbook" and "unit" teaching as I perceive them? I hope that I am not creating two "straw men" just for the sake of contrast, but I see a rather significant difference in these two methods and in their underlying philosophies.

Textbook-centered teaching has a medieval heritage. The teacher

Used by permission of The Social Studies; from *The Social Studies*, February, 1963, 54:43–47.

who could secure a book or commit the contents of a manuscript to memory was "in business." The text was a source of authority, often unquestioned and unchallenged. The more faithfully the learner could return its contents to his teacher, the more approbation he earned. This approach, therefore, has been with us a long time. . . . The facts contained in the single source have some kind of magical intrinsic value—worthy in and of themselves. The assign-study-recite-test procedure is generally followed. The teacher generally originates, directs, and passes judgment upon all learning activity. Only those evaluation techniques which attempt to assess the degree to which the names, dates, places, and events have been "learned" are employed. Motivation is provided by the teacher by way of grades and other extrinsic rewards. The teacher's main aim in life seems to be "covering the text." More and more facts accumulate as research continues over the years and as man's stay on earth is extended; textbooks get larger; and it gets harder and harder for the teacher to reach first Page 523, then Page 678, and later Page 751 by the end of the year. A teacher's life is further complicated by parents who can conceive of no other approach and who believe in "fundamental" learning void of "fads and frills," by administrators who insist that various kinds of standardized tests be given to all groups as a means of comparing teachers or schools, by students who either cannot read the text or are bored by it, and by the fact that his courses seem to be more dull and drab each year they are repeated.

This is not to say that the use of a textbook is wrong. That assumption would be absurd. The textbook can be one of the finest resources available to a class and a teacher. Textbooks are often written by persons who are well qualified both as scholars and teachers. Texts may be well documented and illustrated and may even be graded in an endeavor to meet some of the reading problems. They may even contain suggestions for meaningful activities which can enhance learning. The problem is, however, that too many teachers rely exclusively upon the text and never move out to other green pastures like additional books containing related but varied material and written at different reading levels, pamphlets and booklets, newspapers and magazines, films and filmstrips, recordings, field trips, resource persons, community studies, independent research, *ad infinitum.*

Unit teaching in a more simplified form is not always a radical departure from the most enlightened textbook teaching, nor is it any kind of a final answer; but it does attempt to correct many of the shortcomings of narrowly conceived textbook-centered methodology. Unit teaching at its best can be a thing of beauty, however, and has some unique properties which distinguish it from its more mundane cousin, the textbook approach. Unit teaching attempts to integrate, combine, coordinate, or articulate understandings, skills, attitudes, and appreciations around large significant topics. It seeks wholeness rather than fragmentation, clusters of ideas and data rather than isolated particles, more of a montage than a series of single snapshots taken one by one. The unit approach does not avoid facts, but it does try to build facts into concepts and generalizations which may have more meaning, may be transferable in more situations, and may be more lasting. This method recognizes that any single source of information, however good it may be, imposes unnecessary limitations upon the class and the teacher. Pupil-teacher planning in the drafting of objectives, search for materials, selection of methods of study, and development of evaluative processes is more common. Actual interests, needs, aspirations, and problems of students are tapped and kept in mind, and greater student involvement and identification with objectives of learning tends to upstage intrinsic rather than extrinsic motivation. The unit may deal with material similar in content to that which the textbook approach gives its allegiance, but there is no pressure to cover any given text. Unit teaching encourages creative, independent, critical thought rather than memorization for its own sake. It relies on a variety of evaluation techniques in addition to the typical standardized and teacher-made tests. We could go on, but the basic thing, it seems to me, is that the unit teacher is after more *meaning* in what goes on in a classroom.

I believe that one of the reasons the unit approach has not found its way into more social studies classes is that the distance from basic textbook teaching to full-blown unit teaching is too great to travel all at once. I propose that the teacher already used to the text begin there. The first step is to make the most of the textbook, to get more meaning out of it, to emphasize relatedness. Later, a few added resources may be brought in and some activities with a "unit flavor" blended in. Still later, a simple unit could be worked out with the students, and so on until a complete unit approach is attempted in the spring.

This article begins with and stops at the first stage of this process—using the text as a more unified teaching tool. The steps for the procedure are outlined below:

1. Let us assume for the sake of this illustration that it is a few weeks before the start of the school year. Taking the

basic textbook for the course, the teacher might begin by writing the chapter titles on separate 3 x 5 cards. It is sometimes useful to jot down a few of the sub-topics under the chapter title just to have a reminder of some of the basic things included in the chapter. The cards should be separated into several stacks by priority. Some chapters which the teacher considers to be of primary importance will fall into the "essential" pile; others of secondary importance will fall into the "helpful" stack; and still others which may have doubtful value for a particular class would go into a "possible," "hold," or "delete" group. . . .

2. Next, the teacher works out a rough approximation of the number of teaching weeks in the school year. His purpose for doing this is not to see how much material—regardless of its importance—he can cram into the course but to work out *areas of emphasis* or "unit" topics. Now he roughly divides the total number of weeks into blocks of approximately five weeks. Later, as actual "units" emerge they may vary from three to six weeks in length depending on the teacher's objectives, the interest of the class, and other factors. In a typical school year, there would be from six to eight of these textbook units. Glancing quickly at the 3 x 5 cards in the "helpful" stack and thumbing more carefully through those in the "essential" pile, the teacher tries to list from six to eight over-all problems, topics, or content areas around which the units can be constructed.

3. The remainder of the 3 x 5 cards in the top priority group, probably most of the cards of secondary importance, and perhaps even a few of the cards in the third questionable pile may now be separated under the basic unit copies. This unit distribution may or may not follow the organization of the textbook. The important thing is whether the over-all topics make sense to the teacher and the students. The order of the unit topics can be arranged chronologically, logically, psychologically, or developmentally according to the teacher's perception of the nature of the class and the content discipline. The first unit might be so placed because it is fundamental or foundational in its content, interest arousing, more concrete or understandable, or for some other reason.

4. Now the teacher is ready to build the first of the units. He takes the 3 x 5 cards in the group assigned to the initial topic and notes the chapters they represent. (Each unit

would include from about three to six chapters in the typical social studies text.) It is at this point that a rather tedious, but rewarding, process begins. The teacher carefully reads only those chapters which will be used for the first unit. On fresh, additional 3 x 5 cards he writes down the *crucial, basic* facts contained in each chapter, using one card for each factual statement. Just "any old facts" will not do! These must be facts with lasting importance, facts which will lead to significant understandings, attitudes, and appreciations. Altogether, though it is not possible to assign a magic number, the teacher might have from one hundred to two hundred essential facts.

5. The "fact" cards are now separated into three basic piles, "understandings," "attitudes," and "appreciations." The "understandings" pile will probably be the largest by far.

6. The cards in the "understandings" pile are again subdivided. The teacher tries to find groups of facts which support a given concept. A concept is a class of related information, a "basket" which holds a cluster of facts and gives them real meaning. A given unit might contain from ten to twenty concepts each of which would be supported by from five to ten basic facts which "add up to something." One last refinement is necessary, however, to complete the treatment of "understandings." This is the formulation of from one generalization up to five generalizations. A generalization is the interrelationship of two or more concepts and should emerge quite naturally when the teacher analyzes the concepts already developed. One of the most important goals in social studies education is the ability to generalize, to fit particulars into a configuration, to draw inferences from data, or to perceive applications. The generalization, therefore, is the cognitive capstone of the unit. It is the vein of gold which is the product of all of the digging which the students and the teacher do throughout the unit.

7. A single unit may lead to only one or two important attitudes and appreciations. The "attitude" pile may contain only two or three concept cards and the group of fact cards which buttress the concepts, and a similar situation usually exists with the "appreciation" pile. Attitudes and appreciations are mixtures of both facts and feelings, cognitive and emotive elements. They carry the values, predispositions, and aesthetic elements of the unit.

8. The teacher is now at the "blueprint" stage of building a

textbook-oriented unit. He takes a large piece of butcher paper and divides it into three columns. At the top and center of each of the three columns he prints "Content," "Activities," and "Evaluation" from left to right, respectively.

9. In the "Content" column the teacher prints a complete structural outline of the material he has gathered on the 3 x 5 cards. A Roman numeral is assigned to each generalization, attitude, and appreciation. Capital letters are given to supporting concepts which go under each generalization, attitude, and appreciation. Arabic numbers are assigned to the facts which undergird their respective concepts. Now the teacher can "see" what he is after, where he is going, what he wants to build. This view can be quite satisfying, for it gives a textbook teacher a sense of purpose which he may have missed before.

10. In the "Activities" column the teacher prints *over-all activities* which will serve the purposes and content of the unit like reading from the text, group discussion, etc. and *specific activities* like student panels, individual student papers, etc. which match up on a one-to-one basis with particular generalizations, attitudes, and appreciations or individual concepts which support them. Later, these more traditional activities may be augmented with procedures typical of a full-blown unit approach. The teacher could begin this expansion process on the second unit by having students write for free and inexpensive materials, by ordering several films, by forming a few research committees, by securing a resource person, etc.

11. In the "Evaluation" column the teacher would again list both general and specific procedures for assessing student growth on the unit as a whole and on given generalizations, attitudes, appreciations, or underlying concepts. During the first trial "unit" the teacher might be contented with just teacher-made essay tests, multiple choice tests, etc. In later units, the teacher may include inventories, check lists, observation, open-ended procedures, etc.

12. The final step in the process is for the teacher to ditto copies of the "unit" for all of the students. A cover with a "catchy" title and a clever illustration can help a great deal to interest the students. The teacher should write a one paragraph over-view of the nature of the unit to secure student involvement. A group of basic unit objectives might be listed.

This time they will be the teacher's, but later they will come out of class discussion. Also included would be a copy of the teacher's outline of content, activities, and evaluation so the students have a "preview of coming attractions." The first dittoed unit might contain daily assignments with some options for differences in students interests and capacities. Students will read selectively from the text and use it as a genuine resource. Additional enrichment activities could be suggested too. Culminating, or wrap-up activities might be planned by the students themselves after they have a feeling for this approach. This would also initiate some pupil-teacher planning. Finally, if the teacher has caught the spirit by now, the unit might have a brief bibliography for the students so they could start getting in the habit of consulting other sources.

. . . The "bridge" suggested probably bears a closer resemblance to a log dropped across a creek than a sleek, steel suspension bridge, but it is a beginning. The rest of the construction task is up to the dedicated teacher who wants to do more for the wonderful, unique, challenging young people who walk through his door.

✍ A LESSON ON THE CONSTITUTION FOR THE FIFTH GRADE *Mildred Howarter*

While many plans for and records of units of study in social studies have been published, daily lessons appear in print much less frequently. The necessity of lessons, however, makes it important for the teacher to give specific attention to these briefer periods of study. In this selection a teacher reports on an interesting lesson in fifth-grade social studies. Several elements identified in the article and the approach described are applicable to other lessons. A special feature of this report is the lesson's inclusion of questions regarding content for subsequent periods of study.

ANNIVERSARIES OF HISTORIC events furnish opportune occasions for teaching understanding and appreciation of our heritage. Although

Used by permission of the author and the National Council for the Social Studies; from *Social Education*, 25:199, April, 1961. Miss Howarter is an elementary teacher in Galesburg, Ill.

the following device was used by the author as a Constitution Day activity, with only a few minor revisions it could easily be implemented as part of a unit on the Constitution.

Before the day on which the teacher planned to discuss the Constitution with her fifth-grade social studies class, she made it a point to secure a number of one-dollar bills. With the understanding that they would be returned to her at the end of the period, she distributed the bills among the pupils. In this way, she not only made sure of captivating class attention, but she provided her students with an opportunity to study at close range the Great Seal of the United States, both sides of which are reproduced on a one-dollar bill.

The teacher discussed with the class the significance of the seal as it is explained in *Compton's Pictured Encyclopedia*. She called attention to the fact that the eagle is pictured powerfully bearing the shield without other support, suggesting that the new United States meant to be self-reliant and strong. She explained that the eagle holds the olive branch and arrows in its talons even as Congress bears the power of peace and war in its hands. She interpreted with her class the meaning of the scroll, "*E Pluribus Unum*," the thirteen stars and stripes.

In studying the reverse side of the seal, the teacher was able to lead the group to associate the great, enduring pyramids with strength. The Roman numerals MDCCLXXVI on the base of the pyramid were converted to 1776, the date of the Declaration of Independence. The meanings of the Latin phrases as translated in the encyclopedia reference were discussed.

Up to this point, the teacher had been careful to make no mention of the Constitution or of Constitution Day. She now placed the following subtraction problem on the blackboard.

$$\begin{array}{r} \text{September 17, 1960} \\ -\text{September 17, 1787} \\ \hline 173 \end{array}$$

"Does anybody know of anything that happened 173 years ago on September 17?" the teacher asked. No one knew. By way of a clue, the teacher suggested that the students examine carefully some of the documents posted on the walls of the classroom. One little girl found what she was looking for in the words printed at the bottom of a copy of the Constitution, "Done in convention by the unanimous consent of the States present the 17th day of September in the year of our Lord 1787. . . ."

The teacher then asked the pupils to consider in what ways

the Constitution was important to them, and discussed with them such of the "freedoms" as could be appreciated by fifth graders. Using as a source book, *You and the Constitution of the United States* by Paul Witty and Julilly Kohler, she presented some of the important ideas set forth by George Washington, James Madison, and Benjamin Franklin at the Constitutional Convention.

In order to keep the information the children had gained from their study of the Constitution and the Great Seal fresh in their minds, the teacher compiled a list of questions to be used in class question bees throughout the year:

1. Give a reason why the Constitution is important to you.
2. When did the Constitutional Convention meet?
3. Where did the Constitutional Convention meet?
4. Name three men who attended the Constitutional Convention.
5. Tell the significance of three things which are portrayed on the Great Seal of the United States.

∽§ DEVELOPING SOCIAL SCIENCE CONCEPTS IN THE KINDERGARTEN   *Bernard Spodek*

Although unit plans and records of units taught are widely available in elementary social studies curriculum guides, resource units, methods textbooks, and other publications, it may well be worthwhile to examine an illustration of unit teaching. In this instance special attention was paid to the nature of the content chosen and to evaluation of the children's learning. While the stated conclusions, based on that evaluation, should be applied only to the reported instance, they identify elements and emphases that deserve experimentation with other subject matter, with children in various age and ability groups, and in varying types of schools. The reader may note also the author's use of the term "concepts" as equivalent to what many other authorities refer to as "generalizations."

WITH THE CHANGES that have taken place in our society and with the increases in the amount of knowledge that has been made available in recent years, the curriculum of the schools has been the

Used by permission of the author and the National Council for the Social Studies; from *Social Education*, 27:253–256, May, 1963. Dr. Spodek is on the faculty of the School of Education at the University of Wisconsin in Milwaukee.

subject of much controversy. The question of what to teach children at what age level has been raised anew. Growing out of the questioning, new ways of organizing the curriculum at all levels of education are being suggested. The social studies has become one of the important areas of this reinvestigation.

USING BASIC CONCEPTS IN THE CURRICULUM

From several sources the suggestion has come for using key concepts or basic concepts of the various areas of knowledge as the organizing principles of that which should be taught at all levels (1). These "basic concepts" are those big ideas which unify a field of inquiry and give meaning to the various facts that are collected by scholars who work within the field. The basic concepts of each area of knowledge would be taught at every stage in the education of children, beginning with the first experiences of school and continuing on up into college and the graduate school. Facts and information would be presented at each level, not for the inherent value of this information, but rather because they exemplify or illustrate the larger basic concepts in some way. The outcome of a curriculum organized in this fashion has been labeled a "spiral curriculum," since big ideas would be visited again and again by the child in his school career, with each visit adding more meaning as the idea is investigated in greater depth and breadth.

The research project here discussed grew out of this idea and was developed to test the possibility of beginning such a "spiral curriculum" in the social studies at the kindergarten level. The hypothesis tested was that kindergarten children could begin to attain significant concepts in the social sciences that could become the foundation for later learning at succeeding grade levels. Selected areas of history and geography were explored in this research project.

Although the basic concepts of the fields of history and geography were not isolated for the study, the following significant concepts from these fields dealing with the topic, "New York as a Harbor," were defined with the aid of scholars and became the basis for our program.

CONCEPTS ABOUT NEW YORK AS A HARBOR

A. Man can understand the geographic aspects of a harbor by analyzing the following factors in that area:
  1. Site (the physical characteristics of the harbor)
     a. A large, almost land-locked body of water
     b. Large amounts of land frontage on navigable waterways to serve as dock space

  c. A short distance from piers to open ocean
  d. Deep channels, with water near shore also deep
  e. Tides of sufficient height present to keep channels free of sediment
  f. Moderate enough climate to be ice-free the year round
  g. Adequate land area available on which to build a city
 2. Situation (the relationship of the harbor to its service area)
  a. Good inland transportation systems available
 3. Facilities
  a. The availability of docks
  b. The availability of facilities for rapid loading and unloading of ships
  c. The availability of facilities for moving goods from ships to other means of transportation
  d. The availability of facilities for storing goods
 4. Functions (the interrelationship of other aspects of the city to the harbor)
  a. The variety of industries in relation to the harbor
  b. The variety of jobs related to the harbor
  c. The location of industries in relation to the harbor
  d. The location of home-sites in relation to the harbor
B. Man is able to represent the world and its parts symbolically.
 1. Areas can be located in the world by measurements of distance and direction.
 2. A map is a symbolic representation of the world, or a part of the world. It is drawn to scale, and it shows distance and direction.
 3. There are many different kinds of maps which are used for different purposes.
C. Man can place occurring events into a framework of chronological time.
D. Changes that have taken place in the harbor can be understood in relation to changes in technology and changes in the needs of people.
 1. Ships have changed in design, size, and power used.
 2. Facilities in the harbor have changed.
 3. The availability of other means of transportation has changed. (These changes have brought about changes in the use of the harbor and its facilities. They have also brought about changes in the utilization of various site factors.)
E. These changes that have taken place in the harbor can be understood in the framework of time and space.

These significant concepts were later broken down into more specific understandings that, it was felt, kindergarten children could attain. A program based upon these concepts was implemented over a period of two and one-half months in the kindergarten of the Agnes

Russell Center, a service school of Teachers College, Columbia University. The choice of the topic used to illustrate these concepts, "New York as a Harbor," was made on the basis of children's interest as well as its significance for study in the social sciences.

The program itself was developed in a spiral fashion rather than as a single unit of work. Periods of two weeks' duration, separated by periods similar in length, were set aside for the program in the kindergarten. During the interim periods no new information or experiences were developed although the children could utilize materials left over from the previous period's work. The social studies segment of the program was integrated within the regular kindergarten work. Many of the materials and techniques already familiar to the kindergarten were used in this part of the program, sometimes with minor differences. New materials were also added and trips were planned which would augment the social science learnings. When the social studies program was presented during the activity period, however, there were also other activities available which the children could choose. In this way there were no activities eliminated from the normal kindergarten program.

In order to collect evidence on the children's attainment of the desired social science concepts, a test interview was devised using pictures and models as stimuli. As a measure of control, items dealing with farm concepts were included and were also scored. The test was administered before and after the program to the entire class of 19 children, but since one child could not be adequately tested due to language difficulties, the total number of scores finally used was 18.

RESULTS OF THE STUDY

The children's scores on the pre-test ranged from ten to 34 with a mean of 19.4. In the post-test the scores ranged from 17 to 39 with a mean of 30.1. A *t* test of the difference of the means of the two tests resulted in a score of 16.3, indicating that the changes in score were significant at the 1 percent level of confidence. This difference would not occur by chance more than once in a hundred times.

On the items dealing with farms, the children's scores ranged from one to five in the pre-test with a mean of 3.7. On the post-test the scores ranged from one to six with a mean of 3.9. This difference was not found to be significant. From a comparison of these two portions of the test it was inferred that the changes in score on the experimental items was due to the children's experience in the program and could not be attributed to chance or to maturational factors. We concluded from this that kindergarten children could successfully begin to attain significant concepts in the fields of history and geography.

In addition to the evidence on children's concept attainment, evidence was collected on the process by which the children attained these concepts. Four observers recorded the behavior of children during the experimental program. One of the observers was always available in the classroom and would record behavior of the children that was significant to the program both during the times that experiences were developed and after they were developed. These observations were broken down into learning episodes similar in many ways to the behavior episodes used by Barker and Wright (2). These episodes were categorized by area of the topic covered and were also organized chronologically. Through an analysis of these episodes it was possible to determine the way in which the children attained the objectives of the program.

Using the results of the tests together with the observations, we were able to arrive at certain conclusions about what kindergarten children can learn and the way in which they achieve these learnings.

CONCLUSIONS OF THE STUDY

The conclusions gathered from this research project can be summarized as follows:

Kindergarten children can begin to develop significant social science concepts. From our work we found that children can begin to approach the social sciences in the kindergarten. It seemed to us that the ability to attain the significant concepts was not determined by the proximity or remoteness of the phenomena studied, but rather by the abstractness or concreteness of the phenomena. The "here and now" concept of social studies did not seem to hold true for these children. It seemed more important that the children were able to deal with concrete objects, real or representational, which enabled them to gain meaning from the experiences.

Kindergarten children bring a background of knowledge with them to school. Even before we started developing our program there was evidence that the children were already knowledgeable about certain aspects of the social sciences. They all knew what a map was and they could make some elementary differentiations among map symbols. They had some knowledge of the long ago and the changes that have taken place in their world in time. Some of the information the children had was, of course, inaccurate, and there were some misconceptions in the children's thinking. Sometimes these misconceptions seemed to stem from stereotypes observed through the mass media. Sometimes they were caused by confusion arising from language usage. We found, however, that the children could work out these confusions and that misconceptions could be clarified. All of the knowledge the children brought with them, however, had to be taken into account as we planned our program.

Kindergarten children gather information in many ways. There was no single avenue for gathering information upon which we could wholly rely. A variety of sources had to be employed. Sources of information in the classroom were important. These included books, films, discussions, and a variety of concrete materials that were developed. One of the most important of these was a three-dimensional map, built to scale, that the children could use in their play. Unit blocks were also important in allowing the child to construct recreations of geographic areas and play through ideas in this way. Equally important were the sources of information available outside the classroom. Trips around the neighborhood, to the tops of tall buildings, to harbor installations, and to museums were valuable in feeding information to the children.

Kindergarten children can deal with ideas over long periods of time. Contrary to the popular notions about short attention and retention spans of young children, we found that extending our program over a long period seemed to enhance, rather than detract from its effectiveness. Children remembered what had occurred in past periods of programing during succeeding ones. As a matter of fact, the opportunity to revisit an idea, and to review an experience after it had been intellectually digested, seemed to be an aid to concept attainment.

Kindergarten children use the tools of the social scientist. The physical tools as well as the intellectual tools of social scientists were used by the kindergarten children in our study. Maps, the tools of the geographer, were used by the children to understand geographical space. Although chronological time, the tool of the historian, could not be used by the children, they were able to use sequential time as an aid in understanding the past.

Kindergarten children transfer their understandings in approaching new situations. The children are able to use understandings developed about one set of phenomena in learning about new phenomena. At times these may seem inappropriate from the adult's point of view, but when seen in the light of the information available to the children, they are quite logical. Sometimes the transfer is made using inappropriate criteria which can lead to misconceptions.

From this study it was possible to arrive at some tentative guidelines for developing social studies programs for young children that, although still untested, seem fruitful for further investigation. In developing these new programs for the kindergarten there will have to be further study in the ways of organizing the total program and in the ways that materials and equipment can best be utilized by the children. New materials, such as simple three-dimensional maps and other manipulable material, will have to be developed to enable the children to attain the specific goals of these programs. Additional studies will have to be made to see how the other social sciences can be approached by young children. Social studies programs in the kindergarten can become more closely related to the programs in the rest of the child's school career. Children in the kindergarten can begin to develop social science concepts that are being dealt with by scholars.

References

(1) Association for Supervision and Curriculum Development. A *Look at Continuity in the School Program*, 1958 Yearbook. Washington, D.C.: The Association, a department of the National Education Association, p. 134; Jerome Bruner. *The Process of Education.* Cambridge, Mass.: Harvard University Press, 1960, p. 22–26; Philip Phenix. "Key Concepts and the Crisis in Learning." *Teachers College Record* 59:140; December 1956.

(2) Roger C. Barker and Herbert F. Wright. *One Boy's Day.* New York: Harper and Brothers, 1951.

⋐ CONDUCTING CLASS ELECTIONS

Joseph F. Hannan

Few writers of books on elementary schooling have recalled their experiences with such keen perception and expressed them as humorously as does the author of this selection. It would be easy merely to enjoy his delightful comments. For teachers who wish to develop serious application of democratic principles, however, the writer's recognition of the characteristics of children that must be faced in teaching workable democracy is relevant.

SOME TIME EARLY in his career a new teacher will become stifled by the multiplicity of duties which occupy time better used on cor-

From *Never Tease a Dinosaur* by Joseph F. Hannan, pp. 23–24. Copyright © 1961, 1962 by Joseph F. Hannan. Reprinted by permission of Holt, Rinehart and Winston, Inc. Mr. Hannan is an elementary school teacher in New Jersey.

recting papers or checking the scratch sheet. He will hit upon the idea of class officers. A class president could take attendance, conduct opening exercises and maintain discipline while the teacher finishes his mid-morning coffee. A vice president will backstop his chief (it's always a problem finding chores for vice presidents).

The class treasurer can take over the nasty little duties such as collecting for the many worthy causes which arise during the school year (paying for windows broken in baseball games is just one such cause).

The class secretary also has quite an important job, at least the class secretary in my class does. One of her many duties is to see that each and every child has his daily supply of notices to take home. If this responsibility is placed on my shoulders, it is quite apt to be forgotten. The result is an invitation to the PTA meeting getting home two weeks after the meeting night. When my secretary handles notices, they go home daily in twos and threes and not ten or twelve every Friday as when I'm in charge.

In addition to these very valuable services the election of class officers gives the children a chance to take an active part in democratic procedures, thereby preparing them for life in these United States.

Left to their own devices the children soon discover how our elections work. They find that a vote has value, and unless checked, will vote for the highest bidder. They also find that votes for a friend can be rounded up by discreet distribution of bubble gum, threats of a physical nature, or logrolling.

Stuffing the ballot box is not unheard of in sixth grade. It would appear that political chicanery is an inherited trait. The teacher who discovers 53 votes have been cast for a candidate when the class population is only 32 need not be too shocked. Remember that, although lying and stealing are known to be evil even to first-graders, political dishonesty is accepted by a good segment of the adult world. But teachers in general are a naïve crowd—and after preaching the values of political integrity, he throws out the old election and calls for a reform government. The children, anxious to be honest and upright, will do as requested and vote for those they like best.

Now any practical politician will tell you it's great to vote for your friends but who says they will make good officers? Teachers, being as far removed from practical politics as anyone, are well pleased with the idea of friendship and loyalty playing a part in the campaign. Disillusionment will set in when they discover who has been elected to help govern the class.

President—The lad who has broken every class rule.
Vice-president—His best friend, the strongest boy in the room.
Secretary—A sweet little girl who can't write a coherent sentence.
Treasurer—A nice lad with lots of friends and this psychological
   thing about Arithmetic.

At this point a teacher prone to panic might be frightened into abandoning democracy as a way of life and begin to stump for a dictatorship. No need to despair, all you have to do is play the modern Machiavelli.

The first step is to dump the incumbents. A *coup d'état* is necessary and easily accomplished. The whole election is declared null and void because it took place on Thursday and everyone knows that Tuesday is Election Day in the United States. The teacher declares a new Election Day and goes to work on a list of qualifications for candidates designed to eliminate all but those he wants. In other words, he rigs the whole election.

Even after the election, the problems are not all solved. Children granted authority tend to become ultra-officious. This, combined with a natural, childlike ruthlessness, tends to create friction in the classroom.

Let's take a hypothetical case.

Doreen, heretofore a pillar of classroom society has violated one of the cardinal principles of the Class Constitution: she left her lunch box in the aisle.

If the teacher were dealing with this case he would merely point out the transgression, which would immediately be corrected. No such slipshod police work will be tolerated by the class officers. Doreen is found guilty and is given the usual sentence for such a violation. She has to write the class motto, "Safety is Nice," five hundred times. That night Doreen falls off her back porch and breaks her writing arm. Do her judges have mercy upon her? They certainly do. She is given an extra day to finish because she writes so slowly with her left hand. That's the way it is with kids.

EVALUATION IN THE SOCIAL STUDIES OF THE ELEMENTARY SCHOOL   J. D. McAulay

Some of the professional writing on evaluation of children's learning stresses theoretical elements that are not easily applied to classroom practice. While such treatments serve a valuable function, the teacher often finds it refreshing to have specific attention given to practical aspects of evaluation and other instructional processes. In this selection the author begins by reporting findings of a survey of evaluational practices used by teachers in the middle grades. He then provides suggestions to aid teachers in appraising children's learning of social studies, thus answering the following questions: How are standardized tests used and useful in elementary social studies? What kinds of evaluation are applicable to a social studies lesson? What are suitable means of appraisal in unit teaching?

A SURVEY ON CLASSROOM evaluation practices was made of 300 elementary school teachers grades four to six. The survey indicated that arithmetic was tested most frequently, spelling took second place, science third, language arts fourth, music and physical education tied for fifth place. Social studies, with art, was seldom if ever evaluated in the classroom. Twenty-eight teachers of the 300 surveyed indicated they had never given tests in the social studies nor attempted an evaluation of that content area. Realistically it should be that area of the curriculum most frequently evaluated.

There would seem to be four tools for evaluating the social studies: the standardized test, the weekly and semi-weekly quiz, the unit test and incidental evaluation.

STANDARDIZED TESTING

It would be profitable if the classroom teacher would spend a few dollars of her incidental equipment fund to purchase a package of good standardized social studies tests at the beginning of the school year. To give the tests at the beginning of the year will help her determine the children's social studies background in skills and information. The results from such standardized testing can give her some indication of how she should plan the social studies for the school year. If the results indicate the children lack certain essential skills and information, the teacher can select particular units to meet these needs and deficiencies.

If the children are above the national average in the results, the teacher can plan to cover a greater number of units and enrich them accordingly. A standardized test, given at the beginning of the school

Used by permission of The Social Studies; from *The Social Studies* for November, 1961, 52:203–205.

year, can help the teacher chart her yearly program for the social studies.

There are some good social studies tests on the market today selling at a reasonable price. Level 4 of the Cooperative Test Division . . . would seem to measure adequately understandings and abilities to read and interpret social studies material such as maps, graphs and the printed word. Observing relationships among basic facts, trends and concepts is also measured. The material for this particular standardized test is drawn from social studies content common in the fourth, fifth and sixth grades. The National Achievement Test, form A, grades four to six, gives some indication of the child's achievement in understanding human relations, life situations, social problems, products and peoples and the meaning of events. The Progressive Tests in social and related sciences, Parts one and two Elementary Battery Form A, for grades four to eight, evaluate the American heritage, people of other lands and times, geography and the basic social processes. Unfortunately there are no standardized social studies tests suited particularly for . . . grades one, two and three.

THE DAILY EVALUATION

The children should expect an evaluation in the social studies at least twice a week but preferably more often. This might be verbal, such as a quick evaluation at the conclusion of the social studies period or a quick account of what is to be accomplished in today's social studies period based on what was completed yesterday. A weekly evaluation might come on the Friday afternoon when the teacher and the children discuss what was accomplished in the social studies during the week, what plans should be developed for the following week and how the work for the following week might be improved on the basis of present accomplishments.

But the evaluation may be written on the day following a field trip to a local mill or factory. The teacher might ask the children to quickly list on narrow sheets of paper passed down the aisle, three ways in which the factory or mill helps the community. The children may be planning to have a child from Latin America visit the class from another grade to describe the games played in his country. Again the teacher may ask each child to list on a sheet of paper three things he would do to help a child from another country feel at home in the class. Thus the teacher might secure an immediate evaluation of attitude development.

Some of the daily quizzes should have the surprise element, some should be routine and expected. The quiz is to gather and knot small areas of learning in the social studies. It is a short pause to summarize a skill, a fact, an attitude, an appreciation, and to calculate the next step to be taken in the learning procedure.

THE UNIT TEST

The unit test should evaluate the completed unit. Its chief purpose is to determine how successfully the objectives of the unit have been achieved; how thoroughly they have been accomplished and completed. . . .

The unit test should emphasize that area of the unit which has been stressed. If fifty per cent of a unit on Canada had been devoted to an understanding of that nation's government, then a similar proportion of the unit test should be devoted to this topic. For the slower or below-average student the knowledge that the unit test is to be given is most beneficial. The announcement of a coming test motivates the learning and activity of the slow child. For the average student the taking of the test is most beneficial and for the gifted child the return of the corrected test is of most advantage. Thus the children should know approximately a week in advance that the unit test is to be given. The test should be given under the most favorable of circumstances, preferably in the middle of the morning. No interruptions should be allowed. If at all possible the test should be graded that evening and returned to the children the following day. Once the test has been returned the teacher should go over the questions with the class. If the unit test is thus organized, all ability groups will benefit.

A good social studies unit test should have variety in the type of questions given. For the second grade a unit test should have three types of questions—a completion question and an essay question (such as, "tell one way the farmer helps us") and perhaps simple recall questions. A third and fourth grade should have a fourth type of question, perhaps multiple choice. Fifth and sixth grade children should have five types of questions on the unit test. Matching questions might be the fifth type added. Alternative response questions have no place on a social studies test. The content of the social studies is never sufficiently certain to be valid or reliable as material for alternative response questions.

Too often unit tests for the social studies emphasize facts and memorized knowledge. Too often the test does not evaluate the child's awareness of the social problems he has attempted to solve during the unit, nor does it weigh the attitudes and appreciations, the social behavior he has acquired during the progress of the unit.

Such learnings are often felt to be too intangible to measure by a unit test.

Often the essay question can partially determine if the child can think through a social problem. By transposing the same social problem discussed through the unit to a different framework the teacher can roughly gauge the child's development and growth in understanding of this particular unit. If the fourth grade had discussed, during the Thanksgiving unit, why the Pilgrims left comfortable England and settled in the wilderness of America, the question based on the unit test might be "man is trying very hard to visit the moon or one of the planets. Tell why you think he wants to leave this beautiful earth to visit a strange, different and perhaps very dangerous place in space."

The attitudes and appreciations and social behavior, learned through the unit, might be evaluated through sociodrama. Perhaps the sixth grade, in its study of Latin America, has discussed the deep poverty of most of the population. Then the children might be asked to illustrate spontaneously, as part of the unit test, how American tourists should behave when visiting a particular Latin American country. Another group of children might personify a United States Government trade commission conferring with a group of Brazilian coffee plantation owners. The teacher might call on other children to indicate, by a sociodrama, how they would build better relations with the illiterate of Latin America.

Through such methods the teacher can determine if those attitudes, appreciations and behavior, set out in the objectives of the unit, have been achieved.

INCIDENTAL EVALUATION

The teacher should be evaluating, continually, the process and progress of the social studies unit. . . .

Acquiring more efficient work habits might be one objective of the unit. The teacher, heading a sheet of paper with the name of a particular child, may observe the work and study habits of that child during a social studies period, listing favorable and unfavorable actions. This procedure would be repeated for the same child, and other children, several times during the unit. The teacher would thus evaluate during the progress of the unit, the success or failure of that particular objective.

Work projects must also be evaluated. As the year progresses, are the murals for the social studies becoming more creative, more enriched, more sympathetic? Are the maps becoming more exact, more informative, more scientific? Is the research wider, deeper, more concentrated? Are the children becoming more enthused, more alert, more informed concerning the problems centered in the social studies? Are they searching for social studies materials outside the classroom, with less motivation from the teacher? Are they organizing and planning their social studies projects with less direction from the teacher?

Evaluation is the key to successful social studies teaching. Without it the social studies is without a rudder, without a compass. Of such evaluation the alert and professional teacher will be constantly aware. Always she will say to herself, "How could I improve on this unit—what weaknesses in this unit must I correct in the one that follows?"

❧ THE PROBLEM OF EVALUATION IN THE SOCIAL STUDIES   *Robert L. Ebel*

The enthusiasm that appears in some discussions of evaluation of learning in social studies is frequently uncritical and ill-based. To balance such poorly founded discussions, the teacher will find a thoughtful analysis in this selection. In it an outstanding specialist on evaluation recognizes several basic weaknesses and lacks, as well as some progress, in attempts to develop sound means of evaluation suitable for social studies. He furnishes lucid answers to a number of fundamental questions about such evaluation. What is the status of efforts to find reliable and pertinent techniques for evaluating students' attainment of objectives in social studies? How does and should evaluation vary in relation to each of understanding, attitudes, and skills as major types of learning in social studies? What can and should the teacher do in view of the limited progress that has been made in developing needed means of evaluation?

YOUR APPROACHES to the teaching problem, and to the evaluation problem, are basically sound. Both the maintenance of good educa-

Used by permission of the author and the National Council for the Social Studies: from *Social Education*, 24:6–10, January, 1960. Dr. Ebel is vice-president of the Educational Testing Service, Princeton, N.J.

tional programs and the improvement of educational procedures require good evaluation. Good evaluation, in turn, can only be made in relation to the goals of instruction. Too often when teachers make tests they forget their goals and remember only the subject matter they used in trying to achieve those goals.

I should warn you, however, that my answers to your question are going to be more complex and less satisfying than either you or I would wish them to be. The plain fact is that we do not have many evaluation instruments which will do the job you want done. What is even worse, our disappointing experience in trying to measure some of these outcomes is beginning to convince us that part of the job simply *cannot* be done. I even suspect that part of it *should* not be done. On the brighter side, there is much more we can do, and do better, than we are typically doing in evaluating student progress in the social studies.

Three broad categories of educational achievement are reflected in various degrees by the listed objectives:

I. Objectives primarily concerned with knowledge and understanding
    A. Transmit our cultural heritage
    B. Teach important historical facts and generalizations /
    C. Teach time and space relationships
    D. Acquaint students with basic historical references
    E. Provide instruction and practice in locating information
II. Objectives primarily concerned with attitudes, values, and feelings
    F. Promote moral and spiritual values
    G. Promote the attitude that history is interesting and useful
    H. Promote good mental health
    I. Promote aesthetic sensitivities
    J. Develop democratic citizenship
III. Objectives primarily concerned with instruction and practice in intellectual skills
    K. Writing notes from lectures and references
    L. Writing essay examinations
    M. Judging the validity of evidence
    N. Drawing sound conclusions from data
    O. Working in a group
    P. Facility in oral expression

The overlap among these three categories is substantial. Most of us have attitudes, feelings or values attached to much of the knowledge we possess. Conversely, most of our attitudes, feelings, and values have some basis in knowledge and understanding. Intellectual skills are heavily loaded with knowledge, and also have values attached to them. Thus some of the differences among the three categories are differences in the relative contributions of knowledge, feeling and practice to the attainment of the specific goals.

You may have noticed that my grouping omits entirely the second objective in your list, "Provide intellectual exercise for the discipline of the mind." The notion of mental discipline has been the target of considerable psychological criticism. Its most naive form, which assumes that the mind is analogous to a muscle that can be strengthened by exercise in learning anything, especially something difficult to learn, has been generally discredited. Even the notions of general mental *functions* such as memory, reasoning, and will, which were supposed to be separate faculties independent of mental content, have been generally discarded. Modern studies of human and animal learning, and of brain function, suggest that the mind guides behavior by serving as a semi-automatic ready-reference storehouse of ideas derived from experience and reflection. The effectiveness of a mind seems to depend on how many of these ideas are stored in it, how accurately they represent the world outside the mind, and how easily they can be made available for recall and recombination when the occasion demands.

If by intellectual exercise is meant increasing the store of ideas, and if by discipline of the mind is meant improved accuracy and increased integration of these ideas, then this is indeed an important objective—so important, in fact, that it encompasses most of the others. If this is not what is meant, some further clarification may be required. In any case, I cannot suggest any tests which might be used to make a separate evaluation of it.

KNOWLEDGE AND UNDERSTANDING

For the measurement of knowledge and understanding in the social studies a number of excellent tests are available. The Cooperative Test Division of the Educational Testing Service offers social studies tests in its series of Sequential Tests of Educational Progress, and in its end-of-course achievement tests. The World Book Company offers tests in world history and in American history as parts of its Evaluation and Adjustment series. Science Research Associates distributes the test of Understanding of Basic Social Concepts from the Iowa Tests of Educational Development. Oscar Buros' *Fifth Mental Measurements Yearbook* lists 60 tests in the social studies, with critical reviews of 23 of them. Not all of the tests listed are of high quality. The reviewers are rather critical of some. While the reader must occasionally discount the idiosyncrasies of particular reviewers, their comments are usually unbiased and always informative. This is the best available guide to educational tests of all kinds. It should be consulted by anyone who seeks better tests for specific goals.

You may have hoped for a more specific recommendation of a few tests exactly suited to measure achievement of the goals you listed. Unfortunately, this is not possible. In only a few cases have these particular goals been made the focus of specific test construction efforts. Even if tests of each goal were available, it is unlikely that the test author would conceive of these goals precisely as you do. So many facts and ideas are involved in our cultural heritage, and there are so many different value judgments that can be made of them that tests from different sources are almost certain to differ widely. Hence, even in this easiest area of educational measurement, you are not likely to find ready-made tests to meet your needs.

What, then, is to be done? One solution is to make tests of your own, based on a very specific definition of each goal in the area of knowledge and understanding. This is a difficult task. In the absence of substantial expert assistance (and liberal finances) it is not likely to be done very successfully.

Another solution is to get along with the published tests that come closest to covering the goals as you have defined them. This will be cheaper, and cost less effort, but may not be any more satisfactory in the end. What is really needed, it seems to me, is some nationwide effort by social studies teachers and other educators to agree on a definition of basic goals in this and other areas of common educational concern. Then the effort to build really good tests of the agreed upon goals would be justified, and we would have a means for making sound evaluations of the achievement of our common goals. Unless a teacher foolishly devoted his whole teaching to the attainment of these common goals, completely suppressing his own special interests and disregarding local conditions and individual pupil needs, this would place no strait jacket on the curriculum. But if we are committed to the defense of the freedom of states, schools, teachers, or even pupils, to define all their own goals in whatever way they think best, then the task of getting meaningful measures of the degree of achievement of these diverse goals becomes almost impossible. The price we pay for what may be an excess of freedom seems rather high.

ATTITUDES, VALUES, AND FEELINGS

Adequate measurement of achievement toward goals in the realm of attitudes, values and feelings present other, and still more difficult, problems. There is the problem of getting agreement on a clear definition of just what is meant by "democratic citizenship" or "aesthetic sensitivities." There is the problem of obtaining valid indications of the students' true attitudes, values and feelings. Direct questions in a test situation indicate mainly how the student thinks he *ought* to feel. Indirect, disguised tests are often low in relevance and reliability. The instability of pupil behavior from time to time and from situation to situation makes any single observation quite limited in significance. Finally, it is very difficult to create a test situation which is realistic enough to give valid indication of a student's probable behavior in a natural non-test situation.

For these reasons, good tests in the area of attitudes, values and feelings are quite rare. I know of none in the realm of moral and spiritual values. . . . There are some tests of civic knowledge. There have been some attempts to predict good civic behavior, but here again the problems of trait definition and test validity have been so troublesome that no existing test can be recommended.

This lack of good, ready-made instruments is bad enough. What is even more discouraging is the lack of any promising techniques for the measurement of attitudes, feelings and values. It is gradually becoming apparent that the difficulties of measuring these traits with paper-and-pencil tests are inherent in the nature of the traits, and in the limitations of formal, written tests. Techniques of testing which are reasonably effective in measuring knowledge and understanding may never be even passably effective in measuring an individual person's attitudes, values and feelings simply because these are specific to situations which cannot be realistically reproduced by any test. Further, deficiencies in these traits can easily be hidden from the prying questions of the tester, behind a mask of conventionally correct' responses.

Does this mean that teachers should abandon the pursuit of goals in this area? To some extent, yes. Many widely approved goals with respect to attitudes, values and feelings are generally acceptable only when they are left undefined. What consensus could we get in defining the activities of a good citizen, or the nature of ideal spiritual values? People in different localities, and of different political, religious, or philosophical persuasions would define them quite differently. Is tolerance a virtue or a fault? No teacher can avoid influencing pupils to adopt his own particular attitudes and values, but I doubt that these should become formal goals of teaching, or objects for testing, unless they are the predominant view of the culture, or unless they can be supported as rational consequences of valid knowledge about the world and man.

This suggests that of some of our attitudes, values and feelings are determined by the knowledge we possess. I am persuaded that this cognitive basis for feelings is very influential, and that it constitutes a proper and productive focus for teaching and for testing. Consider the goal of good mental health. How can a teacher promote good mental health? One way is to understand mental hygiene and the causes of mental illness well enough so that most of his acts in dealing with students tend to improve rather than impair the student's (and the teacher's) mental health. Another is to teach a knowledge and an understanding of mental health to the students themselves. Good tests of this kind of knowledge can be built. But no paper-and-pencil test is likely to do an adequate job of assessing mental health or diagnosing mental illness. That is a task for the specialist who knows how to use complex clinical procedures.

Similarly, one could build good tests of knowledge about good citizenship, about aesthetics, about moral and spiritual values and about the uses of history. Imparting of relevant knowledge does not guarantee development of desired attitudes, values and feelings, but it surely must contribute substantially to their development.

The chief alternative to the development of desirable attitudes, values and feelings via knowledge is to develop them by indoctrination or conditioning. Many of our most cherished feelings were developed in this way. As children we learned acceptable social behavior largely through a complex system of rewards and punishments, and only secondarily on the basis of rational understanding of the *why* of the correct form (if indeed it was rational!). Indoctrination is almost the only way of teaching very young children, but it becomes progressively less necessary and less desirable as their minds develop. It is a more appropriate technique in the home than in the school. I seriously doubt that teachers, especially teachers of the social studies at the high school level and beyond, should intentionally have much to do with indoctrination or conditioning. Their attempts to develop desirable attitudes, values and feelings should have mainly a cognitive, rational base, depending on knowledge and understanding.

This emphasis on knowledge, rather than on attitudes, values and feelings, troubles some teachers greatly. Knowledge alone is not enough, they say. It is what a person does with his knowledge that counts. . . . But they err, I think, if they assume that instances of misbehavior are caused mainly by deficiencies in attitudes, values and feelings which the school could correct if it only would try hard enough. Character traits are important determinants of behavior, but so are environmental circumstances. Teachers err if they assume that character is largely independent of knowledge, or that the same techniques of teaching and testing that have served for knowledge will serve also for attitudes, values and feelings. There is little in the experience of teachers or testers to support such assumptions. To evaluate individual achievement in these non-cognitive areas we may have to settle for measurment of relevant knowledge of how one ought to feel. We do not yet have good tests to do even this job, but we know how to make them.

For the rest of our evaluation of typical behavior, as influenced by attitudes, values and feelings, we may have to rely on systematic but informal observation of pupil behavior in real, non-test situations. This does not relieve us of defining clearly the traits we wish to observe. It does not promise to yield reliable measurements with little effort. But techniques for observing and recording typical behavior seem to offer more promise than any test-like instrument designed to probe a student's attitudes, values and feelings. . . .

Today many of us are less sanguine. The experiences of 30 years of generally unproductive efforts are beginning to convince us that we have set ourselves an impossible task, like squaring the circle or building a perpetual motion machine. . . .

Since 1942 an enormous amount of work has been done on personality testing. A great many tests have been developed. Some interesting findings have been reported, and some interesting theories proposed. But much of what goes on in the name of personality assessment is not much better than horoscope casting or tea leaf reading. We still have no personality test of demonstrated value that is practically useful in measuring the effectiveness of learning or teaching in the classroom. We may never have. It may be that our search for the "structure" of personality, and our attempts to "measure" its dimensions will be as fruitless as previous attempts to find the fountain of youth, or the philosopher's stone. Perhaps the problem needs to be reformulated. It may be that the really basic, stable determinants of behavior, so far as behavior is internally determined, are not attitudes, values and feelings, but ideas—rational, cognitive, teachable, testable.

INTELLECTUAL SKILLS

The third category of goals was concerned mainly with intellectual skills. Here again there are no good, ready-made tests that can be recommended. To the extent that these skills rest on knowledge—and this is a considerable extent—they can be tested by conventional paper-and-pencil tests. To the extent that they rest on facility gained through practice, performance tests judged with the help of rating scales offer the most promise. The best solution may be a combination of knowledge and performance tests as a basis for evaluating skills in note taking, essay examination writing, effective group participation, and oral expression.

There are two objectives in this area—judging the validity of evidence and drawing conclusions from data—that may be so greatly conditioned by a student's background knowledge that the influence of generalized skill on his behavior may be relatively unimportant. I wonder if there are broadly applicable rules for judging the validity of evidence, principles which do not depend on the particular nature of the evidence under consideration. I wonder if the interpretation of data is an abstract procedure, like the diagraming of a sentence, that can be applied with reasonable uniformity to all kinds of data. If so, knowledge about these rules and procedures can be taught and tested *as abstract principles*. But I am persuaded that attempts to test these skills by asking a student to judge specific evidence or interpret specific data will reveal mainly how much he already knows about the source of the evidence or data, its meaning, and the problem to which it applies. In short, I wonder if these are important enough as abstract skills to deserve the status of goals of instruction.

RECOMMENDATIONS

What, then, would I recommend for the evaluation of student progress toward the goals of teaching in the social studies?

First, that goals be defined specifically enough so that one can judge how satisfactory a given test will be.

Second, that goals which cannot be defined specifically and with general acceptability, or which hypothesize traits of dubious independence from other more obvious and easily measurable traits, be eliminated or de-emphasized.

Third, that goals which have statewide or nationwide, not just local, validity be emphasized.

Fourth, that command over essential knowledge be emphasized as a primary goal of instruction, even in the areas of attitudes, values, feelings and intellectual skills.

Fifth, that social studies teachers continue to search for, or to construct, evaluation instruments of acceptable validity in terms of specifically defined goals.

Sixth, that the *Fifth Mental Measurement Year-book* be consulted for guidance in judging the usefulness of available tests.

Seventh, that social studies teachers recognize and accept the necessity of building some new tests, whose quality will depend on how much effort and money they are prepared to spend on them, and on how much expert help they get and accept in creating them.

That I have completed this discussion without clearly recommending a single specific test for you to use is something I regret very much. It reflects the complexity of some problems of educational measurement. Even more, it reflects our failure to be realistic in setting our goals, and to be objective and precise in defining them. I am persuaded that the main reason why educational measurement sometimes seems inadequate is that we persist in setting impossible tasks for it to do. But I am also persuaded that if we concentrate on the right problems, and work on them energetically and intelligently, we can improve educational measurement substantially.

☙ Measurement of Growth in Skills

Dana G. Kurfman and *Robert J. Solomon*

In the busy life of the elementary school teacher there often is little time for reconsidering the basic elements in the processes of schooling. Teachers who can and will consider the fundamentals of measuring pupils' learning in social studies will find this selection especially helpful. Though the article concentrates on the measuring of pupils' development of skills, much of it applies to evaluating their learning generally in social studies. A variety of illustrative devices for measurement appears in the original source.

FOR BOTH TEACHERS and students, education is a continuous process of growth. Measurement is the means of obtaining the information necessary to improve this process—to see what has been accomplished and to find out what needs to be done to insure the growth that is desired. This chapter attempts to suggest certain basic considerations in the measurement of skills and to furnish examples of how certain skills may be tested.

GENERAL CONSIDERATIONS

In his efforts to develop social studies skills, the teacher of social studies needs to learn how well his instructional techniques and materials have helped him to achieve his objectives. He needs to know whether, as a result of instruction, his classes have developed

Used by permission of the authors and the National Council for the Social Studies; from its Thirty-Third Yearbook, *Skill Development in Social Studies*, 1963, pp. 274–278. Both Dr. Kurfman and Dr. Solomon are staff members of the Educational Testing Service at Princeton, N.J.

the desired skills; and he needs to know, also, whether they have achieved a satisfactory level of competence in each of those skills. Moreover, he needs to be able to assess the skill development of each student as well. Most important for his role as a teacher, perhaps, he needs to be able to diagnose the relative strengths and weaknesses of each student.

With few exceptions, teachers recognize these needs. They know, too, that measurement is that phase of the instructional process that serves these needs. They recognize, also, that measurement is as continuous as education itself, that on an informal, almost intuitive, level it is going on all the time. The problem for most teachers is to make certain that measurement and the evaluation that stems from it are *relevant* and *reliable*.

In insuring that measurement be relevant, one principle is paramount. It is that there can be no essential substantive difference between instruction and measurement. The latter may involve a reformulation in more systematic and precise terms of the goals and processes of instruction, but it is not concerned with different goals or processes. Thus, the consideration of relevance in measurement starts at the point where the teacher begins planning his instruction. It requires that in explicit and unambiguous terms the teacher identify, in this case for the area of social studies skills, the student behaviors that are the desired outcomes of instruction. To measure and assess the outcomes of instruction, there is a need to know first exactly what the outcomes are intended to be.

. . . Each teacher defines for himself the kinds and levels of skill development appropriate for his students. The teacher needs to use this definition and, if need be, to expand it, in order to identify exactly what it is that he wishes to measure.

For example, developing skills of map reading is a social studies objective which is common to many grade levels. In any particular grade, however, it has a special meaning. The fourth grade teacher does not define the skill of map reading for his students in the same way that the ninth grade teacher does. For any particular social studies class there are specific skills of map reading that students in that class may be expected to master. Should they be able to use a scale of miles to determine distances between points on a map? Should they be able to determine the size and location of bodies of land by use of latitude and longitude? When the desired student behavior is made explicit, the definition of what is to be measured and evaluated has also been made explicit. Indeed, the tasks to be presented to students as the means of measurement have suggested themselves.

Although the defining of tasks for instruction and the setting of standards for achievement by grade levels are necessary and important to a sound program of skill development, teachers must recognize also that students at any grade level will vary widely in their competencies. Hence, the degree of competency in a particular skill expected for most students in a particular grade has to be interpreted flexibly for some individuals.

Another example may be taken from the area of reading skills. In deciding what to measure, the teacher will need, in addition to defining the kinds of material that students may be expected to read, to decide if students may be expected to identify the main point of a passage, or the author's purpose in writing it, or the author's underlying assumptions. Should the student be expected to separate statements of fact from statements of judgment? Should he be expected to apply outside information to the evaluation of the author's conclusions—and, if so, what outside information?

The purpose of instruction in the area of social studies skills, as in other areas of social studies instruction, is to effect desired changes in behavior. A concern for relevancy in the measurement of growth in skills demands, therefore, that the desired behavior be specifically identified and defined. But specifying the behavior to be measured, although essential, is only one step that needs to be considered. Of equal importance is the need for instruments that actually measure the critical aspects of that behavior. Otherwise, measurement may lose relevance despite a generally clear comprehension of objectives. Thus it is crucial for relevant measurement not only that the desired behavior be identified, but also that the student be required to perform tasks that elicit that behavior. If instructional goals are well-defined and if the actual techniques of measurement replicate as far as possible the behavior sought, the teacher's ability to evaluate performance is made relatively simple. The success or failure of the students to behave in the manner defined by the measure offers the best direct evidence of student development.

Almost any situation in the educational process provides a basis for gauging achievement. However, taking one's soundings, so to speak, where one finds them is not likely to produce relevant results. Also . . . not all situations produce results that are equally reliable. In selecting a situation that will provide useful insight the teacher may rely on direct observation, using such techniques as an anecdotal record or a rating scale. The direct observation may take place during an everyday classroom activity or it may occur as a result of an activity specially created to produce the desired behavior. However, direct observation in a classroom situation, natural or contrived, often produces ambiguous results. Often, many variables are operating at once. Even if the teacher can concentrate on one student at a time, the problem remains of controlling the individual's performance or the observation of it, so as to isolate only the critical behavior that is to be measured. If one wishes to judge the class as a whole, the problem is even more complex.

To measure critical behaviors it is almost essential that the evaluation situation narrow its focus. In the area of skills, particularly, it seems more sensible to obtain a work sample of the desired behavior. Such work samples may be specially designed assignments, to be done in class or as homework; or they may be more formally administered tests. Many of the examples for measuring growth in skills that are given later in this chapter are presented as test exercises, although clearly they may also be used in less formal classroom situations because they have the advantage of focusing on a work sample of the student's that may be restricted to a particular skill at a defined level of difficulty.

As we noted earlier, in addition to the relevancy of the instruments of student achievement, sound measurement depends also on the reliability of those instruments. Relevancy has to do mainly with what is measured; reliability has to do with how it is measured. No matter how relevant a measure may appear, it will be of little use—indeed, it may be better not to use it at all—if the method of measurement produces an inaccurate or distorted picture of student achievement. Reliable measurement requires a systematic sampling of the student's behavior. If the sampling is inadequate or inappropriate, the measurement that results will be biased in such a way that another somewhat different sample of the same student's behavior will yield different results. If, for example, an analysis of writing ability is based on one composition at one point in time and on one topic, it will come as no surprise to experienced teachers that the results obtained thereby may be substantially different if another estimate is based on another composition at another time. The more samples of writing obtained, the less likely is the estimate based on them to change radically when one more sample is added. The same may be said of the measurement of any skill.

Related to the need for systematic sampling is the need for equally systematic rating of the samples. Using again the example of the measurement of writing ability, every experienced teacher knows how difficult it is to apply similar standards to the examination of the writing of several different students or the writing of the same student at different points in time. In any measurement of skills where the judgment of a scorer is involved, such as in the rating scales or essay tests, it is essential that the scorer, before he begins, define in precise terms the standards that will be used to judge the performance of every student. By such a procedure, each student is rated on the same basis as every other student and the differences appearing in their performances may be said to represent student differences and not scorer differences.

The measurement of students' skills may also be less useful than desired if the situations used are too difficult or too easy for the students. For example, if the purpose of a test is to ascertain whether students have achieved a defined level of competence, the test should be constructed so as to demand, as exactly as possible, the level expected. For students who have developed the desired skills, such mastery tests will be relatively easy; for those who have not, the tests will be difficult. However, tests may also be used to diagnose or to rank students' achievement. In this situation, the test should include questions giving each student an opportunity to demonstrate the extent of his development. (If a diagnostic test is used, each of several skills is tested separately.) The first kind of test may be considered a hurdle; the second, a ladder. In the first, the test questions are deliberately fixed at a defined level of difficulty; in the second, the level of difficulty needs to be appropriate to the group so that each student can demonstrate his strengths and weaknesses. In the first, all the students may pass or fail. In the second, most students should be able to answer a few questions; a few ought to be able to answer most questions.

In all areas of education, the vital consideration is knowing why a step is undertaken and what is expected of it—and in structuring it so that the means are consistent with the reasons for undertaking it. Measurement provides the basis for the re-examination of the objectives of instruction and the restructuring of the techniques of instruction. In essence, the teacher continuously puts to the test all he knows about effecting desired changes in student behavior, and, based on what he discovers through his systematic collection and appraisal of information about the results of his previous efforts, he modifies his next effort and again studies the results.

Instructional Materials, Equipment, and Resources

TANGIBLE PROGRESS in the social studies, as in most other fields, has been both evidenced and partly caused by continuing improvement in the quality and growing variety of instructional material. Unfortunately, these resources do not automatically find their way into the classroom, and many children struggle through social studies with a bare minimum of material. More satisfactory ways must be found to provide children with accurate and adequate sources of facts and ideas about society, if the social studies are to furnish more than a cursory glance at human relationships. Meanwhile, continuing effort should be devoted to the improvement of the sources that students use in social studies. Sources of content which are simply better than yesterday are insufficient, for the world of tomorrow will demand much more and better.

The selections in this part give appropriate recognition to the merits of various instructional materials. Further, the authors make practical suggestions for utilizing such resources, and provide aids to identifying deficiencies and strengths in both the materials and uses made of them. The readings deal entirely with material that is pertinent to the content of elementary social studies: textbooks and other reading materials, audiovisuals with special attention to television, programmed materials, maps and globes, and local resources of social significance.

◄§ ENRICHING SOCIAL STUDIES WITH TRADE BOOKS
Helen Dzur

As basic material for learning, especially in such fields as elementary social studies, books are scarcely surpassed. Schooling that is based entirely on textbooks, however, can be sterile. It is, therefore, refreshing and practically valuable to find in this selection reminders of specific values that children can gain from using books in the social studies. The article provides,

*further, an excellent bibliography to aid teachers and librarians
who seek desirable reading material for pupils.*

Now THAT THE TERM "social studies" includes geography, history,
current events, economic problems, community services, citizenship,
occupations, the relation of people and places, and the study of
minority groups, trade books have become vital aids to the social
studies program. Consider for a moment how adult reading habits
coincide with the era. In these times of world crises which lead to
feelings of uncertainty and insecurity, adult reading trends have
swung toward histories, historical novels, biographies, and discussions
of scientific developments, foreign countries, and racial equality.
These reading interests of adults are reflected closely in the reading
interests of children.

It is a wise teacher who implements such interests by encouraging pupils to read widely and thoughtfully from the multitude of
trade books on the library shelves. But there is a problem which
presents itself. How can teachers keep up with the publication of
trade books to aid children in selecting them? And how can they
make worthy suggestions for purchase of books that will supplement
and enrich their program? What are some of the guidelines on which
teachers can base decisions or make recommendations of books?

If it is historical fiction, first, the story should be authentic.
The facts presented must be accurate. Second, the story must be
realistic. The characters, setting, and plots created should be as
believable as those of the present. Third, the story must be basically
interesting with details falling into a logical sequence. Fourth, the
situations or problems of the story should give a background for
current problems.

These four points should supplement the general criteria used
for the selection of any children's book: a strong theme to support
an active plot; convincing, non-stereotyped characters with faults
and problems; a distinctive style that has a natural flow of dialogue
and is not flagrantly dramatic; and a beautiful format with accurate,
colorful illustrations that complement the text.

Some teachers have serious misconceptions as to where the
teaching of social studies concepts should begin. A social studies
text is generally introduced in third grade although many schools
have a limited number of texts in first- and second-grade rooms for
reference. (The textbook is not always necessary, as most primary

© Copyright by F. A. Owen Publishing Company. Reprinted from the March,
1963 issue of *The Instructor*, 73: 99–101, by permission of the publishers. The
author is elementary library consultant in the schools of Elkhart, Indiana.

teachers realize, since much of the curriculum is built around the children's interests and daily situations.) Children are even introduced to, and become interested in, social studies learnings long before they enter school. These concepts come into a child's life as soon as he learns the street on which he lives, drops coins in his savings bank, observes a bus or a train transporting people or materials, or hears a relative speak of his travels in Europe.

Picture books with large, well-defined illustrations can do much to broaden a child's comprehension of the world around him. With this in mind, the kindergarten teacher actually begins the teaching of social studies concepts. This is why she wants a large selection of picture books to coincide with the child's interests.

Elkhart City Schools initiated a program in economic education three years ago for the primary grades. This program is totally dependent upon trade books, and units developed by school personnel, to establish such concepts as the distribution of labor, family living, community services, consumer buying, and duties of school personnel. The program has met with much success and is one of high interest to children.

As the child advances, his interests broaden. Social studies, as such, becomes a more formal part of the curriculum. The emphasis upon the study of people creates great interest in the reading of biographies. Since many biographies are appearing in series form, some caution is suggested. Often each book in a series has the same pattern of development: The hero is always a success and has few faults. Some children enjoy this oversimplification of life, and for the slow reader such a series often develops an enjoyment of reading. Teachers should guide their good readers to books that are more challenging. Frequently the challenge for the youngster is only that of trying to read every book in the series.

It might also be pointed out that an *entire* series does not have to be purchased, though usually it costs a little more to buy individual titles. Care should be exercised in the selection and use of series in the social studies program.

If your budget for social studies materials earmarks less than a third of the money to be spent for trade books, you may want to re-examine your expenditures. For they can contribute more than a third of the ideas children acquire in their reading.

Source Books

ARBUTHNOT, MAY HILL, *Children and Books*, Revised Ed. (Scott, Foresman, 1957). Covers most fields of children's literature with summaries of books within chapters. Extensive annotated bibliographies.

ARBUTHNOT, MAY HILL, and others, *Children's Books Too Good to Miss* (Western Reserve University Press, 1948).

Children's Catalog, 10th Ed. (H. W. Wilson, 1961). Yearly supplements.

Huus, Helen, *Children's Books To Enrich the Social Studies* (National Council for the Social Studies, 1961). Contains 618 carefully selected titles to fit any social studies program; suggests grade level; completely annotated.

JOHNSON, EDNA, and others, *Anthology of Children's Literature* (Houghton Mifflin, 1959).

LARRICK, NANCY, *A Teacher's Guide to Children's Books* (Charles E. Merrill, 1960). Contains a very fine chapter on social studies. Bibliographies listed according to units giving reading level for each title.

MATHES, MIRIAM SNOW, *A Basic Book Collection for Elementary Grades* (American Library Association, 1960). Bibliography lists all types of children's books but emphasis is on basic needs for small school libraries.

RUE, ELOISE, *Subject Index to Books for Intermediate Grades* (American Library Association, 1950). Lists both trade books and textbooks without annotations.

TOOZE, RUTH, *Your Children Want to Read, A Guide for Teachers and Parents* (Prentice-Hall, 1957). Describes hundreds of books with suggestions for introducing them to children.

TOOZE, RUTH, and KRONE, BEATRICE PERHAM, *Literature and Music as Resources for Social Studies* (Prentice-Hall, 1955).

Annual Publications

Best Books for Children, compiled by *Library Journal* and *Junior Libraries* (Bowker).

Recommended Children's Books, compiled by E. Louise Davis (Bowker).

Starred Books from The Library Journal, Peggy Melcher, Editor (Bowker).

❧ BIOGRAPHY AND PERSONALITY DEVELOPMENT

Ralph Adams Brown and *Marian R. Brown*

Testimonials abound to exalt the values of books, as witness the variety of favorable citations in this selection devoted specifically to biographical works. Some critics, however, question the extensive time used for reading materials, and contend that other types of resources and aids should have a larger share of the students' time. The authors of this article recognize also some recent research that questions the purported value of biography as an aid to developing readers' personalities. While

> *long tradition and widespread practice favor using biography*
> *for that purpose, teachers may well avoid uncritical acceptance*
> *and indiscriminate use of such materials.*

THE TOTAL IMPLICATIONS of Carlyle's Great Man theory of history, that history has been shaped by great personalities, seem to be generally rejected in the twentieth century. Yet down through the years teachers and biographers have frequently written on the value of biography to young people in terms of the shaping of their personality. . . .

The contribution of biography to the personality development of the student has never been adequately explored, yet we feel sure that biography can help students realize the universality of their own problems, encourage understanding of the role of cause and effect in personal development, increase understanding and appreciation of the problems facing leaders in the students' own time, and enable students to identify with, and to emulate, admirable figures from the past.

There is a real need among boys and girls of ten to fifteen for "hero worship." The preadolescent desires to *know* men and women who can be admired and respected. Arbuthnot, an authority on children's books and reading, has written "No other reading can ever quite approach the effective moral implications of a good biography. Emulation, encouragement, faith in human nature, and faith in ourselves are some of the by-products of reading such books." (1) Writing in *Century* magazine three decades ago, Gamaliel Bradford noted that the supreme educational value of biography "is for the conduct of our lives. It teaches us to understand the lives and motives of others, and nothing is more helpful to us in living our own. . . ." (2) Andre Maurois once wrote that "The cult of the hero is as old as mankind. It sets before men examples which are lofty but not inaccessible, astonishing but not incredible, and it is this double quality which makes it the most convincing of art forms and the most human of religions." (3)

In 1939, Chaffee pointed out that most adolescents need more contacts with adults (4). Certainly we know that people working in child psychology are alarmed at the increasing isolation manifested by children as they become more and more removed from the adult world. Adolescent need for identification with adult per-

Used by permission of The Social Studies; from *The Social Studies*, 54:144–148, April, 1963. Dr. Brown, of the State University of New York College at Cortland, and his wife have served as book review editors for *Social Education*.

sonalities has long been apparent to the psychologist, the psychiatrist and their fellow-workers. . . .

Kenworthy comments on this agreement among psychologists and educators that children need heroes. He suggests that in the lower grades children usually select their heroes from among the people they know, but that in the middle and upper grades, perhaps from the ages of ten to fifteen, they often choose heroes and heroines from the people about whom they read (5). . . .

A school librarian has expressed the belief that teachers frequently assign biographies to be read by their students with the idea of stimulating the student to want to succeed in life (6). Commenting that junior biographies, unlike their adult counterpart, never passed through the debunking stage, Sonneborn adds "How could they when so often their aim was to inspire young people to 'read this and do likewise?'" (7) She notes, however, that more and more junior biographies give the boy or girl readers credit for "the ability to accept and evaluate the weaknesses as well as the strengths of human beings." . . . (8)

Klee asks and partially answers a question that is very pertinent to this entire matter of personality adjustment and the value of biography in this connection. She writes (9),

> May the issue of the relative emphasis on child development and content which represents the needs of society be at least partially resolved by identifying the inherent relationships between the 'needs' and then by making the most effective use of the content of the social studies as a whole by *relating* that content—the experiences of men and women of today as well as those of other times and places—to the problems of young citizens in the middle grades in American schools?
>
> [Some] teachers . . . believe that the content of the social studies, biography for instance, can be used to help children resolve some of their own problems of personal and inter-personal relationships.

. . . Sonneborn sums up her comments on this aspect of the use of biography by noting that (10),

> In the final analysis, we must try to understand what there is about another person's life that most interests young readers and what they get out of it besides information and fleeting enjoyment. Pre-teen-agers and teen-agers, for whom most of the biographies are written, are struggling to understand themselves. Through identification with an honest portrayal of personality they can and do gain self-knowledge. . . . Young people in particular need an opportunity to share the dreams and hopes of the men and women who have

made outstanding contributions to the world. And in so doing they may go on to shape dreams and hopes of their own.

This emphasis upon personality adjustment and the creation of person-objects worthy of emulation is, of course, getting very close to the old argument that the study of biography would produce "good" persons. Most writers in this field seem to have taken for granted the desirability and usefulness of biography in this connection. Few have pointed out that the "good" person of one generation is not always the desirable person of the next. Two writers have, in the last few years, challenged the effectiveness of biography in this connection. One of these is Helen C. Lodge. She introduces her report on research in this area with the following significant comment (11):

> Numerous writers on adolescence and curriculum workers endorse biography as constituting a type of literature which adolescents like and an excellent means whereby the adolescent may find a coherent code of ethics, worthy models with whom to identify, and guidance in expanding his conceptions of personal worth. Attempts to determine empirically how or how often such changes take place in the moral ideology of the adolescent as a result of reading biography are few, probably because such phenomena are extremely difficult to measure and instruments with a high degree of validity and reliability are few.

Lodge's study was made in two California high schools, and involved six classes with a total of 160 pupils. For two and a half weeks they spent 90 minutes a day on a unit on biography. The students were checked for their attitudes, values, etc., before the unit began, at the unit's end, and eight weeks later. The students were all in the eighth grade.

Attempting to determine experimentally whether an adolescent's concept of moral character could be influenced by the reading and discussion of biography, Lodge formulated seven hypotheses. The first was: "The intensive reading and discussion of biographies would make for changes in identification in the persons reported as 'The Person I Would Like to Be Like.'"

After an evaluation of her data, Lodge came to the conclusion that all seven of her hypotheses were not justified, and that any influence on the value systems of the 160 boys and girls was very slight.

Tressa Banks and her associates worked with a group of senior high school students in an effort to test a fairly common belief (12):

If boys and girls can be taught to develop a reasoning admiration for outstanding American historical personages, they will, to a measurable degree, incorporate into their own behavior patterns some of the outstandingly desirable characteristics of these same historic personages.

The teachers working with Miss Banks devoted a semester to the experiment. They incorporated heavy doses of biography into their American history courses. . . .

At the end of the semester, Miss Banks and her associates found no evidence to support any of the hypotheses.

. . . Recently drawn conclusions that few college students change their values as a result of college work may have significance here. Perhaps the senior high school is also too late for such changes to take place readily. Lodge worked with eighth-graders. Is it also too late at that age level? The answer may be that if biography is to result in a change of values, it must be used in the middle grades of the elementary school.

Again, we may question the brevity of the period with which Lodge worked on biography. Two and a half weeks is a short period of time. Perhaps her results would have been different if the experiment had been conducted over a longer period of time. Neither do we know how effective the instruction was. Adolescents dislike being lectured to; one doesn't change their values nor arouse their admiration by directing too closely.

Three decades ago Lorenzo A. Williams conducted some research at the University of California into *The Person-Consciousness of a Selected Group of High School Pupils* (13). He concluded that "Students need to know intimate details of the saying, actions, accomplishments, weaknesses, and all problems which confronted these persons. Out of these facts they will select those experiences which they can weave into their own reaction to their world of affairs." (14) This would seem to suggest several conclusions: students need to be exposed to biography over a long period of time, and allowed to think about what they have read; students will select those ideas, qualities, values that seem to have significance to their own problems, and they will take their own time for the weaving of these into the fabric of their own personality; and finally, these writers would suggest the probability that the importance of biography in terms of personality change and value acceptance can never be measured by any objective instruments.

Sigrid Bennett suggests that (15),

. . . biographies are being rather widely used and recommended for remedial reading cases because of their therapeutic value.

Children whose reading difficulties are related to a sense of insecurity and inadequacy derive great satisfaction from learning that even some of our greatest heroes also had problems as children. This beneficial result need not be confined just to children with reading difficulties. . . . it is a good idea to remember that the best results are achieved when the child senses the kinship—not when it is spelled out for him either by the book or the teacher.

Thus Miss Bennett is suggesting that children gain confidence in themselves and a sense of security, as they read about other people and the problems that others have had, the successes others have gained.

It would seem indisputable that the use of biographical materials has value in terms of personality development. Whether such study will result in a basic change of values, or at what age such changes take place most readily, must be explored by careful scholars, working with more students and over longer periods of time than did either Lodge or Banks.

References

(1) Quoted by Mary McCrea, "Using Biography to Stimulate Reading," *The Instructor*, Nov., 1957. Vol. LXVII, No. 3, p. 89.

(2) Quoted by Robert Partin, "Biography as an Instrument of Moral Instruction," *American Quarterly*, Winter, 1956. Vol. VIII, No. 4, p. 308.

(3) *Ibid.*, p. 315.

(4) Everett Chaffee, "Adolescent Needs and the Social Studies," *Social Education*, Vol. III, p. 544. See also: J. H. van den Berg, *The Changing Nature of Man; Introduction to a Historical Psychology-Metabletica* (New York: W. W. Norton & Co., 1961). Dr. van den Berg, a Dutch psychiatrist, in a chapter titled "Neurosis and Sociosis" states that today's separation of the child from "everything belonging to the adult's life" has kept him from achieving that maturity into which in the 18th century, the child slid effortlessly during his 'teens.

(5) Leonard S. Kenworthy, "World-Minded Heroes," *Social Education*, April, 1952. Vol. XVI, No. 4, p. 163.

(6) Learned T. Bulman, "Biographies for Teen-Agers," *The English Journal*, Nov., 1958. Vol. 47, No. 8, p. 487.

(7) Ruth A. Sonneborn, "These Were Their Lives," *Saturday Review*, Jan. 21, 1961, p. 74.

(8) *Ibid.*

(9) Loretta Klee, "An Analysis of Some of the Issues" (In Loretta E. Klee, ed., *Social Studies for Older Children; Programs for Grades Four, Five and Six*. Washington: National Council for the Social Studies, 1953), pp. 26–27.

(10) Sonneborn, "These Were Their Lives," p. 75.

(11) Helen C. Lodge, "The Influence of the Study of Biography on the Moral Ideology of the Adolescent at the Eighth Grade Level," *Journal of Educational Research*, Dec., 1956. Vol. L, No. 4, pp. 241–55.

(12) Tressa Banks, *et al.*, "We Tested Some Beliefs About the Biographical Method," *The School Review*, March, 1951. Vol. LIX, No. 3, pp. 157–63.

(13) Berkeley: University of California Press, 1931. University of California Publications in Education, Vol. 6, No. 2, pp. 85–138.

(14) Paraphrased by Martha Lois Smith, "The Teaching of Biography in School and College." George Peabody College for Teachers, 1941. Doctoral Dissertation. 327 typed pp.

(15) Sigrid Bennett, "Use Biography To Help You Teach," *The Grade Teacher*, Nov., 1956. Vol. LXXIV, No. 3, p. 72.

❧ Needed: A Revolution in the Textbook Industry

Vincent R. Rogers and *Raymond H. Muessig*

The best-established of all instructional materials, the textbook, has numerous and varied critics. Many teachers join in voicing repeated criticisms of textbooks, but most of these teachers continue to use texts with their classes. Rather than looking for the impossible in texts, the authors of this selection offer a serious and fair-minded, as well as vigorous, analysis of textbooks—their contents, status, and other features. Recognizing many merits in modern texts, these analysts also forthrightly suggest improvements they believe desirable. Readers will find help in answering such questions as: What are the most fundamental defects in textbooks for elementary school social studies? Are these defects consistently found in present-day texts? What variations should be made in the contents of the textbooks? Can text material be presented in a more desirable format that is still sound, teachable, and inexpensive?

THE TEXTBOOK HAS been a part of the educational scene for a long time, and there is every reason to believe that its future is assured for some time to come. An acquaintance with the history of education and a little common sense should compel any teacher to agree that the textual source has made a significant contribution to man's knowledge yesterday and today and that it can perform a vital service tomorrow. It is true that there have been, and still are, some practices associated with the use of the textbook in the classroom which provided justification for extended wailing and

Used by permission of *The Social Studies*; from its October, 1963 issue, 54:167–170.

weeping; but it is also a fact that some creative, perceptive, intelligent teachers have made good use of this resource. In too many instances, teachers have been compelled by legislation, administrative fiat, a persisting attitude in a given community, financial conditions, lack of professional education, or other factors to stick rather closely to a single text. Proposing the elimination of the textbook as a means to correcting various abuses would be rather naive and short sighted. All of the gains which have been made in textbook publication and methodology associated with textbooks would be lost. Rather, the writers recommend that teachers and publishing houses "accentuate the positive" and try to "eliminate the negative," as the song goes. Therefore, the function of this article is to suggest some specific problems related to texts and textbook teaching and a few remedies which seem to be in order. Comments here are focused upon the *philosophy* of the textbook and its content rather than upon format or other mechanical details.

The first basic problem with many current texts is the failure to establish some clear-cut guidelines with reference to carefully identified concepts, generalizations, attitudes, appreciations, and skills. Too many texts represent merely an aggregation of names, places, dates, products, and terms appropriate to the social sciences *without leading anywhere*. Many texts seem to be trying to be all things to all people; to say most of the things which have been said so many times before with a few "new" things added; to hit some Aristotelian mean based upon a nonexistent picture of what all fifth or sixth grades are supposed to be like; and to satisfy all of the hazy objectives which may or may not be appropriate for children in the elementary grades. Even the most attractive covers and sparkling illustrations cannot cover up the fact that the *idea of one, large, all-embracing textbook is invalid*.

The solution to this problem of getting to *specific* understandings, attitudes, appreciations, and skills appropriate for *each individual* child does not reside in the practice of publishing two or even three editions of the same book where each edition tries to say about the same things in general but is adjusted by vocabulary, word count, degree of abstraction, number of supporting details, and type of related activities. This may be better than the single text in make-up but it does not remedy the problem of an underlying purpose. Even three "different" texts, published by three different houses, and chosen in such a way that one is "difficult," another "average," and a third "easy" is a dodge rather than a confrontation with the real issue. The total text is still an example of the proverbial "jack of all trades and master of none." Or, if the reader can stand a mixed metaphor for just a moment, the "complete" text bears a resemblance to an "automated cafeteria" with rows and rows of 10¢ and 25¢ vending machines. It dispenses ten cents worth of this and twenty-five cents worth of that whether the mixture is good for the consumer or not. Rather, the authors propose by way of analogy a specific, individualized, balanced, wholesome "diet" for each child composed of selected educational "foods."

Instead of a large, single text (or large graded editions of the same basic text or separate texts), the authors favor a series of small booklets. Each series of booklets would be based upon a significant topic, unit, problem, theme, generalization, or some similar over-all concern appropriate for the area of elementary social studies. A given topic might be studied for a period of from three to seven weeks depending on its importance, the needs, interests, and abilities of the children in a class, and other related factors. Children could center their attention upon from approximately seven to eleven units. Textbook publishers might offer about twenty-five topics from which teachers and children could select their limited group. Instead of publishing a single booklet for each child, the printing house would offer from four to seven booklets for each area of study. Each of the booklets would cover a different aspect of a problem, have unique content, and be planned for ranges in abilities. Each child would have something which would be meaningful to him and would have a chance to add to class discussion. Small work groups, committees, panels, symposia, and so forth could be organized around each booklet. Children would have an experience in *breadth* through sharing what they have learned in small groups with the total class and an experience in *depth* based upon the dimension of the unit which they have studied in detail. In addition, a single objective or limited group of objectives could be realized in each of the large unit experiences. One series might develop a given understanding, another a particular attitude or appreciation, and still another a specific skill or related skill. For example, one topic might serve as a vehicle for developing an ability like outlining or scanning or separating fact from opinion or finding pertinent material in the library. A second unit might reinforce the democratic attitude of respecting the dignity and worth of the individual human personality or that of balancing freedom with responsibility or that of ensuring basic human rights and equalities while protecting open opportunity for each person to achieve some measure of self-realization. A third series might facilitate the understanding of a given generalization like the one that man is both shaped by his environment and can shape aspects of his environment or that whenever men live in groups they must develop and abide by certain rules and laws. Many other examples could be given, but the point is that each series would have a clear purpose and would stimulate activities which would move children toward that purpose. Both teachers and children could see the "why" of their efforts. In the past, too many teachers have put their trust in the belief that as a result of their study of a large textbook a whole complex of things "might happen incidentally" to children. In this proposal, objectives are clear, individual differences are respected and fostered, activities would lead toward something specific, a multiple-materials approach would be assured and would lead easily to the inclusion of additional materials, and the evaluation of learning would be greatly facilitated.

If textbooks (or the smaller topical sources we have proposed) are to be improved, a second basic problem which deserves to be identified is the lack of social reality which seems to pervade so many books used by children in elementary social studies classes. Too many texts are still filled with slanted "facts," stereotypes, provincial and ethnocentric attitudes, and superficial, utopian discussions which skim over conditions as they actually exist in life today. Texts which have sections devoted to "life in our United States," for example too often portray "Americans" as white, Anglo-Saxon, Protestant, white collar, and middle class. Perusing a number of books, one gets the impression that all Americans live on wide, shady streets in clean suburban areas, occupy white Cape Cod style houses, drive new automobiles, have two children (a boy and a girl, of course) and own a dog. Characters in texts have first names like Bill, Jim, and John, rather than Sid, Tony, and Juan and last names like Adams, Hill, and Cook rather than Schmidt, Podosky, and Chen. California is a land of orange groves and sunshine, movie stars and Cadillacs, and Disneyland and Donald Duck; and books seem to gloss over the problem of non-English speaking migrant workers, smog, water shortages, crowded housing, and traffic jams. Pioneers all too often appear as the "good guys"—courageous, honest, and altruistic; while Indians are left with a counter part. When Negroes are mentioned in texts, it is more frequently in connection with the slavery issue than it is with contributions in science and technology, diplomacy, law, and education. Portraits of India in word and picture recall mendicants walking in streets where sacred cows, disease, and starvation keynote the way of life; while the inevitable tulips, windmills, and wooden shoes are associated with Holland. Other examples are not necessary. The point is that while textbooks have come some distance toward objectivity, they still have a long way to go.

Still a third reform in textbooks which seems to be indicated is the need for writers and publishers to view information as a means rather than an end, to see education as a process rather than a product, to offer a variety of open-ended data rather than just hardened conclusions, to organize content psychologically as well as logically (which too often means chronologically). Material in textbooks should be viewed as a source of stimulation and motivation, a point of embarkation, or—to borrow a current phrase—a launching pad. Textbooks should trigger a variety of classroom activities other than just assign-study-recite-test, should spark reflective and creative thought, and should cause mental and attitudinal "itches" as well as "scratching" them.

A fourth service textbook publishers can and should perform would be to offer teachers packets filled with a variety of free and inexpensive audio-visual materials to supplement the basic text. Various items to be used for bulletin boards and class scrapbooks, pictures for opaque projector, transparencies and transparent overlays for the overhead projector, filmstrips, recordings, and so forth might be included. Annotated bibliographies and supplementary academic content material would be welcomed by many teachers who feel the need to "brush up" or "beef up." Publishers might even consider sponsoring inservice workshops as an investment in the education of our young people and in good public relations with those who use their products.

Finally—and many other things could be mentioned—publishers must consider means of keeping texts up to date. While the life of bindings and papers may have been increased, little has been done to keep content fresh. Many means of replacing sections of books, adding essential chapters which were overlooked initially or which have become necessary due to changes in the world scene, and relating subject matter of a rather enduring nature to current events, could be developed.

⮜§ VITALIZING THE SOCIAL STUDIES

William H. Hartley

The need for numerous and diverse materials to provide for adequate learning about a complex and changing society may easily overwhelm the busy teacher or the school on a limited budget. Fórtunately, quite a few worthwhile materials may be obtained free or inexpensively to complement those already available to the school. Teachers can find special uses for quality audiovisuals that can be secured free or at low cost. This article identifies several examples and offers practical suggestions for using such material. Questions answered in this selection include the following: What extent and variety of free materials are available for social studies? With what kinds of topics in social studies do such materials deal? How can desirable instructional aids be selected and secured?

NEVER IN OUR HISTORY has there been a greater need for social studies instruction characterized by challenging, stimulating vitality. To meet this need, America's schools must have teachers who are able to breathe life into the learning situation. Such meaningful teaching and learning demand vigor, imagination, and careful preparation. They also require the very best available teaching materials. Some of these materials are costly and strain the limited school budget. A surprising amount of valuable learning resources is free. All that is necessary is a letter of request from the teacher. More teachers, undoubtedly, would make use of suitable free material if it were not so difficult to locate. . . .

What type of material is available to social studies teachers? There is first of all a wide variety of motion pictures which help the class to overcome the barriers of time and space. True, in many instances it would be better to take the class to visit places of interest and to see at first-hand modern processes. This desirable practice is not always possible. The time available for the education of America's youth is too limited to permit trips to all the faraway places they need to know about. Then, too, there is the considerable obstacle of expense which causes the practical teacher to turn to possible alternatives. The motion picture, as one classroom film producer expresses it, brings the world to the classroom.

. . . [There] are motion pictures of such divergent topics as Canada, our national parks, Indian life, lobster fishing, Latin America, Boston, Florida, gold mining, the various states, the Far East, nations of Europe, American industries, the armed forces, the Merchant Marine, story of great rivers, social problems, and many others.

Used by permission from *Educators Guide to Free Social Studies Materials,* Randolph, Wisconsin: Educators Progress Service, 1962, pp. x–xii. Dr. Hartley is a professor of education at Towson State College, Baltimore, Maryland.

There is scarcely a unit in the social studies that can not be vitalized through a useful free film. Most of these films run for approximately 10 to 25 minutes and fit well into the usual class period. An occasional film such as *Song of Mid-America,* which relates the growth of the area served by the Illinois Central railroad, takes 45 minutes to show. It is worth taking the entire class period to show an exceptionally good picture which may be referred to frequently during the course of a unit.

Motion pictures serve three specific phases of the learning process. First, they may be used to introduce or to motivate a unit of work. Properly presented through thought provoking questions preceding the showing, and a lively discussion following, a film will arouse interest, raise questions and send members of the class to reference books in search of further information. The thirty-one-minute color film, *Nevada and Its Natural Resources,* for example, will plunge the viewers into a worthwhile study of the problems of conserving the non-replenishable resources of the country.

Next, motion pictures contribute facts upon which generalizations may be formed. *Schools in Japan,* a film available from the Consulate General of Japan, contains a survey of the way in which children in Japan learn from kindergarten through higher education and vocational training. A fifth grade class studying geography from a world point of view, or a tenth grade World History class may profit and learn from this film presentation. The film is used here as a resource for learning facts, for developing appreciations, and for the development of observation and analysis skills.

Finally, the film may be employed as a summary or conclusion to a unit of work. A film selected for this purpose should draw together a number of the unit's main threads and weave them into a pattern which shows the situation as it exists today and perhaps gives some indication of trends. *TVA and the Nation,* a 20-minute color film, sums up the national benefits of the Tennessee Valley program and shows how strengthening a region adds to the national strength and security. This picture could well sum up a unit on rural electrification. *Mainline, U.S.A.,* could be shown at the end of a unit on transportation to stress the important job railroads perform for agriculture, industry, and trade.

Sets of slides, and filmstrips may be used to achieve many of the purposes served by the motion pictures. While they are not as dynamic as "movies" they possess the attention-attracting advantage of all projected pictures and their static nature is really a virtue when details of the picture need class attention. They stand still to be examined and discussed, and to contribute to learning. Furthermore, they are flexible. They may be held upon the screen as long as the teacher considers necessary. Also, they do not have a "canned" commentary, which makes it possible for the teacher to suit his explanation, questions and comments to the needs of the class. Filmstrips such as *You'll Find It in New Zealand* are invaluable for studying life in the land "down under." History may be enlivened with strips such as *Causes of the French Revolution, The Story of American Whaling,* and *Historical Slides of Texas.* There are also a number of slides and filmstrips which are useful in civics, problems of democracy, and elementary social studies units.

Variety is likewise brought to the classroom through the use of the many transcriptions and tapes which may be borrowed and played for the pupils. Like other multi-sensory aids to learning, these auditory aids are not just frills or frosting on the educational cake. Youngsters should and can learn from them. They will make maximum contributions to learning if they are employed like any other good resource material. The teacher should "pre-hear" them, making careful notes on possible ways of introducing them to the class and planning questions to be asked before and after the presentation to make sure that the information and ideas they contain get across to the class. Depending upon the nature of the recording, pupils will want to take notes during the playing, listen for answers to the questions, or write a summary of the main ideas after the listening experience. Some teachers have found it helpful to have a student act as a secretary and write certain information on the chalkboard as it is given on the recording. Recordings may be stopped at certain points and discussed, or certain portions may be replayed to emphasize particular points. Treat the record or tape as a flexible aid. Make each serve the purposes and needs of your class.

Further, no classroom needs to be barren and unattractive as long as suitable posters, charts, and maps may be had for the asking. These graphic devices help to brighten the classroom, create an atmosphere of interest in a topic, and in many cases, add to the knowledge about a person, place, or thing. The Aerospace Industries Association will send a chart which explains time changes around the world. The United Air Lines will give schools a set of pictures on the history of mail. The Australian Consulate distributes maps of Australia. These and other materials may be used on bulletin boards, in scrapbooks, and in pupil reports, or may be integrated into the daily lesson by the teacher. Of course such material should be chosen with care and not used just because it is free and available. Each teaching tool should be subjected to the tests of *accuracy, freedom from objectionable propaganda, technical excellence, grade level suitability,* and *contribution to the educational objectives* of the class.

The mass of available materials described in the above paragraphs, properly used, should help the cause of quality education. Pupils who have the advantage of a wide variety of learning devices should learn faster and better. Whether they will become more efficient in problem solving and in the vital skill of critical thinking depends greatly upon the skill of the teacher. But any teacher has a better chance of success if he has good, up-to-date, authoritative materials at hand.

In bringing the very best possible education to the boys and girls in our schools there is another plentiful adjunct to the textbooks which is too often neglected. It is the pamphlet, folder, or brochure which helps to bring a subject up-to-date and to supply details which can not be included in the limited pages of the text. Practically every country, through its information bureaus, makes available facts and figures concerning its people, industries, trade and tourist attractions. Trade associations, chambers of commerce, and publicity bureaus are glad to send out fact sheets concerning cities, states, businesses and various "causes." The National Education Association, for example, will send you copies of *"How to Write a Letter to Your Congressman."* The Veterans of Foreign Wars National Headquarters publish and distribute a booklet on *"Etiquette of the Stars and Stripes."* The Office of the Commonwealth of Puerto Rico supplies schools with a leaflet of *"Facts About Puerto Rico."* The list of such materials is quite extensive.

Many school libraries keep a pamphlet file for pupils and teachers. A classroom library of pamphlets also makes good pedagogical sense. Some teachers keep a reading table in the room on which a display of supplementary reading materials is kept temptingly before the students. Outstanding leaflets are often fastened to the bulletin board and make that display space a place of active learning. A very successful social studies teacher hangs pamphlets, articles and similar materials from a wire fastened just underneath the chalkboard ledge. Students are most likely to take advantage of the opportunities such materials offer if they are within ready reach.

The urgent needs of our nation, referred to at the beginning of this article, call for a well-educated and able citizenry. The social studies teacher can ill afford to overlook promising materials or practices. The wise and judicious use of free materials will add vitality to the educative process, enhance learning, bring variety into lessons, and help to produce better educated citizens. But they are not a panacea. They will not do the job unaided. Such materials do not replace the text or the teacher. They complement and extend the other resources in the learning environment.

ᛋ THE CHANGING SOCIAL STUDIES CURRICULUM— WHAT DOES IT MEAN FOR AV?

John P. Lunstrum,
Maxine M. Dunfee, and Beryl B. Blain

During the past generation audiovisuals have assumed an increasingly large role in schooling. This is especially true of the motion picture film. Now additional types of audiovisuals are appearing. Teachers will find helpful this summary of major audiovisual aids to more effective learning in social studies. The article also provides selected, specific examples of each type of audiovisual material. Pertinent to the uses of advancing audiovisuals in the changing social studies are the following questions dealt with in this article: What audiovisuals best reflect contemporary social development? How can audiovisuals best be used in relation to current changes in the social studies curriculum and instruction?

SINCE WORLD WAR II, audiovisual materials produced for the social studies have increased in great numbers. A glance through publications listing these materials shows a wide variety of subjects on every grade level. Some lists indicate the correlation of audiovisual materials with units of work or with portions of the textbook. Although technological advances make it difficult for the AV producer to keep abreast of changes, these advances also provide the means.

When present-day events produce new focal points of interest, these focal points are reflected in the media. In the study of countries, the point of emphasis today is the emerging African nations.

Reprinted from the October, 1961 issue of *Audiovisual Instruction*, pp. 381–386. Used by permission of the authors and the Department of Audiovisual Instruction, a department of the National Education Association. All three of the co-authors hold positions in teacher education at the Indiana University.

Newer film and filmstrip titles, such as *Nigeria—Giant of Africa*, reflect this emphasis. (A precautionary note is sounded here, lest in the race to keep abreast, we sacrifice quality for the sake of keeping up to date.)

If more school systems develop units of study bearing on the culture concept, materials will be developed on all grade levels to bring about these understandings. A start has been made in this direction with *People Are Taught To Be Different*, a series of kine-scoped television programs which is being distributed to adult and college groups by the National Educational Television Film Service.

When new approaches are taken to the way in which subject-matter is organized for presentation, this, too, will produce media oriented toward this newer organization. Some producers are already experimenting in this direction. Several years ago *World Without End* was produced under the auspices of UNESCO. This film compares Occidental and Oriental civilizations to make the point that the needs and aspirations of peoples around the world are not too different. More recently, a four-part film, *Four Families*, shows certain aspects of child care in a Japanese, Indian, Canadian, and French family and relates child care to the development of national character. Although some comparisons are made, more is left to the audience's own interpretation. The effect of modernization on cultures is treated in *New Lives for Old* and *The Fisherman*.

MOTION PICTURES

The advent of the 8mm sound motion picture, which some film producers view as a means to reduced production costs, should stimulate production of shorter films similar to *Four Families* in content structure, with each presenting a single concept. Such materials will help to eliminate the too frequent criticism that content is not representative of life in a given country.

In order to give the teacher flexibility in using filmstrips, some producers make a series treating a single country. An example is *The Republic of India: A Regional Study*, consisting of such titles as *The Historic Background*, *The People of India*, *Natural Resources and Government*, and so on. The International Communications Foundation and other organizations are producing kits of audiovisual materials for the social studies. The kit on Iran, for example, has a set of filmstrips, colored study prints with explanatory captions, artifacts, a phono book and record, a teacher's study guide, and supplemental literature. Similar kits have been assembled for Turkey, Pakistan, and Afghanistan. Filmstrip series and teaching kits of this type make it possible for the teacher to use a topical approach to the study of individual countries as well as the customary regional approach. With reduced costs, motion pictures, too, may follow such patterns.

Another pattern of content organization is the "open-ended" material, designed to stimulate finding answers rather than giving them. Information given in these open-ended materials could be centered around problem-solving situations. For example, several series of materials, each demonstrating past colonial structures of the new African nations could provide clues as to why some have pro-Communist leanings and others not.

Today, technological advances have made it possible to record a moment of history as it occurs, as for instance, the film and TV coverage of the recent astronaut flights into space. Because much of history was made before recording devices were invented, it is necessary to re-create many such moments. Film, and TV whether live or recorded, not only bring the past to life, but carry a great impact of reality. These same devices can also be used to preserve the record of a country that is rapidly being lost in modernization efforts.

Reconstructed historical sites and historical museums provide excellent sources for the study of American historical and cultural development. With travel on the increase, these sites provide first-hand experiences as well as background for the production of authentic materials. Children as well as adults often carry their own cameras on these excursions, and the teacher usually finds that she can draw upon the resources of her pupils and patrons as well as upon her own resources and those of her colleagues. A boom in school tours has also resulted from this national interest in preserving the past.

As more people recognize their importance, reconstructions and restorations can be expected to increase both through private and governmental financing. For example, the village of Appomattox Court House is being restored under *Mission 66*, a program of the National Park System (Department of the Interior). Through the National Capital Parks, a division of the National Park System, the old Chesapeake and Ohio Canal has been partially restored, permitting visitors to take summer tours in an old-time, mule-drawn barge. Colonial Williamsburg is a classic example of restoration through private funds.

TELEVISION

Television, of course, plays a major role in on-the-spot viewing of important current events and out-of-school viewing of special programs pertinent to the social studies curriculum. Kinescopes make possible the use of these programs for more careful classroom examination and for study at more appropriate times than the original telecast. Programs such as *Face the Nation, NBC Reports,* and *Meet the Press* not only bring a body of useful background knowledge but also provide up-to-the-minute news coverage.

Most experts will agree that educational television as a direct teaching method calls for further experimentation before its full potential can be realized. The social studies curriculum offers vast opportunities to test the ETV medium as a means of developing powers of reflective thinking and skills in problem solving. One type of TV lesson for government and civics classes can be patterned after the "pro and con" type of network program, drawing on local resources to present varying viewpoints of a community problem. This type of program can provide the stimulation for numerous problem-solving and reflective-thinking activities, and like the open-ended film, stimulate students to search for answers rather than to passively accept them.

Besides the film, filmstrip and TV program, other kinds of visual materials are increasing in number and taking on new dimensions, as evidenced, for example, in the advertisements of map and globe manufacturers. Rainfall maps, thermal maps, polar projection maps, slated globes, raised relief globe sections, and especially designed satellite orbit demonstrator globes are cases in point. Some geographers see advantages in globes that are constructed with interlocking parts like a jigsaw puzzle so that they can be disassembled for purposes beyond the customary use.

The application of mass production techniques to transparencies can affect pictorial representations in charts, maps, and textbook illustrations. For example, a basic map of the United States with a series of preceding transparencies, each showing a later territorial expansion, would provide for easier comparison than several series of maps with each devoted to a different territorial acquisition. Some reference materials and teaching manuals are already using this technique.

WESTERN TV PROGRAMS AND ELEMENTARY SOCIAL STUDIES   *J. D. McAulay*

Instructional use of television has thus far concentrated on educational television (ETV) programs. Commercial television broadcasts have found only limited use in schools. Quite a number of commercial programs, however, relate to topics that pupils study in social studies. Among such programs, the "westerns" predominate. This selection reports the results of a study in which almost a thousand school children answered questions about their reactions to "western" programs. The author judges that television "westerns" do aid in developing children's understanding of the westward movement. But it is not clear that the questions on that topic listed at the end of the article were used in this investigation, or, if they were, how answers were appraised.

A TOTAL OF 973 third-, fourth-, fifth-, and sixth-grade children answered the questionnaire that furnished the raw data for this report. These children came from two different communities: 470 from Community A, a professional residential area; 503 from Community B, which depended, economically, upon a steel mill. Since the two communities had different socio-economic backgrounds, it was assumed that the children of Community A might secure somewhat different understandings from TV Westerns than the children from Community B. As to grade distribution, 227 children were in the third and fourth grades, 746 in the fifth and sixth grades.

One purpose of the questionnaire was to determine what TV Westerns children preferred, and why. Another purpose was to discover to what extent, if any, the TV programs contributed to the children's knowledge and understanding of the Western movement. The questionnaire contained seven questions:

1. Do you have a TV set at home?
2. What is your favorite Western TV program?
3. Give a reason why this is your favorite Western TV program.
4. How many Western TV programs do you think you watch in one week?
5. Who is your favorite Western TV actor?
6. Name some things you have learned from Western TV programs about the pioneers who moved to the Western territories.
7. Why would you like to have been a pioneer going to the West?

Ninety children in the classrooms selected for this study reported that they did not have TV sets in their homes.

The children's preferences generally followed the adult pattern (1). *The Rifleman*, first choice with the children, stood fourth

Used by permission of the author and the National Council for the Social Studies; from *Social Education*, 24:169–171, April, 1960.

in the Nielson TV rating. *Wagon Train* was second choice with the children, second also in the Nielson rating. *Maverick*, the children's third choice, was rated fifth by Nielson. *Have Gun Will Travel*, fourth in popularity with the children, stood third with the adults. *Gunsmoke*, fifth choice of the children, secured the top place in the Nielson rating.

The popularity of TV personalities paralleled the popularity of the programs. Chuck Connors of *The Rifleman* received the largest number of votes from all four grades, with James Garner of Maverick a close second. This would indicate that there is a close correlation between a highly popular personality and the popularity of the program on which that personality appears. (It is interesting to note that those children in the third, fourth, fifth, or sixth grades whose preferences for both programs and personalities fell outside the group concentrations had I.Q. scores of 118 or higher.)

There seemed to be no significant difference in program preference between third- and fourth-grade children as compared to fifth- and sixth-grade children, except in the echelons of popularity, nor between children of Community A as compared to children of Community B. Seemingly third- and fourth-grade children have difficulty distinguishing the principal actor (or performer) on a Western TV program from the program itself, since 20 percent of the children confused the name of a performer with that of a program, indicating the total action of the program made more impression than the individual parts.

Fifth- and sixth-grade children from Community A (the professional community) viewed nine programs per week as a mean average, compared to a mean average of 14 in Community B (the industrial community). Third and fourth graders viewed four Western TV programs as a mean average per week. There was no appreciable difference between third- and fourth-grade children of one community as compared to another in the number of Western TV programs viewed. These figures are considerably less than those indicated by some authorities (2).

Answering the query as to why a particular Western TV program was popular, fifth and sixth graders indicated such reasons as: I like the way the hero handles his gun (80 votes); the program is humorous and comical (67 votes); the program has thrills and excitement (56 votes); the program is entertaining and has plenty of action (53 votes); I like the way he shoots his gun (33 votes); it is full of action (27 votes).

Fifth- and sixth-grade children preferred a particular TV Western program mainly because of its entertainment value, but third- and fourth-grade children preferred a particular Western TV program mainly because of a specific action. However, the reasons given by third and fourth graders for preferring a particular program, although fewer in number, were not too different from those given by fifth and sixth graders. Children in Community B were more specific in their reasons for preference of a particular program than were the children of Community A.

Asked to name some of the things they had learned from Westerns, fifth and sixth graders listed such understandings as: the Western pioneer had Indian trouble (167 children); the pioneers had many hardships (165 children); pioneers had to join together to protect themselves (164 children); epidemics often wiped out a wagon train or settlement (162 children). Third and fourth graders listed such understandings as: not the same kind of houses, clothes, food, and guns as we have today (72 children); never point a gun because guns are dangerous (63 children); many Westerners had to know how to drive cattle and round up horses (43 children).

Children in the fifth and sixth grades seemed to have secured from Western TV programs a depth of understanding of the day-to-day life of the pioneers, their food, means of transportation, clothing, amusements, difficulties, dangers, and hardships. There seemed to be no significant difference between boys and girls, between children of Community A and Community B (in the fifth and sixth grades) as to what was learned of the Western movement.

The number of understandings of the Western movement secured by third- and fourth-grade children from Western TV programs were not so many or so complex as those secured by fifth- and sixth-grade children—nor were they so accurate (16 children, or 3.5 percent, believed pioneers liked to shoot people) but they were more concrete and realistic.

The mean number of understandings of the Western movement secured by fifth- and sixth-grade children from Western TV programs was 5. The mean number of understandings secured by third and fourth graders was 2.

Fifth- and sixth-grade children, when asked why they would like to have been pioneers, indicated the following reasons: would have been allowed to have a horse (208 children); always something exciting happening (170 children); allowed to shoot a gun (168 children); could fight off Indians (167 children). Seventy-one third- and fourth-grade children indicated they would like to have been pioneers because they could have driven horses, 35 because they could have fought Indians, 28 because they could have used a gun.

However, 111 fifth and sixth graders would not like to have been pioneers because there were no conveniences, 63 because the pioneers had to work too hard, another 63 because they had no law, 57 because it was too easy to be killed. Forty-three third- and fourth-grade children decided they would not like to have been pioneers because it took too long to get any place; 20 because life was hard; 18 because Indians were always attacking.

Children seemed to have secured a sympathy for and an empathy with the pioneers through viewing Western TV programs. Although the main reasons for such sympathy and empathy may be personal (the desire to own a horse), many children seemed to have secured an understanding of the difficult but adventurous life of the Western pioneer. Third- and fourth-grade children gave reasons for wanting to be a pioneer concerned with personal action. Fifty percent of the girls of Community A, by indicating they would not like to have been pioneers, realized the difference in ease and convenience between modern life and that of the Western pioneer.

Did the lessons the children learned from watching Westerns on TV have any relationship to what they learned about the Western movement in their classrooms?

One way to answer the question is to measure what the pupils learned from TV against a list of specific questions such as those listed below. It is reasonable to assume that these questions point to the minimum knowledge and understanding a fifth-grade pupil should acquire from an organized unit on the Western movement.

1. How did the United States get the lands west of the Mississippi River?
2. Who settled in various parts? Where did they come from?
*3. How did the people from the East travel to the Western lands?
4. Why did the United States want more land?
*5. How did the people make a living in the early West?
*6. Why did the early people of our land want to move to the West?
7. Who sent Lewis and Clark to explore the Oregon country? Why were they sent?
8. Why did the new settlers follow the path blazed by Lewis and Clark?
9. Why did the discovery of Gold in California increase the population of the West? What are the ways in which we can still see this influence?
10. Who first settled the West coast? Where did they come from?
11. What routes did the Forty-niners use? Why?
*12. How did the miners of that time live? What did the term "The Golden West" mean?

After examining the answers the children gave to the questionnaire, it was evident that they (particularly the fifth and sixth graders) had learned enough from their TV experiences to answer those questions, in part at least, checked with an asterisk. It is important to note, however, that the questions which the children did *not* answer accurately were those requiring a larger knowledge of history or geography than they evidently possessed.

Since children spend a substantial amount of time watching Westerns, and since out of this experience they do acquire a certain amount of knowledge and understanding of the Western movement, teachers organizing and working in the classroom with units on the Western movement would do well to build upon the children's experiences, developing understandings in geography and history which the TV programs, with their emphasis upon plot and action and entertainment, do not attempt to develop.

References

(1) *Time Magazine.* March 30, 1959. p. 52.

(2) Paul Witty and Henry Bricker. "Your Child and Radio, TV, Comics, and Movies." Chicago, Ill.: Science Research Associates, 1952.

⊷§ Does Television Help Us?   *John R. Palmer*

This selection contrasts with the favorable report in the preceding article, providing a critical analysis of children's television viewing. The author does not regard present television practices as conducive to preparation for the kind of adult society needed in a democracy. His article, based on a number of useful studies, provides answers to such questions as the following: How extensive is children's viewing of television? What types of programs do they chiefly watch, and what types do they generally ignore? To what extent does children's selection of television programs contribute to their learning about society? Is the understanding they gain sufficiently realistic and accurate?

Used by permission of the author and the National Council for the Social Studies; from *Social Education*, 25:361–363, November, 1961. Dr. Palmer is a professor of education at the University of Illinois.

POWERFUL AND AFFLUENT forces are promoting educational television, and educators across the country are probing into the wonders and mysteries of its teaching potential. Our concern here, however, is with the type of television which is already firmly established—public commercial television. This is no longer new, strange, and wonderful, for most children and adults have come to accept it as a part of normal living. Commercial television has served and will continue to serve as an educational device for the majority of youngsters. It is the bearing on social studies teaching of this unplanned and largely unconscious educational influence that we wish to examine. The many research studies which deal with television as a significant social and cultural phenomenon provide the stimulus for these observations (1).

The statistics related to television viewing have been widely reported, but they are still rather startling. Eighty percent of all children in this country are regular users of television by the time they reach kindergarten, and the figure goes to 90 percent during first grade. Children average over two hours a day with their electronic companion. From age 11 through 13, the peak years, viewing averages over three hours a day. No other mass media commands nearly this much attention. It consumes one-sixth of the child's waking hours, and during the first 16 years of life the total time devoted to television is greater than that spent in school (2).

Obviously this is an enormous commitment of time to one activity for a child. The significance of these figures, however, is in their qualitative dimension. Television has to be considered along with the home and the school as a major influence on the social development of the child. Nationally it is certainly the chief source of common experience for children.

The television fare available is very diverse with a wide variety of programs being offered during the long television day and on the several stations operating in most densely populated areas. The first two weeks of April, 1961, to select a brief period at random, one could have seen shows devoted to the Eichmann case, time-lapse photography of animal and plant life, a Leonard Bernstein concert, Russian films of oceanic life, a dramatization of some of Lincoln's wartime problems, and many regularly scheduled news and current affairs reports. The potential instructional value of these television presentations is obvious. But there is one serious difficulty. According to the studies that have been made of viewing habits, most children simply don't turn the dial to shows of this type. Their overwhelming favorites are children's variety shows, adventure programs, Westerns, situation comedy, crime programs, and the like (3). Schramm, Lyle, and Parker, after analyzing these shows that consistently rank high with four-fifths of our children, conclude that they consist chiefly of fantasy materials. "Reality material"—material related to public affairs, fine arts, and serious attempts to understand the world about us—is available on television but it is not sought out by most children or adults (4).

It appears that children watch television primarily for "the passive pleasure of being entertained, living a fantasy, taking part vicariously in thrill play, identifying with exciting and attractive people, getting away from real-life problems and escaping real-life boredom." (5) Such activity promotes the withdrawal of the child from the life around him, escape from the private or public problems of the day, and passive behavior. Undoubtedly this meets certain needs of children or they would not spend their time in this manner. They crave fantasy, and they readily assert that they want more of the same. It is difficult for them to imagine television offering them anything else.

Children do learn from television. However, because of the nature of the programs they watch and their reasons for watching them, most of this is incidental learning not consciously sought after. The vocabulary level of the young child is increased considerably through television, although this advantage is lost after a few years of schooling. Grooming, styles of dress, and many personal mannerisms are picked up. Undoubtedly children acquire from television many of their ideas and stereotypes about frontier America, criminals, law enforcement, social justice, sex roles both in and out of the family situation, the activities of the social elite, and a number of other things. In the great bulk of cases, however, this information is acquired incidentally and in a context of fantasy.

Research indicates that relatively few children go to television in search of information (6). They conclude very early that books, newspapers, and magazines are informative while television is entertaining. This would be merely an interesting item of information if it were not for the fact that most children devote themselves so overwhelmingly to the picture tube as compared to the printed page. Only about one-fifth of our children appear to be "reality oriented" in their selection of television shows. That is, this number tend to watch the shows that are centered in realistic materials and situations, invite cognition and activity, and continually refer the viewer to problems of the real world. However, unless an educational channel is available, virtually no shows of this type are shown during the late afternoon and early evening (except for brief news reports) when children are most apt to be viewing. This prime time for children consists of a series of exciting and fast moving fantasy presentations with large doses of broad humor, romance, and violence.

A primary aim of social science and history is to portray the world both past and present in all of its actuality—to present the truth of the matter to the extent that our intellectual skills and research tools permit. It would be foolhardy to contend that we are as yet able to present such a world view, but it continues to be our goal.

In any time and place, children come to school equipped with a large complement of facts, concepts, and generalizations about their world together with an accompanying value syndrome. They have a certain understanding of their social environment and cultural heritage which has been picked up at home, on the playground, in church, and elsewhere. Some of this material is in accord with the best knowledge available; much of it is not. A fundamental objective of social studies teaching is to replace the folklore students have acquired through informal learning with social science knowledge in those areas where the two are in conflict. Even where there is no conflict, a careful examination of the grounding of a belief or attitude now taken at its face value often proves instructive. In a diffuse and frequently confused culture such as ours, the teacher must stand firmly on scholarship and research whenever possible or risk being pulled apart by the shifting currents of public opinion, the pressures of group interest, and the tribal myths passed on from generation to generation.

If the research into the television viewing habits of children has accurately appraised the situation, it appears that most children now acquire heavy and repeated doses of social folklore via the fantasy material they seek out and consume. They do learn occasional bits of information about social reality, but these are usually highly fragmentary and difficult for the naive child to relate to his environment.

Every normal child and adult craves imaginative literature, daydreaming, and other forms of escape from time to time. The disturbing things about the current situation are the degree to which children seem to be given over to escape and the influence this may have on our future as a society. One does not have to accept Toynbee's theory of challenge and response to believe that societies continually face difficult problems which demand wise solutions if the vigor of the society is to be maintained. Social action and social responsibility in a democracy rest with the masses of the people. It is not enough for a few to be reality oriented. If Mannheim's analysis of the increasing difficulty of any individual being able to bring the total society into focus is correct, then the task of orienting each potential citizen is becoming increasingly difficult. However, democracy, at least as we have traditionally conceived it in this country, demands it.

It is quite probable that children are only reflecting adult attitudes and apprehensions when they seek escape. Television is rarely cited as the cause of such tendencies. It merely provides an inexhaustible and easily accessible source of fantasy experiences. But whatever the reasons, it is imperative that social studies teachers assess the situation carefully. Dealing with the misconceptions and lack of understanding of social reality that children carry about with them is largely the burden of the schools under present circumstances. The problem is a perennial one, but commercial television appears to be making it more difficult.

Some writers have expressed concern over the fact that youngsters may be forced to "look life in the eye" too early because of television and classroom discussions of such things as crime probes, racial violence, totalitarian oppression, and the threat of war and atomic annihilation (7). Of course, it is possible to destroy faith without rebuilding, to project the feeling that nothing can be counted on anymore. But the purpose of teaching and learning knowledge verified by scientific procedures is not to destroy myth for the sake of destruction but for the sake of building. Neither a nation nor an individual can function in a constructive manner if he is out of touch with reality. Try as we will, wishing will not make it so.

If one really must choose between the dangers that may be associated with prolonged escapism and those associated with an early introduction to "real life," the latter seems much the better risk. And the risk is slight indeed if the teacher is a mature, intelligent individual.

It appears that the child in our culture now uses commercial television in such a way that it prolongs his infancy, encourages his withdrawal from current problems rather than participation in their solution, promotes the learning of social folklore, and encourages acceptance rather than critical thinking. All these tendencies go counter to the aims of social science teaching and make the task of the teacher increasingly difficult.

References

(1) For those interested in exploring the research, an excellent annotated bibliography of many important studies is included in Wilbur Schramm, Jack

Lyle, and Edwin B. Parker, *Television in the Lives of Our Children*. Stanford, California: Stanford University Press, 1961.

(2) W. J. Clark. *Of Children and Television*. Ohio: Xavier University, 1951, passim; Schramm, *op. cit.*, passim; Jack Greenstein, "Effects of Television Upon Elementary School Grades," *Journal of Educational Research*, 48: 161–76; 1954; Paul A. Witty, "School Children and Television. Summary of the Results of Ten Yearly Studies of Children's Television Viewing in the Chicago Metropolitan Area." Distributed by the Television Information Office, New York, 1960.

(3) Hilde Himmelweit, A. N. Oppenheim, and Pamela Vince. *Television and the Child*. London: Oxford, 1958. Chapter 9. Published for the Nuffield Foundation; Schramm, *op. cit.*, p. 37–45; Witty, *op. cit.*

(4) Schramm, *op. cit.*, p. 60–69. Similar analyses are given in Eleanor E. Maccoby, "Why Do Children Watch Television?" *Public Opinion Quarterly* 18: 239–44; 1954; and Lottie Bailyn, "Mass Media and Children: A Study of Exposure Habits and Cognitive Effects," *Psychological Monographs* 73: 1–48; 1959.

(5) Schramm, *op. cit.*, p. 57.

(6) Schramm, *op. cit.*, p. 76.

(7) A recent example: Dorothy Barclay. "Children Who Grow Old Too Young." *The New York Times*, Magazine Section. July 16, 1961, p. 26.

✑ History by Television   *Joseph F. Hannan*

> *Can the teacher compete with television performers? This additional competency may eventually be thrust upon even the unwilling teacher in an era when the average child views more than twenty hours weekly of commercially sponsored television programs. Because quite a number of television programs have themes or settings of social significance, what the children get from these broadcasts has much import for the teacher of social studies. Here Hannan reports on the matter in his characteristically humorous style.*

Before you attempt to teach a Science lesson on the birth of a hurricane you must remember that you're in competition with Dr. Frank Baxter and Richard Carlson reinforced by a whole platoon of cartoon characters. The classroom teacher must suffer by comparison to such a cast.

But the problem of dramatics or the lack of them is secondary to the problems confronting History teachers. History is by definition a systematic record of past events. History, in so far as we can judge, is based on truth as recorded through the ages. Television history is another matter.

In the interest of selling more cigarettes or deodorant, the television writer resorts to the "based on" technique. As an example we'll take the undisputable fact of Paul Revere's ride. This historically valid seed must be expanded into a one-hour show. "The story as it stands wouldn't make a bad poem," mused the writers. "But we'll have to jazz it up a little if we want that spot on the 'Important Events in American History' program."

So they set out to make the story a little more "gutty," that is, they ring in sex. Ignoring Paul's marital status at the time of the ride, they give him a girl in Concord. Also this girl is being wooed by a captain in the British regulars. So Paul's ride, although ostensibly patriotic, is really done for much more basic reasons.

Paul comes in the back door of the girl's house as the redcoat captain enters the front. Then a scene ensues in which the dastardly acts of the dastardly British are pointed out. A fist fight follows. It would seem that swords would make a better scene but the writers' historical integrity is inviolate. Research has shown that Paul rode without sword and he won't be given one for the sake of drama. After a three-minute sequence in which every antique in the house is shattered, Paul lays the lobsterback low with a well-aimed pewter tankard. Then, amid a hail of bullets from arriving British infantry (the captain's amatory impatience causing him to lead his troops by a good few blocks), Paul and his girl, riding double on his wind-broken but gallant steed, make for Boston. They arrive just in time for the war bond kickoff banquet at the Old North Church which had been delayed because some prankster had hung every one of the Church's lanterns in the belfry. As the story ends Paul and his girl are being married in defiance of the British imposed three-day waiting period then mandatory in Massachusetts.

After that little story, the textbook version of Paul's ride seems drab even to the teacher, but in an attempt to rescue something, you question those who were lucky enough to see "Important Events in American History." "What did you think of Paul Revere?"

Everyone's eager to answer. "He was great. Did you see him bop that guy with the beer mug?"

"Yeah. And how about at Concord when he jumped off the barn that was on fire onto his horse! Wow!"

You try to steer things your way. "How about what happened at Lexington?" Blank stares till finally someone remembers.

"Oh yeah, that's where his horse lost the shoe and the blacksmith was a Story or Lory or something and Paul knocked him through the window onto the water wheel and down he went into the lake."

You nod. "Yes, that happened but how about the other thing at the bridge. You know when the farmers stood up to all those British soldiers. What did you think of those farmers?"

"They looked pretty corny to me, no uniforms or nothin'."

"Hey," chimes in another, "how about those British uniforms with the white strap. They were keen!"

"You shoulda seen it on my color set, red coats and all! Boy!"

You see what we teachers are up against? Wagon trains which took two months to cross the Great Plains back in the 1880's now take thirty-two weeks with an occasional time out for a special feature. The Alamo rises and falls; Richard the Lion-Hearted shuttles back and forth between England and the Holy Land and every battle of the Civil War is reworked, its ending changed according to the birth state of the writer. So far television has confined itself to historical mutilation and has steered clear of other subjects. Still, if the shortage of material gets any more acute, the writer may feel a need to tamper with Math or Spelling.

"Let's throw a saddle on this and see how it rides. Everyone knows that two and two are four. But suppose—just suppose someone finds out that two and two are five. Get the significance here. Every calculation made by man since the beginning of time is off by one. See the picture? Now here's the . . ."

I've heard of an opening in a one-room school up near Hudson's Bay. It only pays eleven hundred skins a year (usually beaver) but I'm considering the idea.

◄§ PROGRAMMED INSTRUCTION AND THE TEACHING OF SOCIAL STUDIES SKILLS   *Lauren B. Resnick*

Automated learning materials may be considered reading materials as properly as they may be classified as audiovisuals. It is nonetheless important to consider this resource, however classified. Most of the limited writing on programming for social studies has stressed material for developing understanding of concepts. Therefore this selection, concentrating on the programmed development of social studies skills, is practically unique. The article also reports on the general nature

*of programming and its present status in the social studies.
Because of space limitations, the illustrative material in the
original article has been omitted. Readers may wish to consult
it and to note the annual review of programmed materials
for social studies that appears in* Social Education *each winter.*

FEW OF THE CURRICULAR and technological innovations of the past
several years have been the subject of as much interest and debate
as "programmed instruction" and "teaching machines." Some advocates of automated instruction have claimed that the techniques
of programing could and should be applied in all curricular areas,
and that such application could be expected to revolutionize education. Others have been more cautious in their claims; while some
educators have been altogether skeptical about the possibility or advisability of programing any but the most routine kind of material.

Until recently, social studies teachers have been involved only
peripherally in this debate, for the very simple reason that few attempts to program social studies material had yet been made. For
example, only seven social studies programs were listed in *Programs,
'62* (1). Similarly, NEA's 1962 paper on programmed instruction devoted only 1 page out of a total of 19 pages of program listings to
the social studies (2). The situation is now beginning to change,
however, and we can expect in the next few years to see more and
more social studies programs becoming available commercially, as
well as more attempts on the part of school systems and other
educational groups to prepare programed materials in the social
studies.

In light of these developments, several questions concerning
programed instruction are pertinent for social studies teachers to
consider. First, how adaptable are the techniques of programed
instruction to the social studies field? More particularly, are the
techniques appropriate to the teaching of social studies skills; and
if so, what kinds of skills can be most easily handled? Finally, to
what extent can school systems or individual classroom teachers
expect to be successful in writing their own programs rather than
depending upon commercially prepared materials?

Used by permission of the author and the National Council for the Social Studies;
from its Thirty-Third Yearbook, *Skill Development in Social Studies,* 1963, pp.
252–273. Dr. Resnick is a lecturer in the Office of Research and Evaluation, City
University of New York.

NATURE OF PROGRAMMED INSTRUCTION

. . . Programed instruction may be considered an attempt to approximate without a live teacher certain critical features of good tutorial instruction. The fundamental condition of such tutorial instruction is continual interchange between an individual student and his teacher. Participating in this exchange, the student is always active, his attention always on the task at hand because he is asked to respond at every step. The teacher, for his part, is closely "tuned" to the student, speeding up or slowing down as the student does, framing his questions and explanations so that the student will be able to respond appropriately, prompting and encouraging where necessary. As a result of continual exchange with his teacher, the student always knows where he is, never waiting more than a moment or two to learn whether his responses are correct. What is more, the student is likely to be correct most of the time; for effective tutorial instruction does not present the student with a difficult problem and leave him to his own devices. Instead, it attempts to help him along, step by step, each step building on the last, until he is able to solve the more difficult problems or perform the more complex skills.

In approximating the features of tutorial instruction, a self-instructional program breaks down the material to be taught into small units, generally called "frames." Each frame of a program presents some information or other material and then requires that the student respond to the material in some way. Having responded, the student is immediately informed concerning the accuracy of his answer or he is presented with the correct answer, which he compares with his own. Only after this evaluation does he go on to the next frame, always proceeding through the program at his own pace. A "teaching machine" is no more than a device for presenting these frames one after another, exposing the correct answer only after the student has made his own response, and maintaining a record of the student's responses at each step. There are on the market and in experimental use a very large number of teaching machines, ranging from simple mechanical devices (the machines most widely in use) to elaborate electronic mechanisms that automatically choose the next frame for presentation according to the student's response. In addition, there are "programed texts," in which programs are bound in ordinary book covers (3). Thus, programed instruction does not necessarily involve the use of elaborate equipment, although the use of machines, as opposed to paper-and-pencil forms of instruction, sometimes offers an important measure of control over the student's behavior. In any case, it is the quality of the program, not the nature of the presentation device, that will ultimately determine the effectiveness of programed instruction. . . .

SPECIFICATION AND ANALYSIS OF SOCIAL STUDIES SKILLS

. . . In keeping with the psychologist's definition of learning as an observable change in behavior, terms such as "understanding," "comprehension," and "knowledge" must be redefined by specifying the behaviors performed by the child as he gives evidence that he understands, comprehends, or knows. In addition, the stimuli, or appropriate occasions, for each of the behaviors must be specified. Such a detailed set of statements about a student's behavior in very specific situations constitutes a set of "behavioral specifications" for a program (4). The techniques of programed instruction will be applicable to the social studies only insofar as behavioral specifications of this kind can be set forth for the various skills and concepts one is interested in teaching.

Programed instruction relies for the development of its teaching procedures on an analysis of the behaviors to be taught such that each of the smaller units of behavior that contribute to or constitute the desired "terminal behavior" is specified. Beginning with a behaviorally stated objective, this analysis asks what other things a child must be able to do in order to do what is stated as the terminal behavior. Five or six sub-behaviors may be identified in this way. For each of the sub-behaviors, the same question is then asked. Using this procedure, it is possible to generate a set of "nesting" behavioral specifications in which several smaller units of behavior serve as components of a larger one, and the behaviors become less and less complex as one describes smaller and smaller units. This analysis will to a great extent serve to determine the nature and ordering of the teaching process. Students will not be asked to perform the more complex behaviors until it is certain that they can perform the simpler component behaviors. The simpler behaviors, depending upon the students, may be either assumed or taught. Teaching begins with the simplest behavior that is not assumed, and proceeds through the "nests," or levels of analysis, to the most complex, or terminal, behavior. The exact nature of behavioral specification and analysis will vary, of course, according to the kind of concept or skill to be taught. . . .

THE NATURE OF THE TEACHING PROGRAM

Assuming that the necessary analyses of behavior can be performed, what will teaching programs for these skills look like? Following the tutorial model, a good self-instructional program must have features that provide for active responding, individual pacing, and immediate reinforcement of responses. These requirements set certain limits on the forms that programed instruction may take; but in fact the limitations are much less strict than is generally supposed. Format, for example, may be varied according to what is being taught. There is nothing either necessary or permanent about the small, one-or-two sentence frames that are typical of most linear programs. Frames may be as long or short as is appropriate to the task, just as a teacher may sometimes require a student's response after a very brief statement, and sometimes, equally appropriately, after a rather long lecture. Similarly, there are teaching tasks for which multiple-choice formats are appropriate, and others which require responses constructed by the student. Some subjects and some children may require the use of mechanical or electronic devices, others may be taught quite adequately with pencil-and-paper arrangements. There are many arrangements for presenting programs and reinforcing responses that have been explored thus far in only a limited way.

Use of display panels. In much skill teaching, programs must provide for actual practice in reading or interpreting various kinds of material. This can be most simply done through the use of what are called "panels." Panels are displays of some kind: maps, charts, pictures, reading material—whatever is appropriate to the task. The student may be given a different panel every item or two; or he may use the same one for an entire program. The panels can appear within the program, or apart from it in a separate booklet or some kind of display feature. Many of the commercially available teaching machines have provision for panel display. . . .

An extension of the notion of the panel would be to provide objects for manipulation, according to directions given in the program. These might be as varied as globes, books, construction paper, or rulers. Alternatively, it may be possible to direct the student to do something away from the program, and then return to the program to record his results and have them evaluated. Such a procedure might turn out to be particularly useful for the teaching of library skills. Rather than trying to duplicate certain aspects of a library in its panels, a program might send students to actual card catalogues, shelves, and indexes. In geography, two or three large globes or maps in a classroom might allow for more effective teaching than a miniature map or globe for each student. To the best of the author's information, such a procedure has not yet been tried in connection with programed instruction.

Teaching complex performances. The need for immediate reinforcement makes self-instruction difficult for certain complex skills,
such as writing. Two possibilities for meeting the problem should
be mentioned, however. Both are largely unexplored as yet. The
first is to use programed instruction to train the student to discriminate good from bad work, using the productions of others. He can
then be asked to apply his discriminatory powers in judging and
improving his own work. The second possibility is to use programed
instruction only in the teaching of some of the simpler component
behaviors for the skill. Reinforcement of the simpler behaviors often
poses no particular problem; and the more complex behaviors can
be built up from these components. . . .

The discussion of the nature of the teaching program has been,
of necessity, more concerned with possibility than actuality. Programers have thus far been relatively unadventurous in exploring
possible arrangements for organizing instruction and guiding learning. It is only as more of these possibilities are explored, however,
that any definitive answers concerning the kinds of skills appropriate
for programed instruction can be given. Obviously, a self-instructional program that students follow in isolation from one another
will not be an effective means of teaching discussion skills or any
kind of skill in which social interaction forms an integral part of
of the terminal behavior. For most other skills, however, there is
a strong likelihood that inventive programers can develop techniques
that will allow them to apply the basic principles of programed
instruction.

EVALUATION AND PREPARATION OF PROGRAMS BY TEACHERS

While only a skilled programer will be able to judge the finer points
of programing technique, there are certain questions that teachers
can ask themselves in trying to decide which, if any, of the programs
available at a given time will best serve their needs. Does the program, for example, emphasize description or actual performance of
a skill? Is practice provided in precisely the kind of skilled performance with which one is concerned? Are the assumptions made
about what students can already do appropriate to one's classes?
These questions can be answered by an intelligent scanning of the
program itself, but the teacher should also ask to see data from
pre-publication trials. "Error rate"—the number of errors made in
the program itself—should be low. . . . However, it is quite possible for programs with very low error rates to produce little learning, or learning of the wrong sort. Therefore, the teacher should
examine data on test performance. First, he must ask if the be-

haviors sampled in the test are those he is interested in teaching. If so, he can compare scores on tests given before and after administration of the program. Significant improvement in post-test as compared with pre-test scores means the program is teaching effectively (5).

As is perhaps inevitable in a field so rapidly expanding and so competitive, few of the currently available commercial programs appear to be based on extensive and detailed behavioral analysis. In their attempts to provide broad coverage of a subject or skill area, programs are frequently superficial in their treatment of the specific component behaviors. Frequently, too, they follow the relatively easier path of having a student talk about or describe a skill rather than actually perform it. While some of these programs—particularly for the less complex skills—may nevertheless prove useful as aids to the teacher, they probably cannot be expected to show the marked superiority over conventional methods that is often claimed for programed instruction.

Given this situation, many teachers and school systems are becoming interested in preparing programs on their own, to meet their own requirements and fit their own curricula. Formal programing, however, is a demanding discipline, and probably cannot be successfully undertaken by the isolated teacher working casually in his spare time. Frequent consultation with content specialists and psychologists or skilled programers is needed if behavioral analysis and self-instructional presentation are to be of the highest quality. This means that a school system wishing to prepare good programed materials must be willing to make a major commitment to the task. It must somehow provide large blocks of free time for the teachers who are programing, and the funding necessary to obtain high quality consultation services at frequent intervals, to the teachers who are programing. Further, it must be willing to maintain the project over a long period of time, even when progress is slow. Without such an extensive commitment, programing is likely to prove a rather discouraging task for the teacher whose standards of instruction are high.

CONCLUSION

Programed instruction as it bears upon the social studies must be assessed as a field of great potential and little realization. While there are presently few programs in social studies, and fewer still in skills, there is every reason to believe that the principles of programing can be effectively applied to the teaching of a wide range of social studies content. However, it should be clear by now that programed instruction is no quick and easy panacea for the ills of education. The task of producing programs both significant in their content and effective in their teaching procedure is an imposing one. For the moment, behavioral analysis and specification are probably the most pressing—and the most difficult—tasks. With the aid of adequate analyses, the techniques of programed instruction can perhaps be applied to the teaching of the most complex skills. Whether or not the goal of complete self-instruction is reached, however, good behavioral analyses should prove of immense benefit in the design of instructional procedures of all kinds.

References

(1) Center for Programed Instruction, in cooperation with U.S. Department of Health, Education, and Welfare, Office of Education. *Programs, '62: A Guide to Programed Instructional Materials Available to Educators by September 1962.* Publication No. OE3415. Washington, D.C.: U.S. Government Printing Office, 1962. 383 pp.

(2) Finn, James D., and Perrin, Donald G. *Teaching Machines and Programed Learning, 1962: A Survey of the Industry.* Occasional Paper No. 3. A report prepared for the National Education Association, Technological Development Project. U.S. Department of Health, Education, and Welfare, Office of Education. Publication No. 34019. Washington, D.C.: U.S. Government Printing Office, 1962. 85 pp.

(3) For a classification and description of the various kinds of presentation devices, including programed texts, see Stolurow, Lawrence M. *Teaching by Machine.* Cooperative Research Monograph No. 6. U.S. Department of Health, Education, and Welfare, Office of Education. Publication No. 34010. Washington, D.C.: U.S. Government Printing Office, 1961. pp. 4–50.

For a description of machines and a directory of those commercially available, see Finn and Perrin, *Teaching Machines and Programed Learning,* pp. 20–49.

(4) Mager, Robert F. *Preparing Objectives for Programmed Instruction.* San Francisco: Fearon, 1961. 62 pp. A branching-style programed text providing an introduction to the process of behavioral specification for programing purposes. Essentially the same process has been discussed with reference to test construction in Furst, Edward J. *Constructing Evaluation Instruments.* New York: Longmans, Green and Co., 1958. 334 pp. For an application in the field of testing, see Bloom, Benjamin S., *et al. Taxonomy of Educational Objectives, Handbook I: Cognitive Domain.* New York: Longmans, Green and Co., 1954. 192 pp.

(5) It should be pointed out that tests are frequently included in the program itself as the final series of frames. This is generally accepted procedure, but it is then necessary to consider performance on these final frames apart from performance on the program itself. It is unfortunately the case that very few publishers of programs today provide data of the kind discussed here. Such information, however, is extremely important for the evaluation of a program. Publishers will perhaps be encouraged to supply it as more and more teachers make their demands known.

✄§ DEVELOPING MAP SKILLS IN ELEMENTARY SCHOOLS

Harriett Chace

This selection well illustrates that a school faculty really desiring to improve children's map skills can certainly do so. In this case, testing was used as an aid in appraising pupils' learning of map skills. While the test results are not detailed here, they were also utilized in the development of the school's program of map skills. The article thus serves the additional purpose of exemplifying a carefully conceived attempt to improve a specific phase of social studies instruction in one school.

TWO YEARS AGO the teachers of a small elementary school in Centerville, Massachusetts, undertook to study the effectiveness of their efforts to teach selected skills in the social studies at successive grade levels and to develop better articulation among the grades in relation to these skills. Through careful organization of subject matter and experiences, through a study of the stages of child growth, and through a cooperative teacher-pupil planning technique that broke down grade barriers, they hoped to learn more about *what* skills could be taught *where* and *when* and *how*.

At the beginning of the experiment the teachers made a number of basic assumptions: 1) Each child can only be expected to develop according to his own capacity. Some children start with many well-developed skills and others with scarcely any. It is necessary to study each individual and each group in order to know where a pupil stands and how he can be expected to grow. 2) It should not be expected that students exposed to the same learning situations will all develop in the same way and at the same time. A skill must be a goal toward which growth is directed rather than an end product. 3) All that a school can do is to provide situations, instructional materials, and personal relationships that will help each child to advance at his own rate and in the desired direction.

Used by permission of the author and the National Council for the Social Studies; from *Social Education*, 19:309–310, November, 1955. Dr. Chace is former supervisor of elementary education in Harwich, Orleans, Chatham, and Eastham, Massachusetts.

Among the general or "basic skills" selected for the experiment was that of map skills. In a broad sense these map skills were aimed toward two major objectives: 1) training in map reading, and 2) using maps as sources of information.

It was then necessary to determine the specific skills which were part of the general skill; to help the children to use these skills in classroom and other real-life situations; and to seek evidence of the extent to which these new skills were being mastered and used by the students. We proposed, therefore, to break down map skills into specifics; tentatively to grade these skills in relation to assumed difficulty; and to use standardized and improvised tests to establish individual levels of ability in using the specific skills. In this way, we hoped to find a working level for each class, although no assumption was made that any child because he had arrived at a certain grade level had of necessity arrived at a certain proficiency in a skill.

Under the general heading of "Map Skills" the staff isolated the following:

1. Using a map index.
2. Interpreting map scales.
3. Using map keys and symbols.
4. Interpreting weather maps, relief maps, route maps, political maps, air maps, historical maps, and product, industry, population density or other special type of map.
5. Map construction: copying maps, drawing maps from realia, drawing maps from written accounts, making sand table maps, making maps with clay and similar material, making maps outdoors with natural material.
6. Drawing maps from memory.
7. Locating places on maps.
8. Using an atlas.
9. Using a globe: interpreting a globe, locating places on a globe, finding distances on a globe.
10. Using polar projections.

Having agreed upon the specific skills to be taught, the staff of the Centerville School held meetings and conferences to: 1) discuss skills and the range of skills in various grades; 2) discuss individual child growth and development; 3) work out sequences of skills based on pupil progress; 4) compare work and records at different levels; 5) discuss planned activities, methods of presentation, equipment, and materials of instruction; 6) make summaries of accomplishments. This cooperative planning proved invaluable in the establishing of an effective program.

PRE-TESTING

Before our experiment could really get under way, it was necessary to test the students to be sure that individuals and groups were placed at their proper levels. The first maps asked for in this testing were a series of free-hand drawings to show map concepts. No instruction was given before the children were asked to draw these maps, and no helpful materials were provided for the youngsters' use. If a grade as a whole had a reasonably mature concept, the group continued up the scale until failures resulted.

In the upper three grades it was possible to use the Iowa Every-Pupil Tests of Basic Skills in Map Reading. The results were compared, keeping in mind pupil ages, intelligence quotients, and scores. The I.Q.'s were Binet or Pintner-Cunningham. The information gained from this testing was then set up in the form of tables similar to the following:

CODE NAME	SEX	AGE	I.Q.	SCORE IN GRADE LEVEL
6A	b	10–9	122	11–2
6B	g	10–9	110	5–8

The Iowa test on reading graphs was also used in grade six, and an improvised test on graphs was administered to grades three, four, and five. The results showed ability in graph reading starting at the third grade level.

In the work with memory maps we found that: 1) political maps were remembered better than other types, and 2) pupils with high intelligence quotients were not necessarily best in constructing maps from memory although the Iowa test results showed that they excelled in the reading of maps.

When we analyzed the testing program we noted that there was a positive, if low, correlation between age and map ability. There was a wider range of ability within a single grade than between adjacent grades, and more than the range in chronological age would suggest. Since there seemed to be so little correlation between the factor of age and intelligence and the factor of the selected skill, we felt that interest and self-initiated previous experience with maps must be of prime importance. From the test results we concluded that although it would not be possible to make a definitive list of skills at grade levels, it would be possible to grade skills in order of difficulties so that they could be taught at workable levels. . . .

GRADING

In the past it had usually been assumed that first graders were not mature enough to be taught map skills. The experiment in the

Centerville School, however, bore out the idea that the system of grading skills as well as materials becomes essentially a problem of presentation which was precisely the point Henry Johnson made many years ago (1). It was possible for pupils to learn to draw and read maps of the immediate environment in grade one, to learn symbols on maps as easily as reading and writing, and to understand directions and locations. Planned work in teaching map skills may be started at first grade level provided the work seems like play, the maps are simple, and all concepts are within the pupils' actual experience. The Nineteenth Yearbook of the National Council for the Social Studies supports this conclusion.

> Children will begin early and without direction to represent places they have seen by reproducing them with blocks. . . . The same principle continues in force at all levels of instruction. The child must have the concept that is expressed by a map symbol or the symbol will be meaningless (2).

Although in the second and third grades the children should still do most work from direct observation, models, movies, and still pictures are valuable aids, it is not until grade four that transition is noticeable from complete dependence on oral and visual sources to the comprehensive use of written sources.

In the upper three elementary grades, geographies, histories, fiction, picture and more advanced encyclopædias, atlases, dictionaries, and periodicals are useful. These will supplement direct purposeful experiences and help the children to form the habit of using appropriate printed sources of information. Map indices can be used, map scales can be read and constructed, and symbols can be changed gradually from those that appeal merely to the imagination to the more abstract and conventional ones. By the time a child has completed grade six, he should be able to interpret the majority of maps using keys and symbols, and to use various projections.

At the close of our experiment we found that we had compiled a useable list of skills graded in order of their apparent difficulties, and had reached the following conclusions.

Planned work in map skills may be started at the first grade level if the right presentation is used. Symbols, too, will be accepted at this grade level. As the age group advances the children can visualize larger areas, develop greater accuracy, and work with more abstract symbols.

In map work at all levels there should be constant appeal to the child's own environment and to his experiences. The transition from concrete to abstract should be gradual. Maps for a single purpose should be used until the child reaches the upper grades. Symbols should be introduced in order of reality—pictures, semi-pictorial representation, and abstract representation. As printed material is introduced in other work, printed symbols may be introduced in map work and indices may be used.

References

(1) Henry Johnson. *Teaching of History*, Revised edition. New York: The Macmillan Company, 1940. Chapter 4.

(2) Katheryne Thomas Whittemore. "Maps." *Geographic Approaches to Social Education*, Nineteenth Yearbook. Washington, D.C.: National Council for the Social Studies. 1948. p. 120.

✍ IMPROVING THE USE OF MAPS IN THE ELEMENTARY SCHOOL   *Rose Sabaroff*

Better teaching with maps requires thoughtful planning of ways for children to learn, step by step, how to interpret what maps show. This selection contains abundant suggestions carefully worked out to accomplish that objective. It provides both sound and practical answers to the following questions: What are some of the major misconceptions to be overcome in teaching map usage? What techniques and steps are most useful in teaching skills for locating places? How can children best learn to use map symbols? How should use of map scales be developed? In what ways can awareness of relative location be learned with maps? How can maps be more closely related to children's understanding of their real physical and cultural environment?

A MAP IS A SHORTHAND record of a mass of geographic knowledge which would require many pages or even a volume to record in words. Almost anything concerning an area may be shown on a map—the form, the size, the location, direction, topography, transportation, vegetation, industries, etc. This "shorthand record" is like a foreign language. Children cannot be faced with a conventional map and be expected to read it without any prior preparation. We would not expect a child who had never been taught to read to be able to open

This article first appeared in the April, 1961, issue of the *Journal of Geography*. Used by permission of *The Journal of Geography* from 60:184–190, April, 1961. Dr. Sabaroff is on the faculty of the Graduate School of Education, Harvard University.

an adult book and read it, not even if it were a simplified version. Yet, with maps, we do this continually. At the fourth grade level, many social studies textbooks include maps which assume a skill with a "language" that may never have been taught.

Furthermore, we do not wish children to study maps merely to understand them. We have children study maps in order to understand relations about the earth and its inhabitants. A map symbol does not stand for a word. A child does not understand a map symbol when he has learned to name it. Should we be content when a child calls a wiggly line a river and a dot a city? This kind of learning breeds many common misconceptions, such as:

> Belief that a plain is flat as a floor.
> Confusion of *mouth* and *source* of rivers.
> Ignorance of *upstream* and *downstream* direction of rivers.
> Incomplete concept of climate, thinking it is synonymous with temperature alone or thinking it can be adequately described as "good" or "bad."
> Confusion of *north* with *up*, *south* with *down*.
> Thinking that it never rains in a desert.
> Thinking that farther and farther south (all the way to the South Pole) the climate is warmer and warmer (1).

It becomes quite obvious that only when a map symbol calls forth a mental image in the mind of the child, can he use the map "shorthand" with any significant meaning. Just as a trained musician can look at a score and hear the music, so a person skilled in the use of maps can look at one and bring forth imagery of the landscape—the hills and rivers, arid and growing regions, fields of wheat. He can feel the heat and the cold, the dryness and the dampness. Furthermore, the cultural symbols: highways, railroads, cities, etc., tell him something of what the people have done with their land and their climate. What then are some of the skills our pupils need if maps are to be a useful tool to learning?

FIVE BASIC MAP SKILLS

Research in the literature offers us many lists of map skills. I have settled on the following five skills as the ones most necessary for our pupils if we are to have the kind of literate citizenry our times demand. First, we must be concerned with location, including orientation and direction. The second basic map skill is a knowledge of symbols, both physical and cultural. The third requisite is some understanding of scale. Fourth, pupils need to develop an awareness of relative location. Fifth, the globe should be recognized as a model of the earth. We begin to provide experiences for teaching each of these skills in their simplest form from first grade on. As the children mature and enrich their background, we can extend our expectations.

EXPERIENCES NECESSARY TO DEVELOP THE SKILLS

Location. We want children to become increasingly oriented in space. We can encourage them to orient themselves in relation to familiar landmarks: "near the park," "beyond the store," "by the river."

Very early we want to encourage the use of *up* as meaning away from the center of the earth; *down,* as meaning toward the center of the earth. . . . If we have children associate up and down properly right from the start, we may avoid the confusion of misusing up for north and down for south when we discuss cardinal directions. . . . Children will not have difficulty picturing a river flowing north.

In order to build some understanding of North, South, East, and West in reference to maps, children should experience these directions first in relation to the earth. By planning a series of outdoor lessons, we can call children's attention to the different position in which we see the sun at different times of day. . . . We should encourage children to use cardinal directions in their speech.

We also want children to understand that shadows help them know cardinal directions. . . . Encourage the children to check the direction of their shadows in the morning, at noon, and at recess. Have them check the shadows thrown by posts, trees, buildings, etc. With distributed practice throughout the primary grades, children will learn to determine approximate direction from studying sun position and shadows. . . .

It is wise to hang North, South, East, and West labels on the walls of the classroom. In the primary grades, all maps should be kept in a horizontal position, either on the floor or on a table top to help pupils relate cardinal directions on maps to directions on the earth's surface. All maps should be labelled with cardinal directions. The North arrow should also be introduced. It might be wise to use both the four direction labels *and* the North arrow until the concept of the North arrow is mastered. In-between directions can be used in speech as the children become able to grasp them.

On the globe, we are concerned with establishing north as toward the North Pole, south as toward the South Pole. Then we introduce the Equator as an east-west line lying halfway between the poles and also establish north and south in relation to the equator. On a map, children can use streets and roads as a grid for determining direction. "The house is north of Third Street." "The school is east of Maple Avenue."

Symbols. In teaching symbols we are most anxious that a child not be confronted with a symbol on a map for which he has no mental image. There is a certain progression in teaching of map symbols that is in keeping with good learning theories. We move from the known, the concrete, the near at hand to the unknown, the abstract, the far away. In the use of maps this means we start with the observable environment. Take the children on a trip around several blocks near the school, to a park, or some other place of interest. . . . When they return to the classroom, the children, with the help of the teacher, will then reproduce the landscape on a floor map, or table model, roughly laying out streets, streams, etc. in proper orientation. Toys, blocks, and other props can be used as symbols and placed in correct relation to each other and to the base map. This three-dimensional reproduction of the observed landscape is the first step in mapping. The second step would be to reproduce on paper what they have seen in order to produce a more permanent record. When they decide on the pictorial symbol they will use to represent the school, a house or other building, a street or railroad, they can then plan a legend so others will also understand the symbols they have used. Making of maps *following* observation of the landscape is the one way of insuring that the feature symbolized has a true image behind it. Eventually, under the teacher's guidance, the pupils can replace their pictorial symbols with more conventional symbols. This would be step three. However, the child has arrived at the abstract symbol through his own experience. Now, if he should see a map made by others using the same abstract symbol, he is prepared to invest that symbol with a correct image. The maps thus developed by children can be reproduced in smaller scale and mimeographed by the teacher. Perhaps another trip can be taken using their map to plot the trip.

It is not always possible to take a trip. The same three steps in mapping can also be done starting with a picture. It is best to choose a picture that was taken looking down at the features of the landscape. Many pictures in the new social studies books lend themselves to such mapping. . . . A legend should be placed in the lower left-hand corner of the map, which is its proper position. Cardinal directions should be labelled. . . .

As children study their environment and draw their maps, they should be helped to see the relationship between the cultural feature and its physical base. Children should study effects before causes. They should study human activity before physical conditions. For example, children might be taken to see a dam and the lake formed by it which is now used for irrigation. They should then have their attention called to the physical environment that helped bring it into being. . . .

When children have had ample opportunities to observe their environment and study well-selected pictures, when they have had adequate experiences with three-dimensional, pictorial, and abstract mapping, they are ready to begin the study of maps made by others. The maps they study should follow a similar sequence. The first maps children see should be large-scale base maps made by the teacher showing areas which they have observed first-hand or in familiar pictures. To these base maps, children add their three-dimensional symbols, pictorial symbols, and then abstract symbols. The children are now ready for very simple teacher-made or textbook maps on which these familiar symbols appear. They should have many experiences with pictorial and semi-pictorial maps which are kept simple and uncluttered. . . . Land and water relations are very difficult for children to visualize even when they observe them in their own environment. How can children understand that an island is the top of an almost submerged piece of land? How can children understand the direction of flow of a river? The only way I know of adequately clarifying such relations is with a three-dimensional model which can be flooded and drained.

Scale. When a person wishes to study a map, there are three things he must establish immediately: cardinal directions related to this area on the map, the symbols used as depicted in the legend, and the scale of the map. If some sort of scale is not established, there is no way of knowing how large the area is nor the distances between features.

Scale becomes important very early. When children lay out a floor map of an area, a very rough idea of scale is involved since the floor scheme is smaller than the original landscape. Relative distance must be considered as each object is placed to represent the actual feature seen. Children compare distances between places on the same map: "The store is nearer to home than to school." "The park is half-way between school and the highway." . . .

Children can learn to measure distance by use of a scale chosen in relation to the landscape or area they wish to represent. For example, a given-sized wooden block can stand for a city block or an acre or a square mile out in the country. As they represent the same area on different-sized sheets of paper, the concept of scale is being developed. Even on their pictorial maps, children can be helped to think in terms of scale: so many blocks to the store, so many feet, yards, or miles to the river. Finally, children may be able to recognize the scale of a map not of their own making, and use that scale to compute distances. . . . Large maps of small areas should be studied first and then placed in the context of a map of a larger area which includes the smaller area.

Children can be helped to understand the principal of scale by looking down at a landscape from a height and taking careful note what happens to size as they get higher and higher above it. They may make estimates of the size of a given feature as seen from a height and then measure it as they come closer. This might help them see why features get smaller as more and more area is covered on a map.

In working with globes, children can learn that different sized globes reproduce the same earth. The poles can be located; the equator can be described as being half-way between the poles. The idea of latitude may be introduced, but only as distance north or south from the equator toward the poles.

Relative location. The location of any place on a map is only the beginning. What counts is the comprehension of the functional significance of that location. . . . Where is our community located? In the mountains? On a river? Is it hot or cold? Is there much rainfall? When do things grow? Is it in a desert or near a mine? Are we near corn or cattle country? Are we a manufacturing community?

It is obvious that children living in a cotton-growing area will find different content as they investigate their local community, than will children living in a large trading center or in an isolated mountain community. However, the *influence* of "relative location" would be equally significant in investigating any area.

Even within the community, important differences arise due to relative location. In a large city, for example, it will make a difference whether children live in a congested apartment area or in the suburbs. There will be important variations in fire and police protection, work of parents, kinds of transportation and communication used, opportunities for aesthetic and religious expression, number of parks and libraries, kinds and amount of recreation available, number and crowding of schools, etc. In an agricultural community, it will matter greatly whether soil is fertile, when the rains come, what the major product is, how many or few roads there are, how far apart people live, what means are available for aesthetic, religious, recreational and educational functions.

In making their maps, children will discover where certain features are located and how these relate to railroads, waterways, physical features and land-use. At a very elementary level, children may be checking to discover where fire hydrants occur or how far it is to the nearest park for children located in different neighborhoods. They may discover that this was a good year for one crop and a difficult year for another crop. A river may flood, and they may discover that the slope of the land makes a big difference; perhaps their best friend's home was inundated while their own remained untouched because the ground level was higher. If children are led to analyze the relative location of every place being studied, they will build a background for understanding events in our world today.

References

(1) Isabelle K. Hart, *The Teaching of Geography*, The Thirty-Second Yearbook of the National Society for the Study of Education, Bloomington, Illinois, 1933, Chapter XXIX, Part II, "A Classification of Common Errors in Geography Made by Teachers and Pupils," pp. 478–483.

◄§ Observing Geography in the Local Environment   *G. H. Gopsill*

This selection highlights a distinctive example of instructional use of community resources in the social studies. The author analyzes some basic features of successful method in teaching geography, then deals with children's observations as a particularly worthwhile activity in that subject. The tangible elements of environment and the specific procedures that the author identifies can be of considerable practical help to teachers.

The method which a teacher employs depends upon the aim which he adopts. If his aim is to impart facts for some extraneous purpose such as the passing of an examination or the acquisition of a store of useful knowledge, then his method will consist principally of formal didactic instruction. But if his aim is to stimulate an enthusiasm for the subject and to lay firm foundations for personal study, then the cardinal principle of his method will be to demonstrate at every opportunity that geography deals with the realities of life as the children can see it round about them, and there will be far more opportunity for children actually to participate in the work which is done.

Used by permission from the Macmillan Company Ltd., London, from the author's *The Teaching of Geography*, 1956, pp. 12–15, 24–27.

Where the first of these two methods is used exclusively, the facts learned soon disappear when the immediate need for them is passed. Moreover the sum total of facts which a child can learn during his school life is limited and this limit represents but a fraction of the body of knowledge which geography has to offer. Very much remains to be learned whether in the pursuit of a profession or merely as an enrichment of one's personal life, long after the guiding hand of the teacher has been withdrawn. So the incentive provided by the second method has far more lasting value, and children finish up, not only better informed, but better students since they have made first acquaintance with systematic personal study. This is not a new idea. Another glance at the 1880's will show that even then there were some few persons who were much concerned with the necessity of basing the study of geography on principles which were psychologically sound. . . .

I cannot stress too strongly that a teacher's philosophy should so direct his method that his children are actively engaged in *pursuing* knowledge instead of sitting and waiting for it to come to them. This means that he has to be enterprising in providing the necessary sources or pointing out where they may be found. He must be skilful in directing children how to make the best use of them, and vigorous in his own personal teaching. I hope to translate this into practical terms in the chapters which follow.

For the present I should like to add just one word of caution on the interpretation to be placed on the term "actively engaged." This does not necessarily imply activity in the physical sense, nor an excess of exuberance or informality. As I understand it, children are actively engaged if they are intelligently occupied on any sort of occupation which happens to be appropriate for the task. A class of young children busily engaged upon some communal undertaking which involves a certain amount of movement as well as thought, is "actively engaged." But so also is a sixth form listening intently to a discourse from a learned speaker, and subsequently engaging him in his arguments. This class, too, is "actively engaged" even though the activity is almost wholly intellectual. There are times when either or both types of activity may be appropriate, and it is important to remember that "activity" in this sense ought always to be present even in the ordinary lesson which forms the greater part of daily routine.

The success of a method is reflected in the attitude which children bear towards the subject after they have spent some time at it. I do not suggest that they must become parochial towards it to the exclusion of other interests, acquiring what is sometimes described as a *geographical attitude*. Indeed, I am not quite sure what a geographical attitude is. It is easier to understand an *enquiring* attitude which helps a pupil to seek and find, or an *enthusiastic* attitude which serves him as a powerful incentive, or a *scientific* attitude which enables him to seek his facts and to reason about them when he has found them. Any one of these attitudes may serve a pupil well in the study of geography and conversely, when the subject is well taught, it is probable that they are actively encouraged. It is also probable that such attitudes may apply to other subjects as well, and habits of work thus become established. The arguments surrounding formal discipline seem to suggest that a skill acquired in one subject is not necessarily carried over to another. But it appears more evident that attitudes and systematic habits of study are more general in their effect. These things are the things that endure, and if they are established aright from the beginning, and the children can say: "We have enjoyed doing this; let us find out more about it" —then something really positive has been achieved, a stimulus has been given, and facts soon follow. . . .

OBSERVATIONS BY CHILDREN

Observations made by very young children are necessarily limited. On the other hand it is remarkable how penetrating intelligent children can be when once their curiosity has been given that initial impetus by a teacher who is himself enthusiastic for this kind of work.

Work in the local district is often confined to social observations of a somewhat superficial character which fail to stress the importance of maintaining a geographical emphasis. From the geographer's point of view human activities are necessarily related to, and frequently derived from, the physical structure of the region. Therefore observations of natural features of a simple kind should be undertaken first as for example, the shape of the ground: some is higher, some lower; some hills are steeper than others; some are exceedingly steep, some indeed are *cliffs* or *escarpments* and these terms are introduced naturally into the working vocabulary when such features are observed along with other simple descriptive terms such as *hill*, *knoll*, *ridge*, *valley*. It does not take long to notice that water runs down these hills and not up; that it tends to collect in *streams* which join together as *tributaries* to form *rivers*, some of which run more swiftly than others; and generally speaking the swifter running streams occur where the slopes are steep whereas broad sluggish-flowing rivers *meander* slowly across the plains below. It is perhaps possible to trace a *tributary* back to its *source* if it is within reasonable distance, and then another fact will emerge—that *springs* flow more freely at some times than they do at others. It is but a step to relate this to the weather observations which the children keep recorded on a chart in the classroom and to the fact that prolonged rain, free-flowing springs and floods in the lower valley occur together, whereas prolonged *drought* goes with restricted or intermittent flow and parched fields.

In these elementary observations the pupils have made a beginning in the study of physical geography not *in vacuo* but from living samples in their own neighbourhood. They have taken new words into their geographical vocabulary, not in a sterile list, but quite naturally and incidentally as the occasion demands them.

Another very simple but quite fundamental physical feature to notice is the colour of the sub-soil. It may be exposed to view in cliffs, railway cuttings, quarries, gravel-pits, or simply in trenches dug in the road for repairs to cables or watermains. It may be red and some-what sticky as in the case of Keuper marl; or white and very hard on the chalk; yellow in the Cotswolds; black in the Fens. These differences in colour and texture are important as the children will see when they pass on to the next stage in their observations—the life and work of men. What use have they made of the land? Is it agricultural? If so, what sort of agriculture is practised? Is it indus-trial? Are there coalmines, brickfields, quarries or gravelpits in the neighbourhood? What of the roads and the railways—how do they avoid or overcome natural obstacles such as the steepest hills, or rivers, or land liable to floods? These and similar questions soon capture the imagination of children and the material which they discover is invaluable as a starting point for further studies. But more important than this, children so trained are learning to *open their eyes*, to see that the neighbourhood will disclose a wealth of interesting matter if only they know how to look for it.

Another aspect of method shown here is the fact that we have begun to teach physical geography by using real examples—the simpler land forms which can actually be seen. This is a principle which may well be continued whenever physical geography is dealt with. I regard this as most important, for so often the teaching of physical geography and of land forms in particular, is done from models of hypothetical examples with impeccable symmetry, divorced from their context and which bear little relationship to living features. In my view it is most necessary for children to understand from the beginning that physical features are not isolated elements which stand alone and that one does not build up a landscape piece by piece by adding together so many separate components like the bits of a jig-saw puzzle. Rather they should learn that a landscape is an entity of itself with its own individuality and that it contains certain distinctive features. It is convenient to call these features by specific names, on occasions to isolate them temporarily and to simplify them by means of diagrams or models so that their shape may be observed or their evolution more closely studied. . . . It is legitimate to do this when the features are taken from the landscape for examination and "put back" as it were, afterwards. But it is misleading for children and gives them a wholly wrong impression of physical geography when the "bits" are taken first and added together afterwards.

Using local material in this manner is not always easy. In the first place varieties of topography or of physical structure do not always occur within the immediate neighbourhood. Some areas are rich in potentialities, others more uniform, offer less scope for a study of the physical background to man's life and work. This is particularly true in towns where physical structure is so masked by building. Further, it is rarely possible in the time available, frequently to take whole classes out of school to make such observations. There are many other things to be done and school life is short. In any event there is no reason why forty children in a body should be engaged in school hours on a task which a couple could do equally well in their spare time. Instead, after the teacher has drawn attention to the possibilities inherent in their surroundings, a more practical arrangement is for individual children or pairs of children to go out, observe, and record their observations. Later, they place their results before the remainder for more systematic study in class. It is well to set definite limits to such an enterprise and to lay down beforehand precisely what is to be looked for.

WITH THE SCHOOL AS A CENTRE

As an example of the kind of work which can be done locally with young children, a series of four journeys can be arranged going in each direction from the school, north, south, east and west for as far as children can conveniently walk in an hour. Four pairs of children undertake these journeys in their own time. They are instructed to observe according to a schedule drawn up with the class before they go out, e.g. Starting from school, walk to the *west* (1) along Scardale road for about an hour:

(i) How far do you go?
(ii) Do you go uphill or down?
(iii) Is the hill steep? Can you see any steeper?

(iv) As you go, do you see on the road sides: houses, or fields? Or any of these: a colliery, or a gravel-pit, or a brick-works?

(v) Is there anywhere on the journey where you can see the soil exposed? What colour is it? Is it sticky, or hard or soft? Bring some back.

(vi) Do you cross, or can you see, any rivers? etc., etc.

There are similar instructions drawn up according to the detail which the teacher knows is likely to be met, for the parties which set out from the school to the east, to the north, and to the south. With the school as a hub, these four parties go their separate ways for an hour, each covering approximately a mile and a half.

They observe and record what they see. They may illustrate with a little sketch map which again is a matter for specific instruction from the teacher. I emphasize this matter of instruction. Local study can so easily degenerate into aimless wandering, wasting much time and energy from lack of a little direction beforehand. It should always be borne in mind that schools are places where work is done, and the teacher's first task is to direct it.

Subsequently the reports are presented to the class.

References

(1) Or to the north, or south, or east for other parties.

Professional Improvement of the Social Studies Curriculum

PRECEDING PARTS of this volume have presented, described, illustrated, and analyzed curriculum and instruction in elementary school social studies. Pertinent problems have been considered, and proposals for improvement have been suggested. This part concludes the volume with a group of selections that look toward the future of elementary social studies—the need for and means of moving toward that future. These readings provide special stimulus and guidance for groups committed to planning or revising the social studies curriculum, to individual teachers who desire to improve their teaching, and to other interested persons who wish to help in the development of improved ways of relating children to their society.

∼§ THE CURRENT CHALLENGE   John U. Michaelis

The concluding group of readings opens with a selection that stresses the theme of this entire volume. One of the nation's authorities provides a succinct enumeration of outstanding reasons for redoubling efforts to improve curriculum and instruction in elementary social studies. The article then quotes a carefully worked out statement of criteria for an effective social studies program. The challenge here is to curriculum makers to plan programs that more nearly meet these criteria, and to individual teachers to bolster those components of the social studies appearing in the grades they teach.

THE CHALLENGE TO develop outstanding programs of instruction in the social studies has never been greater. Responsibilities of citizen-

Used by permission of the author and the National Council for the Social Studies; from the "Introduction" to its Thirty-Second Yearbook, *Social Studies in Elementary Schools*, 1962, pp. 1–4. Dr. Michaelis is a professor in the school of education of the University of California at Berkeley.

ship continue to increase as human problems become more complex both at home and abroad. The rapid growth of man's knowledge in basic disciplines and swiftly-moving changes in human affairs offer opportunities heretofore not possible in selecting content, activities, and materials for inclusion in the program. The current emphasis upon the problem of achieving quality in education while at the same time meeting the problem of increasing enrollments has lead to a critical examination of existing programs. Increasing attention is being given to intellectual outcomes such as critical thinking ability, depth and breadth of understanding, and insight into the ways of thinking and living of other peoples. The impact of television and other mass media of communication upon children's development of concepts and understandings has opened up new possibilities for improving children's learning. Laymen and educators alike have shown increased concern for developing programs of instruction that truly lead to the achievement of basic objectives of the social studies.

This challenge is particularly urgent in democratic countries. One group has stated that the record of accomplishment in democratic countries offers no guarantee for the future (1). The dangers of the totalitarian challenge must be faced realistically. Programs of education in non-democratic countries are designed to indoctrinate the young systematically and thoroughly. On the other hand, education in an open society is designed to liberate intelligence, to develop allegiances and loyalties based on reason and understanding, and to nurture critical thinking abilities. The social studies and other areas of the curriculum must be considered in relation to this challenge! As never before there is need to develop the understandings, abilities, attitudes, and appreciations that are needed to live effectively in our times.

The social studies can make significant contributions to the meeting of this challenge only if great effort is put forth in planning, developing, and evaluating the instructional program. The study of man in relation to his social and physical environment must be kept in central focus. Instruction must be guided by clear-cut purposes that teachers understand and use as they work with children. The instructional program must be rooted in the social and psychological foundations of education and be organized to provide for depth, breadth, and continuity of learning. A critical selection of content must be made from geography, history, political science, economics, anthropology, sociology and other disciplines, and from current affairs of greatest importance. Instructional resources, learning activities, and evaluative procedures must be selected and utilized in accord with criteria and principles designed to facilitate the achievement of basic values that are of the essence in promoting human dignity in our times.

Tasks such as these need to be approached in a framework that gives a sense of direction to educational planning at all levels of instruction. Basic characteristics and fundamental purposes of effective social studies programs need to be identified. With a statement of characteristics and purposes in hand, it is possible for school personnel at the local, county, and state levels to work with a sense of common purpose in improving the social studies yet achieve the diversification that is needed to meet local needs and conditions.

CHARACTERISTICS AND PURPOSES OF EFFECTIVE SOCIAL STUDIES PROGRAMS

What are the characteristics and purposes of effective social studies programs? This is a difficult question, but one that should be answered as steps are taken to improve the social studies. Although a statement of desirable characteristics and basic purposes will vary from situation to situation in terms of existing values, problems, and conditions, certain basic elements should be discernible because of the many common needs, issues, and problems that exist in schools throughout the country.

The statement that follows grew out of a five-year statewide study (2). It is illustrative of basic considerations to keep in mind as efforts are made to design and evaluate social studies programs that will make significant contributions to the education of children in our times.

A social studies program is effective if:

1. It is based upon the spiritual, moral, intellectual, emotional, and physical development of the individual and upon the needs of the society in which he is a member.
2. It applies the best available information about the learning process and its relation to the development of children and youth, and it challenges the capabilities of each individual.
3. It emphasizes the *American way of life* and provides individuals with continuous opportunity to experience democratic living.
4. It emphasizes the importance of moral and spiritual ethics and provides for the acquisition of those ethical values cherished in American culture.
5. It promotes particularly the dignity of man and the ideal in our free society that people of all races and creeds shall have equal opportunities to excel.
6. It gives attention to current and persistent problems and utilizes contributions from the social sciences in formulating suggested solutions for those problems.

7. It stimulates creative thinking and reasoned action based upon an objective study of controversial issues.

8. It provides many opportunities for individuals and groups to use problem-solving techniques and to develop skills for effective thinking.

9. It provides a series of experiences which help individuals understand and appreciate that the rights and privileges of American society entail attendant responsibilities and duties.

10. It balances the contributions of the several social sciences and emphasizes the interrelatedness of social, political, economic, and spiritual forces in the United States and in the world.

11. It emphasizes the fact that democracy is a process through which ideas and institutions are submitted to public discussion and debate and it places value on the contributions of Americans to the development of their traditions.

12. It develops understanding and appreciation of other peoples and ways of life and of the reciprocal contributions to civilization made by individuals and groups of our own and other nations.

13. It illustrates how science and technology have made peoples of the world increasingly interdependent and have, at the same time, created many social, economic, and political problems that are international in scope.

14. It promotes an awareness of basic human needs and the development of skills and attitudes that enable individuals to contribute positively towards improved human relations in family, school, and communities.

15. It gives adequate attention to the development of the varied skills and competencies that are required for effective citizenship in a republic.

16. It utilizes and interrelates other areas of the curriculum in order to further its purposes.

17. It provides for continuous evaluation of the achievements and progress of individuals in terms of behaviors, understandings, competencies, values, and attitudes.

18. It is flexible enough to meet the individual differences of pupils in varying environments, yet maintains a continuity of purpose and content that gives direction to the program at all levels.

19. It develops from kindergarten through the fourteenth grade, reinforcing and expanding content, skills, and attitudes at each level, and it encourages an appropriate variety of emphases and approaches to learning at different educational levels.

20. It provides for revisions to incorporate new research findings and to meet the emerging demands of our changing society and of the individuals therein.

21. It is taught by persons who have the breadth and depth of preparation that will enable them to teach effectively the wide range of topics which comprise the social studies.

The foregoing statement was not prepared for direct transfer to courses of study. Rather, it was planned for use as a guide to a) the formulation of specific objectives in courses of study and units of work, and b) the evaluation of social studies programs. . . .

References

(1) *The Power of the Democratic Idea.* Special Studies Project Report VI, Rockefeller Brothers Fund. Garden City, New York: Doubleday and Co., 1960. p. 1.

(2) *Report of the State Central Committee on the Social Studies to the California State Curriculum Commission.* Sacramento: California State Department of Education, 1961. 92 p.

✎§ QUESTIONS TO CONSIDER IN EFFORTS TO IMPROVE THE SOCIAL STUDIES CURRICULUM
Jonathon C. McLendon

What are the main aspects of the social studies that need attention? What are the chief questions that should be considered in planning or revising a social studies curriculum? The author of this selection undertakes to suggest questions about a social studies program that need answering. The list is more extensive and specific than that given in the preceding selection, and the questions parallel the arrangement of elements of the social studies as they are typically dealt with in curriculum guides.

OBJECTIVES

1. Do they identify kinds of learning achievable to a significant degree in social studies?
2. Are various appropriate types of learning specifically identified?
3. Are particular grades and courses designated as concentrating on particular objectives?
4. Have all or most teachers met (in small groups or large) during the past three years to formulate or otherwise consider both the objectives and their attainment?
5. Do they include basic values of American democracy?

Used by permission of The Macmillan Company, from "Professional Development of and in the Social Studies" in *Social Studies in Secondary Education*, 1965, pp. 525–529.

6. Do they include some balance among knowledge and under-standing, skills and abilities, and appreciations and other at-titudes?
7. Are the skills included likely achievable in social studies?
8. Are the attitudes selected likely affectable to a significant extent through the social studies?
9. Do the objectives accord with major values and interests of con-temporary American society?

CONTENT OR SUBJECT MATTER

1. Does it concentrate on social rather than scientific, technical, personal or individual, esthetic, spiritual, or other asocial inter-ests and activities of people?
2. Does it emphasize basic elements of society, especially of demo-cratic, American culture?
3. Does it relate to contemporary and emerging changes in the social world?
4. Does it reflect accurate and up-to-date scholarship in the social sciences?
5. Does it stress relationships rather than facts, elements, and entities as such in the social world?
6. Does it include a careful selection of socially significant, as dis-tinguished from relatively less important, facts and concepts and generalizations?
7. Does it contain sufficient treatment of relationships among in-dividuals, individual to group, group to group, and group to society?
8. Is it sufficiently limited in scope to facilitate learning in depth throughout the grades?
9. Does it include adequate motivational and illustrative material to stimulate and facilitate learning at each age level?
10. Does it provide for students carefully drawing conclusions from social data and not merely memorizing ready-made generaliza-tions?
11. Does it repeat in higher grades human relationships dealt with in the lower grades in such ways as to facilitate really advanced learning without needless and wasteful duplication?
12. Does it reflect the rising importance of underdeveloped areas and newly emerging nations of the world?
13. Does it reflect important characteristics and interests of the local community and region without succumbing to provincialism and anti-social prejudices and pressures?

14. Do teachers individually and collectively at each school level have and exercise freedom to try variations?
15. Are individual students at each level encouraged and aided in pursuing topics that are important to them?

LEARNING ACTIVITIES AND TEACHING PROCEDURES

1. Are they identified specifically and thoroughly enough to be understood by teachers?
2. Are they adaptable to teachers of varying backgrounds, interests, and talents?
3. Do they facilitate efficient and effective development of knowledge and understanding?
4. Do they include gathering, organizing, and reporting information on political, economic, and other social relationships?
5. Do they emphasize practices of social, economic, and civic utility?
6. Do they include counterparts of research methods used in the social sciences?
7. Do they involve more complex or advanced levels of performance both within grades and in successively higher grades?
8. Do they provide sufficiently for practice of previously developed levels of performance of basic skills, without merely repeating needlessly and wastefully what students already know how to do?
9. Do they include provisions for class study in depth on one or more topics or aspects of topics?
10. Do they include techniques designed to motivate students' interest?
11. Do they include provisions for individual, independent study by pupils?
12. Do they include sufficient variety in each grade or course to facilitate achievement by the students of varying backgrounds, interests, and levels of skill development?
13. Do they include special, advanced study procedures for gifted, high ability, or highly motivated students individually and in designated classes or small groups?
14. Do they include special study procedures for low ability students or underachievers?
15. Do assignments to be performed out-of-class adequately involve out-of-class sources, facilities, and situations?
16. Does the planned curriculum facilitate coordination, among teachers and classes, in the development of designated basic skills within and among the grades without restricting unduly the initiative, abilities, and interest of each teacher and class?

INSTRUCTIONAL MATERIALS, RESOURCES, EQUIPMENT

1. Are sources, types, and individual materials specifically identified in recommendations to teachers?
2. Is a sufficiency of each of the following types of material included:
   a. basic reading materials?
   b. complementary reading materials?
   c. other independent study materials (workbooks, programmed materials)?
   d. audiovisuals?
   e. community resources?
3. Are the recommended materials appropriate to designated grade levels and inclusive of suitable materials varying in approach difficulty at each grade level?
4. Does the curriculum provide for students' use of major types of instructional material at designated grade levels?
5. Does the curriculum provide for students' developing advanced skills in using materials at successively higher grade levels?
6. Does the curriculum provide for students' developing skills in rejecting or discarding after examination the less valuable, as well as in selecting for use the most appropriate, materials?
7. Does the procedure used in textbook selection facilitate securing the variety of textbooks needed?
8. Are arrangements or recommendations offered for a continuing flow, to and among teachers, of information about new and other potentially useful material, including:
   a. contacts between teachers and librarian and supervisor or curriculum director?
   b. formal and informal exchange among teachers of information concerning materials?
   c. files and other collections of material contributed by and accessible to several teachers, perhaps cooperating with librarian?
   d. materials purchased by school funds and stored in a school or elsewhere in a school system?
   e. up-to-date card or other information files identifying used and usable materials, community resources or audiovisuals?
   f. easily accessible published directories and bibliographies identifying worthwhile materials?

EVALUATIVE PROCEDURES AND DEVICES

1. Are they used to appraise students' progress directly toward the major objectives of learning in social studies?
2. Are both objective and subjective means of evaluation used?

3. Are specific procedures and devices recommended to illustrate to teachers the development of effective and appropriate techniques and instruments for evaluation?
4. Do the testing procedures provide for balance among the points to be tested that matches the emphases in subject matter that the students study?
5. Do they provide for ascertaining both breadth and depth of students' learning about society?
6. Do they correspond to the types of learning activity most used?
7. Do the rating types of procedures suit specifically the kinds of performances and products to be rated?
8. Are appropriate standardized tests that are devoted to or inclusive of the social studies utilized?
9. Are they used so as to encourage and help students become skillful in appraising their own learning?

GENERAL FEATURES OF THE SOCIAL STUDIES CURRICULUM

1. Is it concentrated on learning about society?
2. Does it contain desired portions of the following ingredients: basic elements in human relationships? recent or current trends? the foreseeably emerging future?
3. Does it sufficiently reflect up-to-date information, interpretations, and methodology in the social sciences?
4. Does it possess desired unity in the directness of relationship between objectives and other ingredients?
5. Does it possess unity and balance in the interrelationships among subjects, procedures, and sources?
6. Do teachers at each school level, and among the school levels, cooperate frequently in coordinating social studies content, methods, and materials?
7. Is it broad enough to widen progressively the students' learning about society and, at the same time, sufficiently selective to facilitate depth in learning?
8. Does it adequately relate to the developmental characteristics of children at each age level, to an increasing range of individual differences, and to the growing variability within each individual?
9. Is it practical as regards the necessity of teaching to groups and of learning by individuals?

◄§ The Importance of Teaching the Social Studies in an Age of Science

Robert E. Jewett

Emphasis on science and technology, in schools as in modern life more generally, was already great and growing when the advent of the Space Age stimulated a further rapid spurt. It is especially timely, then, to recognize that technical and scientific developments often cause, involve, or facilitate the emergence of social conditions and situations that require more than scientific means to cope with them. In a sense, as Jewett's analysis shows, the expansion of science calls for more, not less, attention to social studies. The study of society needs to deal specifically with the very elements and problems that the increasing influence of science has brought in human affairs.

Perhaps it would be wise . . . to define the term democracy. The meaning I am giving the term is well stated by Robert M. MacIver in the following definition: "Democracy is . . . primarily a way of determining who shall govern and, broadly, to what ends." (1) This definition carries with it the corollaries that there shall be a free flow of conflicting opinion and freedom of assembly for purposes of discussion and organization. Note that this definition expresses the meaning of the concept of democracy solely as a political process. Under this definition of democracy, the majority can adopt any ends except those which would violate a continuation of majority rule, free speech, and free assembly.

MASS COMMUNICATION

Now let us examine some of the conditions created in our society by the growth of science which have created the need for a greater emphasis on the teaching of the social studies in the schools. For one thing, the growth of science and technology has brought extensive change in the area of mass communication. This development has made possible the extension of democratic government over

Used by permission of The Social Studies; from *The Social Studies*, 52: 163–166, October, 1961. Dr. Jewett is a professor of education at Ohio State University.

larger geographic areas. At the same time, the development of the means of mass communication has made the maintaining of democratic government more difficult. It is easier to indoctrinate a whole population through methods of propaganda. This has been demonstrated forcefully to us in our time by totalitarian governments of Germany, Italy and Russia. Mussolini's Italy was fashioned with the aid of the printing press and the microphone. Hitler's regime relied heavily upon techniques made possible by the age of science and invention.

If democratic government is to be maintained, therefore, the individual must be self-directing. He must be able to detect indoctrination. Here the social studies, drawing upon the disciplines of semantics and logic, have a decisive role to play.

Pupils in social studies classes must be taught to recognize dangerous forms of indoctrination and to discount them as they examine important problems in the culture. They must, for example, come to recognize such propaganda devices as card stacking, glittering generalities, middle-of-the-road arguments, the undistributed middle term, guilt by association, and repetition.

Because of the tremendous power of the mass means of communication, it is essential that pupils be made aware of the necessity of keeping these communicative channels open to the free flow of conflicting opinions. . . .

In developing the pupil's skill in detecting propaganda devices, the classroom should increase the pupil's ability to think reflectively. Briefly, this entails increasing the pupil's skill in recognizing and defining problems, formulating possible solutions, and testing these hypotheses against relevant facts. In this effort to increase the pupil's ability to carry forward the reflective act, his attention should be directed to those important problem areas of the culture which are normally closed off from a critical examination in the media of mass communication.

POWER STRUCTURE

Another effect of the growth of science upon society is that science has placed in the hands of government, whether authoritarian or democratic, overwhelming military power. This fact has grave implications for democracy—both on the domestic scene and in the area of foreign affairs. Prior to the quite recent advances of science and technology—approximately the last 50 years—an informed majority with a deep democratic tradition could maintain their sovereignty. When the squirrel rifle was equal in fire power to the weapons possessed by the government, numbers were decisive. The majority ruled, partly because in the last analysis the majority had the preponderance of military power.

For the first time in modern history we are faced with the problem of preserving democracy in a society in which governments possess military power vastly superior to the armaments available to the private citizens. This fact means that the majority finds it increasingly difficult to resort successfully to revolution, or the threat of revolt, in order to maintain, or secure, democratic government. It is imperative under these circumstances that the rank and file of the population understand the nature of democracy. The individual citizen, therefore, must see clearly what he has at stake in the preservation of democracy. Today the moral conviction of the individual citizen is his major weapon.

Furthermore, it has become increasingly important that the citizen understand the proper role of the military in a democratic government. If democracy is to be preserved, the citizen must understand that policy making must remain in the hands of the civil government, that the military is an agency of policy, not a determiner of it. Many young citizens today have never experienced a time when the military was not a dominant force in the life of the nation.

Given our present power structure, it is vital that the voters select men for public office who have a deep commitment to the democratic process. Men in public office, by the very nature of the present power structure, may be more tempted than men in earlier times to destroy rule by the majority; and they will find it easier to do so. . . .

FOREIGN POLICY

There is a general realization today that large scale atomic warfare is unthinkable. Unfortunately, while this realization is a strong deterrent to war, it does not preclude the possibility of such a conflict. The details of negotiation often are complex, calling for technical knowledge. The role of an informed public, therefore, would seem to be that of passing judgment on the results of the negotiation; judgment based upon the consequences of the negotiation. This judgment usually will take the form of voting in national elections.

When the public is uninformed concerning foreign affairs, the demagogue acquires great influence in the area of foreign policy. A "Big Bill" Thompson can threaten to punch King George V in the nose and gain votes by the statement. Father Coughlin can prevent U.S. entry into the World Court with a single radio address—when, and only when, the public is uninformed in the area of foreign policy. Conversely, responsible, able statesmen can act courageously and wisely only when they are supported by an intelligent public.

Since the advent of the guided missile and the atomic bomb, we can no longer afford the luxury of demogoguery in foreign affairs nor the paralysis of decisive, intelligent leadership by the narrow, uninformed views of an ignorant electorate.

If we are to preserve democracy, therefore, the public school must give pupils insights into economic, sociological, psychological, geographical, political and historical concepts which are essential to a basic understanding of foreign policy. Furthermore, the school must do all in its power to develop in its pupils the habit of suspended judgment, the habit of weighing the facts, the habit of examining the consequences, as they discuss problems in the area of foreign policy.

It is too much to expect that the social studies curriculum will make its pupils experts in foreign affairs. This is not possible, nor is it necessary. But the social studies class may aid the pupils in building broad concepts which they can apply in judging specific proposals and acts of government officials.

CHANGE OF SOCIAL STRUCTURE

The growth of science has led to an increasingly complex and diversified economic and social system. Primary communities are giving way to secondary ones. Adults tend to associate with other members of their own profession, craft, or business, rather than with their neighbors—school teachers associate largely with school teachers, financiers with financiers, lawyers with lawyers, etc. This association is both organized and informal. Teachers have their organizations, as have lawyers, doctors, laborers, etc. These groups, moreover, tend more and more to widen the scope of their interests. Labor unions, for example, formerly largely confined their interests to the wages, hours, and working conditions of their members. Today, while continuing their efforts in these matters, they are taking a stand on such subjects as domestic politics, race relations, consumer education, and foreign policy. And they are conducting extensive educational programs for their members that reach far beyond the technical concerns of their craft. . . .

A large percentage of our children are growing up in a home environment in which they "pick up" a single pattern of social, economic, and political beliefs. The effect of the home environment on the child in our interest-group-oriented society is to make him a product of a single socio-economic class. He tends to think and act within the limits of a class. His imagination and intellect are limited in their operation to the confines of class boundaries.

This situation has heightened the importance of the public school in our culture. One single fact stands out concerning the nature of the American public school system: it serves all the children of all the people. The students represent various socio-economic classes, various religious faiths, varying national backgrounds, and different races.

As he lives in the school, under competent teachers the child may come to realize that there are people who hold values different than his: people who have different beliefs and who possess skills and knowledge which he does not have. In his classes, the pupil enters— or should enter—the arena of conflicting opinion. Thus he experiences the meaning of freedom of speech.

In the social studies class, he may enter into critical discussion of social, economic and political issues. Many of the beliefs which he has picked up in the home may be challenged by material he reads and by the beliefs, experiences, and information of other pupils. This type of environment will encourage the pupil to examine his beliefs; examine them in the light of new facts.

The fact that in the school, and particularly in the social studies classes, the pupil is sharply confronted with the desires and goals of other pupils (pupils with different socio-economic backgrounds) will tend to sharpen his imagination and his sympathies. The conclusions which he arrives at will incorporate, to a degree at least, these wider considerations.

The pupil should be helped to think about the ideas he has picked up in his secondary environment. He may then be expected to emerge from the social studies classroom with tested ideas that are relevant to the nature of the social order. The child is unlikely to secure tested ideas concerning the nature of society outside the school.

The function of the school is neither to destroy the beliefs children hold nor to substitute different ones. The former practice would leave the child with no sense of direction; the latter practice would make of the school an instrument of an authoritarian state. . . .

References

(1) MacIver, Robert M. *The Web of Government.* New York: The Macmillan Company, 1947. Pp. 198.

~§ A BASIC BIBLIOGRAPHY ON ELEMENTARY SOCIAL STUDIES

AMBROSE, EDNA, and ALICE MIEL, *Children's Social Learning.* National Education Association, Washington, 1958.

BERELSON, BERNARD, and GARY A. STEINER, *Human Behavior: An Inventory of Scientific Findings.* Harcourt, Brace & World, Inc., N.Y., 1964.

BERG, HARRY D., *Evaluation in the Social Studies.* National Council for the Social Studies, Washington, 1965.

CARPENTER, HELEN M., ed., *Skill Development in Social Studies.* National Council for the Social Studies, Washington, 1963.

CARTWRIGHT, W. H., and R. L. WATSON, eds., *Interpreting and Teaching American History.* National Council for the Social Studies, Washington, 1961.

CHASE, STUART, *The Proper Study of Mankind.* Harper & Row, Publishers, N.Y., 1956.

Economic Education in the Schools. Committee on Economic Development, N.Y., 1961. (See also *Economic Literacy for Americans,* 1962, and *Study Materials for Economic Education in the Schools,* 1961.)

Education for Freedom and World Understanding. Bulletin OE-10016, U.S. Office of Education, Washington, 1962.

Educator's Guide to Free Curriculum Materials in Social Studies. Educator's Progress Service, Randolph, Wisc., annual.

EISENSTADT, S. N., *From Generation to Generation.* Free Press of Glencoe, Inc., N.Y., 1956.

ENGLE, SHIRLEY, ed., *New Perspectives in World History.* National Council for the Social Studies, Washington, 1964.

ERICKSON, ERIK, *Childhood and Society.* W. W. Norton & Company, Inc., N.Y., 1950.

FAY, LEO, *et al., Improving Reading in the Elementary Social Studies.* National Council for the Social Studies, Washington, 1961.

GIBSON, JOHN S., *New Frontiers in the Social Studies.* Lincoln Filene Center for Citizenship and Public Affairs, Medford, Mass., 1965.

GINZBERG, ELI, ed., *The Nation's Children* (3 vols.). Columbia University Press, N.Y., 1961.

GROSS, RICHARD E., and W. V. BADGER, "Social Studies," *Encyclopedia of Educational Research.* The Macmillan Co., N.Y., 1960.

GROSS, RICHARD E., *et al., The Problems Approach and the Social Studies.* National Council for the Social Studies, Washington, 1960.

A Guide to Content in the Social Studies. Report of the Committee on Concepts and Values, National Council for the Social Studies, Washington, 1957.

HARRIS, RUBY M., *The Rand McNally Handbook of Map and Globe Usage*. Rand McNally & Co., Chicago, 1959.

HILL, WILHELMINA, ed., *Curriculum Guide for Geographic Education*. National Council for Geographic Education, Normal, Ill., 1963.

HILL, WILHELMINA, *Selected Resource Units: Elementary Social Studies*. National Council for the Social Studies, Washington, 1961. (See also *Unit Planning and Teaching in Elementary Social Studies*. Bulletin OE-31003, U.S. Office of Education, Washington, 1963.)

HILL, WILHELMINA, *Social Studies in the Elementary School Program*. Bulletin OE-31000, U.S. Office of Education, Washington, 1960.

How-To-Do-It Series. National Council for the Social Studies, Washington, various dates.

HUUS, HELEN, ed., *Children's Books to Enrich the Social Studies*. National Council for the Social Studies, Washington, 1961.

JAMES, PRESTON E., ed., *New Viewpoints in Geography*. National Council for the Social Studies, Washington, 1959.

JAROLIMEK, JOHN, *Social Studies in Elementary Education*. The Macmillan Co., N.Y., 1963.

JAROLIMEK, JOHN, and H. M. WALSH, *Readings for Social Studies in Elementary Education*. The Macmillan Co., N.Y., 1965.

JOHNSON, HENRY, *Teaching of History*. The Macmillan Co., N.Y., 1940.

Journal of Geography. National Council for Geographic Education, Normal, Ill., monthly during school year.

KELTY, MARY G., *Learning and Teaching History in the Middle Grades*. Ginn and Company, Boston, 1936.

KENWORTHY, LEONARD S., *Introducing Children to the World*. Harper & Row, Publishers, N.Y., 1956.

KENWORTHY, LEONARD S., *Social Studies Curriculum and Methods*. National Council for the Social Studies, Washington, 1963.

McLENDON, JONATHON C., *A Guide to Curriculum Study: Social Studies*. North Carolina Board of Education, Raleigh, N.C., 1959.

McLENDON, JONATHON C., *What Research Says to the Teacher: Teaching the Social Studies*. National Education Association, Washington, 1960.

MASSIALAS, BRYON G., and FREDERICK R. SMITH, *New Challenges in the Social Studies: Implications of Research for Learning*. Wadsworth Publishing Co., Inc., Belmont, Calif., 1965.

MEAD, MARGARET, *The School in American Culture*. Harvard University Press, Cambridge, 1951.

METCALF, LAWRENCE E., "Research on Teaching the Social Studies," *Handbook of Research on Teaching*. Rand McNally & Co., Chicago, 1962.

MICHAELIS, JOHN U., *Social Studies for Children in a Democracy*. Prentice-Hall, Inc., Englewood Cliffs, N.J., 1963.

MICHAELIS, JOHN U., ed., *Social Studies in Elementary Schools*. National Council for the Social Studies, Washington, 1962.

MICHAELIS, JOHN U., and A. MONTGOMERY JOHNSTON, *The Social Sciences: Foundations of the Social Studies*. Allyn and Bacon, Inc., Boston, 1965.

MILLER, NEAL E., and JOHN DOLLARD, *Social Learning and Imitation*. Yale University Press, New Haven, 1951.

MUESSIG, RAYMOND H., and VINCENT R. ROGERS, eds., *The Social Science Seminar Series* (6 vols.). Charles E. Merrill Books, Inc., Columbus, Ohio, 1965.

NOAR, GERTRUDE, *Teaching and Learning the Democratic Way*. Prentice-Hall, Inc., Englewood Cliffs, N.J., 1963.

PATTERSON, FRANKLIN, ed., *Citizenship and a Free Society: Education for the Future*. National Council for the Social Studies, Washington, 1960.

PEATTIE, RODERICK, *Geography in Human Destiny*. Henry Stewart, Inc., E. Aurora, N.Y., 1940.

PEATTIE, RODERICK, *Teaching of Geography*. Appleton-Century-Crofts, Inc., N.Y., 1950.

PRESTON, RALPH C., chrm., *Social Studies in Elementary Schools*. National Society for the Study of Education, Washington, 1957.

PRESTON, RALPH C., *Teaching Social Studies in the Elementary School*. Holt, Rinehart & Winston, Inc., N.Y., 1958.

PRESTON, RALPH C., *Teaching World Understanding*. Prentice-Hall, Inc., Englewood Cliffs, N.J., 1955.

PRICE, ROY A., ed., *New Viewpoints in the Social Sciences*. National Council for the Social Studies, Washington, 1958.

RAGAN, WILLIAM B., and JOHN D. MCAULAY, *Social Studies for Today's Children*. Appleton-Century-Crofts, Inc., N.Y., 1964.

Social Education. National Council for the Social Studies, Washington, monthly during school year.

Social Studies. The Social Studies, Brooklawn, N.J., monthly during school year.

SOWARDS, G. WESLEY, ed., *The Social Studies: Curriculum Proposals for the Future*. Scott, Foresman & Company, Chicago, 1963.

TABA, HILDA, *School Culture*. American Council on Education, Washington, 1955.

TAVEL, DAVID Z., *Developing Reading and Study Skills in Social Studies.* Lynn Press, Denver, 1960. (Available from the author at the University of Toledo, Ohio.)

THRALLS, ZOE S., *Teaching of Geography.* Appleton-Century-Crofts, Inc., N.Y., 1958.

TIEGS, ERNEST W., and FAY ADAMS, *Teaching the Social Studies.* Ginn and Company, Boston, 1959.

TOOZE, RUTH, and BEATRICE KRONE, *Literature and Music as Resources for Social Studies.* Prentice-Hall, Inc., Englewood Cliffs, N. J., 1955.

TYLER, RALPH W., chrm., *Social Forces as Affecting American Education.* National Society for the Study of Education, Washington, 1961.

WESLEY, EDGAR B., with MARY A. ADAMS, *Teaching Social Studies in Elementary Schools.* D. C. Heath, Boston, 1952.

WILLCOCKSON, MARY, *Social Education of Young Children.* National Council for the Social Studies, Washington, 1956.

ᏬᏣᎦ Directory of Social Studies Projects
John U. Michaelis

Bailey, Wilfred, and Marion J. Rice, Development of a Sequential Curriculum in Anthropology for Grades 1–7, Department of Sociology and Anthropology, University of Georgia, Athens, Ga. 30601.

Becker, James M., Foreign Relations Project, North Central Association, First National Bank Building, Suite 832, Chicago, Ill. 60603.

Brown, Richard, and Van R. Halsey, History and Social Studies Curriculum Materials: Average Terminal, College Bound, and Adults, Amherst College, Amherst, Mass. 01002.

Collier, Malcolm C., Anthropology Curriculum Study Project (Secondary), 5632 So. Kimbark Ave., Chicago, Ill. 60637.

English, Raymond, Social Science Program (K-12), Educational Research Council of Greater Cleveland, Rockefeller Building, Cleveland, Ohio 44113.

Feldmesser, Robert A., Sociological Resources for Secondary Schools, Bartlett Hall, Dartmouth College, Hanover, N.H. 03755.

Fenton, Edwin, A High School Social Studies Curriculum for Able Students, Carnegie Institute of Technology, Pittsburgh, Pa. 15213.

Frankel, M. L., Economic Education Activities (1–12), Joint Council on Economic Education, 2 West 46th St., New York, N.Y. 10036.

Helburn, Nicholas, High School Geography Project, Association of American Geographers, Montana State College, Bozeman, Mont. 59715.

Hill, Wilhelmina, Committee on Curriculum Guide (K-12), Geographic Education, U.S. Office of Education, Washington, D.C. 20202.

Lee, John, New Approaches to and Materials for a Sequential Curriculum on American Society, Grades 5–12, Social Studies Curriculum Study Center, Northwestern University, 1809 Chicago Ave., Evanston, Ill. 60201.

Lee, Marvin, Economics Education Committee of the Southern States Work Conference, College of Education, West Virginia University, Morgantown, West Va. 26506.

Leppert, Ella C., The First Three Courses in a Sequential Social Studies Program for the Secondary School, Department of Education, University of Illinois, Urbana, Ill. 61803.

Used by permission of the author from "A Review of New Curriculum Developments and Projects," in *The Social Sciences: Foundations of the Social Studies*, John U. Michaelis and A. Montgomery Johnston, eds. Allyn and Bacon, Inc., Boston, 1965.

LERNER, DANIEL, The Development of a Basic Social Science Course for Undergraduate Students in the Natural Sciences and Engineering (College), Massachusetts Institute of Technology, Cambridge, Mass. 02139.

LONG, HAROLD M., Improving the Teaching of World Affairs (K-12), Glens Falls Public Schools, Glens Falls, N.Y. 12801.

MAHER, JOHN E., Development of Economic Education Programs (K-12), Joint Council on Economic Education, 2 West 46th St., New York, N.Y. 10036.

MICHAELIS, JOHN U., Preparation of Teaching Guides and Materials on Asian Countries for Grades I–XII, Department of Education, University of California, Berkeley, Calif. 94720.

MORISON, ELTING E., A Program of Curriculum Development in the Social Studies and Humanities (1–12), Educational Services Inc., 108 Water St., Watertown, Mass. 02172.

MORRISETT, IRVING, The Social Science Education Consortium (1–12), Department of Economics, Purdue University, Lafayette, Ind. 49707.

OLIVER, DONALD, A Jurisprudential and Social Science Curriculum for Grades 8–10 Focusing on the Analysis of Controversial Public Issues, Graduate School of Education, Harvard University, Cambridge, Mass. 02138.

PATTERSON, FRANKLIN, The Lincoln Filene Center for Citizenship and Public Affairs (Secondary), Tufts University, Medford, Mass. 02155.

PRICE, ROY A., Identification of Major Concepts from the Social Sciences, Development of Materials and Techniques for Teaching Them, and Evaluation of Their Applicability and Utility in Grades V, VIII, and XI, Department of Education, Syracuse University, Syracuse, N.Y. 13210.

RADER, WILLIAM D., Elementary School Economics Program, Industrial Relations Center, University of Chicago, Chicago, Ill. 60637.

RIDDLE, DONALD H., Secondary School Project, Eagleton Institute of Politics, Rutgers University, Woodlawn, Douglass College, New Brunswick, N.J. 08901.

ROSWENC, EDWIN C., Basic Concepts in History and Social Science (Secondary), Department of American Studies, Amherst College, Amherst, Mass. 01002.

RUNDELL, WALTER, JR., Service Center for Teachers of History (Secondary), American Historical Association, 400 A St., Washington, D.C. 20003.

SENESH, LAWRENCE, Elkhart Indiana Experiment in Economic Education (1–12), Department of Economics, Purdue University, Lafayette, Ind. 47907.

SHAPLIN, JUDSON T., Development of a Model for the St. Louis Metropolitan Social Studies Center, Grades K-12, Graduate Institute of Education, Washington University, St. Louis, Mo. 63130.

SHAVER, JAMES P., Development of Economic Curricular Materials for Secondary Schools, Ohio State University, Social Studies Curriculum Center, Columbus, Ohio, 43201.

SPERLING, JOHN G., and SUZANNE WIGGINS, Development and Evaluation of a 12th Grade Course in the Principles of Economics, Department of Economics, San Jose State College, San Jose, Calif.

STAVRIANOS, L. S., World History Project (Secondary), Department of History, Northwestern University, Evanston, Ill. 60201.

TOY, HENRY, Civic Education Project (1–12), American Heritage Foundation, 11 West 42nd St., New York, N.Y. 10036.

WEST, EDITH, Preparation and Evaluation of Social Studies Curriculum Guides and Materials for Grades K-14, College of Education, University of Minnesota, Minneapolis, Minn. 55455.

RELATED STUDIES

BARNACK, ROBERT S., The Use of Electronic Computers to Improve Individualization of Instruction Through Unit Teaching, School of Education, State University, Buffalo, N.Y. 14205.

BECKER, JAMES, Experimental Statewide Seminars in Teaching About Democracy and Totalitarianism, Foreign Relations Project, First National Bank Building, Chicago, Ill. 60603.

COLEMAN, JAMES S., Research Program in the Effects of Games With Simulated Environments in Secondary Education, Department of Social Relations, Johns Hopkins University, Baltimore, Md. 21203.

DAVIS, O. L., The Usefulness of Graphic Illustrations in the Social Studies, Kent State University, Kent, Ohio.

EASTON, DAVID, and ROBERT D. HESS, Study of Political Socialization, Department of Political Science, University of Chicago, Chicago, Ill. 60637.

JOHNSON, CARL S., and CHARLES A. DAMBACH, Survey of Printed Materials on Conservation Education, Research Foundation, Ohio State University, Columbus, Ohio 43201.

JOYCE, BRUCE, and CARL WEINBERG, Sociology in Elementary Social Studies, Department of Education, University of Chicago, Chicago, Ill. 60637.

OJEMANN, RALPH H., Preventive Psychiatry Program, W 613 East Hall, University of Iowa, Iowa City, Iowa 52240.

SANDERS, NORRIS, Use of a Taxonomy of Questions to Increase the Variety and Quality of Thought in the Classroom, Manitowoc Public Schools, Manitowoc, Wis. 54220.

SHINN, RIDGWAY F., JR., An Investigation Into the Utilization of Geography and History as Integrating Disciplines for Social Studies Curricular Development in a Public School System, Department of History, Rhode Island College, Providence, R.I. 02904.

TABA, HILDA, Thinking in Elementary School Children, Department of Education, San Francisco State College, San Francisco, Calif. 94127.

WING, RICHARD L., The Production and Evaluation of Three Computer-Based Economics Games for the Sixth Grade, Board of Cooperative Educational Services, Yorktown Heights, N.Y. 10598.